W9-CLG-423

COLLECTED WORKS OF ERASMUS

VOLUME 20

THE CORRESPONDENCE OF
ERASMUS

LETTERS 2803 TO 2939

May 1533–May 1534

translated by Clarence H. Miller †

with Charles Fantazzi

annotated by James M. Estes

University of Toronto Press

Toronto / Buffalo / London

The research and publication costs of the
Collected Works of Erasmus are supported by
University of Toronto Press

ISBN 978-1-4875-0585-1 (cloth)
ISBN 978-1-4875-3284-0 (EPUB)
ISBN 978-1-4875-3283-3 (PDF)

Library and Archives Canada Cataloguing in Publication

Title: Collected works of Erasmus.

Names: Erasmus, Desiderius, –1536, author.

Description: Includes bibliographical references and indexes. | Contents: vol. 20.
The correspondence of Erasmus: Letters 2803 to 2939, May 1533–May 1534

Identifiers: Canadiana (print) 74006326x | ISBN 9781487505851 (v. 20)

Subjects: LCSH: Erasmus, Desiderius, –1536 – Correspondence. |
LCSH: Bible. New Testament – Commentaries – Early works to 1800. |
LCSH: Bible. Psalms – Commentaries – Early works to 1800. |
LCSH: Authors, Latin (Medieval and modern) – Netherlands – Correspondence. |
LCSH: Humanists – Netherlands – Correspondence. |
LCSH: Scholars – Netherlands – Correspondence. |
LCGFT: Correspondence. | LCGFT: Sources. |
LCGFT: Personal correspondence.

Classification: LCC PA8500 1974 fol. | DDC 199.492 – dc19

University of Toronto Press acknowledges the financial assistance
to its publishing program of the Canada Council for the Arts
and the Ontario Arts Council, an agency of the Government of Ontario.

Canada Council   Conseil des Arts
for the Arts   du Canada

ONTARIO ARTS COUNCIL
CONSEIL DES ARTS DE L'ONTARIO

an Ontario government agency
un organisme du gouvernement de l'Ontario

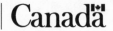

Funded by the   Financé par le
Government   gouvernement
of Canada   du Canada

Canadä

Collected Works of Erasmus

The aim of the Collected Works of Erasmus
is to make available an accurate, readable English text
of Erasmus' correspondence and his
other principal writings. The edition is planned
and directed by an Editorial Board, an Executive Committee,
and an Advisory Committee.

Contents

Illustrations

Preface

This volume comprises the correspondence of Erasmus for the period May 1533 through May 1534. The thirteen months in question were ones in which Erasmus' sharply deteriorating health restricted his ability to work, to receive guests, and to travel. This turned his mind to thoughts of approaching death, but it did not rob him of his determination to promote good causes and defend his good name.

Having abandoned Basel for Freiburg in 1529, Erasmus was immediately prey to the thought that he should have moved somewhere further away from the turmoil and threat of violence that the Reformation brought with it, and the thought stayed with him as the religious polarization in Germany continued to get worse and civil war seemed ever more likely. After years of uncertainty and hesitation that amounted to dithering, Erasmus finally decided to return to his native Brabant, where Queen Mary of Hungary, regent of the Netherlands, held out the prospect of an extremely comfortable and secure old age in which he could devote himself to his scholarship. Brabant, moreover, had the advantage of being safely remote from Germany but not so far from Freiburg (or so Erasmus hoped) as to prevent a frail old man from undertaking the journey. So in February 1533, Erasmus let it be known that if he received a formal letter of invitation from Queen Mary and was provided with travel money, he would return to his native land. In reply, Erasmus was informed that the invitation would be issued as soon as the approval of the emperor, who was away in Spain, had been received. That is where matters stood at the end of the period covered by CWE 19.[1]

In July 1533, Queen Mary, having received the emperor's approval, was able to send a formal letter of invitation to Erasmus.[2] The letter was

* * * * *

1 For a more detailed account of the decision to move, see CWE 19 xiii–xvi.
2 Ep 2820

carried by Erasmus' one-time famulus Lieven Algoet, who was now in the service of Nicolaus Olahus and who brought with him the money for Erasmus' journey.[3] Lieven returned to the Netherlands on the assumption that Erasmus would soon follow. But the notice that the invitation was forthcoming (March 1533) had coincided with the onset of the siege of chronic illness that would last for the rest of Erasmus' life. In addition to severe digestive disorders, he suffered recurring attacks of excruciating pain in his feet, hands, and indeed his entire body that he almost invariably referred to (with partial accuracy) as 'gout.'[4] As a result, he was too ill to undertake the journey to Brabant. In August 1533 he spoke of the matter as having been put off until the spring,[5] and in November of that year he assured Olahus that nothing had changed with regard to his proposed return.[6] But on 22 April 1534 he reported to Olahus that, after a brief respite at the beginning of the month, the 'enormous pain' had struck again and not gone away, that he had not set foot outside his house for five months, and that he feared the journey would result in paralysis.[7] Writing to Erasmus in June 1534, Olahus expressed genuine concern about Erasmus' health but once again urged him to return to his native land.[8] That, however, was the end of the surviving correspondence between Erasmus and Olahus as well as of any serious talk of Erasmus' return to the Netherlands.

Meanwhile, the situation in Germany that had made Erasmus eager to leave it seemed as threatening as ever. It was not yet clear that the truce between the emperor and the Protestant estates concluded at Nürnberg in 1532 would endure until 1546.[9] In the spring of 1534, moreover, the peace of the Empire was dramatically if briefly shattered by Landgrave Philip of Hessen's reconquest of Württemberg on behalf of its hereditary ruler, Duke Ulrich. In 1519 Ulrich, guilty of a series of crimes that culminated in the forcible annexation of the free imperial city of Reutlingen to his principality, was driven into exile by the army of the Swabian League. In 1520 the league ceded Württemberg to Charles v, who in 1522 incorporated it into the Austrian domains of his brother Ferdinand. The problem with this was that neither

* * * * *

3 Ep 2870:22–3
4 See Ep 2818 n1.
5 Ep 2865:1–2
6 Ep 2877:22–3
7 Ep 2922:6–11
8 Allen Ep 2948:6–16
9 Ep 2702 n2

the Swabian League nor the emperor had the right arbitrarily to dispose of
a principality that in imperial law still belonged to its hereditary ruler. As a
result, the Hapsburg acquisition of Württemberg was widely viewed, in the
duchy itself as well as in Germany at large, as a usurpation that deserved
to be undone. Chastened by his exile, Ulrich became a far more responsible
man as well as a theologically articulate adherent of the Reformation who
found in Landgrave Philip of Hessen a champion of his cause. Always eager to strike a blow in support of the rights of territorial princes, to weaken
the Hapsburgs, and to advance the cause of the Reformation, Philip raised
an army that was paid for largely with money advanced by that mortal enemy of the Hapsburgs, Francis I of France, and in May 1534 easily conquered
the poorly defended duchy, where Ulrich was received as its rightful ruler.
By the Peace of Kadan (June 1534), Ferdinand recognized Ulrich as duke of
Württemberg and conceded his right to introduce the Reformation, which he
immediately set about doing.

Erasmus received reports of these events from correspondents, one of
whom, Johann Koler in Augsburg, feared that they presaged 'a huge storm'
that would 'devastate and crush Germany.'[10] Erasmus' own surviving comments on the reconquest are, however, found in letters written some months
after the event and thus fall into the chronological compass of CWE 21. In
August 1534 he reports that Ulrich had 'struck terror into Germany,' but that
'the storm has passed more quickly than we thought.'[11] From an earlier letter,
written in July, we learn that Freiburg (in the Hapsburg Breisgau and dangerously close to Württemberg) had hired soldiers to defend itself against
a feared attack by Philip of Hessen.[12]

As was already clear at the time, the reconquest of Württemberg was
significant not simply as a vindication of princely rights against the over-
mighty Hapsburgs; it was also a huge victory for the Protestant cause, bringing with it the immediate introduction of the Reformation by Duke Ulrich
and, within a few years, the establishment of Württemberg as the bulwark of
orthodox Lutheranism in southern Germany. By 1535 the Catholic mass had
been banned from the duchy, an event that Erasmus cited as one evidence
(along with Henry VIII's persecution of opponents of the royal supremacy,

* * * * *

10 Ep 2937:54–71; cf Epp 2917:52–3 with n9, 2936:75–90, 2937:54–71, 2939:9–11, and
   Allen Ep 2947:9–37.
11 See Allen Ep 2961:94–6, and cf Allen Ep 2955:30.
12 See Allen Ep 2955:31, and cf Allen Ep 2947:10–12.

Francis I's fierce crackdown on heresy, and the emergence of the Anabaptist 'kingdom' at Münster) that 'we are witnessing a deadly revolution in human affairs.'[13] What, if anything, could be done to remedy this dangerous situation, and what could Erasmus contribute to the effort?

In Germany there were many princes who, more interested in peace and order than in clearly formulated doctrines, viewed the rapid advance of religious polarization as a threat to the internal stability of their territories and to the peace of the Empire as well and thus strove to overcome it. Known to historical scholarship as 'the confessional neutrals,' they were unable to believe that there was any real obstacle to a compromise settlement of the religious dispute. Their response to the perceived threat to peace was twofold. In their own territories they strove to satisfy the demand for reform while avoiding an open break with the old church. To this end they enacted measures intended to be tolerable to everyone except Anabaptists and other radicals. At the national level they supported the revival of the efforts towards a negotiated settlement that had failed at the Diet of Augsburg in 1530. There was thus an obvious affinity between their politically motivated efforts and the religious aspirations of the Erasmian humanists active as advisers at many of their courts.[14]

Among the most prominent of the confessionally neutral princes was John III, duke of Jülich-Cleves, whose most influential counsellors included Erasmus' friends and correspondents Konrad Heresbach and Johann von Vlatten. The duke's territorial church ordinance of 1532–3 made provision for better training and supervision of the parish clergy and stipulated that preaching was not only to be based on Scripture and the early Fathers but to be free of polemics as well. Traditional ceremonies (cleansed of abuses) and traditional doctrines (formulated with the maximum possible imprecision) were to be observed. This was the embodiment of what was already known as 'the middle way' (*via media*) in religious reform. Twice consulted about the church order by its authors (September 1532, May 1533), Erasmus gave it his blessing, but privately, lest the Paris theologians have a pretext for accusing him of being the founder of a new sect known as 'the moderates.'[15]

* * * * *

13 See Allen Ep 3000:32–5.
14 For a brief summary of the scholarship on the confessional neutrals, virtually all of it in German, see James M. Estes *Peace, Order, and the Glory of God: Secular Authority and the Church in the Thought of Luther and Melanchthon, 1518–1559* (Leiden 2005):138–40.
15 See Epp 2728 n24, 2804 introduction, 2845:1–6.

Nevertheless, having thus evaded public endorsement of Duke John's church order, Erasmus soon issued a public statement endorsing the general principles incorporated in it, doing so in response to the friendly urging of interested parties in both religious camps.

In the autumn of 1532, Philippus Melanchthon, since 1530 the chief spokesman for the Wittenberg theologians and the government of Electoral Saxony in all efforts towards a negotiated religious settlement, had urged Erasmus to use his influence to promote peace and to dissuade those in authority from resorting to war.[16] Erasmus had already received a similar request from his friend Julius Pflug, the jurist at the court of Duke George of Saxony who was rapidly emerging as the chief Catholic advocate of a compromise religious settlement based on mutual concessions and the toleration of differences. Harbouring the false hope that Melanchthon might be 'moved to intervene and persuade his followers to agree to many things that in themselves are not acceptable but must be tolerated in the circumstances,' Pflug exhorted Erasmus to persuade the princes that 'controversy can be removed from religion,' and that 'certain prescriptions of the church can be changed,' so as to make them less severe.[17] Erasmus' response was the *Liber de sarcienda ecclesiae concordia*, first published in the summer of 1533, with a letter of dedication to Pflug.[18] Boiled down to its essentials, the treatise was a justification of what had already been tried at the territorial level in Jülich-Cleves. It called for agreement based on the use of language vague enough to satisfy all parties; the subordination of interim agreements to the decision of a general council; the recognition that some questions could be left to individual judgment; the maintenance of the status quo in cases of doubt; and the practice of mutual accommodation.[19] Examples of the kind of accommodation on controversial subjects that Erasmus recommended can be found in Ep 2853, which is essentially a summary of the final section of the treatise.

* * * * *

16 Ep 2732:13–16. Ever since the anonymously published *Consilium* of 1520 (CWE 71 108–12), Erasmus had consistently promoted the idea that contentious religious issues should be settled by a commission of the most learned experts on both sides, and that, pending final settlement at a council, both sides should maintain peaceful unity. Whenever it seemed possible that such discussion might actually take place, he came under pressure to state his views anew, as at the Diet of Augsburg in 1530 (CWE 17 xii).

17 See Ep 2492:38–52, and cf Ep 2806:19–42.

18 Ep 2852

19 See CWE 65 129–30 (introduction to *De concordia*).

Within a year *De concordia* had been reprinted six times and twice translated into German. Certain Roman cardinals, preferring harsher measures,
were said to have been displeased and offended by it.[20] Some of Luther's
followers, by contrast, reacted favourably to the peaceful intent,[21] but Luther
himself, in a document of uncertain date that was not published until 1534,
dismissed the work as useless. While admitting that Erasmus and his disciples were 'perhaps' sincere in their desire for peace, he accused them of not
understanding that there is no 'middle path' between scriptural truth and
error, and that Christian souls cannot find peace in 'doubtful and uncertain
doctrines.'[22] At the time of the publication of *De concordia*, however, Luther
had long since made up his mind to launch a much more virulent attack
on Erasmus.

Though he had refrained from public criticism of Erasmus ever since
the publication of *De servo arbitrio* in 1525, Luther had continued to read his
works with some care, particularly his biblical scholarship. This confirmed
him in his view that Erasmus was an incompetent theologian whose studied
ambiguity on matters requiring clarity and commitment marked him as a
sceptic who only pretended to believe fundamental Christian doctrines (like
the Trinity) while in fact he took delight in undermining them. Erasmus'
influence was thus pernicious, and he needed to be discredited. Early in
1533 Luther announced to a group of students that he had resolved 'to slay
[Erasmus] by the pen.' The opportunity to do so came about a year later. Since
1532 Georg Witzel, a one-time Lutheran pastor turned Erasmian Catholic,
had been defending the Catholic doctrine of good works in a heated debate
with the Wittenberg theologian Justus Jonas. Hearing that Luther intended
to get involved in the debate between Witzel and Jonas, Luther's friend and
fellow theologian Nicolaus von Amsdorf wrote to him (28 January 1534) arguing that since Witzel stole everything he said from Erasmus, the appropriate target of Luther's attack was Erasmus himself. Several weeks later
(c 11 March) Luther responded at length to Amsdorf in a letter that, together

* * * * *

20 See Ep 2906:5–6, 22–4, but cf Ep 2935:3–10.
21 Notably the Hessian pastor Antonius Corvinus, in his *Dissertatio quatenus ex-
    pediat Erasmi de sarcienda ecclesiae concordia rationem sequi* (Wittenberg: Nicolaus
    Schirlentz 1534), written in the form of a dialogue between Corvinus himself
    and Julius Pflug
22 This was in Luther's preface to Corvinus' *Dissertatio* (see preceding note),
    which he said had been 'extorted' from him by the printer (WA 38 276–9).

with Amsdorf's letter, was published in March 1534 under the title *Epistolae Nicolai Amsdorfii et D. Martini Lutheri de Erasmo Roterodamo*.[23]

Taken entirely by surprise and deeply offended by the most vehement assault upon him that anyone had ever published, Erasmus responded with his *Purgatio adversus epistolam non sobriam Martini Lutheri*, which was in print before the end of April 1534. Replying point by point to what he called Luther's lies and misrepresentations, he firmly defended and explained his position in every case, though with a moderation of tone that disappointed his friend Johann Koler in Augsburg. The work enjoyed a wide circulation. In addition to the original Froben edition, there were six reprints in 1534 alone, including one at Augsburg arranged by Johann Koler, who sent two copies to Rome, one for the pope and one to be forwarded to the emperor. Even before he had seen a copy of Erasmus' *Purgatio*, Luther announced that he intended to continue the controversy with Erasmus. In the end, however, he did not do so, in large part, it seems, because of the restraining influence of Philippus Melanchthon, who had been 'displeased' with the vehemence of Luther's *Epistola*.[24]

Although the letters in this volume are liberally sprinkled with references to many of Erasmus' other controversies with his critics,[25] the controversy with Luther was the only one that came back to life in 1533–4 and led to a renewed exchange of published works. Indeed the *Purgatio* was the penultimate apologia of Erasmus' career.[26]

Apart from *De sarcienda ecclesiae concordia* and the *Purgatio adversus epistolam Lutheri*, Erasmus published only one further work in the period covered by this volume: *De praeparatione ad mortem*, which appeared early in 1534. Written at the request of Thomas Boleyn and dedicated to him, it dealt with a theme much on Erasmus' mind, preparing for death. With twenty Latin editions and eight vernacular translations in the space of six years, *De praeparatione* became one of Erasmus' most popular works. The original Basel edition acquired additional importance because of the sixteen previously unpublished letters that were appended to it, making it the penultimate edition of letters to be published by Erasmus himself.[27]

* * * * *

23 See Ep 2918 introduction.
24 Again, see Ep 2918 introduction.
25 See especially Epp 2806:15–24, 2892:76–125 (Agostino Steuco), 2807:9–21 (Frans Titelmans), 2810:83–6 (Julius Caesar Scaliger), 2810:95–110 (Alberto Pio), 2873:3–8 (Diego López Zúñiga).
26 For the final one, see Ep 3032.
27 See Ep 2884 introduction.

We come finally to the subject of money. Always a major theme in
Erasmus' correspondence, it is an unusually prominent one in this volume.
As had been the case since 1525, the collection and transmission of the income
from Erasmus' livings in the Netherlands and England were in the capable
hands of the Antwerp banker Erasmus Schets. Unfortunately, for the period
covered by this volume only four letters of Erasmus to Schets are extant,[28]
while none of those from Schets to Erasmus has survived. We are thus deprived of information that might have made some features of Erasmus' financial affairs easier to understand. Nevertheless, the surviving letters to
and from other correspondents tell us a good deal concerning Erasmus' anxieties about money, his difficulty in understanding the transactions involved
in dealing with it, and his propensity to jump to the conclusion that he was
being cheated. In addition to that, they provide a valuable record of the provisions that he made for the disbursement of his money after his death.

Erasmus had reason to fret about disruptions, real or only feared, in
the payment of the income from his livings in the Netherlands and England.
Payment of his Courtrai pension came to him via Pierre Barbier, who, cursed
with meagre income and high expenses, was frequently tardy with the payments. This led Erasmus to conclude that Barbier was colluding with several
others to rob him of his pension, and he imagined Barbier having a laugh at
his expense as a result.[29] When William Warham, archbishop of Canterbury,
died (August 1532), Erasmus feared that payment of the income from the
two livings that Warham had granted him would cease. Not until the summer of 1533 did he receive firm assurance that Warham's successor, Thomas
Cranmer, would continue the generosity that Warham had shown him.[30] In
the meantime, Erasmus had twice dispatched his servant Quirinus Hagius
to England to expedite the payment of sums owed him there by Warham
and others.[31] Quirinus seems to have done his job competently, particularly
so on his second journey,[32] but by the beginning of 1534 Erasmus, for reasons that are entirely obscure, had come to the conclusion that the young
man had cheated him of some of the money collected and had also spread

* * * * *

28 Epp 2896, 2913, 2924, 2933
29 See Barbier's rather opaque letter in his own defence (Ep 2842), and see also
    Epp 2851:34–43, 2896:9–11.
30 Epp 2815:8–19, 2879:30–7
31 See Ep 2804 n7.
32 See Ep 2815:13–19.

malicious gossip about him, an offence never to be forgiven.[33] A bit later, in May 1534, Pieter van Montfoort, a young man with whom Erasmus had been on friendly terms for several years,[34] visited him at Freiburg to deliver an honorarium that the six Estates of Holland had voted him.[35] At the time, Erasmus wrote letters of recommendation for Montfoort to Queen Mary and to her secretary Nicolaus Olahus.[36] But their friendship was destroyed when confusion over the amount of the gift from the Estates led Erasmus to conclude that Montfoort had siphoned off some of the money for himself.[37] In stark contrast to what happened with the honorarium from the Estates of Holland, generous gifts of money from Duke John III of Jülich-Cleves, King Ferdinand, Ferdinand's chancellor, Bernhard von Cles, and Thomas Boleyn managed to reach Erasmus without causing any misunderstanding or injured feelings.[38]

While worrying about money owed him and losing friends in the process, Erasmus established two funds from which his money was to disbursed 'for pious purposes' (for example, scholarships for poor students, dowries for poor virgins) after his death. One fund was entrusted to the care of his friend Bonifacius Amerbach, professor of law at Basel, with whom he deposited sixteen hundred gold florins for the purpose.[39] A second fund of comparable value and identical purpose, established at the same time as the first, was entrusted to another friend, Conradus Goclenius, professor of Latin in the Collegium Trilingue at Louvain. Unfortunately, the language of the letter granting Goclenius authority over the money deposited with him (Ep 2863) was susceptible of being read as a deed of gift, a simple bequest with no strings attached, rather than as a deed establishing a trust with clear instructions about the disbursement of the money. When Goclenius suddenly died intestate in 1539, having distributed very little of the money in the fund, there ensued a legal battle among three claimants to the money (the treasury of Brabant, the University of Louvain, and Goclenius' seven brothers) in which the brothers, citing Ep 2863, claimed that Erasmus' money had been 'donated' to Goclenius without restriction and that they were therefore entitled to

* * * * *

33 Epp 2896:21–2, 2906:100–3, 2918:28–32
34 See Ep 2389 introduction.
35 Ep 2818:15–21
36 Epp 2812, 2813
37 Epp 2819:1–19, 2913:10–21, 2922:41–55
38 Epp 2804:1–13, 2808:1–11, 2824:20–3, 2851:71–2
39 See Ep 2855 introduction.

it as his heirs. The claim of the treasury was quickly eliminated, whereupon the university, assisted by documents supplied by Bonifacius Amerbach (as trustee of Erasmus' will) demonstrated that both Erasmus and Goclenius had understood Ep 2863 not as a deed of gift but rather as a deed creating a trust, and that the brothers therefore had no claim to the money, which had to be disbursed for the purposes that Erasmus had specified. What little evidence survives indicates that this is what happened. Because the documentation essential for the correct understanding of Ep 2863 was too bulky to be presented in the form of notes to a short letter, Allen put together an appendix to his volume x that includes the fourteen surviving documents (letters and memoranda, 1533–9) relevant to the dispute over the 'donation.'[40] We have duplicated Allen's arrangement of the material.[41]

Of the 134 letters in this volume, 68 were written by Erasmus and 66 were addressed to him. These surviving letters include approximately 100 references to letters that are no longer extant. Since some of these references are to an unspecified number of letters, no exact total of letters known to have been written during the period covered by this volume can be determined, but 270 would be a cautious estimate. Of the surviving letters, 12 were published by Erasmus himself. Of these, one was printed at the end of *De sarcienda ecclesiae concordia* (1533), and eight were printed in the epistolary appendix to *De praeparatione ad mortem* (1534). Two were the prefaces to the works just mentioned, and one was the preface to the work of another scholar. The remaining letters were published by a variety of scholars in the period from 1544 to 1941. Nineteen of them were first published by Allen. To allow the reader to discover the sequence in which the letters became known, the introduction to each letter cites the place where it was first published and identifies the manuscript source if one exists. Allen's text and his numbering of the letters have been followed. Seven letters have been redated. Two of them, published by Allen as Epp 2259 and 2509, appear here as Epp 2873A and 2917A. The other five, published by Allen as Epp 2902–3, 2907–8, and 2931, will appear in CWE 21 as Epp 2989A, 2992A, 2995A, 2997A, and 2966A.

All of Erasmus' correspondents and all of the contemporaries of Erasmus who are mentioned in the letters are referred to by the version of their name that is used in CEBR. Wherever biographical information is supplied in the notes without the citation of a source, the reader is tacitly referred

* * * * *

40 See 'The Donation to Goclenius (Ep 2863)' Allen x 406–24.
41 See 303–33 below.

to the appropriate article in CEBR and to the literature there cited. The index
to this volume contains references to the persons, places, and works mentioned in the volume, following the plan for the Correspondence series in
CWE. When that series of volumes is completed, the reader will also be supplied with an index of topics, as well as of classical, scriptural, and patristic
references.

As with all the other volumes in this series, the basis for translation
and the starting point for annotation is the edition of the *Erasmi epistolae* that
was founded by P.S. Allen. This is, however, the fourth of the volumes in the
CWE Correspondence series to be based on volumes IX–XI of Allen's edition, which were completed after his death (1938) by his widow, Helen Mary
Allen, and H.W. Garrod, who had been his collaborators on earlier volumes.
At the time of his death Allen had, with few exceptions, collected and pro-
visionally arranged all the letters in those volumes, but had done the notes
for only twenty-seven of them. The remaining work of annotation had to be
done by H.M. Allen and Garrod. In many cases, therefore, 'Allen' is used in
the notes as shorthand for 'the Allen editors.' Where their work has needed
to be corrected, updated, or expanded – far more often in their case than
in that of Allen himself – I was able to rely on the advice and assistance of
distinguished colleagues here in Toronto and elsewhere. The great majority
of the classical and patristic references that were not supplied by Allen were
supplied by Charles Fantazzi. Amy Nelson Burnett and Timothy J. Wengert
read the entire manuscript and supplied information that filled gaps and
corrected mistakes in the notes. Jacqueline Glomski, Robert Sider, David
Starkey, John Guy, Wolfgang Ernst, John Grant, James K. Farge, and James K.
McConica responded most helpfully to inquiries about difficult questions of
history, bibliography, or translation. The notes on money and coinage were
contributed by Lawrin Armstrong.

This is the second of the two volumes of the Correspondence (CWE
19–20) translated by the late Clarence H. Miller (d 21 June 2019). Already
in 2016, just as the annotation of CWE 19 was getting under way, Professor
Miller found it necessary to withdraw from further participation in the project. Responsibility for the final revision of the translation of both volumes
having thus fallen to me, I sought and found the help of my colleague on
earlier Correspondence volumes, Charles Fantazzi. He kindly read the entire
manuscripts of both volumes, found answers to the many questions concerning the translation that Professor Miller himself or I had raised, and made
helpful suggestions for further changes and corrections as well. Without his
help, neither CWE 19 nor CWE 20 could have been brought to publication.

As ever, two libraries were of special importance in the preparation
of this volume: that of the Centre for Reformation and Renaissance Studies

at Victoria College in the University of Toronto, and that of the Pontifical Institute of Mediaeval Studies on the campus of St Michael's College in the University of Toronto. To Natalie Oeltjen, Assistant to the Director of the Centre for Reformation and Renaissance Studies, and to William Edwards, reference librarian of the Pontifical Institute, I am indebted for a degree of support and assistance that amounts to special treatment.

The volume was copyedited with typical thoroughness and care by Mary Baldwin.

JME

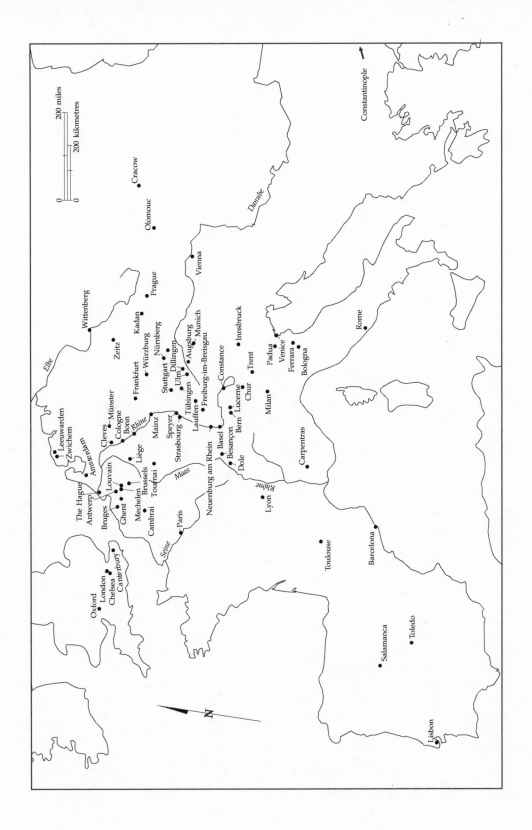

200 miles

200 kilometres

0

0

Cracow

Olomouc

Danube

Constantinople

Vienna

Elbe

Wittenberg

Prague

Kadan

Zeitz

Frankfurt

Würzburg

Nürnberg

Munich

Innsbruck

Rome

Leeuwarden

Zwichem

Münster

Cleves

Cologne

Bonn

Rhine

Stuttgart

Ulm

Dillingen

Augsburg

Freiburg-im-Breisgau

Constance

Trent

Padua

Venice

Ferrara

Bologna

Amsterdam

Liège

Mainz

Speyer

Tübingen

Lauffen

Basel

Chur

Lucerne

Bern

Milan

The Hague

Antwerp

Louvain

Brussels

Mechelen

Toumai

Strasbourg

Maas

Neuenburg am Rhein

Besançon

Dole

Carpentras

Bruges

Ghent

Cambrai

Paris

Seine

Rhône

Lyon

Oxford

London

Chelsea

Canterbury

Barcelona

Toulouse

N

Salamanca

Toledo

Lisbon

THE CORRESPONDENCE OF ERASMUS

LETTERS 2803 TO 2939

DES. ERASMVS ROTERO∙

damus Ioanni Agricolæ Hammonio, rei Me∙
dicæ & Græcæ linguæ profeſſori
Ingelſtadij, Suo. S. D.

FFECTVS ANIMI TVI MIHI
gratiſſimus eſt, & utiliſſimis tuis la∙
boribus humaniſſime Agricola ex
animo, ut par eſt, faueo: huiuſmodi
enim ingenijs ſemper unice ſum de∙
lectatus. Nec uideo quo ſpecioſiorę
titulo memoriã induſtriæ tuæ poſteritati ualeas com=
mendare. Hoc nanɋ nomine tua uirtus multo erit ce=
lebratior, quod primus ſtrenuam operã nauaris in hac
Therapeutica Galeni methodo elaboranda. Galenum
uero in omni medicina ſummum eſſe, tot eruditorũ ho=
minum iudicia, qui ex hoc authore ueræ medicinæ ſe=
minaria hauſerunt, honorificentiſſimis teſtimonijs cõ=
probãt. Hinc eſt quod ſperem futurũ, Ioannes ornatiſ=
ſime, ut per hos conatus accedat & cenſus & dignitas
tuæ doctrinæ tuisɋ laboribus debita. Sed utinã quod
tu cupis Theſeum præſtare queam. Hic nuncius prope
rabat, & eodem tempore pluribus erat ſcribendũ, ut
mihi uix ſemihoræ ſpacium ſupereſſet, Sunt autẽ hæc
propemodũ quæ per immenſa negocia licuit indicare.
　　Duo uerſus Græci: quos Galenus lib. 1. ca. 2. citat:
ſunt in Oreſtε Euripidis, pagina ab initio fabulæ quiṅ∙

A ii

Prefatory letter by Erasmus in
Johannes Agricola's *Scholia copiosa in therapeuticam methodum*
Universitäts- und Landesbibliothek Düsseldorf

2803 / To Johannes Agricola   Freiburg, 3 May 1533

This letter was printed at the beginning of Johannes Agricola's *Scholia copiosa in therapeuticam methodum, id est, absolutissimam Claudii Galeni Pergameni curandi artem* (Augsburg: Philipp Ulhard 1534). The year-date of the letter is confirmed by the reference in lines 41–3 to Georgius Agricola's *De mensuris et ponderibus* (Ep 2782 n1).

Johannes Agricola (1496–1570) was born in the Franconian town of Gunzenhausen, south and west of Nürnberg. He studied at Ingolstadt, where, after extensive travels, he became professor of Greek (1515) and of medicine (1531), positions he seems to have held for the rest of his life. His *Scholia copiosa* on Galen was one of several translations with commentary of Greek medical authors. Agricola also published (1539) a work on medicinal plants (*Index copiosissimus simplicius pharmacorum omnium*) notable for its reliance on personal observation as well as for its dedication to the Augsburg banker and patron of scholars (including Erasmus) Anton Fugger. This letter, Erasmus' answer to one now lost, is the only extant record of contact between him and Agricola.

DESIDERIUS ERASMUS OF ROTTERDAM SENDS GREETINGS
TO HIS FRIEND JOHANNES AGRICOLA AMMONIUS,
PROFESSOR OF MEDICINE AND GREEK AT INGOLSTADT
Your frame of mind is most pleasing to me, and I heartily approve of your extremely useful labours, my very kind friend Agricola, as is only right. For 5 I have always taken a particular delight in talents of this nature. And I do not see by what more brilliant distinction you could commend the memory of your efforts to posterity. For your ability will be much more celebrated because you are the first to have accomplished the difficult task of elaborating this *Therapeutic Method* of Galen. In fact, according to the most honorific 10 testimony of learned men, who derive the principles of true medicine from this author, he is judged to be the leader in all branches of medicine. For that reason I hope, my most accomplished friend Johannes, that your efforts will bring you the remuneration and the esteem that befit your teachings and your labours. I only wish I could provide the Theseus you want.[1] This mes- 15 senger was in a hurry, and at the same time I had to write to quite a few other people, so that I had hardly a half hour left over. But these are essentially the observations I could make in the midst of endless occupations.

* * * * *

2803
1 A 'Theseus' is someone who provides outside help (*Adagia* I v 27); cf Ep 2794:10 with n3.

The two Greek verses that Galen cites in book 1, chapter 2 are in Euripides' *Orestes*,[2] the fifth page from the beginning of the play. I do not 20 know whether the third line is Greek verse, but it is certainly not a metrical line in Latin. If it is verse, Galen added it on his own. So the dream of Orestes is nothing but a meaningless dream, as those of madmen are. They are the words of Electra to Orestes, who in his madness thinks he sees things he does not see. But I am surprised that the translator gave *scire* [to know] for εἰδέναι, 25 since *videre* [to see] or *cernere* [to discern] would be more correct.[3]

The Tabiae, whom Galen describes in book 5, chapter 12 are mentioned by Stephanus in his *De urbibus*,[4] indicating that they are a people in Italy among whom Remus was brought up. I have no doubt that more can be discovered in the geographers. But I had no time for it.   30

Cribris in se transfusis[5] means just 'a mixture and blending of many substances.'

Likewise, in book 6, chapter 3 I think Galen applies to men lacking good judgment the term κριομύξους, that is, 'like drivelling rams,' for sheep always have runny muzzles.   35

For the rest, there was no time to inquire into other questions, nor did I have at hand what you asked me about. Some other time I will do that carefully. At the moment there is nothing more to discuss with you; for as I wrote this I was more than overwhelmed by my other labours. And so let this letter serve as a recognition of both your singular kindness and your extraordinary 40 good will towards me. In some matters the very learned scholar Georgius Agricola will supply what you need; the work he has finished in five books

* * * * *

2 Euripides *Orestes* 258–9
3 The Allen editors, who accuse Erasmus of an 'imperfect knowledge of Greek,' claim that he is wrong to suggest that εἰδέναι should be translated 'to see' or 'to perceive' rather than 'to know.' (Gerlo echoes Allen.) It is true that this perfect infinitive of of the verb εἴδω is usually translated as 'to know,' but the root meaning is 'to have perceived with the mind.' Erasmus is simply stating accurately that in this context the verb should be translated 'to see' rather than 'to know.' Orestes is hallucinating, seeing things that are not really there.
4 The Greek grammarian Stephanus of Byzantium (probably sixth century) was the author of *Ethnica* (sometimes called, as here, *De urbibus*), an alphabetical list of place names along with the adjectives derived from them. It survives only in an epitome, an edition of which had been published at Venice by Aldo Manuzio in 1502.
5 Literally 'sieves pouring their content into one another' (Galen book 3, chapter 2)

on weights and measures is now being published at Basel.[6] In it he presents many shrewd arguments against the opinions of Guillaume Budé, Portis, and Andrea Alciati.[7] He also touches on the weights and measures of physicians. 45 If you ever get my letter (for I hear many complaints about letters not only having the seal broken or being torn open, but also being completely intercepted), I beg you to offer my special greetings to Master Mattheus Kretzer,[8] a precious treasure in an earthen vessel. I intensely admire the splendid gifts of God in that man.   50

Farewell from Freiburg im Breisgau, 3 May in the year 1533 after Christ's birth

Written extempore

2804 / From Johann von Vlatten   Hambach, 3 May 1533

This letter was first published as Ep 183 in Förstemann / Günther. The autograph was in the Burscher Collection of the University Library at Leipzig (Ep 1254 introduction). Erasmus' reply is Ep 2845.

Johann von Vlatten (Ep 1390), vice-chancellor of Duke John III of the United Duchies of Cleves-Mark-Jülich-Berg, was one of the group of ardently Erasmian councillors who formulated and implemented the duke's policies. Of the other members of the group the most influential were the chancellor, Johann Gogreve (Ep 2298 n5), and the tutor to the future Duke William V, Konrad Heresbach (Ep 1316). Only recently united under a single ruler (1521) but maintaining their distinct existence, the duchies were not only difficult to administer politically but also fragmented religiously among the adherents of Catholicism, Lutheranism (especially in the cities), and Anabaptism. The response of the duke and his councillors was to exploit the duke's *ius reformandi* (his legal right as ruler to regulate religious affairs in his territories) to turn the United Duchies into the home *par excellence* of an Erasmian attempt to satisfy the demand for religious reform while preserving the unity of the church. Their efforts, summarized briefly in the *Kirchenordnung* (church order) of 11 January 1532 and elaborated in the *Erklärung zur Kirchenordnung* (Declaration Concerning the Church Order) of 8 April 1533, focused on broadly formulated Catholic doctrines, traditional

* * * * *

6 Georgius Agricola's *De mensuris et ponderibus* (cf Epp 2529:21–2, 2781–2) was published by Froben in August 1533.
7 The reference is to *De asse* of Guillaume Budé (1515), *De sestertio, pecuniis, ponderibus et mensuris antiquis* of Leonardo de Portis (c 1520), and the *Libellus de veterum ponderibus et mensuris* of Andrea Alciati (1530).
8 Erasmus means Matthias Kretz (Ep 2402), but gets both first name and surname wrong.

ceremonies cleansed of abuses, the avoidance of polemics, better training of the clergy, and close governmental supervision through visitations. We know that Konrad Heresbach visited Erasmus at Freiburg in September 1532 to consult with him on the reforms in progress (see Redlich 255 n1 and cf Ep 2728 n24). The present letter was carried by Karl Harst (n1 below), who brought with him a Latin translation of the *Erklärung zur Kirchenordnung* for Erasmus' comments (see Redlich 278:15–20). There is no record of what Erasmus actually said to Heresbach or Harst. It is clear, however, that although he cautiously avoided public endorsement of the church order, for fear of providing ammunition to his enemies, he privately expressed his approval (see Ep 2845:1–7). As reward for his services Duke John bestowed on Erasmus an annual pension of thirty Rhenish gold florins, the first instalment of which Harst brought with him (lines 7–9 below).

I send you greetings. The most illustrious prince of Jülich sincerely recognizes that your faithful, prudent, and wholesome advice concerning affairs of the faith and the Christian religion in his territories has turned out very well for his commonwealth, which has been badly weakened in many places. Hence he does not see how, in his mortal life, he can respond adequately 5
to your immortal kindness. Nevertheless, lest he should be thought to be completely ungrateful, he has decided to assign to you an annual pension of thirty Rhenish gold florins for as long as you shall live (which we pray may be for a long time). However munificent or generous this is, you should interpret it favourably as emanating from the very devoted affection and love 10
for you on the part of a most noble prince. Our friend Karl Harst will present you in person with thirty truly minted gold coins and will deliver to you the order of the prince that this should be regularly done in perpetuity.[1] He will also show you the chapters of the ordinance,[2] and will express the desire that you be not unwilling to share at some time with our preachers a clear and 15
succinct presentation of your work on the Lord's Prayer,[3] the Creed,[4] and

* * * * *

2804
1 In 1530 Karl Harst, Erasmus' former famulus (1524–5) had entered the service of Duke John III of Jülich-Cleves; see Ep 2231 n4. The gold coins were almost certainly Rhenish florins; if so, the pension was equivalent to £7 7s 6d groot Flemish, slightly less than a year's wage of a fully-employed Antwerp master mason/ carpenter (£8 8s 1d) at 9.05d per day and a year of 230 days (CWE 12 650 Table 3, 691 Table 13).
2 Harst's Latin translation of the *Erklärung zur Kirchenordnung* (see introduction above)
3 *Precatio dominica* (Ep 1393 introduction)
4 *Explanatio symboli* (Ep 2772 introduction)

the commandments of the Lord,[5] since this would seem to be not only most pleasing to our prince but also acceptable to God in his goodness and power, and also necessary and useful for these territories.

There have crept into our territories (alas!) some execrable and sacrile- 20 gious corruptors of the word of the Lord who, much to the distress of pious minds, vilify the great, sacred gift of Christ, the sacrosanct body of the Lord, and treacherously pervert it into something base and spurious.[6] God, in his immense compassion for us, will one day avert this evil.

The reason I am writing this rather late is that I had intended to entrust 25 its delivery to Quirinus Hagius, when he had returned from England, since he is a faithful servant of yours who can be trusted in such matters.[7] But since he has remained in England to manage your affairs, I wanted to make sure that these matters were entrusted to our friend Harst. As for what remains, he will tell you in person. Our chancellor,[8] a man who is greatly devoted to 30 you, wanted to write a few words to indicate his readiness to be of help to you; when he has returned from his embassy, he will write at greater length. Your friend William, a prince of excellent and unmatched character,[9] prays for your happiness and prosperity and sends you greetings a thousand times over. Farewell, and continue in your affection for me, as you do, and make use 35 of Vlatten as a discreet friend. Written extempore from Hambach, 3 May 33

Johann von Vlatten, scholaster, etc,[10] your friend

To the most fully accomplished gentleman Master Erasmus of Rotterdam, theologian, a friend to be respected reverently

* * * * *

5 In his reply to this letter (Ep 2845:15) Erasmus says 'commandments of the Decalogue,' ie the Ten Commandments, a subject treated in the concluding section of the *Explanatio symboli*.
6 The language here is sufficiently imprecise to cover the views of both Anabaptists and Spiritualists on the Catholic mass.
7 Quirinus Hagius (Ep 2704 n6), was currently on his second mission to England in the attempt to expedite the payment of sums owed to Erasmus by his patrons and friends. He seems to have made it back to the continent (Brussels) at about the end of June (Ep 2828:41–3), was in Tournai on 9 July (Ep 2842:32–3) and in Ghent on 12 July (Ep 2843:5). He arrived back in Freiburg at some point before 25 July (Ep 2846:120–1).
8 Johann Gogreve (see introduction)
9 William v, duke of Cleves, the dedicatee of *De pueris instituendis* (Ep 2189 introduction)
10 Vlatten was scholaster (head of the chapter school) at St Mary's in Aachen, where he was a canon.

2805 / To Bonifacius Amerbach   Freiburg, 3 May 1533

This letter (= AK Ep 1748) was first published in the *Epistolae familiares*. The autograph is in the Öffentliche Bibliothek of the University of Basel (MS AN III 15 48).

Greetings. You have never abused my good nature. But some people are trying to abuse your generosity.[1]

I had a good laugh at your reply to Herwagen about *De oratore*. That saying of Terence immediately came to mind: 'Not this [door], so far as I know.'[2] You could simply have said, 'Nothing was sent, however much it   5
was promised.'[3]

If the Portuguese has been troublesome to you, I am sorry about that.[4] To keep that from happening I did not want to recommend him, though he seems to be a man of good character and education.

About that untamed individual I will tell you a long tale,[5] but in person,   10
which I hope will soon be convenient for you. In the meantime keep what I wrote to you confidential. There is no character with whom I would like less to be at odds than with him. He is rotten to the core.

A certain theologian in the Collège de Navarre is lecturing on the Epistles of Paul to a large audience,[6] from time to time taking me to task,   15
drawing upon the ignorant and quarrelsome *Collations* of the Franciscan

* * * * *

2805
1 The reference to Cicero's *De oratore* in the following sentence suggests that Allen was right to see here an allusion to the importuning of both Erasmus and Bonifacius by Johann Herwagen for help with his edition of Cicero; see Epp 2765:13–21, 2768:1–11, 2769:18–21, 2775:1–5, and 2788:14–15.
2 Terence *Adelphi* 641. This is the response of Aeschinus, nephew of Micio, when his uncle, who has just emerged from a prostitute's house where he heard someone knocking on the door, asks Aeschinus whether he was the one knocking at the door. Since we do not know what Herwagen's question was, the meaning of Erasmus' imagined response is obscure.
3 Erasmus here plays with the words *missum* 'sent' and *promissum* 'promised' in a way that cannot be duplicated in English.
4 Probably Damião de Gois; see Ep 2826 introduction.
5 Possibly Ludovicus Carinus (Ep 920), an old friend with whom Erasmus had had a serious falling out (Ep 2111 n2), and who had recently sent Erasmus a letter full of 'the venom of long-standing enmity' (Ep 2788:30–5). The description of him as *indomitus* 'untamed,' 'wild,' 'ungovernable' may stem from Carinus' unseemly brawl with Erasmus' servant Felix Rex (Ep 2112:32–45).
6 Undoubtedly Jean de Gaigny; see Ep 2807 introduction.

Titelmans,[7] to whom I responded a while ago in a little book that was printed at Antwerp.[8] If you can get that book there, I beg you to send it to me. I myself cannot find any copy of it.[9]

Farewell. Freiburg, 5 May 1533   20

Erasmus of Rotterdam

To the very renowned gentleman Master Bonifacius Amerbach, doctor of laws. At Basel

2806 / From Julius Pflug   Zeitz, 5 May 1533

> For Julius Pflug, counsellor to Duke George of Saxony, see Ep 2395 introduction. Erasmus published this letter, Pflug's answer to one from Erasmus that is no longer extant, on pages 114–20 of *De sarcienda ecclesiae concordia* (Basel: Froben 1533), a work dedicated to Pflug (see Ep 2852). The final pages of what Allen describes as the original letter (from 'Camillo' in line 52 to the end) survive in the Landesbibliothek Stuttgart (ms Cod Hist folio 889) and were published by Gustav Bossert in the *Archiv für Reformationsgeschichte* 17 (1920) 233–5.

TO THE MOST LEARNED GENTLEMAN MASTER DESIDERIUS
ERASMUS OF ROTTERDAM, A MASTER TO BE GREATLY RESPECTED,
JULIUS PFLUG SENDS GREETINGS

Love for the church, to which I am committed, causes me never to cease thinking about her general state, even though I myself may not be able to of- 5 fer her any help. And from that very fact I derive much benefit, whether what comes to mind consoles or terrifies me. I am so absorbed in this thought that in the one case my mind is refreshed, but in the other it is fortified against impending adversities. For when an evil has been long foreseen it is usually easier to bear when it actually occurs. Added to this is a certain special bond 10 of duty. For since I hold public office in the church,[1] even though my abilities are not capable of maintaining it, I must still be willing to try to make every effort to do so. Therefore, since I can find no other way of fulfilling my duty, I am easily moved to implore the assistance of you and others like you, who

*****

7 Cf Ep 2807:9–11.
8 *Responsio ad Collationes* (Ep 2206 introduction)
9 Bonifacius seems to have sent a copy immediately: Erasmus forwarded it to Gaigny with his letter of 11 May (Ep 2807:80–1).

2806
1 As provost of Zeitz, as well as canon at Merseburg, Mainz, and Naumburg

are preeminent in learning and authority. I write this to make you under-   15
stand that, in addition to the purpose I share with all good men, I also have
a private duty, so that if I am excessively importunate, you will forgive me,
because the feeling that has carried me away is not at all unjustified.

As for the state of religion, what you wrote is absolutely true: for I have
experienced it myself. And at the present moment there is nothing to relieve   20
the anxiety of my spirit, especially because we never put an end to those
crimes that caused God to inflict such woeful miseries on us – quite justly so.
As for your inclination to take the wooden sword,[2] this will never be permitted by the God who gave you the power to have such an extraordinary effect
on mankind. Even less so because, just as the last song of a swan is usually   25
the sweetest, so too the last words uttered by some holy man with his last
breath are usually the holiest. And so, though you have your reasons for rejecting the demands of printers, you will still not find any way of satisfying
him who has every right, as it were, to give orders except by obeying.

But what am I doing? Somehow I am speaking to you as if your old age   30
were not occupied to such an extent that I hope it will last for a long time. In
fact, when I consider the splendid works that you continue to produce for us,
I understand very well that your old age is not only not deprived of the works
that every good man desires to have from you but is even more productive.
For all the powers that enable you to further Christianity are flourishing, per-   35
haps even more so than in your prime. This gives us reason to hope that you
will long render service to the church to which you manifest such devotion.
Inspired by your most affectionate letter, I thought I should write in this manner, not that an inexperienced young man like me should give advice to a
man of your age and authority, but rather in order to continue the discussion   40
you had initiated. In doing so, in the course of avoiding brevity, I have been,
in some way or other, more verbose and inept than was proper.

I come now to Giulio Camillo and Agostino of Gubbio: the former I knew
by appearance only when I was at Venice;[3] but the latter I met and spoke to on
many occasions. He made me particularly indebted to him because he made   45
it possible for me to frequent the library of Sant' Antonio whenever I wished.[4]

* * * * *

2 Ie 'retire from the fray.' On retirement a Roman gladiator was given a wooden
   sword (*Adagia* I ix 24).
3 For Giulio Camillo, see Ep 2632:154–80.
4 Agostino Steuco of Gubbio (Ep 2465 introduction) was librarian of the Grimani
   family collection in the convent of Sant' Antonio at Venice.

As for the amphitheatre of Camillo,[5] if it could be as useful as he promises
it will be, I would willingly become one of the spectators in it. And if he is
pleading a case in your court, Eloquence has already won. For if I know you
well, you will never pronounce sentence against her, because it is by her   50
gift that you are so great as to be a living presence in the eyes of the whole
world. And so Camillo accomplished nothing by casting her at your feet.[6]
Instead he should have come to terms with those who say that knowledge
cannot be joined with eloquence, as if, in fact, speaking in a debased style
constitutes wisdom.   55

I read a long time ago your letter to Steuco, in which you give him
advice in a friendly way and with great earnestness.[7] I only wish he had followed it. For it almost always happens that the pleasure won by insult is lost
by ill repute. And such an outcome conforms perfectly to the impartiality of
justice. So I am all the more surprised that it should enter into the man's head 60
to direct such scorn at our entire nation.[8] But if he did not wish to take your
excellent advice, had he but consulted his own good sense he would not so
shamefully have spewed that poison upon us.

Certainly there are in every nation some who under the semblance
of human beings act with the brutality of beasts. Likewise there are some   65
who excel in both intelligence and virtue. Anyone who denies this is truly
ignorant of human affairs or completely shameless. And so if someone reproaches an entire nation because of the deficiencies of certain members of
that nation, how, I ask, can he have the impudence to do such a thing? Why
doesn't he praise it instead because of the virtues of some of its citizens? That 70
conforms more closely to the proper role of a good man. Doesn't one who
makes such reproaches understand that he is disparaging his own country
and condemning it with a silent judgment, as it were, because it is guilty
of the same or similar crimes? But what if he does not so much condemn
vices as twist virtues into the kindred vices – for example, by attributing   75

* * * * *

5 See Ep 2632 n20.
6 Ie making her a suppliant seeking mercy from a judge, a common device of the
  advocates of defendants in the legal proceedings of the ancients
7 Ep 2465
8 Although Steuco's hostility to Germans is referred to in Erasmus' correspondence with him (Epp 2465:463–83, 2513:121–52), it is more amply documented
  in book 2 of Steuco's *Pro religione christiana adversus Lutheranos* (1530), where he
  describes the Germans as perennially inclined by nature to heresy and hostility
  to the papacy and thus susceptible to Luther's errors. Pflug's indignation was
  based on his reading of that work; see Pollet i 299–300 n4.

the lofty spirit and courage of our countrymen, which shines forth in the
face of dangers, to bestial ferocity. Then if one of the Germans, to whom
Steuco denies intelligence, should want to display his cleverness in this kind
of game, couldn't he easily use the force of his own oratory to make the most
outstanding qualities of Steuco look shameful? For there is no virtue that   80
does not have a kindred vice, so that what is upright and good can easily be
spoken of so as to be falsely portrayed and made to seem wicked.

    And so you are quite right to require prudence from Steuco, since there
are certainly many of our nation who, if they should once be aroused, would
make him understand that Germans do not lack intelligence or oratorical   85
skill or profound knowledge. Actually the facts themselves speak for our
people even if they do not say a word. For there are many indications, and
clear ones, not only of their intelligence but also of their extraordinary learning. Consider also that Steuco's state of life seems to be at odds with his bitterness. For what could be more alien to the duty of a Christian, a priest, and 90
a theologian than, in the very process of professing to defend the religious
life, to pour forth such bitterness and, quite contrary to the law of loving one
another, to inflict such manifest injury on many good men who deserve no
such thing? But let Steuco himself see to these matters. For my part, I would
wish he had refrained from this sort of slander. For I am concerned about the 95
man's honour. If he had done so, he would undoubtedly have derived more
benefit from his efforts and would not have called into doubt his own reputation, which he was so eager to defend.

    I was especially pleased by what you wrote about Guillaume Budé.[9]
For he so conducts himself and contributes so much to us that he seems to   100
me to have been born to shed lustre on true studies. And so I am delighted
that this great man is continuing in the course that has brought him great
glory for such a long time. If he gains as much authority among his countrymen as is due to his learning and virtue, which are unanimously celebrated, all good men should certainly rejoice, and that applies especially to the   105
French themselves.

    This almost takes care of your letter. But, lest you be unaware of what
is happening here, you should know that religion is more disturbed than
it used to be, and that some native of the region has recently arisen who is

* * * * *

9 Probably one of Erasmus' standard expressions of respect for Budé as a justly
  renowned scholar, paired with the insistence that there had never been any
  serious quarrel between them. See, for example, Ep 2448:5–15.

trying to introduce a new evil. For he says that Christ's words of consecra-   110
tion are not necessary to the Eucharist, and that in fact the appearance of the
bread and wine are not necessary, but that it is sufficient if the Eucharist is
received with an interior motion of the heart. Thus when he refers everything
to a spiritual eating, he does it so that he can completely take away the sacrament itself.[10] Nevertheless, God in his mercy has looked down upon us and   115
by his divine gift the author of this heresy was thrown into chains and it was
suppressed before it spread among the common people.[11]

* * * * *

10 Erasmus seems to have had this passage in mind when he wrote in *De concordia*:
    'Indeed, just recently someone has appeared on the scene who has dreamed
    up a view of this sacrament so wicked as to remove its whole sacramental na-
    ture, since what is performed only by mental processes and with no external
    sign is not worthy of the name of sacrament' (CWE 65 211). Cf Epp 2825:16–17,
    2845:23–5.
11 Cf Ep 2845:22–5, where Erasmus identifies Frankfurt as the place where these
    new doctrines were being taught. Accepting this at face value, the Allen editors
    tentatively identify the author of the heretical views in question as Dionysius
    Melander (c 1486–1561), a Dominican of Ulm who had been appointed evan-
    gelical preacher at Frankfurt (1525). But Melander's views on the sacrament
    were essentially those of the Strasbourg reformers Martin Bucer and Wolfgang
    Capito (see CWC 2 310, introduction to letter 346). In January 1533 Luther pub-
    lished an open letter admonishing the Frankfurt pastors to avoid 'Zwinglian'
    teachings, to which Melander and his fellow pastors responded in an open let-
    ter written by Bucer and published in March (see WA 30/3 554–71). Though
    Melander was criticized for the violent iconoclasm that accompanied his suc-
    cessful campaign for the abolition of the mass in the winter and spring of 1533,
    he was never arrested for any reason, and he left Frankfurt voluntarily in 1535
    at the call of Landgrave Philip of Hessen to serve as court preacher at Kassel.
    Pflug's language here indicates that he is in fact referring to the 'spiritual' view
    of the sacrament advanced by the Silesians Valentin Crautwald (1465?–1545)
    and his colleague Kaspar Schwenkfeld (1490–1561); cf CWE 65 211 n402, and
    see Douglas H. Shantz 'Crautwald, Valentin,' in OER I 451–2. Schwenckfeld left
    Silesia in 1529 and moved to Strasbourg, where there was still a community of
    Anabaptists and other dissidents, and lodged with Wolfgang Capito. Although
    Schwenckfeld refused to join any of the sects and maintained a discreet si-
    lence about his own views, he also refused to join the established church, thus
    eventually alienating Martin Bucer and the other preachers. When this letter
    was written, however, Schwenckfeld was still in Strasbourg and had not been
    'thrown into chains,' nor would he be so before leaving the city in 1534; see R.
    Emmet McLaughlin 'Schwenckfeld, Kaspar von' OER IV 22. As for Crautwald,
    who never left Silesia, he was never 'thrown into chains' either. The identity of
    the person to whom Pflug is here referring thus remains a mystery.

Otherwise I know of no news at all to write about, and I think this more
than enough, especially when writing to a man like you who has little free
time. But I preferred to be expansive rather than not demonstrate that I was 120
delighted by what you wrote. It was like talking with you, and from my
reluctance to stop talking you can easily understand the pleasure that I experienced. And so you did not seem to me to be garrulous (the word you used)
but to speak with great deftness and substance, and the longer your letter
was, the more intensely you seemed to love me. Thus I feel myself bound to 125
repay your kindness as much as anyone possibly could. And since nothing
could be more fitting than that I give evidence of my gratitude to you in any
way I can, you will be doing me a great favour if you indicate to me in what
way you would wish me to fulfil my obligation to you.

    Farewell. Zeitz, 5 May 1533 130
    Julius Pflug

2807 / To [Jean de Gaigny]   Freiburg, 11 May 1533

The surviving manuscript of this letter, first published by Allen, is an autograph rough draft with no heading in the Royal Library at Copenhagen (MS GKS
95 Fol, folio 182). The person addressed is clearly the 'theologian in the Collège
de Navarre ... lecturing on the Epistles of Paul' referred to in Ep 2805:14–15.
Allen reluctantly endorsed the 'plausible' speculation of Herminjard III 58 that
the unnamed theologian was Étienne Loret (d c 1541), who at the time was
grand master of the Collège de Navarre. But, as Allen noted, there is no evidence for this in the letter itself. There is, however, good evidence that in 1532–3
the theologian Jean de Gaigny (d 1549), lectured on the Epistles of St Paul at
the Collège de Navarre; see Farge *Biographical Register* 178. We conclude that he
was the addressee of this letter.

    Born in the diocese of Paris, Gaigny studied arts at the Collège de Navarre from
about 1516, taking his MA around 1520, teaching arts for several years, serving
briefly as rector of the university in 1531, and attracting notice for his proficiency
in the three languages. He received his doctorate in theology in March 1532 and
was for a time actively involved in the affairs of the faculty. Around 1536, however, he came under the patronage of Francis I, to whom he became chaplain,
almoner, and librarian, and through whom he received a long list of ecclesiastical
preferments and lucrative benefices. As royal librarian he enthusiastically collected books and manuscripts that he found lying neglected in monasteries and
priories, and in a number of cases he either edited them for publication himself
or fostered the efforts of others to do so. Also a prolific author of works in both
French and Latin, he even set up a printing press in his own house. For details
and a list of his many publications see Farge *Biographical Register* 179–83.

I am especially pleased that you, who are accurately and meticulously learned in the three languages, are lecturing to a large audience on Paul, that extraordinary Doctor of the church. I do not mind that you sometimes disagree with me. You have a right to do so. For the truth has priority over everything, especially in Holy Scripture, and I would not want anyone to   5
favour me so highly as to do any damage to Holy Scripture in order to advance my reputation. Moreover, even when you do this with exaggeration and pique, it is right for me to forgive your zeal, which I think is far removed from any guile or malice. But that you take your criticisms and bad temper in great part from the *Collations* of the Franciscan Titelmans shows, believe me,   10
that you are not following the best source.[1]

Since he wrote these things when he was young, he was too little trained for the task, not sufficiently skilled in the Latin language, and had only a smattering of Greek. I wish he had brought to this undertaking as much learning and judgment as high spirits and selfconfidence. It is difficult to believe how   15
much arrogance lurked under the sackcloth and ashes and the semblance of humility. And so those fathers, not without reason, curbed him with a bit.[2] But if such a great doctor as you did not hesitate to read the *Collations* of Titelmans, I beg you not to be unwilling to read my replies to them, even though I wrote them with a light touch, as they say;[3] I even suppressed his   20
name, lest I irritate further a young man who was already too ardent.[4]

I have often testified that I undertook the translation of the New Testament against my own inclination. But however reluctant, I was driven to do so by those who were more interested in the advantage of the printer than in my reputation.[5] And even so I never cease to insist that my translation   25
was not undertaken with the aim of replacing the old translation or of having it read publicly, but rather of making the old one better understood through comparison and showing clearly how much the readings of the orthodox

* * * * *

2807
1 For Erasmus' controversy with the Louvain Franciscan Frans Titelmans, see CWE 16 xvi–xvii. The work by Titelmans referred to here is *Collationes quinque super epistolam ad Romanos* (1529).
2 The faculty of theology had attempted to prevent publication of Titelmans' work; see Ep 2089:2–6.
3 Literally 'with a light arm' (*Adagia* I iv 27)
4 Erasmus entitled his 1529 apologia against Titelmans *Reply to the Collations of a Certain Young Teacher of Old Men* (*Responsio ad Collationes cuiusdam iuvenis gerontodidascali*) and did not mention him by name in it.
5 Cf Ep 2758:12–18 with n2.

Greeks differ from those of the Latins.[6] And this was practically inevitable
because of the Greek commentaries, which frequently do not correspond   30
with the Latin edition. Furthermore, if they think I wanted to undermine the
old translation, which has been accepted for so many centuries, they are deceived in their imagination. Even if the pope had wanted that, I would have
opposed it with all my might. Others are also deceived who do not distinguish between the version of the Old Translator and the errors of scribes or   35
others,[7] between the fountain of the Scriptures and the puddles polluted by
human ignorance or carelessness. Others are wrong if they read my translation without the Annotations.[8] In the translation it is possible to express only
one meaning; in the commentary various interpretations can be given and
the reader is free to choose whichever he wants to accept. In the Annotations   40
I propose whatever meaning seems to me to be closest to the apostolic sense.

Now just as those who change a true reading betray Scripture, so also
those who twist it to a false meaning do not deserve well of it. But I have
pointed out some places where the ancients have done both these things, either
to avoid giving scandal to the unlearned multitudes (for at that time Scrip-   45
ture was accessible to ordinary people)[9] or to oppose heretics. Furthermore,
it seems to me that Scripture owes a great deal to one who restores its true
reading or who points out the true and genuine meaning by exposing a violent distortion of the meaning. But if it is not allowable that anyone translate
any passage in Scripture in a different way than the ancient translators did,   50
especially when they are fighting against heretics, then first of all the ancients
do not always agree among themselves, and then too it is a fact that some
interpretations (and they not merely a few) proposed by Ambrose, Jerome,

* * * * *

6 By 'the old translation' Erasmus means the Vulgate, universally used in the
  Latin West for public worship.
7 The Vulgate New Testament was based on the 'Old Latin' version by an anony-
  mous 'Old Translator,' whose work St Jerome revised to make it correspond
  more closely to the original Greek. Erasmus was adamant that Jerome's revision had, over the centuries, been extensively corrupted by scribal error and
  editorial malfeasance. Cf Ep 2172 nn2 and 5.
8 Erasmus' editions of the New Testament had three parts, the original Greek text,
  Erasmus' Latin translation, and his critical notes (the Annotations) keyed to
  the Vulgate and commenting on its adequacy as a translation. The Annotations
  were his chief contribution to New Testament scholarship.
9 Because it was in their own language

and Augustine as pious and worthy of belief have been clearly rejected by the
scholastic theologians. 55

Since I have pointed out some of these difficulties in their proper places,
it is not necessary to repeat them here. But one of them is, in my opinion,
inexcusable: Augustine (among others) interprets the words of John 'Unless
you eat the flesh of the Son of Man, etc'[10] as if it said that the baptism of infants is not effective unless they receive the body and blood of the Lord, and 60
that before this Christians were not accustomed to kiss the hands of the
infants, as if they did not recognize them as members of the church until
after they had received the other sacrament.[11]

There remains, then, some scandal, which is not inconsiderable, but not
to the degree that truth is to be silenced. Jerome was not unaware that a new 65
translation of the Old Testament would cause some disturbance, but that did
not deter that holiest of men from his enterprise. Now, however, since such
matters are discussed by learned men in the absence of the people, there is accordingly not much danger. And if any scandal arises, it should be attributed to
those who make a public outcry to the ignorant crowd without having exam- 70
ined the matter: 'Lo, someone has arisen who would change "Magnificat,"'[12]
'Lo, he corrects the Gospel of John, reading "In the beginning was Speech."'[13]

I have written these things, my eminent friend, not to object in any
way to your most holy labours, but rather to lend my assistance. For one

* * * * *

10 John 6:53
11 See the annotation on Rom 5:12 CWE 56 149 with nn66–8 (page 159). See also *In
psalmum 38* CWE 65 48 with n182.
12 In his annotation on Luke 1:46, the first verse of the Song of Mary, which begins
Magnificat anima mea and is commonly referred to as the Magnificat (Luke 1:46–
55), Erasmus observes that *magnificit* 'esteem highly,' 'make much of' would be
a 'more apt' translation of the Greek than *magnificat* 'to extol,' 'honour.' It is not
clear who, if anyone, complained about this particular annotation with its extremely fine distinction. The recorded complaints concerning Erasmus' treatment
of the Magnificat make specific reference only to verse 55, where he was falsely
charged with changing 'Abraham and his seed' to 'his seeds.' See Ep 948:101–7.
13 In the second edition of the New Testament (1519) Erasmus translated the opening verse of the Gospel of John as *In principio erat sermo* 'In the beginning was The
Spoken Word / Speech' instead of *In principio erat verbum* 'In the beginning was
the Word.' Although this was hardly a novelty in the history of efforts to render
the Greek word *Logos* accurately into Latin, it caused a storm of criticism from
conservative theologians in England, Louvain, and Paris. Erasmus defended
himself in the *Apologia de 'In principio erat sermo'* (1520). See CWE 62 xii–xix.

who advises helps to a certain extent, according to the saying of Plautus.[14] 75
Then again, the more restrained you are in taking up this subject matter, the
more profit your hearers will gain, and the more favour you will acquire in
the eyes of God and men. You have beheld the tumults stirred up by certain
people, and you see how no profit comes from them.

I am sending you the only copy I had of the book,[15] which I suspect you 80
have not yet seen. In your kindness you will take my solicitude in good part
as arising from the best of intentions. Farewell.

Given at Freiburg, 11 May 1533

2808 / From Johann Löble   Augsburg, 11 May 1533

This letter was first published as Ep 184 in Förstemann / Günther. The manuscript, in a secretary's hand but signed by Löble, was in the Burscher Collection
of the University Library at Leipzig (Ep 1254 introduction). For Löble, a high
official in the Austrian Hapsburg treasury and landlord of the house at Freiburg
in which Erasmus had lived in the years 1529–31, see Ep 2497 introduction.

Greetings to you, most learned and honourable sir, together with whatever
effort and service I can provide. Yesterday Ferdinand, the most serene king
of the Romans, etc, my most gracious lord, having also sent me his letter for
this purpose, ordered that I should send in his name as a gift to your Lordship
150 gold florins of the Rhine, and also to Master Henricus Glareanus 50, and 5
to this sum my most reverend lord the cardinal of Trent added in his name
50 gold florins to be paid out to you.[1] You will receive this money at Strasbourg
from Johann Ebel and Hieronymus Hirschkoren, (formerly the business associates of Friedrich Prechter),[2] to whom I write in the present document,
and order that whenever you request it they should pay out to you 250 gold 10
florins, which I am quite confident they will do without any delay.

* * * * *

14 *Curculio* 460: 'Qui monet quasi adjuvat.'
15 This is presumably the copy of the *Responsio ad Collationes* that Erasmus had
    asked Bonifacius Amerbach to send to him; see Ep 2805:16–19.

2808
1 For the background of these payments, see Ep 2801.
2 Friedrich Prechter (documented 1485–before 1546) was a leading businessman and banker in Strasbourg, a major producer of paper and a partner of the
   Fugger banking house. Johann Ebel, about whom little is known, was his son-
   in-law. Hieronymus Hirschkoren has not been identified.

Moreover, I was told, most learned sir, by Master Johann Koler, the provost of Chur, how your Lordship recently wrote him that you were once more troubled by my agents in Freiburg concerning the payment of the rent for my house,[3] though I had certainly forbidden them many times to require 15 anything from you, but that they should only determine how much money had been agreed with you as rent for the house, since his most serene Majesty did not want the amount you owed me to be collected from you but rather that it should be assigned to him and his royal Majesty would give it to me. I was most annoyed (and rightly so) that you should be troubled by my agents 20 (which was quite improper) since I not only want you to be free and clear of this obligation, but I am also ordering that if in the future anyone should disturb you any further about this matter you can show him this letter as proof that you owe me nothing whatever. Indeed, far be it from me to ask anything from you or to demand anything from you in any manner what- 25 soever. I would rather that all my resources should be at your disposal, in whatever way they could be of use to you. In sum, I want to assure you that I want nothing so much as to deserve very well of you and to provide for your comfort, however I may be able to devote myself to it. Farewell.

Given at Augsburg, 11 May, in the year of our salvation 1533 30

Very truly yours, with sincere friendship, Johann Löble, signed in my hand, written by a secretary[4]

To the most renowned and learned doctor of sacred theology, Desiderius Erasmus of Rotterdam, his cherished friend. At Freiburg

2809 / To Johann Georg Paumgartner   Freiburg, 12 May 1533

Erasmus published this letter in the epistolary appendix to *De praeparatione ad mortem* (Basel: Froben and Episcopius 1534) pages 143–4. For Johann Georg Paumgartner, a young Nürnberg patrician currently studying in Padua, see Ep 2683 introduction. This is the last of the three surviving letters in Erasmus' correspondence with him.

* * * * *

3 The letter to Koler is not extant. For the complicated business of Erasmus' move (in 1531) from the house 'zum Walfisch,' which Löble owned, to the house 'zum kind Jesu,' and the claim of rent still owed to Löble, see Epp 2462 introduction, 2470, 2497. For Koler's intervention on Erasmus' behalf, at the behest of Christoph von Stadion, bishop of Augsburg, see Ep 2505:11–30.
4 The text reads 'p.m.p.s.'; we take this to mean 'per manum [meam] per secretarium.' Cf Ep 2497:38 with n7.

DESIDERIUS ERASMUS OF ROTTERDAM
TO JOHANN GEORG PAUMGARTNER, GREETINGS

If you want to see the book I dedicated to your father,[1] then you should ask him for it. For here no one is available to who would be a responsible carrier of a packet. There is no reason, my fine young man, for you to worry about 5 the duty of repaying me. Among those who belong to the federation of the Graces duties are mutually exchanged, but there is no system of rewards. Even so, your very kind father of his own accord undertook to repay this little favour of mine, even though I had been careful not to give any indication that I expected a return payment. He sent me a gilded cup,[2] a fitting gift 10 for a Dutchman, but one who is now hardly a drinker in the Dutch fashion. I find your devoted fondness for me, my dearest Georg, most gratifying indeed, and it is only right that I should have the same feelings for you. But if I have done you any favour – which I certainly consider to be nothing or of no great importance – you cannot return the favour in any better way than to 15 strive to improve yourself every day, that is, to become more like your excellent father. But in fact, since of your own volition you are already running eagerly in the race, you do not need to be goaded by my encouragement. Do not apologize for your desire, as you do in your letter, and I will not apologize for my advice. For that reason I urge you time and again to select 20 the best from the best authors. In that list there is no place for Erasmus, who perhaps seems finer to you than he actually is, because you are seduced by your love for him, since to you what is not beautiful seems beautiful, as that famous Sicilian poet says.[3]

Farewell. Freiburg, 12 May 1533   25

2810 / To Viglius Zuichemus   [Freiburg], 14 May 1533

This letter, Erasmus' reply to Ep 2791, was first published in LB III/2 1756–8 *Appendix epistolarum* no 372. Since 1936 the autograph, which P.S. Allen consulted in London in 1909, has been in the Central Library at Rotterdam (MS 94 D 2). For Viglius Zuichemus, at this time lecturing on civil law at Padua, see Ep 2101 introduction. The letter bears his endorsement: 'Delivered on 26 June 1533.' His reply is Ep 2854.

* * * * *

2809
1 *Aliquot homiliae Chrysostomi* (Ep 2774)
2 See Major 57 n32.
3 Greek in the text; Theocritus 6:18–19

Viglius Zuichemus
Cabinet des Estampes, Strasbourg

You are mistaken if you think you know even the thousandth part of the troubles that I have to put up with, apart from the inconveniences of old age and bodily infirmity. But even the gods do not fight against necessity.[1]

The Maecenas of Alogos[2] wrote a most kindly letter, and sent a cup, which I have not yet received, though it was sent a year ago.[3] In my last letter 5 to him I complained somewhat about the effrontery of the man's tongue, but with the greatest moderation, otherwise than he deserves.[4]

I cannot guess who that archbishop is, since you do not reveal the name, unless perhaps it is William Knight, which I would certainly hope that it is.[5] Once again I have sent my servant Quirinus Hagius to England, 10 for the last time I sent him he returned emptyhanded; and now I do not expect anything different.[6]

It pains me that the situation in England presages serious conflicts. Nor are things in the Low Countries any more tranquil. The pope commands the king of England to live with the queen as man and wife until Rome has 15 pronounced on the case. But everyone understands that there will be no end to the dispute as long as the parties to the marriage are alive. It is eight years now that this affair has been going on, and the king's conscience is burdened, not without reason, since two hundred doctors have proved with arguments from Scripture that entering into that marriage was impermissible according 20

* * * * *

2810
1 Greek in the text. See *Adagia* II iii 41.
2 The nickname (Greek in the text) of Georg von Logau (Ep 2716 n3), the Latin form of whose surname, *a Logus*, made possible the pun on Greek *alogos*, meaning 'without eloquence,' 'unreasonable,' 'stupid.' Cf Ep 2791 n3. His Maecenas (Ep 2815 n6) was Stanislaus Thurzo, bishop of Olomouc.
3 The letter is Ep 2699. As for the cup, it did eventually arrive and was recorded in the inventory of Erasmus' possessions; see Ep 2699 n2.
4 The most recent surviving letter to Thurzo, Ep 2608, contains no such complaint about Logau.
5 Cf Ep 2791:17–19. Erasmus had evidently not yet received the news that Thomas Cranmer had succeeded William Warham as archbishop of Canterbury. William Knight (1476–1547) studied at New College, Oxford from 1491, and at some point Erasmus appears to have met him (see Ep 534:73n). Trained in canon law, he became chaplain to Henry VIII (1515), protonotary apostolic (1516), and the king's secretary (1526). In 1541 he became bishop of Bath and Wells. From 1514 he had a distinguished diplomatic career, during which he shared a number of missions with Thomas More, whom he came to know well.
6 See Ep 2804 n7. The current mission would in fact produce encouraging results; see Ep 2815:8–19.

to both human and divine law.[7] But if the pope annuls the marriage, he will
first of all offend the emperor,[8] and then he will condemn the see of Rome,
because it granted an illegal dispensation. Such cases, which bring a great
deal of money to Rome and which render princes subject to our most holy
Father, do not usually come to an end. And perhaps there is something else   25
smouldering in the mind of the king that he does not want to be revealed.[9]

Now I move on from England to Friesland. It is extremely difficult to
maintain a friendship with Cammingha.[10] He is supremely cunning and
is deeply offended by a word or two spoken in a straightforward way. He
wrested several letters from me, which I am now ashamed to have written.[11]   30
In his view no praise is sufficient, and I have no doubt that he is severely angry with me. He was indignant because when I wrote to others I did
not deign to send him a letter.[12] It was clearly a declaration of war if I did not
make honourable mention of him in the letter to Hoxwier. That mention was

* * * * *

7 There is a heavy dose of irony here. Henry VIII's claim was that his marriage to
   his brother's widow, Catherine of Aragon, was contrary to divine law and that,
   consequently, pope Julius II had had no right to issue a dispensation allowing
   the marriage. By 1531 Henry VIII's agents had secured and published favourable *determinationes* from eight French and North Italian universities (including, by a narrow margin, the Paris faculty of theology); see Scarisbrick 255–8;
   Ep 2413 n15. But Erasmus, who was devoted to Queen Catherine, did not find
   Henry's argument persuasive, though he refrained from saying so publicly;
   see Ep 2256:39–63, and cf Ep 2267:46–143. He knew perfectly well, moreover,
   that many of his English friends, including Thomas More (see Ep 2735:42–4),
   were opposed to the divorce. And he would doubtless have smiled at Conradus
   Goclenius' mockery of the 'virtue and wisdom' shown by the Paris theologians
   ('Sorbonnic heroes') in their *determinatio* on the royal divorce (Ep 2573:10–11).
8 Charles V was the nephew of Queen Catherine.
9 In mid-January 1533 Anne Boleyn, Henry's chosen replacement for Queen
   Catherine, had been found to be pregnant, and c 25 January she and Henry
   were secretly married. On 23 May – nine days after the date of this letter –
   Archbishop Cranmer declared Henry's marriage to Catherine of Aragon void,
   and on 1 June Anne Boleyn was crowned in Westminster Abbey.
10 For Haio Cammingha and the disintegration of Erasmus' friendship with him,
   see Ep 2766 introduction.
11 The only surviving letter to Cammingha himself is Ep 2073, published in the
   Opus epistolarum but not again in Erasmus' lifetime. Two other letters, Epp
   2261–2 (to Haio Herman and Gerard van Herema), were also withdrawn from
   publication after their initial printing in the *Epistolae floridae*, on the ground that
   they contained passages complimentary to Cammingha; see Allen's introduction to Ep 2261.
12 See Ep 2766:3–6, 16–19.

removed in my published letters and in his place Viglius was substituted.[13]   35
O heavens! O earth!

About the attitude of the other one I am not greatly concerned.[14] When
he came back from Italy and was seeking a position at court (and, by virtue of
the commendation of that title, a well dowered wife),[15] in elaborate letters he
entreated from me elaborate letters of recommendation to the leading figures   40
of the court; he got what he asked for and thanked me for it.[16] It is a wretched
thing to depend on such characters.[17] I suspect, however that Cammingha
did not contribute very much to maintaining the friendship.

I warned the son of the treasurer about my pension from the emperor,
and I beg you to warn him not to write a word to anyone about the pen-   45
sion. I see that he has no notion of the nature of this matter, and his father
cannot do anything about it;[18] Praet and Laurinus could obviously do even

* * * * *

13 In its published form (*Epistolae palaeonaeoi*), the letter to Hector van Hoxwier
   (Ep 2586) includes an encomium of Hoxwier's native Friesland as a burgeoning
   'home of the Muses.' Praised by name for their 'prolific talents' are Haio Herman
   and Viglius Zuichemus, while all mention of Haio Cammingha has been omitted.
14 Haio Herman, for whom see Ep 1978 introduction. The correspondence between him and Erasmus had ceased with Ep 2261. Their friendship may have
   been damaged by Erasmus' failure to mention Haio in the first edition of the
   Ciceronianus, though the omission was remedied in the second edition (Ep 2108).
   Haio's silence eventually led Erasmus to conclude, probably wrongly, that he
   had conceived a mortal hatred of him because of the omission (Ep 2587:57–8).
15 Anna Occo, to whom he was already married by March 1528 (Ep 1978 n1). In
   July 1528 Haio was appointed to the council of Friesland. In February 1532 he
   became a member of the council of Utrecht.
16 The letters of recommendation (to Erard de la Marck and Jean (II) de Carondelet)
   are Epp 2054–5. No letters of Haio to Erasmus are extant.
17 This sounds like an expression of Erasmus' disappointment that Haio's burden
   of administrative duties had prevented him from undertaking what Erasmus
   thought was his duty, namely editing the works of his kinsman Rodolphus
   Agricola, responsibility for which was taken over by Alaard of Amsterdam; see
   Epp 1978:5–18, 2073:79–81, 2091:115–26, 2587:52–6.
18 Viglius' friend and fellow law student, Florens van Griboval, who was living
   with him at Padua, was the son of Pieter van Griboval, treasurer of Flanders (Ep
   2716 n39). Florens had generously offered to appeal to his father for assistance
   in securing payment of Erasmus' imperial pension (Ep 2716:165–75), and in
   Ep 2791:39–44 Viglius reports that Florens had already written to his father and
   would continue his efforts in Erasmus' behalf after his return to the Netherlands
   from Padua. In the meantime, however, Erasmus, having himself written to the
   father, had quickly come to the conclusion expressed here; see Ep 2716 n45.

less.[19] Therefore I would not want the matter to go awry because of his intervention. Still, his affection for me is not at all unappreciated; it is merely that
I would not want to make use of his services in this matter. Even though he   50
is returning to his country, I would not want him to try to do anything.

Brassicanus is either angry about certain matters or is overcome by
shame. He had boasted that there was no lack of proverbs collected after
those of Erasmus, whereas he took almost thirty proverbs from mine.[20] He
has stopped writing to me – which is easy for me to bear.[21] There is nothing   55
more irritating than his letters, and he mixed up his insults with such flattery
that sometimes I think he is out of his mind.

Aleandro is glad to be at Venice; he has been looking for a title under
which he could live more honourably there.[22]

I have not seen anything by Vida.[23] I would be glad to read the books   60
of Ricci if they were published.[24] The canon sent me a manuscript of the
Prefaces.[25] I sent it to Hieronymus so that he could add the booklet to the
Chrysostom, but I do not know yet whether he did so.[26]

* * * * *

19 Louis of Flanders, lord of Praet (Ep 1191), a genuine admirer of Erasmus who
   had long been a member of the privy council of Charles v, was now one of the
   closest advisers of the regent, Mary of Hungary. Marcus Laurinus (Ep 1342),
   dean of St Donatian's at Bruges and son of Hieronymus Laurinus, treasurer
   to Philip the Handsome, had always maintained close contacts with the court
   at Brussels.
20 Johannes Alexander Brassicanus (Ep 1146), whom Erasmus had met at Antwerp
   in 1520, was now a professor at the University of Vienna, where he taught rhetoric, Greek, and civil law. He and Erasmus enjoyed friendly relations until the
   publication in 1529 of Brassicanus' *Proverbiorum Symmicta*. At first, Erasmus
   found the work 'delightful,' but subsequently concluded that a substantial portion of its content had been taken from his *Adagia*.
21 No letters of Brassicanus to Erasmus survive.
22 Girolamo Aleandro, Erasmus' friend-turned-enemy (Ep 1553 n9), was now
   papal legate at Venice (1533–5) and had 'received the office of judging which
   books can be sold publicly' (Ep 2791:47–9).
23 Marco Girolamo Vida; see Ep 2791 n17.
24 Bartolomeo Ricci; see Ep 2971 n19.
25 The canon was Giovanni Crisostomo Zanchi. The 'manuscript of the *Prefaces*'
   was presumably the preface to the life of Cyprian that in Ep 2791:54–7 Viglius
   said he was sending to Erasmus. See the following sentence.
26 Hieronymus Froben had published an edition of Chrysostom's *Opera* in 1530
   (Ep 2359) and a volume of *Aliquot homiliae* in March 1533 (Ep 2774). The manuscript would have to have been received well before the composition of this
   letter in order for it to be appended to the volume of homilies. At all events, it
   was not.

I would not want you, my friend Viglius, to go to the trouble of copying out the life of Cyprian or the sermons of Ambrose.[27] The matter is not impor- 65 tant enough for that. If you can hire someone to copy them, I will see to it that Hieronymus reimburses you.

I am afraid that the architect of the Amphitheatre will not find such ready and easy generosity from the king as he thinks.[28] They write that the reason is the treachery of a moneychanger who went bankrupt (as they say),[29] 70 and ran away, to seek (I think) a pardon from the pope. For two whole years now, the professors of languages have not been paid a cent; so all of them have deserted their professorships, except Toussain.[30]

Everything you write about Bembo I found extremely delightful. I am greatly pleased indeed that you are dear to such a man.[31] Recently I read some 75 of the rhetorical exercises written in his youth, and I found them all most pleasing, especially *Aetna*, which persuaded me that it is no longer active.[32]

I am very pleased that your Greek *Institutes* is being published with favourable prospects.[33] I know that the project at Nürnberg was undertaken

* * * * *

27 See Ep 2791:56–7.
28 For his Amphitheatre ('theatre of memory') Guido Camillo was expecting to profit handsomely from the patronage of King Francis I of France; see Ep 2657:30–71.
29 For 'bankrupt' Erasmus uses the peculiar expression *mensa rupta* (from *banca rotta*). He had recently used the same expression in his exposition of Psalm 38 (ASD V-3 223:959–60).
30 On the foundation of the Collège royale in 1530 and the appointment of the first four regis professors (*lecteurs royaux*), two in Greek and two in Hebrew, see Ep 2456 introduction. Jacques Toussain (Epp 2119, 2421) was professor of Greek. Although it is true that King Francis I had been paying them little attention and no salary (a deficit made up at least in part by the income from ecclesiastical benefices granted them by certain sympathetic bishops), Erasmus' allegation that all but Toussain had deserted their professorships is not true: in 1534 they were all still there, causing anxiety in the faculty of theology. The first to leave was Pierre Danès, the other professor of Greek, in 1535. See James K. Farge *Le parti conservateur au xvie siècle: Université et parlement de Paris à l'époque de la Renaissance et de la Réforme* (Paris 1992) 37, 117–31 (documents VIIA–C).
31 Ep 2791:57–63
32 Pietro Bembo's *De Aetna dialogus* was published by Aldo Manuzio at Venice in 1495.
33 Viglius' edition (published by Froben at Basel in 1534) of the thirteenth-century Greek translation of Justinian's *Institutes* by Theophilus Antecessor, the manuscript of which he had discovered in the library of St Mark's, Venice; cf Ep 2791 n22.

precipitously.[34] I don't want you to offend Aleandro in any way at all – but I know that I admonish you in vain, because he of course has a good memory.[35] You have my reaction to almost all the parts of your letter.

At Paris Scaliger has published some epigrams chosen from three thousand. In his preface he says they have no teeth because by temperament he always shies away from mordacity.[36] He is waiting for a reply from me and has already prepared another invective.[37] But I have not read through all of his book; I just glanced at it.[38] Sepúlveda has returned to his beloved Spain, in the entourage of Iñigo, cardinal and bishop of Burgos,[39] through whose faithful efforts I have obtained the annotations of Zúñiga on the Jerome and on my Annotations on the New Testament, which Zúñiga left behind on his deathbed, not to be published but to be transmitted to me.[40] But that would

80

85

90

* * * * *

34 The reference is to the pioneering edition of the *Corpus iuris civilis* published at Nürnberg (1529–31) by Gregorius Haloander (Ep 2568 n9). Viglius had discovered at Venice a manuscript of the *Novellae constitutiones* (part 4 of the *Corpus*) that was more complete and correct than Haloander's version (Ep 2791:60–3 with n23).

35 Aleandro's legatine and inquisitorial authority at Venice (see n22 above) extended to Padua, so Erasmus warns Viglius of the legate's tendency to detect heresy in Erasmians and never to forget it.

36 This is a puzzle. In 1533 Julius Caesar Scaliger (Ep 2564 n2) did indeed publish at Paris a volume of *Nova epigrammata*, a collection of short, mostly erotic poems that was included in later editions of his *Poemata*. But it had no introduction (at least not in the text published at Heidelberg in 1574 – the only one accessible to us). Moreover, Erasmus appears to be speaking of epigrams in the sense of barbed verses aimed a rivals (a form in which Scaliger was well versed) rather than verses about love. We cannot identify any such epigrams of Scaliger published at this time.

37 The reply that Scaliger was waiting for was one to his *Oratio pro Cicerone contra Erasmum* (1531), but Erasmus refused to write one; see Ep 2564 n2. As far as is known, Scaliger did not start writing his second *Oratio contra Erasmum* until the spring of 1535; see Vernon Hall, Jr *The Life of Julius Caesar Scaliger (1484–1558)* Transactions of the American Philosophical Society, new series 40/2 (Philadelphia 1950) 108. It was not published until 1537, after Erasmus' death.

38 Cf Ep 2736:13–14.

39 Iñigo López de Mendoza y Zúñiga (Ep 2705) cardinal-bishop of Burgos and a diplomat in the service of Charles v, did indeed return to his diocese in Spain in 1533, but there is no evidence that Juan Ginés de Sepúlveda (Ep 2637), who had enjoyed his patronage, went with him.

40 For this transmission to Erasmus of the annotations of Diego López Zúñiga on Erasmus' edition of Jerome and his Annotations on the New Testament, see Epp 2637:24–36, 2701:11–17, 2705, 2729:28–34.

never have been done by Sepúlveda if Iñigo had not diligently seen to it. Sepúlveda is remarkably satisfied with his own work, though there is nothing more stupid.[41] He has not read any of my works; he simply exaggerates stories he has heard about them. But in his own letter to me he confesses that he has said some hateful things against me, not out of anger but to please those who favour Pio.[42] Isn't that a clever excuse? But what was an unassuming man to do? If he didn't do so, they would renounce their friendship. I had a good laugh when he no longer gives me precedence over Lucian but much more so over the blasphemous Averroes.[43] This was an opportunity to display the vehemence of Demosthenes.[44]

When Pio, deceived by the note of some hireling who had written 'Erasmus ridicules anathemas,' spends a whole chapter defending papal excommunications, although I was talking about the waxen images placed in churches according to the Italian custom,[45] Sepúlveda finds me lacking in courtesy, saying 'You should have blamed this fault on the copyist.'[46] But he could not have done it, given that Pio is completely off the mark.

Sepúlveda takes great pains to prove that Pio had no help from anyone,[47] though in fact, out of those whom Pio hired for this task, some wrote to me and some admitted it to me here.[48]

* * * * *

41 The *Antapologia pro Alberto Pio*, published in two editions (Rome and Paris) in 1532. The copy sent to Erasmus was a hand-annotated copy of the Rome edition. See Ep 2637 introduction and n1. We had access to a digitized copy of the Paris edition.

42 Ep 2637:3–23

43 *Antapologia* (Paris edition) 49

44 The oratory of Demosthenes was often described as vehement, especially in his speeches against Philip II of Macedon.

45 See *Apologia adversos rhapsodias Alberti Pii* CWE 84 178 with n428; *Brevissima scholia* CWE 84 365 with n11. The original meaning of *anathema* in Greek was 'an offering,' which is the intended meaning here: a votive offering left at the image of a saint in gratitude for a favour rendered by the saint. The more familiar use of 'anathema' to mean a curse or (in ecclesiastical usage) a formal ban or excommunication, was a later development.

46 These words are not in the Paris edition of the *Antapologia*. They may have been in the hand-annotated copy of the Rome edition that was sent to Erasmus (cf n41 above).

47 *Antapologia* (Paris edition) 26–33

48 There is no record of any of them having written to Erasmus directly, but in Ep 2311:17–35 Gerard Morrhy wrote to Erasmus about Pio's 'hired minions' and named a certain 'Gerard, a Frisian' as one of them. We know nothing of any reports to Erasmus in person.

These people have found a marvellous way to praise themselves. The preface has 'Aldus' in the title, as if we did not know the abilities of Aldus, whom they make my instructor in Greek literature.[49]

I wonder who this Alessandro d'Alessandro is. He knows all the famous Italians, Filelfo, Pomponius Laetus, Ermolao,[50] and who not? He is a familiar   115 acquaintance of everyone, but no one knows who he is. He hates Lorenzo Valla, repeatedly calling him a 'grammarian.'[51]

A certain theologian named Gérard Roussel has become prominent at Paris; he speaks to a large audience at the royal court, preaching the gospel with great freedom but not without rousing the ire of the theologians.[52] The   120 affair seems to presage an uproar. I wish that kings would regulate their conduct so that the commonwealth might suffer no harm.[53] The emperor has preeminent power, and he has at his disposal not only wise counsel but also wealth and weapons.

* * * * *

49 It is not clear who 'these people' were, nor can we identify the work with the preface that had 'Aldus' in the title. All that can be said is that the matter is somehow connected to the claim of Alberto Pio that Aldo Manuzio had been Erasmus' instructor in Greek; see *Apologia adversus rhapsodias Alberti Pii* CWE 84 162.

50 See Epp 23:77n (Francesco Filelfo), 347:369n (Julius Pomponius Laetus), 126:150n (Ermolao Barbaro).

51 Alessandro d'Alessandro of Naples (1461–1523) was a legal scholar who divided his time between Naples and Rome. He was best known as the author of the *Dies geniales* (Rome 1522), a compendium of notes and discussions of philological and legal subjects as well as anecdotes of his friends and experiences. As this passage indicates, Erasmus appears to have been previously unaware of him and took umbrage at his attitude towards Lorenzo Valla. Viglius had presumably included a copy of the book with his letter.

52 For Gérard Roussel, confessor to Margaret of Angoulême, sister of Francis I and Queen of Navarre, see Ep 1407 n22. His sermons at the Louvre in 1531–3 scandalized the conservative theologians but pleased moderates, including King Francis. Cf Ep 2841 n5.

53 The Latin reads *ne quid detrimenti capiat respublica.* This is the language of the *Senatus consultum ultimum,* a decree of the Roman senate during the late Roman Republic removing all limits on the magistrates' authority to defend the republic in a time of emergency. It usually took the form 'let the consuls see to it that no harm come to the republic.' When the Republic became the Empire, such power to defend the state was a routine part of the imperial office and required no emergency senatorial decree. Erasmus is, as always, invoking the duty of Christian kings to see to the welfare of their subjects.

The counts of Rennenberg are living with me; one of them, Kaspar (if I   125
am not mistaken) is writing to you.[54]

To come to an end: if, when you are pursuing your fortunes, you think
there is any way in which I might be of service to you, be assured that whatever I can do is at your disposal. Farewell.

14 May 1533   130

Erasmus of Rotterdam, in my own hand

To the most renowned gentleman Master Viglius Zuichemus, a Frisian,
ordinary professor of law. At Padua

2811 / From Jakub Groffik   Cracow, 15 May 1533

This letter was first published as Ep 32 in Casimir von Miaskowski 'Erasmiana.
Beiträge zur Korrespondenz des Erasmus von Rotterdam mit Polen. Teil II'
Jahrbuch für Philosophie und spekulative Theologie 15 (1901) 195–226, 307–60, and
shortly thereafter as Ep 185 in Förstemann / Günther. The autograph was in the
Burscher Collection of the University Library at Leipzig (Ep 1254 introduction).

Very little is known of Jakub Groffik (d after 1538) of Felsztyn in southern
Poland. He was first a parish priest at Czchow in southern Poland, then preben-
dary at the Cracow cathedral and warden (*custos*) of the collegiate church of St
Giles in Cracow. Everything else that is known of him is found in this fawning
letter. If Erasmus ever wrote a reply, no trace of it has survived.

Since I am not unaware, most eminent and learned sir, that there are very
many people, not only in Germany and Italy but in the whole Christian
world, who are not accustomed to taking account of your highly noble labours, which are so useful to the whole world, and interrupt them with their
letters, and sometimes with almost nothing to say but simply to demonstrate   5

* * * * *

54 The brothers Hermann (d 1585) and Kaspar (1511–44) von Rennenberg were
   from the portion of the duchy of Jülich that is now in the Dutch province of
   Limburg. Both studied law and pursued careers as ecclesiastical administrators
   in the Netherlands. In 1529–30, Kaspar studied law at Bourges, where he and
   Viglius Zuichemus became friends. At the moment of the writing of this letter,
   the two brothers were living with Erasmus at Freiburg, but by June Erasmus'
   poor health had obliged him to ask them to leave (Ep 2818:6–8). Subsequently
   they lived for a time in the house 'zum Walfisch' that had been Erasmus' first
   address at Freiburg (Ep 2919:9–10). The brothers left Freiburg in April 1534, and
   for a time Erasmus lost touch with them (Ep 2924:24–6), though contact appears
   to have been restored fairly quickly (Allen Ep 3031A:8–9). No direct correspondence with either of them survives.

their good opinion and their commitment to you, but I also know that your
kindness is such that there is no one among those who trouble you with their
letters, even if he be of the lowest standing, whom you do not vouchsafe to
answer, even in the midst of so many important engagements. Thus it came
about that I too was encouraged to write you, when I saw our master here,   10
the lord abbot of Mogiła or Clara Tumba, doing so;[1] I was his companion last
year last year when, together with him, I was allowed to visit and greet you in
person, and when I left I could hardly refrain from kissing your right hand, so
worthy of being kissed and venerated by everyone, and (if you will give credence to my words) from bathing it with the tears that welled up in my eyes.   15
     I thought this should be mentioned so that you would not be unaware
of who this Jakub Groffik is, this barbarian unknown to you who has the
audacity to disturb you with his barbaric letter, etc. And what is more, when
I eagerly held your most desired hand and imprinted tender kisses upon it,
you said to me, 'I am not a bishop, am I?' But I kissed your right hand with   20
more desire and piety than I would kiss the feet of all the bishops in this
world of ours or the sacred feet of Pope Clement, from whom we were returning at that time, making a sort of detour through Burgundy and France.
I only wish that I could have kissed not only that right hand that wrote so
much and so well but also the head that dictated it and the heart that con-   25
ceived the thoughts that have inundated the whole Christian world, including our Poland, with the loftiest praise of you and with the glory of your
undying fame among those yet to come, the 'sons of sons and those to be
born of them.'[2]
     I wanted to say this in order to present myself by this sign, namely kiss-   30
ing your right hand, and to thank you for not having been unwilling to put
aside your tasks, to show yourself to us face to face, and to deign to bestow
your sweet conversation on Master Erazm the abbot and indeed on me also.
To us, that alone seemed sufficient recompense for all our efforts and costs in
travelling through so many lands, not without considerable discomfort and   35
expense: namely, to actually see you face to face. We are very proud to have
seen you, and we will also be proud, together with our descendants, for as

* * * * *

2811
1 Erazm Ciołek (Ep 2600 n1), abbot of the Cistercian monastery of Mogiła (Clara
   Tumba). In 1531 he was sent to Rome on an embassy for King Sigismund I.
   There he received from Pope Clement VII a special privilege that allowed the
   abbot of Mogiła to be a member of the cathedral chapter at Cracow. Returning
   to Poland in the winter of 1532, Ciołek stopped at Freiburg and called upon
   Erasmus, who seized the opportunity to entrust to him letters for delivery to
   friends in Poland (Ep 2600). The letter to Erasmus mentioned here is not extant.
2 Virgil Aeneid 3.98

long as we shall live. And may heaven grant that, although the distance of
our separation does not allow us to hear you or speak with you, we may at
least hear that you live as long as possible and always safely. That this may　40
be granted by him from whom comes every best and perfect gift, I myself
will lend help by my intercessions and prayers. For I am, by the grace of
the Lord God, one of the humble priests of the little and little-known chapel
dedicated to St Giles, where I have the priestly function called wardenship,
living with no fame, in fact (if I am not deceived by self-love) living far from　45
all greed or ambition, saying mass here as is proper for priests and acting
as warden, etc. This, I say, is what inspired the audacity to write to you, etc.

If at any time you deign to answer me with a letter written by your own
hand, however brief, that would give me the greatest pleasure and would
take the place of the very greatest gift and greatest kindness. But if you do　50
not, I will attribute it to your occupations, and I will nevertheless besiege God
and the saints with my ceaseless prayers to give you a very long and safe life,
etc. Fare well, live long, noble sir, most worthy of life and immortality.

Cracow, 15 May 1533

Jakub Groffik, warden of St Giles at Cracow　　　　　　　　　　　　55

To Master Erasmus of Rotterdam, a gentleman most eminent and universally learned

2812 / To Mary of Hungary　　　　　　　　　　Freiburg, 1 June 1533

This letter was first published in Ipolyi page 369. The manuscript is page 347 of
the Olahus codex in the Hungarian National Archives at Budapest (Ep 2339 introduction). Together with Ep 2813, the letter was written to recommend Pieter
van Montfoort, who had delivered to Erasmus at Freiburg the honorarium bestowed on him by the six Estates of Holland and who was a candidate for the
provostship of Haarlem; see Epp 2389 introduction, 2818:15–26.

TO HER MOST SERENE MAJESTY, QUEEN MARY OF HUNGARY
AND BOHEMIA, WIDOW, REGENT OF LOWER GERMANY,[1]
ERASMUS OF ROTTERDAM SENDS GREETINGS
In view of the singular favour of your Majesty towards me, most serene
Queen, seeing that I am greatly indebted, so am I greatly pleased to be in-　5
debted, and I also want to be even more indebted. For I consider as expended

* * * * *

2812
1 Ie the Netherlands, often referred to in Latin as *Germania inferior*, as distinguished from *Germania superior* (Upper Germany), where Basel and Freiburg
were located

on me whatever is expended on those who visibly provide something either
useful or ennobling to the realm of my prince. At the present moment I seek
nothing in the way of a new benefit; I do not think there is a need for any
entreaties. I merely wish to attest to my joy that the emperor shares your be-   10
nevolent sentiments in awarding a distinction to Pieter van Montfoort. Since
this estimation of him proceeds from good judgment, it will, I have no doubt,
long endure.

   He is a young man born to a well-known family among his own people
and is endowed with rare human gifts of both kinds, that is, God in his good-   15
ness gave him an excellent bodily dwelling for a mind far more outstanding.
For the wonderful agility of his intelligence, his learning, openness, integrity,
and his other virtues were evident to me a while ago when he spent several
days staying at my home, and the more closely anyone examines him and
the more thoroughly he knows him, the more he will love him and highly   20
admire him. But among the many deliberations proper to a king God has inspired in the mind of the emperor this one in particular, that he chooses with
careful foresight those to whom he assigns public offices. No other ability is
as important for protecting and augmenting the tranquillity and dignity of
cities and kingdoms. Since in this kind of admirable quality you are clearly   25
the sister of the best and greatest emperor, I have no doubt that you will
embrace this young man with the same constancy and eagerness as your
brother, and like him will make every effort to enable him to execute the office so kindly bestowed on him happily and prosperously. For I understand
that his imperial Majesty, in conjunction with your Clemency, has promoted   30
this young man to a commandership of St John at Utrecht.² It seems to me
that this benefice was bestowed quite rightly, that is, on someone who deserves it and will remember it.

   For just as he has so far fulfilled his duties to his Majesty the emperor
in a most satisfactory way in affairs conducted in Germany, so too in the fu-   35
ture, as he gains more authority and experience, he will produce even greater
results. For three years now he has served, not without praise, in the court
of his reverend Lordship the cardinal of Mainz,³ and during that time he
encountered men of both estates;⁴ right from the first in his earliest years
he furnished an extraordinary example of mature prudence and dexterity in   40
handling matters in Germany. So too the most serene emperor had that same

* * * * *

2 Cf Ep 2848:7–11.
3 Albert of Brandenburg (Ep 745)
4 Ie both clerical and secular

MARIA AB AVSTRIA. D.G. REGINA HVNGARIÆ,
CAROLI V IMPERATORIS SOROR, GVBERNATRIX
Mariée à Louis II, BELGICARVM. &. ✝ 1558.
Roi de hongrie. P. de Iode excudit

Mary of Austria, queen of Hungary
Engraving by Pieter de Iode

experience, and for that reason thought he should be honoured with the be-
stowal of the commandership so as to be able to conduct affairs of state even
better. But if some chance prevents him from fulfilling his desire to receive
the commandership – though I hardly think this will happen, since he has   45
the benign favour of both the emperor and of your Majesty – if, nevertheless,
he fails to achieve this, he would at least like to have the provostship of his
native place – that is, Haarlem – bestowed on him, since (as I understand
from the young man) the emperor gave his approval at Regensburg,[5] and
also the man who now holds the provostship is prepared, under equitable   50
conditions, to resign from it. Believe me, this would confer a benefit not only
on one man but on the commonwealth. This young man and I share the same
homeland, Holland, which has always been especially loyal, obedient, and
generous to its prince. I am grievously tormented that it is now afflicted by
storm after storm, through the wickedness of foreign countries.[6] But I hope   55
that the gracious favour of heaven, lending assistance to your piety, will soon
put an end to these evils. May heaven also deign to keep your most serene
Majesty always safe and prosperous.

Given at Freiburg im Breisgau, on the feast of Pentecost 1533

2813 / To Nicolaus Olahus   [Freiburg], 1 June 1533

First published in Ipolyi page 371, this is the second of two letters (cf Ep 2812)
recommending Pieter van Montfoort for the provostship of Haarlem. The
manuscript is page 371 of the Olahus codex in the Hungarian National Archives
at Budapest (Ep 2339 introduction). For Nicolaus Olahus, secretary to Mary of
Hungary, regent of the Netherlands, see Ep 2339 introduction.

ERASMUS OF ROTTERDAM TO NICOLAUS OLAHUS,
SECRETARY TO HER SERENE MAJESTY

If you know Pieter van Montfoort as well as I do, I have no doubt that he is
as dear to you as he is to me. For to me he is very dear indeed, because of
the outstanding qualities, both of nature and of fortune, which I perceived in   5
him when he lived with me. You, a more sharp-sighted man, will have seen
them even more clearly; and, as a man of greater humanity and virtue, you
will, I think, value them all the more.

* * * * *

5 Ie at the Diet of Regensburg in the summer of 1532
6 For Holland's trade war with Lübeck and Denmark, see Ep 2798 n12.

The emperor too seems to have examined the man and, freely and of his own volition, given him a distinguished office;[1] but, as I see it, he is worthy of an even more splendid gift.[2] But since you are not inexperienced in the ways of the court, you know that many harpies gather with open beaks around such booty and that often wickedness prevails over virtue. The emperor and the emperor's sister Mary look on him with great favour, so that I have no doubt whatsoever that this affair of his will be borne along by good winds and waves. But it is driven to the desired port more quickly if a timely admonition is added to it, like the efforts of oarsmen. I would beg you to fulfil that role if I were not confident that you had already undertaken it of your own volition. Concerning the miseries of your friend Erasmus you will learn more from our friend Montfoort than from anything I say.[3] From my servant Quirinus I expect to learn everything about everything.[4]

Farewell, my very dear friend (to reply in Greek to a lover of Greek)[5]
On the feast of Pentecost, 1533

2814 / From Johann Koler   Augsburg, 5 June 1533

This letter was first published as Ep 186 in Förstemann / Günther. The manuscript was in the Burscher Collection of the University Library at Leipzig (Ep 1254 introduction). For Johann Koler, canon of St Moritz in Augsburg, see Ep 2195 introduction.

Cordial greetings. On the day when I sent you a packet with my letter,[1] on that same day (that is, on the eve of Pentecost), Nachtgall came to us here,[2] as unexpected, I thought, as if a white crow had arrived. He explained to me the reason he had come, which I would have thought hardly a good reason for undertaking such a long journey.

* * * * *

2813
1 The commandership of St John at Utrecht; see Ep 2812:29–31.
2 The provostship of Haarlem; see Ep 2812:41–51.
3 Montfoort had just visited Erasmus at Freiburg; see Ep 2812 introduction.
4 See Ep 2804 n7.
5 Greek in the text

2814
1 Not extant
2 Ottmar Nachtgall (Ep 2166 n3)

Nachtgall had a canonry and a prebend here,[3] which at his departure he resigned in favour of a relative of Master Anton Fugger, with the proviso that an annual pension of eighty florins should be paid to him from it.[4] And for that sum Fugger made himself surety and debtor until such time as Nachtgall should be provided with an ecclesiastical benefice of a value equal to that of the pension. But now I understand that a benefice is in hand that is satisfactory to Nachtgall and that constitutes the equivalent of the other pension, so that Fugger is freed from his obligation. But the transaction, as I understand it, has not been completed and Fugger is still legally obligated to Nachtgall.[5]

And it is for that reason and no other that Nachtgall undertook his journey here. Certainly he could not have arrived at a more inopportune time: everything is completely engulfed in tumult and rebellion. Concerning the outrageous manner in which Fugger himself has been treated, I prefer that you learn about it from Nachtgall himself.[6] For to write about it fills me with disgust and shame. In my last letter to you I rehearsed the tragedy, though hastily, and I neither know very well nor wish to reread what I wrote.[7] To sum up, nothing remains to be done but to give the order to pack up our things and depart, leaving behind this beautiful city, our homeland, to be sacked by brutish creatures. The Zwinglian faction is now on the verge of giving us, from the very first day, laws about what ceremonies are allowed; and if we refuse to put up with them we are free to leave here with bag and baggage. But even beforehand we can easily guess what can be, and usually is, prescribed by these Evangelicals. In the meantime, however, we are in suspense, full of fear and not knowing what to hope for.[8]

* * * * *

3 In 1525, through the patronage of the Fugger family, Nachtgall was named preacher and canon at St Moritz in Augsburg and quickly emerged as a principal spokesman for the conservative Catholic faction in a city that was on its way to adopting the Reformation. Forbidden by the city council to continue preaching, he moved to Freiburg, where he was appointed preacher at the cathedral. In 1531 he made an effort to secure the preachership at the cathedral at Augsburg, but the hostility to him of Anton Fugger and his friends precluded his doing so (Ep 2437:45–52).
4 Fugger's friend has not been identified.
5 On this matter cf Ep 2818:45–60.
6 See Erasmus' account of this in Ep 2818:29–43.
7 The letter is not extant.
8 The religious situation in Augsburg was moving steadily, but slowly and with much tension and turmoil, towards the victory of the Reformation and the organization of a new church on the model of that in Strasbourg (Epp 2430:9–18,

If the Swabian League,[9] which was postponed to the feast day of St Lawrence,[10] had been renewed yesterday, as was agreed,[11] we would have had some hope of being safe and undisturbed here. But it is extremely doubtful, and in my mind there is almost no hope and all is lost. And no place is left to which such a huge crowd of priests can migrate and set up new dwell- 35 ings, 'seek distant places of exile in uninhabited lands ... uncertain where the Fates are carrying us or where we may be allowed to rest.'[12]

Though these words were said in jest, I am afraid we are going to act out the play all too truly. My only consolation is that I will have as companions in

* * * * *

2631 n38, 2787 n3). For the moment, the reform party was still divided between Lutherans and Zwinglians, the old church still had prominent supporters (like the Fugger family), and the city council was proceeding with such caution that it had not yet joined the League of Schmalkalden (Ep 2472 n18). The crucial phase of reform instituted by the city council would come in 1534–7. In 1537, the bishop (Christoph von Stadion) and his chapter would move from Augsburg to Dillingen.

9 Founded in 1488 and renewed four times (1496, 1500, 1512, 1522), the Swabian League was an alliance of cities, princes, prelates, and lesser nobles aimed at maintaining peace and order in southern Germany (cf Ep 2269 n2). In that capacity it served as a useful instrument of Hapsburg interests in the area. Although never entirely free of internal tensions (mostly between the imperial cities and their predatory princely neighbours), it was on several occasions able to take effective action against breaches of the imperial peace. In 1519, for example, when Duke Ulrich of Württemberg conquered the free imperial city of Reutlingen and added it to his domains, the army of the league invaded his duchy, drove the duke into exile, and transferred control of the duchy to the Hapsburgs (cf Ep 2917 n9). But the religious differences engendered by the Reformation eventually caused the league to fall apart, its Protestant members seeking political and religious security in the League of Schmalkalden (Ep 2472 n18) and (egged on by anti-Hapsburg France, Hessen, and Bavaria) abandoning their support for the older alliance. On 2 February 1534, after months of futile efforts to renew the league, it was disbanded.

10 10 August

11 4 June 1533 may have been the date on which the Swabian League, last renewed in 1522, was due to be renewed, but we have been unable to verify this. We do know that there was a meeting of the League at Augsburg in April 1533 at which the imperial commissioners failed in their effort to secure an agreement to extend the life of the league, and that there was another meeting in August (see preceding note), also in Augsburg, with the same result; see Brendle 119, 121–2; Klüpfel 352–3.

12 Virgil *Aeneid* 3.4 and 7

exile not only many members of my own station,[13] but all the best and most   40
outstanding members of this city, who will not be able to bear the tyranny
of the heretics. Whatever happens, I will always keep you informed.[14] Nor is
there any reason for you to have any doubts about me. I will always be the
same as I am, and I will always have the same feelings for you, no matter
what place I may be carried off to. And maybe I will see you soon in person.   45
Nachtgall is the same as he always was.

 Mariangelo is gathering up his baggage in preparation for leaving. He
is setting out first for Venice and then for his home city of Aquila. He has
completed here his Ammianus Marcellinus and works of Cassiodorus.[15]

 I myself gave the bundle of your letters to Master Johann Paumgartner,   50
as you directed. He promises to see to it that it gets to Padua soon.[16]

 All that remains is for you to stay well and not cease to return my affection for you. Farewell, my most loving friend Erasmus.

 Given at Augsburg on 5 June 1533

 Your true friend, Koler   55

 To be delivered to the most learned and accomplished theologian
Desiderius Erasmus of Rotterdam

  * * * * *

13 Koler uses the word *ordo*, but he was not a member of any religious order
 in the usual sense of the term. He presumably means the clergy as a distinct
 community.
14 In July 1533 Anton Fugger retired to his estate at Weissenhorn in Swabia. As for
 Koler, when the chapter of St Moritz left Augsburg in January 1536, he and a
 few other canons remained behind. He married the following year and died in
 March 1538.
15 At some point before 1522, Mariangelo Accursio of Aquila (c 1489–1546), a
 scholar at Rome with antiquarian and philological interests, became the tutor and guide of Johann Albrecht and Gumpbert von Hohenzollern, who had
 come to Rome to complete their education. He remained in their service, accompanying them on their journeys to Germany, Poland, France, and Spain,
 until about 1532. He then joined the circle around Anton Fugger in Augsburg,
 where his editions of Ammianus Marcellinus and Cassiodorus were published
 in 1533. He left Augsburg in that year, probably because of the religious turmoil
 in which Fugger was found guilty of sedition for his role in a riot on the feast
 of the Ascension (28 May) and decided to leave Augsburg himself; see Epp
 2818:29–44, 2845:38–46.
16 Letters to Erasmus' correspondents in Padua, including Viglius Zuichemus and
 Johann (ii) Paumgartner's son Johann Georg. The bundle in question may well
 have included Epp 2809–10.

2815 / From Gerard of Friesland   London, 5 June 1533

This letter was first published as Ep 187 in Förstemann / Günther. The manu-
script was in the Burscher Collection of the University Library at Leipzig
(Ep 1254 introduction). For Gerard of Friesland, of whom little is known, see
Ep 2232 introduction.

Greetings. My lord the earl has received with gratitude the *Symbolum* dedicated to him.[1] Two outstanding bishops who have considerable influence
with the king have also added their praise to his: the lord archbishop of
Canterbury, a theologian, to whom the lord of Wiltshire gave it to read,[2] and
the bishop of Winchester, a lawyer,[3] who has learned both letters and 'how   5
to swim.'[4] Our earl promises a great deal; but what he will provide you will
learn from Quirinus.[5]
    In recent months, with the support and recommendation of Wiltshire,
I have defected to the new archbishop of Canterbury, the Maecenas of both
of us.[6] He indeed offers, on his own initiative, a bonus beyond what the   10
other used to offer your Kindness, desiring all the while that you will not
mention him without reason in any written document, for he is a man who
does not like to be either bitten or barked at. At this time he is not sending
a letter, hoping that you will put faith in this one. You will shortly get thirty
pounds that have been counted out in the presence of your servant by Luis   15
de Castro,[7] including twenty paid by Canterbury in the hope of recovering
them from debtors, who say that the previous bishop of Canterbury had collected the whole pension except for the ten that were counted as part of the

* * * * *

2815
1 Erasmus' *Explanatio symboli apostolorum* was dedicated to Thomas Boleyn, earl
   of Ormond and of Wiltshire; see Ep 2772.
2 Thomas Cranmer, the newly appointed replacement for Erasmus' patron,
   William Warham, as archbishop of Canterbury
3 Stephen Gardiner (Ep 1669), at this time secretary to Henry VIII
4 Cf *Adagia* II ii 23: 'I go on foot, for I have not learned to swim,' said of people 'who
   have no experience of important business and deal with less important matters.'
5 See Ep 2804 n7.
6 The name of Maecenas, confidant of Emperor Augustus and the patron of Virgil
   and Horace, became (and remains) the byword for a generous and enlightened
   patron of the arts.
7 Castro was Erasmus Schet's agent in England responsible for the collection and
   transmission of the income from Erasmus' English livings. The servant was
   Quirinus Hagius (see n5 above).

thirty.[8] Farewell. For as long as I live I will watch out for my friend Erasmus
as his most faithful servant.   20
 London, on the octave of Pentecost in the year 1533
 Yours truly, Gerard
 To Master Desiderius Erasmus

2816 / From Jacopo Sadoleto   Carpentras, 9 June 1533

This letter was first published in *Iacobi Sadoleti, episcopi Carpentoracti, epistolarum libri sexdecim: Eiusdem ad Paulum Sadoletum epistolarum liber unus* (Lyon:
Gryphius 1550) page 169. For Jacopo Sadoleto, bishop of Carpentras, see Ep
1511. As indicated in n7 below, the actual dispatch of this letter took place two
months after the date of composition.

JACOPO SADOLETO, BISHOP OF CARPENTRAS,
TO DESIDERIUS ERASMUS OF ROTTERDAM, CORDIAL GREETINGS
Do not think (I beg you), my dear friend Erasmus, that I find anything more
pleasing than your kindness towards me or more weighty than your judgment. For that reason I receive most eagerly all those who arrive from where   5
you are, as long as they bear your greeting or bring news about you, and even
more so if they bring some reminder of your extraordinary intelligence and of
your support and fervour for Christian piety, as evidenced in the many works
that issue from your pen. You must not be disturbed if I reward with a small
gift those who have taken this trouble for my sake.[1] I have such a high opinion   10
of your judgment (as I hope that all the saints will grant me their favour) that I
cannot approve of any of my work, certainly whatever of it pertains to religion
and Holy Scripture, if you have not approved it beforehand. Therefore, when

* * * * *

8 This seems to say that the 'bonus' referred to in line 10 above was ten pounds,
  and that in addition to it he also paid from his own pocket the pension of twenty pounds that had supposedly been collected by his predecessor, Warham, but
  had not been properly credited to the archiepiscopal treasury. The allowance of
  thirty pounds sterling was equivalent to just over five years' wage income of a
  fully employed Oxford master mason/carpenter (£5 15s 0d) at 6p per day and
  a year of 230 days (CWE 12 650 Table 3, 691 Table 13). For Erasmus' two pensions
  from livings in England, see Ep 2332 n10, and for Cranmer's continuation of
  them see Ep 2761 n10.

2816
1 Erasmus must at some point have said, in a letter now lost, that Sadoleto's lar-
  gesse towards those who deliver his letters was unnecessary.

I had completed my commentary on the first epistle of Paul (I will not say how
long and hard I worked on it, for you know well enough how obscure that   15
epistle is) I had decided to rest for a few months and to refrain completely from
thinking and worrying about it, so that I could come back refreshed and renewed as I revise and carefully correct it.[2] Such is my customary practice, and
also that of learned men. And it was my intention not to share it with anyone
until I myself had approved of it. But, thinking of human calamities and how   20
much grief and harm it could cause me if some harsh turn of fortune (which
could certainly happen to either of us) should interrupt the literary exchanges
between us, when the first of the three books had been copied out, I purposely
sent it to you, for that book surely contains the greatest and most beautiful
mysteries of the Christian faith. I beg you, my dear friend Erasmus, and I be-   25
seech you in the name of our extraordinary mutual affection, to read it with the
conviction that you would do me a greater favour if you criticized what you
think should be criticized than if you praised what should be praised.[3]

Certainly I have dared, as you yourself will see, to depart from the worn
and beaten path already followed by others and to take another course, which   30
seems to me to rise up out of the surging questions, and to strive more strongly
and gloriously towards the truth, and I have always prayed that God would
be with me. But I may be mistaken. Therefore, my dear Erasmus, all my hope
is in you. For in your judgment, which you modestly deprecate, I have the
highest confidence, and that quite rightly, for it is now my very refuge and   35
haven. Both the polishing of my whole work and I myself rely on you alone,
as well as on your affection for me and your celebrated virtue and learning.

I want you to be aware that there are not a few places in this book where
additions will be made when I have taken up the work again to scrutinize
it more closely. For there is much that needs to be discussed more fully than   40

* * * * *

2 Sadoleto had first mentioned his intention to write a commentary on Romans
in a letter of 8 May 1532; see Ep 2648:13–17.
3 On 31 August 1533 Erasmus informed Bonifacius Amerbach that Sadoleto's private messenger had delivered 'the book he wants me to correct,' noting that
he had already read the book through and done what Sadoleto wanted; see Ep
2865:13–14. (Allen Ep 2973:22–6 indicates that the manuscript was that of the first
book only and that Erasmus never commented on the remaining books.) There
followed a period of well over a year during which no response from Sadoleto
arrived and Erasmus grew apprehensive that his frank criticisms of Sadoleto's
book (no record of which survives) had offended him; see Ep 2927 (25 April
1534), and Epp 2971 (31 October 1534), 2980 (24 November 1534). Not until the
receipt of Sadoleto's letters of 1 November 1534 (Ep 2973) and 9 December 1534
(Ep 2982), thanking Erasmus for his criticisms and apologizing for the delay
in responding to them, were Erasmus' apprehensions laid to rest.

in the present explanation, and certainly I will collect some appropriate and lucid testimony from Sacred Scripture to be added when I have in mind to publish the work. For at this point I have not even reread the part I sent to you, for fear of becoming prematurely entangled in corrections and erasures, since (as I have said) I put off all such care to another time.   45

As for the printing, I would like nothing better than what you advise, namely that it should be carried out by Froben. I am certain that there is no better alternative anywhere. I would not be concerned about the expense, but I have some scruples because of the kindness and modesty of Gryphius, who is completely devoted to me. There will, however, certainly be time to 50 think about that.[4]

I wish to make this urgent request: you may show this part of the commentary to whomever you wish, but you must not give anyone the opportunity to copy it, for it is clearly not yet completely finished. I am on familiar terms with you, and I think I can safely do this, for I have the highest opinion 55 of your humanity and great faith in your integrity. Hence, if I impose any burden on you, I do it with the desire that you be fully persuaded that there is no one more prepared than I am to offer you in return my support and good will in all your activities.

Although, as I wrote to you, I thoroughly approved of your Clarifica- 60 tions at the first reading,[5] I will nevertheless read them afresh, and I have no doubt that all the changes you made are improvements. I read your commentary on the Creed,[6] with which I was quite delighted. For you have certainly stopped the mouths of the contentious and those who seek undeserved praise by defaming others and whom your preeminent virtue and authority 65 have amply refuted.

Farewell, my most excellent friend Erasmus, and remember me, who can never forget you. I am sending a letter to Amerbach,[7] to whom I especially want my lucubrations to be shown. Once more and again once more, farewell.

Carpentras, 9 June 1533   70

* * * * *

4 Sadoleto's *In Epistolam Pauli ad Romanos commentariorum libri tres* was published in 1535, not by Hieronymus Froben at Basel but by Sebastianus Gryphius at Lyon.
5 Ie the *Declarationes ad censuras Lutetiae vulgatas* (Ep 2552 n10)
6 Ie the *Explanatio symboli* (Ep 2772)
7 Clearly a reference to AK Ep 1770, dated and signed on 10 August 1533 in Sadoleto's own hand. Ep 2865:15–16 indicates that the two letters arrived together, which in turn indicates that the present letter, written on 9 June, was not dispatched until two months later. See Alfred Hartmann's introduction to AK Ep 1770.

2817 / From Levinus Ammonius   Koningdal, 9 June 1533

This letter, Ammonius' answer to Ep 2483, is the last in the surviving correspondence between him and Erasmus. It was first published by Allen from the
autograph in the Bibliothèque municipale at Besançon (MS 599 page 276). For
the Carthusian monk and excellent classical scholar Levinus Ammonius, see
Ep 2016 introduction. Originally in the monastery of St Maartensbos, west of
Brussels, Ammonius had just recently been driven away by a new abbot hostile
to humanist studies and was now at the monastery at Koningdal, outside Ghent.
In this letter, as in the others he wrote to Erasmus, Ammonius occasionally
switches effortlessly from excellent Latin into excellent Greek and back again.

LEVINUS AMMONIUS TO ERASMUS OF ROTTERDAM,
A MOST ACCOMPLISHED THEOLOGIAN, GREETINGS
If our friend Uutenhove, Erasmus most dear to my heart, had persuaded me,
after he returned to his native land,[1] that you took great pleasure in my letter
and desired that I write more often, I would not have been able (I confess) to   5
escape being branded a shirker of my duty, since it took two years before I finally thought of answering. And I would not have written an answer to your
most delightful letter, which Uutenhove faithfully took care to deliver to me,
any earlier than when I saw it printed in your *Epistolae floridae*.[2] But even
though he was completely inspired by Cicero and had lived so long among   10
Ciceronians,[3] he was never able to persuade me. For I myself, well aware of
my deficiencies, had long before come to a judgment of myself which he,
with all his eloquent oratory, could never remove. If he could have done so
– may Christ be my witness – I would not have put off my answer even to
the next day.   15
    For what could I have hoped or sought more eagerly than to gratify
Erasmus, especially in a matter in which I myself would find exceptional

* * * * *

2817
1 In April 1531 Karel Uutenhove, who had been studying in Italy, returned to the
   Netherlands via Freiburg, where Erasmus gave him Ep 2483 to be delivered to
   Ammonius; see Ep 2483 introduction and n1.
2 Published in September 1531
3 Uuthenove had spent two years (1529–31) at Padua, a hotbed of Ciceronianism.
   In March 1530 Erasmus chided him for having written a letter that fell short
   of the standard of excellence expected of someone who had studied there and
   urged him to apply himself more diligently; see Ep 2288:13–20. Erasmus persisted in regarding Uutenhove as a young man of good family but mediocre
   education who had disappointed his hopes; see Epp 2681:2–5, 2682:55–7.

pleasure by that very gratification. For is there anything in all my possessions (if anything can be called mine) of such worth that I would not gladly
abandon if I could be allowed to enjoy a conversation with Erasmus? And 20
though that cannot happen in person, it is not denied in a letter, which acts as
an intermediary between absent persons in such a way that it almost makes
them present to one another.

Therefore, since I was so eager to engage in conversation with you,
what was the reason for putting it off for so long? I will tell you, my dear 25
Erasmus, frankly and as briefly as I can. The reason was partly scrupulous-
ness, as well as a certain naive shyness and an eagerness to show my respect
for you; it was also partly an unhappy chance occurrence in the house where
I was living at the time, the death of the Father Abbot.[4] For I saw that you
were possessed by the indefatigable desire to do good for all men, and that, 30
undeterred by the many slanders of the sycophants who confront you, you
resolutely direct all your will, wisdom, effort, labour, and diligence to that
aim, so that to the extent of your powers you might restore to health both
humane letters, from which true and genuine theology, long deprived, had
entirely deteriorated into scholastic and sophistical disputations, and genu- 35
ine Christianity, which through the ignorance of certain people had been corrupted (alas, what a crime!) by Jewish superstitions.[5] I saw that you pursued
these two aims especially, both in the works that you have previously published throughout the world and also in those that even now you unceasingly present to us in an unending stream, one after the other. 40

In addition to that, I considered, not without much mental distress,
that the ranks of sycophants, joined together from all sides in a conspiracy
aimed at your downfall (though you are entirely innocent), rushing at you
with tongues dipped in hellish poison, were armed not with arguments but
with libellous books, slanders, and blasphemies, and that they would not 45
lay down their ineffective weapons, no matter how often they were refuted
and utterly defeated by clear arguments. And when necessity compelled you
to answer them, I always found it very hard to bear that though you were
occupied with better studies you were forced to do this. Thus it has come
about that, apart from other offspring of your most fertile talent, born for 50
the advancement of the whole church, we are still looking forward with the

* * * * *

4 Ammonius does not turn to the consequences of the abbot's death until line 121
  below. Neither he nor his successor (lines 124–5 below) has been identified.
5 Ie confidence in external ceremonies; cf Ep 2483:23–31.

greatest anticipation to your work on the method of preaching.[6] Even as you were already in labour and on the verge of giving birth, the inauspicious folly of the shoemaker did not allow you to bring the work to an end and bring it forth.[7] But in passing, to defend the cause of good men before you, my excellent friend Erasmus: will you continually allow the effrontery of the wicked to achieve its aim to a greater extent than this long and anxious expectation of those who love you? Who will give me the power of the harpist who once made Elisha to be possessed by God, so that you too, auspiciously inspired by God, might fulfil this prophecy for us?[8]

For you write that your mind would not warm to the task, however often you called upon it to do so.[9] Would that the malignant animosity of those who called you elsewhere when you were engaged in that task had utterly perished! In this regard I was always so inclined that, if I had been closer at hand and able to consult with you, I would never have urged you to respond indiscriminately to everything and to everyone, as you have in fact done up to this time – although it has not escaped me that you have deliberately ignored many (but not, to be sure, Cousturier, Carvajal, or Titelmans),[10] and that you have made them and other scoundrels of the same stripe more mad by not opposing them. Such men, driven either by envy (the worst disease of all – Pindar's saying 'talking is a delicacy' applies to them),[11] could not bear that the glory granted to you in Christ was given justly and by good men everywhere; or through ignorance and sloth, they preferred, contrary to all that is right and just, to slander what, perverted by their prejudices, they could not understand and follow rather than learn.

Not that your apologias will not bear some fruit, although they were certainly written with a light touch, as it were,[12] so that these people need not take any great satisfaction in appearing to have sparred once with Erasmus.[13]

* * * * *

6 Ie the long promised but slowly achieved *Ecclesiastes sive de ratione concionandi*, published in 1535 (Ep 3036)
7 'Shoemaker' (the Greek word for which is used here) refers to Ammonius' fellow-Carthusian Pierre Cousturier (Ep 1804 n65), whose Latin name was *Sutor.* We have no knowledge of what Cousturier might have done to impede the completion of the *Ecclesiastes.*
8 Cf 2 Kings 2:9–15, Ecclus 48:112–14.
9 Ep 2483:54–5
10 See Epp 1943 n7 (Pierre Cousturier), 2110 n10 (Luis de Carvajal), 1823 introduction (Frans Titelmans).
11 Cited in Greek; Pindar *Nemean Odes* 8.21
12 Literally 'with a light arm,' said of 'work not taken seriously' (*Adagia* I iv 27)
13 'They' are presumably the 'sycophants' of line 82 below.

For all posterity will learn of the portents produced in our times, and when Erasmus has ceased to live and has yielded to fate, as he must (though he 80 would otherwise be most worthy of immortality), there will be ready at hand ample proofs against the sycophants (if there are any still living) for those who will undertake to defend the truth and protect the name of Erasmus from infamy. I have never desired at all to be of that number, even if I could contribute anything and should happen to outlive Erasmus. For it seems 85 that they have no slander against you for which you yourself have not fully accounted, and that there is nothing in what has already been written that could not be refuted with no trouble at all.

Moreover, it is also advantageous that, just as everyone thinks his own injury to be the most grievous and (as the poet says) 'the heart is soon free 90 of grief over the grief of others,'[14] so you will hardly find anyone else, even among your closest friends, who will have taken to heart to the same degree the assertion of the truth and the refutation of slanders, especially in defending the writings of others. And though here, as elsewhere, the proverb which claims that among friends everything is shared should apply,[15] almost 95 everyone would have thought either that such slanderers ought to be held in complete contempt, or that, if anyone should finally undertake the task of defending the truth, he would not equal your strength in refuting the assumptions of your adversaries, just as no one would dare to aspire (if I may be forgiven for saying so) to that manifold and incomparable learning of 100 yours. We have seen that time after time.

And so having considered that your labours, however unpleasant they may be to you, are still in one way or another necessary, and also by no means unaware of how much time, which you would otherwise have spent at leisure, is consumed in reading letters to you from all sorts of people from 105 all the corners of the earth, responding to them, signing them, giving them to be delivered (as I see you complain about so often in your letters, and not without reason),[16] I was somehow overwhelmed by scruples in making you expend effort on writings that are hardly necessary, and I reasoned with myself as follows: 'What are you about, you good-for-nothing Ammonius,' 110 I say, 'What are you doing? Will you interrupt the sacrosanct occupations of Erasmus with this inept and useless letter of yours?' What shall I say? 'Don't you see how kind he has been, at times, indeed quite often, deigning

* * * * *

14 Cited in Greek from Pindar *Nemean Odes* 1.54
15 *Adagia* I i 1
16 See Ep 2451:11–13 with n1.

to answer you in letters written in his own hand? Don't you see that he has
numbered you among his friends, something for which you could hardly   115
have even hoped? At least refrain from shaming him and yourself. Do not
drag him down from his lofty studies to such a lowly task. Consider the good
of the whole church, for which he labours, rather than just yourself.' Such
ideas as this I turned over in my mind, and not without reason. And I kept
within bounds the feelings that lured me on to write letter after letter to you.   120
    And then the death of our Father Abbot,[17] who was clearly a man of
splendid character, genuinely pious and most favourable to true intellectual
pursuits, was a severe blow to me, not only because under his rule I was
left undisturbed in my studies, but also because the successor of the dead
man is completely unlike him, uneducated, pretentious, authoritarian,[18] one   125
(I think) who will not tolerate anyone who does anything different from
what he does, and he does nothing but waste his time. Moreover, he is sur-
rounded by those who are very similar to himself, whereas anyone who has
even the slightest taste of good letters is a heretic. Indeed they would all prefer to live the life of sheep, so that, in the general destruction of education, if   130
their own lack of education became known, they could somehow escape the
ignominy of ignorance in that way, as Nazianzus says.[19] Moreover, as long
as I had that protector, who was favourably disposed to the reputation of
Erasmus, I could to some degree hide away from the slanders of others, but
deprived of him it seems I cannot remain unharmed among them any longer.   135
There are many of them who find nothing easier than to cry out 'Lutheran,'
or 'heretic,' or some such label. It is intolerable to hear this when you are
no such thing and at the same time to keep your peace of mind, though it
is especially necessary to do so, if you don't want to live a life full of bitterness. Having reached this decision, I decided that at this juncture there was   140
nothing more desirable than to take counsel with Christ and flee to another
city, wherever I might live more comfortably. And lo and behold! while I was
thinking about it, a splendid opportunity presented itself to me (arranged by
Christ, who never forgets his own), not sought after by me but offered, as it
were, enabling me transfer quite legitimately, with no fuss. I seized it by the   145
forelock, quite aware that to grab it from the back of the head would have

* * * * *

17 See above, lines 28–9.
18 Much of this hostile description of the new abbot is in Greek.
19 Like Allen and Gerlo, we have been unable to identify this reference to Gregory
    Nazianzus.

been impossible.[20] And so it happened, my friend Erasmus, so it happened, I
say, that I left that woodland[21] in which I had spent some twenty-seven years
and betook myself to the Carthusians near Ghent. But I see from what is written on the back of your letter that you were aware of this, as if I had always   150
lived here before. And I wish that it were fully settled that I should remain
here (which I am afraid it may not be).[22] In fact it has turned out very happily,
far more so than I had either hoped or expected. For although in the former
brotherhood some difficulties arose, I had learned to put up with everything
and I hesitated to give any thought to a change of place, partly because I   155
had become accustomed to such difficulties by bearing them for a long time;
partly because I was afraid that even more intolerable difficulties might occur elsewhere (if I made up my mind to do it, I had no doubt that I would be
leaving men thoroughly known from much experience of them and setting
out on my own to join men I did not know); partly because there were men   160
there whom I would not have abandoned except with great regret (for they
were not all bad); and finally, because I understood that it was not an entirely
bad thing for me to be harassed by troubles so as to learn to rise above and
conquer some feelings that even now give me difficulty, and, as if exposed
in a theatre to the eyes and tongues of everyone, plan to live more circum-   165
spectly, knowing that everything, even the slightest fault, would be seized
upon as matter for slander if they ever discovered the slightest peccadillo.
For it is a wonder to see how some people who have never learned the precepts of rhetoric (for they indeed never learned anything worthwhile) have
thoroughly learned in such affairs all the methods of collecting, exaggerat-   170
ing, and intensifying matters, as if they had them all categorized, so that they
can magnify even the tiniest thing and, as they say, make an elephant out of a
mouse.[23] But this community that I have joined seems to be not only tolerable
but such that you can rightly love it. Evidently they have adopted the more
cultivated manners of the people of Ghent (they are located right next to the   175
walls of the city). And their abbot, a prudent man, experienced in human affairs, has trained them liberally and well, with great care and solicitude, and
over a long period has shaped them to a happy sort of monastic life.

* * * * *

20 Said of the goddess Opportunity, who had thick hair at her forehead but was
   bald behind, so that she could not be seized after she had run past (*Adagia* I vii
   70)
21 St Maartensbos (bos = 'wood,' 'forest'); see introduction above.
22 Ammonius subsequently moved to Arnhem, then to Scheut near Brussels, and
   then back to Ghent, where he died in March 1557.
23 *Adagia* I ix 69

And so, when I first arrived here, your servant Quirinus, who had set
out for England and had returned from there, sought me out and came upon   180
me around the feast day of St Martin,[24] when I was very busy arranging the
bundles and books I had taken with me. For moving had somewhat disor-
dered my few belongings. That was the reason I could not write anything
at that time. But when, beyond all my expectations, meeting me once again
when he was setting out for England,[25] he conveyed your greetings to me   185
(I had with me on that day the physician Joachim, whom you saw in your
home not very long ago),[26] I did not think that when he came back here I
could make the mistake of letting him return once more to his master without a letter from me. So I asked him to visit me on his way back to get my
letter or, if something prevented that, to ask for it from Uutenhove. When I   190
asked him, 'Is our Erasmus in good health,' I was grieved to hear him reply
that you had been ill for almost the whole month of March,[27] but he threw
cold water on my distress by saying that you were doing well enough when
he left.[28] I would have wished that you might be unimpaired at your age
(though that age brings with it enough troubles, even if there be no others)   195
so that you might be able to exercise the mental gifts God has generously
bestowed on you to the common good of Christendom. Oh, how often have
I been forced to sigh at the thought of what (among other things) Uutenhove
said you wished, that I might spend my old age with you, something for
which I have also wished thousands of times. If this should happen, how-   200
ever, I would certainly come off better and more learned from being with
you, but I do not see how you would gain anything from me.

But woe is me! I foolishly put my feet into these shackles, before I really knew myself or had any idea what monasticism is, much less knowing
why I made such haste (I am still amazed at it even now), when I was two   205
whole years younger than the age when it is allowed to join this order.[29] For,

* * * * *

24 This passage makes clear that Quirinus Hagius was on his way back to Freiburg
    from his first visit to England around 11 November (St Martin's Day) 1532.
25 Quirinus Hagius' second journey to England commenced at the end of April
    1533.
26 For Joachim Martens and his visit to Erasmus in August 1532, see Ep 2703:7–8.
27 See Ep 2768 n11.
28 To 'pour cold water' on something was to inflame or refresh it, as in throwing
    cold water over a race horse to make it run faster; see *Adagia* I x 51. In this case
    the sense is to stimulate recovery from distress.
29 At the bottom of the page Levinus wrote 'Prover[bia] 20:[25],' giving the Greek
    of the verse from the Septuagint (which differs significantly from that of the
    Vulgate): 'It is a snare for a man to make a sacred vow too quickly and to repent
    of it later.'

though the Carthusian rule forbids that boys or adolescents be accepted but requires that according to the precept of the Lord transmitted by the hand of Moses (and I use his words) men no younger than twenty years of age should proceed to the holy wars,[30] I was scarcely eighteen when I was 210 'captured' (you know the word the priests use), willing enough, to be sure, but not yet of mature understanding. Since I myself have knowledge of all this,[31] I would, if it were possible to talk to you in person, say that there is nothing to compare with this murky business. This is all I can say for the present. I truly hold the wolf by the ears;[32] I cannot hold on without great 215 aversion, I cannot let go without great disgrace, having already devoted so much time to this life. The evil that is known is best.

Nevertheless, my excellent Erasmus, I cannot entirely agree with you about life in these penitentiaries, although otherwise I hardly ever disagree with you. I think that in the beginning they were certainly introduced as holy 220 institutions under divine auspices, but, as almost always happens in the affairs of men, when charity grew cold they degenerated and declined. I think that good seeds were surely well sown, but that nonetheless that schemer Satan secretly sowed (as is his custom) a great many tares among them.[33] And in our times the tares have taken such hold that everywhere 'unproduc- 225 tive weeds and barren oats hold sway.'[34] Everywhere you can see more emphasis on ceremonies and superstition than true piety. And this comes about necessarily when the ordinances of men are considered more important than the commandments of God and derelictions against the contrivances of men are punished more severely than neglect of the law of Christ.[35] 230

See now how far I am from your way of thinking, which has often affected my thoughts as well. But I am persuaded, once and for all, that anyone can live piously in any manner of Christian life as long as long as his heart

* * * * *

30 Num 1:24–45
31 The rest of the paragraph is in Greek.
32 *Adagia* I iv 25
33 Matt 13:24–6
34 Virgil *Georgics* 1.154
35 On the face of it, what Ammonius says in this paragraph is in complete agreement with Erasmus' view that the monasticism of his day was a badly corrupted version of monastic life as practised in the ancient church; see *De contemptu mundi* chapter 12 CWE 66 172–5; Ep 858:548–632 (the letter to Paul Volz that served as the preface to the second edition of the *Enchiridion*; *Moria* CWE 27 130–3 (the section on monks). In light of the paragraphs that follow, however, it appears that Ammonius imagines himself to be more optimistic than Erasmus about the possibility of living a holy life in an existing monastic community, and is unwilling to follow his example by abandoning that life.

is constantly armed to bear all sorts of adversity and his mind is faithfully
devoted to the will of Christ. I have said these things, 'putting my head next   235
to hers so that others may not overhear.'[36] For this way of life brings with it
many opportunities for keeping the mind alert, if one knows how to spend
the leisure of solitude in a way that is not idle.[37] First of all, to say nothing
about amply providing for matters pertaining to the body, such as food and
clothing – something that I certainly value greatly – solitude itself, even for   240
someone who is attending to other things, invites mental tranquillity, since
sight is neither allured nor entranced by bodily beauty nor hearing by the
sweetness of sounds, nor any of the other senses by the things that delight
them. Moreover, the mind itself is much sharper when it is not hindered by
any external bonds, and more capable of intellectual activities, of repress-   245
ing harmful desires, and finally of holding to the pursuit of piety. Certainly
solitude has taught me this, that in all liberal arts and disciplines nothing is
so abstruse, nothing so difficult that the intellect, even the most hopeless,
cannot easily acquire it, as long as it strongly wills to do so. How is that so?
Cannot someone who loves money, honour, fame, pleasure, or possessions   250
be content with little and very easily temper worldly desires once he knows
how to moderate the feelings against which he must struggle and bring them
under Christ's yoke? And who would not be led to the pursuit of piety (if
he really wants it) when, according to the rule itself of living in common, he
hears, reads, and contemplates every day the will of God in Sacred Scripture?   255
For he is required year after year to hear in the appointed common readings
whatever is presented by the Word of God – I was going to say 'even if he
doesn't want to,' but far be it from him not to be most eager to hear it. As for
the readings from the Divine Office which roll by year after year, we are better off than many other monks because we do not have to listen to any old   260
wives' tales. For apart from the most approved writers of the church, and
those mostly the ancient ones, almost nothing else is read to us, except that
during lunch and dinner on feast days (for only on those days do we have our
meals together, otherwise we eat alone) stories or deeds of the saints are read
by the lector. I am quite sure this practice was introduced so that meals might   265
be rendered more cheerful, since there was no other ordinary way – such as
conversation, little drinking bouts, or toasts – to dispel any boredom that
might occur, and meals were adorned with silence. 'Adorned,' I say, because
a practice that might seem depressing to those who are accustomed to jokes

* * * * *

36 Cited in Greek from Homer *Odyssey* 1.157
37 A play on the words *otium* 'leisure' and *otiosus* 'idle'

and games at mealtimes was in my opinion established as a holy custom, so   270
that the mind might always be kept focused on its duty and not wander from
its course even when bodily necessities are being supplied. Then again, I
have always steadfastly and easily endured the choice of foods because I was
endowed with a bodily constitution that can tolerate all such things and a
stomach that can comfortably digest any ordinary human food. In the end, is   275
there anything to be seen in all of this that cannot be observed together with
the pursuit of piety? But there is one thing that is most difficult for me and
that I have always had to struggle against, that is, to put up patiently with
slandering busybodies who for no reason have need to commit evil deeds.[38]
But what can you do? One must accept things as they are.[39]   280

   I often reflect in this way. Wherever I turn, as long as I am to be in
this body, I must have dealings with men. Where in the whole world will
you provide for me a community of men so free of all vices that one who
wants to keep peace of mind does not have to ignore or tolerate many things?
Certainly I wish there were no people who, to get the place of honour, have   285
inflicted on anyone the sort of great tragedies that you describe in your letter.
But it is no wonder that in such communities some are found in whom you
would find the intellect more lacking than the belly, especially because here,
in many of these communities, the highest-ranking member claims intellect
for himself because the others are completely indifferent. But certainly a man   290
would be spending his free time badly in criticizing frivolities of this kind,
which they contrive among themselves, and making them widely known
among the people. For I do not see what fruit can be gathered from that. It
seems to me better to put up with them with magnanimity, or better yet to
scorn them with a certain Democritean laughter,[40] than to lose both free time   295
and peace of mind in examining them. But I would not deny that in these
utterly calamitous times of ours those who pursue good learning have no
little trouble trying to preserve their peace of mind, because feelings are exac-
erbated by the factions, both that of Luther and others, and almost everyone
suspects that those who have set their hearts on humane studies, especially   300
Greek, support one faction or the other; indeed they are quite falsely and
prejudicially persuaded that such factions have arisen from the revival of
good, especially Greek, literature. If someone could wrench this persuasion

* * * * *

38 This phrase is in Greek.
39 This sentence is in Greek.
40 Democritus was known in antiquity as 'the laughing philosopher' because of
   his emphasis on 'cheerfulness.'

from their minds, it would not seem so unpleasant to live among them, as long as he kept Christ as the only goal of his life and directed all his efforts 305 at imitating him.

And so much for that. Your published letters to me,[41] my excellent friend Erasmus, brought me honour (for they brought me friends, who had followed your familiar and heartfelt letters and wanted to get to know Ammonius better) but they also stirred up some animosity against me among 310 some of our people, though I don't care in the least about that. I am rather more concerned that I will not at all live up to the expectation of friends. For they will have found that my behaviour was far below your praises, not to say that I fear they will bring a lawsuit against you, saying that when they met me personally they did not encounter what you had written in your let- 315 ters. However that may be, you most certainly did motivate me to try my best to be, rather than merely be said to be, that person. May Christ inspire my efforts. I am certainly grateful to you, because through you I always come out better in every way. I only wish I had the power to be able to repay you some day. I hope I have the good fortune in my lifetime to meet you face to 320 face on some occasion. If Christ should grant me this, I would by no means be unwilling to have him think that I have received compensation for whatever ill treatment I have suffered for Erasmus' sake. Some people led us to hope that you would come to live closer to us here, but your servant Quirinus dispelled that hope.[42] But I do not allow myself to desire any more than that you 325 should be completely safe, and I would be willing to extend your life at the expense of my own, if it should come to that. I only hope that you will furnish what you promised in the prefatory letter to the Basil: that you would issue from time to time equally faithful and careful translations of the holy Greek Fathers.[43] I read your edition of the Apostles' Creed, but only fleetingly;[44] 330 I will soon reread it. But I was wonderfully pleased by it. May Christ favour all your works most highly, to his own glory and the advancement of the church, my most dear friend Erasmus, and may he fulfil his promise in you. I think I will soon be writing to you again. In the meantime, farewell.

From Koningdal, house of the Carthusian order near Ghent, on the day 335 after the feast of the Trinity

Yours from the heart, Levinus Ammonius

* * * * *

41 Epp 2062, 2483
42 See Ep 2820 introduction.
43 See Ep 2611:186–92.
44 *Explanatio symboli* (Ep 2772)

2818 / To Bonifacius Amerbach   Freiburg, 12 June 1533

This letter (= AK Ep 1756) was first published in the *Epistolae familiares*. The autograph is in the Öffentliche Bibliothek of the University of Basel (MS AN III 15 49).

Cordial greetings. I have never been more dejected than during this summer. An important cause of my malady is this unending bad weather, from which has come much sickness in this city.[1] But for me the principal cause is the lack of the sort of wine I have had up until now. The wine from Beaune that Hieronymus sent last time relieved my nausea somewhat, but it is adulter-   5
ated.[2] I had acquired some companions who were as friendly and agreeable to live with as I could wish.[3] I had to send them away because the proneness of my stomach to vomit prevented me from having any conversation. Two scholars, whom Alciati had recommended in a most friendly letter,[4] came to greet me while I could not get out of bed, in a condition that kept me from   10
reading Alciati's letter, or yours, or Grynaeus'.[5] The next day they came back

* * * * *

2818
1 In the autumn and early winter of 1532–3 Erasmus was, by his own account, in reasonably good health. But in late February 1533 he began to complain of deteriorating health in terms that would remain more or less constant until the last months of his life. The symptoms were recurring periods of excruci-ating pain in his feet, hands, and indeed his entire body (usually referred to as 'gout'), as well as severe stomach problems, all of which caused difficulty eating or sleeping. Given the state of his health, he could not fulfil his avowed intention of leaving Freiburg and returning to his native Brabant (Ep 2820 in-troduction). He found it increasingly difficult to write or even to sign his let-ters, to receive and entertain guests properly, or to leave his house, and he lived in expectation of his imminent death. These developments can be followed in Epp 2770:1–6, 2776:63–5, 2780:79–80, 2782:6–10, 2783:16–23, 2788:2–6, 2818:1–14, 2827:1–10, 2846:13–14, 2858:1–3, 2860:6–9, 2898:4–10, 2906:4–5, 2911:14, 2916:2–10, 2918:37–42, 2920:1–4, 2922:6–11, 2924:2–7. The list continues unin-terrupted into the letters that will appear in CWE 21; see especially Allen Epp 3000:12–29, 3106:11–12, 3108:3–8. For an attempt to explain Erasmus' condition from the perspective of modern medicine, see 'Erasmus' Illnesses in His Final Years' 335–8 below.
2 There is no other record of Hieronymus Froben having sent wine from Beaune. On the effects attributed to the wine, cf Epp 2860:26–7, 2865:2–3, 2870:5–10.
3 Most likely the two counts of Rennenberg; see Ep 2810 n54.
4 The letter is not extant. The 'scholars' were probably students of Andrea Alciati (Ep 1250 introduction) at Bourges.
5 The letters of Bonifacius and Simon Grynaeus (for whom see Epp 1657, 2433) are not extant.

to say goodbye. But my illness made even that impossible. And for that reason I am all the more displeased by my poor health because it has made me not only wretched but also discourteous.

On the same day, Pieter van Montfoort arrived, a very tall young man, 15 a Dutchman whom I think you saw with me at Basel.[6] He brought an honorarium that my native country had some time ago designated for me.[7] If he had wanted to kill me, he could not have come at a more opportune time. He pressed me for letters of recommendation concerning some important matter, to the emperor, to people I know, and to some I do not know.[8] And for 20 that purpose he stayed six whole days. Sometimes, when I tried to converse or dine with him, it brought back the sickness. Now, forsaking everything, I am trying to preserve myself for when I get better. I had decided to see whether a little horseback riding would shake off the queasiness of my stomach, but the weather was unfavourable, and at the same time the pain in my 25 foot came back and kept me from doing it.

King Ferdinand has sent me, in addition to a very kind letter, two hundred gold florins,[9] together with fifty for Glareanus, whom I had recommended.[10]

I think you have already heard of the uprising that occurred at Augsburg on Ascension Day.[11] The occasion was the veneration of an image of Christ 30 hanging from the vault of a church. On the day before the feast the Zwinglians secretly took it away and destroyed it. The opposite party got wind of it and secretly had a new one made. The Zwinglians, in turn, got wind of this and very firmly stopped up the hole in the vault through which the image used to be suspended. The opposite party secretly opened up the hole and hung 35 the new image. This immediately caused an enormous uproar, so violent that it was a wonder that many people were not killed. The Zwinglians climbed up the vault of the church and threw the image down. Finally the city government sent in troops, kept the people out, and closed the church. Some warden of the church was responsible for taking the image down; the leader 40

* * * * *

6　For Montfoort, see Ep 2812 introduction.
7　For this see Ep 2819:1–19.
8　Two of these were Epp 2812–13. The letter to the emperor does not survive.
9　King Ferdinand's letter (cf Ep 2821:2) is not extant, but that from his chancellor, Bernhard von Cles, is. It makes clear that fifty of the two hundred florins were a personal gift from Cles himself; see Ep 2801:4–8. For the delivery of the money see Ep 2808:2–11.
10　For Erasmus' recommendation of Henricus Glareanus, see Ep 2651:60–75. For his fifty florins see Ep 2801:3–4 and n23 below.
11　22 May

of those who put it back was Anton Fugger, who is now accused of inciting a riot. In that respect I find Anton wanting in prudence. He should have yielded to the storm. And the image was not that important.[12] I do not know whether Mariangelo egged Anton on to this misdeed.[13]

Listen now to how Nachtgall was reconciled to me.[14] He resigned his 45 prebend to someone, with the proviso that every year Fugger should pay him fifty gold florins until he had received a benefice of that value or more. But when Fugger learned from Koler that Nachtgall was an enemy of mine, he gave the impression that he would diminish his kindness; at all events Koler caused Anton to have some doubt about Nachtgall. Nachtgall was afraid of 50 this and feigned a reconciliation. I was amazed at this sudden volte-face. But just before the feast of the Ascension,[15] Nachtgall wrote a letter to me,[16] imploring me to use my famed eloquence to recommend him to Anton Fugger, saying that he was now no different than he was when Fugger judged him worthy of his kindness. Indeed he was telling the truth, except that he should 55 have said 'wrongly judged.' What was I to do? Refuse to do my duty to someone who was reconciled with me? I wrote it,[17] but in a highly rhetorical style. He boasted about our friendship. He said many nice things about me. He claimed he was innocent. He added that Erasmus was greatly talented. Why say anything more? He got what he wanted. But he never came to see me. He 60 indicated what he wanted by letter or through a servant. Pelargus does not visit or write, just to let you know that this happens by agreement.[18]

A new commentary by Philippus Melanchthon on the Epistle to the Romans is for sale there.[19] He is pleased with himself, and I confess that he

* * * * *

12 In Ep 2814:16–22 Johann Koler alludes briefly to the events that Erasmus here reports in greater detail. Erasmus returns to the subject in Ep 2845:38–46. For a more detailed account of the incident at the church of St Moritz, written by a supporter of the evangelical cause a few days after it occurred, see CWC 3:118–21 (Gereon Sailer to Wolfgang Capito and Martin Bucer, 26 May 1533).
13 In Ep 2814:47–8 Johann Koler reports that Mariangelo Accursio is packing up to leave Augsburg.
14 On the contents of this paragraph, cf Ep 2814:6–15.
15 See n11 above.
16 Not extant
17 It does not survive.
18 Relations between Erasmus and Ambrosius Pelargus (Ep 2169 introduction) had been severely strained since the autumn of 1532; see Epp 2721–5. A reconciliation was soon to occur; see Epp 2832–40.
19 *Commentarii in Epistolam Pauli ad Romanos* (Wittenberg: Joseph Clug 1532); critical edition in MSA 5

makes some brilliant observations. But much of it is disappointing. He dis- 65
torts many things, he arrogantly rejects Origen and Augustine,[20] he passes
over many points. I have read some quaternions.[21] He seems to have come
upon some work by a scholastic theologian, and discusses his argument.[22] It
does not cost much. You would do me a favour if you sent it to Sadoleto, but
with the caveat that he separate the gold from the dung. 70

If Hieronymus is going to the fair at Strasbourg, I would commission
him to collect from the bankers there the money that the king has given me.[23]

Here there are no almonds except for tiny, unripe, and spoiled ones. I
would be grateful if Hieronymus would send a few pounds here. You can
show him this letter if you wish. 75

Farewell, my incomparable friend. Freiburg, on the feast of Corpus
Christi in the year 1533

Erasmus of Rotterdam, yours by every right

To the illustrious doctor of law Bonifacius Amerbach, an incomparable
gentleman or, in his absence, to Hieronymus Froben. At Basel 80

2819 / To Vincent Cornelissen van Mierop   Freiburg, 12 June 1533

This letter was first published in *Illustrium et clarorum virorum Epistolae selec-
tiores* ed Daniel Hensius (Leiden 1617) 288. The person addressed, Vincent
Cornelissen van Mierop, entered the service of the future Charles v in 1505
and rose through the ranks of the financial administration. In 1531 he became a
member of the council of finance at the court in Brussels, and in 1546 he became

* * * * *

20 See, for example, MSA 5 89, 156 (Origen), and 100, 121–2 (Augustine).
21 A quaternion is a quire consisting of two sheets folded once to folio format. See
Ep 1289 n6.
22 In the commentary Melanchthon takes issue with 'certain scholastic arguments'
(MSA 5 52:28–54:5), which Erasmus may have hastily concluded were the work
of a particular theologian. Or, perhaps, Erasmus noticed that Melanchthon ad-
dresses a series of scholastic arguments whose unnamed source the MSA editor
has identified as Nikolaus Herborn *Locorum communium adversus huius temporis
haereses enchiridion* (Cologne: Eucharius Cervicornus 1528). See MSA 5 37:14n,
47:13n, 96:10n, 116:10n, 132:19n. For Herborn (known to CWE as Nikolaus
Ferber of Herborn) see Ep 2896 n8.
23 Ie the two hundred florins from King Ferdinand and Bernhard von Cles;
see lines 27–8 above. The money had been deposited with a banking firm at
Strasbourg: see Ep 2808:2–11. We have no information about the dates of fairs
at Strasbourg, but the one in question would presumably have been sometime
soon after the date of this letter.

treasurer-general of the Netherlands. In the two letters that Erasmus wrote
to him (this one and Ep 2923) he is associated with the Estates of Holland at
The Hague and addressed (see lines 28–9 below) as imperial treasurer of the
Netherlands 'in Holland.'

Cordial greetings. The most accomplished young man Pieter van Montfoort
found me half-alive, in such a state that I could neither read letters nor engage in conversation.[1] He offered me as a gift the honorarium of Holland,[2]
but when he indicated that the money is in the hands of Erasmus Schets, I did
not want to take it from him. Afterwards, when I was somewhat recovered,   5
I read the letter of Schets,[3] which did not make it clear that the money had
been given to him. And he did not write the letter to me but to Pieter van
Montfoort. The letter of the advocate of Holland did not name the sum that
the Estates of Holland wished to give me.[4] But Schets' letter gave the figure
as two hundred florins. This gift was as gratifying to me as if it had been a   10
thousand florins. For I did not deserve it, but it was clearly written to me that
it was three hundred florins; and Pieter van Montfoort assures me that that
sum had been granted in the meeting of the Estates. He added that in his
own presence the lord of Assendelft had ordered Willem Goes, the advocate
of Holland, to instruct Schets to pay me two hundred and forty florins.[5] Now   15
it has come down to two hundred.[6] I consider the gift to be most ample, as I

* * * * *

2819
1 Cf Epp 2812 introduction, 2813:19–20, 2818:1–22.
2 See Epp 2645 n9, 2818:16–17.
3 Not extant
4 The advocate of Holland is doubtless the person referred to in lines 14–15
  below; see n5.
5 For Gerrit van Assendelft, president of the council of Holland, see Epp 2645
  n9. It was he who was instrumental in arranging the handsome gift from the
  Estates acknowledged in this letter; see Ep 2734. The advocate of Holland and
  West Friesland at the time was Aert van der Goes (1475–1545). Erasmus here
  calls him 'Guilielmus Goesius.' In a letter now lost, Erasmus wrote to Goes
  about the matter of the grant from the Estates; see Ep 2896:3–4, where Erasmus
  once again gets his name wrong, calling him 'Arnoldus.'
6 It is not known where Erasmus got the idea that the amount granted was
  300 florins. The records of the Estates of Holland show that on 16 April 1532
  they had set aside 240 florins for the purpose, and that on 24–5 April 1533 they
  ordered that 200 florins be sent to Erasmus Schets for delivery to Erasmus
  by Montfoort; see CEBR II 450. Writing to Cornelissen in April 1534 (Ep 2923),
  Erasmus reiterated that the amount of the gift had been set at 300 florins and
  that Montfoort had confirmed that. By this time, however, Erasmus' inquiries
  about the matter had resulted in his being assured of at least 240 florins, not

said. Nevertheless, I wanted you to know this, my very good friend, so that, if by any chance there is something underhanded in this business, you can discover and correct it.

A few days ago I wrote to you through Pieter van Montfoort,[7] but I was 20 quite exhausted. I am still not well as I write this to you. The Lord will grant me happier days when he wishes to do so. When I have recovered, I will express my gratitude for the kindness of my native land. From Pieter's report I know how much I owe you. I only wish I had some way of repaying you. I send my best wishes to you and to all who are dear to you.   25

Given at Freiburg, on the feast of Corpus Christi in the year 1533
Erasmus of Rotterdam, in my own hand
To the excellent gentleman Vincent Cornelissen, the treasurer of his imperial Majesty for Lower Germany in Holland

2820 / From Mary, Queen of Hungary and Bohemia   Brussels, 13 June 1533

This letter was first published in Ipolyi page 378. The manuscript is page 349 of the Esterhazy codex in the Hungarian National Archives at Budapest (Ep 2339 introduction).

Ever since leaving Basel to settle in Freiburg in the spring of 1529 Erasmus had been prey to the thought that he was living in a place that was almost certain to be a scene of conflict if, as seemed likely, a religious civil war were to break out in Germany. What he longed for was a friendly, welcoming place that was safely distant from the turmoil in Germany and yet close enough to Freiburg that a frail old man could survive the journey. In the end, after much indecision and procrastination, Erasmus found that the only place that met all these criteria was his native Netherlands, where for years his many friends had been urging his return. So too had the regents Margaret of Austria and her successor Mary of Hungary, both of whom made the resumption of Erasmus' imperial pension conditional on his return. The project of bringing Erasmus home to his native land had the warm support of Queen Mary's secretary, Nicolaus Olahus, who in 1532 enlisted the assistance of the imperial chancellor for the

* * * * *

200 (see Ep 2913:10–21), and he had resolved to be content with that, though fretting nonetheless about the missing 60 florins and forever after suspecting Montfoort of skulduggery. The gift was a generous one: 240 Rhenish florins were equivalent to £59 0s 0d groot Flemish or just under seven years' wages of an Antwerp master mason/carpenter (CWE 12 650 Table 3, 691 Table 13).
7 The letter is not extant.

Netherlands, Jean (II) de Carondelet, in his efforts to that end (see Epp 2689, 2693). In March 1533, having secured from Erasmus a statement of his conditions (Ep 2762), Carondelet sent an official letter of invitation (Ep 2784), cautioning however that nothing could be done until the emperor (absent in Spain) had given his approval. That is where matters stood at the end of CWE 19. For a more detailed history of Erasmus' difficult and much postponed decision to return to the Netherlands, see CWE 19 xiii–xvi.

In a letter of 4 May 1533 the emperor's secretary, Nicolaus Grudius (Ep 2785 n8), informed Olahus and Carondelet that their project of recalling Erasmus to the Netherlands had the approval of the emperor, who had written to Queen Mary to that effect (see Ipolyi pages 354–5, 361–2). Only then could Mary dispatch the present letter, which, along with Epp 2822 and 2828, was carried to Freiburg by Lieven Algoet, Erasmus' former famulus and now Olahus' secretary (Ep 2278 n2). Lieven, who also brought with him three hundred gold florins to cover the cost of Erasmus' journey (Ep 2870:22–3), returned to the Netherlands on the understanding that Erasmus would soon follow. But Erasmus' health was such that he could not risk the journey (Epp 2850:1–4, 2860:3–12). In late July he spoke of the matter as postponed until the spring (Ep 2846:175–8), and in November he assured Olahus that nothing had changed regarding his proposed return (Ep 2877:22–4). In April of the following year, however, he described to Olahus the symptoms that had prevented him from leaving his house even once during the preceding five months, and for good measure he alluded once more to his old fear of the monks in Brabant (Ep 2922:6–15). In reply, Olahus expressed grave concern about Erasmus' health but nonetheless persisted in urging him to return, arguing that in Freiburg Erasmus was in greater danger from the 'savagery' of the 'Lutheran soldiery' than he would be from hostile monks in the Netherlands (Allen Ep 2948:6–16). That was the end of the surviving correspondence between Erasmus and Olahus and of any serious talk of Erasmus' return to Brabant.

MARY, QUEEN OF HUNGARY AND BOHEMIA,
TO ERASMUS OF ROTTERDAM, GREETINGS

Your many volumes, Erasmus, give testimony to how much Christendom and our holy religion owe to you because of your virtues, teaching, and singular learning. For that reason we also hold you and your virtues in high 5
regard, especially since we have been fully informed of how you have always maintained a certain deference towards us, both from the letters you have sent us, and from your other learned writings, and especially from the frequent written and spoken commendations of you by our beloved, faithful servant Nicolaus Olahus, treasurer of Székesfehérvár, secretary and counsel- 10
lor. For that reason we would wish that you return to this your country and

to us, so that we might make use of your intellectual abilities and services
more closely at hand.

Therefore, we urge and beseech you to agree to come to us. The annual
pension that for some time now has been assigned to you by his imperial   15
Majesty, my lord and most loving brother, will be placed completely at your
disposal every year. And we will personally guarantee it by our own hand
and take care that it always be uninterrupted. We will also graciously provide for your other needs, so that nothing will be lacking to you here. We will
also provide for your personal safety and will do so in no ordinary manner,   20
so that you will find that our favour and kindness correspond to your merits
and virtues. And so we beg you, return; and do not delay. The speedier your
return, the more it will please us, and it will also be especially gratifying to
his imperial Majesty.

Brussels, 13 June in the year 1533   25

2821 / From Bernhard von Cles   Vienna, 14 June 1533

This letter was first published by Allen. The manuscript, an autograph rough
draft, is in the 'Correspondenza clesiana' collection of the Archivio di Stato di
Trento: 'Minute, copie e originali di lettere di Bernardo Clesio, 1514–1539.' For
Bernhard von Cles, bishop of Trent and chancellor to King Ferdinand, see Epp
1357, 2007. In this letter Cles appears to be responding to a letter from Erasmus
(not extant) thanking him for Ep 2801, which announced a gift of 150 florins
from King Ferdinand and one of 50 florins from Cles himself.

TO ERASMUS

We were exceptionally pleased that the king's letter and especially our letter[1]
were safely delivered when you were dining with your friend. But we were
sorry to hear that during the following night you suffered from stomach pain
and unremitting insomnia. We are nonetheless confident that you have been   5
relieved of that trouble and are now leading a pleasant life, which we hope
that Almighty God will continue to grant you, so that you may also promote
to the best of your ability what you hope for most of all in this storm of our
princes and lords concerning the peace of the church. For this purpose we
will not cease to exhort you in our letters, even though you are already suf-   10
ficiently inspired.

Vienna, 14 June 1533

* * * * *

2821
1 King Ferdinand's letter (cf Ep 2818:27–8) is not extant.

2822 / From Philippe de Croy   Brussels, 16 June 1533

This letter was first published in Ipolyi page 379. The manuscript is page 379
of the Olahus codex in the Hungarian National Archives at Budapest (Ep 2339
introduction).

In 1514 Philippe de Croy (1496–1549) succeeded his father, Henri de Croy, as
lord of Chateau-Porcéan, and in 1521 inherited the majority of the many lordships and titles of his childless uncle, Guillaume (I) de Croy, lord of Chièvres
(Ep 532:30n), including the marquisate of Aarschot. In the same year Philippe
succeeded his father-in-law Charles (I) de Croy (Ep 956) as captain-general of
Hainault, and six years later, on the latter's death, he became prince of Chimay.
By this time he was the wealthiest lord in the Netherlands. Greatly admired
by both Charles v and his regent Queen Mary, he was appointed to the council
of state in 1531, named president of the council of finance in 1532, and created
duke of Aarschot in 1533 (when that marquisate was elevated to the rank of
duchy). As this letter makes clear, Philippe willingly complied with the request
of Queen Mary that he add his support to the efforts of Nicolaus Olahus and
others to bring Erasmus back to the Netherlands.

THE ILLUSTRIOUS DUKE OF AARSCHOT TO ERASMUS OF ROTTERDAM
You will readily understand from her letter the wishes and the good will
of her serene Majesty the queen towards you.[1] As for me, I do not wish to
promise you anything for the moment. If you come here, as I hope and pray
that you will, you will learn in very fact my high esteem for you. I will never   5
forget both how closely you were acquainted with my brother of blessed
memory, the Cardinal de Croy, and that in your most learned writings you
have made known to posterity our name De Croy.[2] For that reason I confess
that I am extremely indebted to you.

Nor will I be lacking in gratitude when you return. I beg you again   10
and again to do so as soon as possible, according to the wishes of her royal
Majesty and of all of us who are the fervent promoters of your virtue and
reputation. Do not allow us to be deprived of your presence any longer. Here
you will have her royal Majesty to promote your teaching and learning, and

* * * * *

2822
1 Her letter is Ep 2820.
2 There is no evidence that Erasmus dedicated any of his works to any member of
the Croy family. He did, however, publish in the *Farrago* an exchange of letters
between himself and Philippe's brother, Cardinal Guillaume (II) de Croy: Epp
945, 957–9.

Philippe de Croy
Recueil d'Arras, Bibliothèque Municipale d'Arras

I also, among others, will be no ordinary friend and patron and will defend   15
and assist you in whatever other affairs and activities that may arise from
time to time. Make haste, therefore, and do not delay in complying with
the expectations of her royal Majesty, and my own as well, concerning your
return. The sooner you return, the more you will please all of us. Farewell.

Brussels, 16 June in the year 1533   20

2823 / From Bernhard von Cles   Vienna, 18 June 1533

This letter, written by Cles to accompany a letter (not extant) of Fridericus
Nausea to Erasmus (see lines 2–3 below), was first published by Allen. For the
manuscript, and for Cles as well, see Ep 2821 introduction. Nausea's letter replied to one (also not extant) containing advice in which Nausea detected a
note of anger. Erasmus' conciliatory reply is Ep 2847.

TO ERASMUS

Attached to this letter we send you the one we received most recently from
our outstanding and beloved friend, Fridericus Nausea.[1] Perhaps it would
have come into to your hands more quickly if it had been transmitted from
there.[2] But we have made every effort to get it to you there[3] as soon as pos-   5
sible, so that we could please both you and him at one and the same time.

Vienna, 18 June 1533

2824 / From Thomas Boleyn   Greenwich, 29 June [1533]

This letter was first published as Ep 109 in Enthoven. The manuscript, in a
secretary's hand but with line 28 and the signature added by Boleyn, is in the
Rehdiger Collection of the University Library at Wrocław (MS Rehd 254 152).
The year-date is supplied by Boleyn's expression of thanks for the *Explanatio
symboli* (March 1533), and his request that Erasmus write a work on the preparation for death (see nn1, 5 below).

For Thomas Boleyn see Ep 2266 introduction.

* * * * *

2823
1 For Nausea, see Ep 1577 introduction. Allen incorrectly inferred from this letter
  that Nausea was by this time in Vienna, where Cles had secured his appointment as court preacher to King Ferdinand. In 1533–4 Nausea was in fact in
  Rome. Not until his return from Italy in 1534 did he assume his position in
  Vienna.
2 Ie from Rome
3 Ie to Freiburg

THOMAS, EARL OF WILTSHIRE AND ORMOND, SENDS CORDIAL
GREETINGS TO DESIDERIUS ERASMUS OF ROTTERDAM

Since you have bestowed on me, most accomplished sir, such benefits of pious literature as ought to be expected from one who everyone unanimously
testifies is endowed with every kind of humane learning, you have certainly   5
made me most obliged to you, and you have not only justified the general
public opinion about your extraordinary kindness and prompt generosity to
the pious but have far surpassed it.[1] For you should not imagine that the outstanding piety of your character can either be hidden and not spread abroad
on the lips of everyone or not be loudly and widely proclaimed because of its   10
extraordinary usefulness not only to present but also to future generations.

   But if a similar or equal glory is achieved by an author who has undertaken some extraordinary work, or if it is gained by someone who labours
with all his strength to keep his work from perishing in the long, devouring
ruins of time, then it really seems to me that you should rightly be advanced   15
to the greatest honour and praise. But what could have been more pleasing
to me or more desirable to everyone than that he presented the most certain token[2] of our salvation and adds as it were a very strong anchor to the
Christian religion?

   But lest it should seem unfair not to confer any reward on someone   20
from whom I have received such a great benefit, I have sent to you by the
bearer of this letter fifty gold crowns,[3] not as a little gift but as a token[4] of
my gratitude to you; I will send more later, but in the meantime I implore
you again and again to take care to finish a little book on the preparation for
death, as soon as you can.[5] And if there is anything in which you think you   25
could use my help, I will strive in every way to comply with your wishes.

   Farewell. Greenwich, 19 June 1533

* * * * *

2824
1 Erasmus had dedicated his commentary on Psalm 22 to Boleyn (Ep 2266), and
   more recently the *Explanatio symboli* (Ep 2772).
2 Here and in line 22 below, Boleyn uses the word *simbolum* (usually spelled *symbolum*, from Greek σύμβολον), which means 'sign' or 'token,' but in ecclesiastical
   Latin means 'creed' or 'confession of faith.' This plays on the title of the work
   that Erasmus had dedicated to him; see the preceding note.
3 The rose crown, a gold coin that in 1533 was worth 60d. Fifty crowns (£12 10s 0d
   sterling) were equivalent to 500 days' or almost two years' wages for an Oxford
   master mason (CWE 12 650 Table 3, 688 Table 11).
4 *simbolo*; see n2 above.
5 *De praeparatione ad mortem* would be published c January 1534 (Basel: Froben
   and Episcopius), dedicated to Boleyn (Ep 2884).

I beg that you number me among you friends.
Thomas of Wiltshire and Ormond

2825 / To Pier Paolo Vergerio   Freiburg, 20 June [1533]

First published by Allen, this is a passage from a letter of Erasmus to Vergerio
that the latter quoted in a letter, dated 20 June 1533 at Vienna, to Jacopo Salviati.
The manuscript is in the Vatican Archives (Nunziatura di Germania, vol 56 folio 54).

Born in Capodistria (south of Trieste in Venetian territory), Pier Paolo
Vergerio (1498–1565) studied and practised civil law at Padua (doctorate in
1524) while engaging in humanist pursuits in the circle of Pietro Bembo. In
1532 he entered the service of Pope Clement VII, who immediately sent him on
diplomatic missions, first to Venice to promote a league against the Turks, and
then in 1533 as nuncio to the court of King Ferdinand, where he gathered his
first impressions of the political and religious problems in Germany. His reaction to the German 'heretics' at this time was hostile. In 1535 Pope Paul III sent
Vergerio once again to Germany to assess support for the calling of an ecumeni-
cal council. Returning to Italy in 1536, confidently expecting to be rewarded for
his services, he was nominated to the bishopric of Capodistria, a see with disap-
pointingly meagre revenues. While the appointment was pending, he accepted
the hospitality of a variety of Italian princes and prelates, visited the courts
of Francis I and Margaret of Angoulême, and in 1540–1 attended (as unoffi-
cial agent of Francis I) the colloquy at Worms aimed at reuniting the church in
Germany. During these travels he came increasingly under the influence of proponents of Catholic reform who were influenced by Protestant reformers and
the idea of justification by faith alone. In the summer of 1541 Vergerio, newly
ordained as a priest, took up residence in Capodistria and undertook to imple-
ment his ideas of reform. His vigorous, often tactless efforts to instruct his flock
and to root out abuses in religious houses aroused the opposition of friars and
of persons who had the ear of the pope, and in 1545 he found himself excluded
from the Council of Trent as well as on trial for heresy before the patriarch of
Venice and the papal nuncio. In 1549, having abandoned hope of establishing
his innocence, he left Italy and the church, fleeing first to the Grisons (a haven
for exiled Italians). Following a brief sojourn in Basel (1549–50), where he matriculated at the university, met Bonifacius Amerbach, and encountered other
exiled Italian reformers, he returned to the Grisons, where he became a pastor at
Vicosoprano. In 1553 he accepted the call of Duke Christopher of Württemberg
to enter his service at Tübingen, which was the centre of his activity for the rest
of his life. From there he undertook several diplomatic journeys (1556–60) as
an enthusiastic propagandist for Duke Christopher's policy of promoting the

Protestant cause, particularly in eastern Europe. But he devoted most of his time and effort to writing and publishing Protestant propaganda aimed primarily at his countrymen in Italy. (In addition to the article on Vergerio in CEBR III 387–8, see that by Anne Jacobson Schutte in OER IV 228–9.)

This fragment of a letter, written during Vergerio's first nunciature in Germany, is the only surviving evidence of the 'good friendship' between Vergerio and Erasmus. The passage in italics is Vergerio's introduction (in Italian) to the quoted passage.

The passage below is from a letter of Erasmus, with whom I am joined in good friendship, and we often write to one another. He is currently in Freiburg, and writes on 20 June.

Everywhere there are various disturbances and threats, so that the plans of men are in tumultuous confusion, which Homer compares to squadrons of 5 flies.[1] But the unknowable wisdom, goodness, and mercy of the supreme celestial artisan give me firm hope that all these things will be turned to the profit of the devout and his own glory.

There is now a rumour here that a truce has been concluded between King Ferdinand and the Turks with sufficiently fair conditions, namely, 10 that Hungary should belong to Ferdinand, as it once did to Louis (who is deceased).[2] The evangelicals carry on as if they were throwing dice. What happened at Münster and at Soest would take a long time to tell.[3] No doubt

* * * * *

2825
1 Homer *Iliad* 2.469
2 Following the death of King Louis II of Hungary at the battle of Mohács in 1526, there was intermittent warfare between Sultan Suleiman I, the victor at Mohács, and Ferdinand of Austria, who claimed Hungary as the brother of Louis II's childless widow, Mary of Hungary. In 1529 and again in 1532 the Turks came close to taking Vienna. In June 1533, after months of difficult negotiation, a truce was signed between Suleiman and Ferdinand. Ferdinand recognized the sultan as his suzerain, agreed to pay an annual tribute, and abandoned all claim to rule outside 'Royal Hungary,' the narrow strip of territory in the west over which he had managed to maintain control. The rest of Hungary was ruled from Buda by John Zápolyai, Suleiman's puppet king. Renewed conflict in the 1540s left the situation of Hapsburg 'Royal Hungary' unchanged.
3 It is too early for this to be a reference to the Anabaptist kingdom of Münster (1534–5), though it was at this time that Anabaptist preachers, expelled from the Netherlands and Jülich, began to arrive in town and to reinforce radical tendencies already there (OER III 97). For Soest, see n5 below. Erasmus' source of information about events in Münster, like that about events in Soest, may have been Konrad Heresbach, counsellor to the duke of Jülich-Cleves; see Ep 2780:77–8 with n26.

you have already learned what happened at Augsburg.[4] The uproar at Soest
was caused by a Dominican who had fled from many places because of 15
theft.[5] At Frankfurt someone very like him is sowing new dogmas about the
Eucharist.[6] Lübeck has declared war on Holland, etc.[7]

2826 / From Damião de Gois   Antwerp, 20 June 1533

This letter was first published as Ep 188 in Förstemann / Günther. The autograph was in the Burscher Collection of the University Library at Leipzig (Ep
1254 introduction). Erasmus' reply is Ep 2846.

Born at Alenquer into a family that belonged to the lower nobility, Damião de
Gois (1502–74) became a page at the court of King Manuel I of Portugal in 1511.
In 1523, Manuel's successor John III appointed Gois secretary of the Indiahouse
at Antwerp, the Portuguese establishment that looked after the king's commercial interests in the Netherlands. Gois also undertook diplomatic missions
on behalf of King John to many parts of Europe, including Denmark, Prussia,
Poland, and Russia. Meanwhile, he was greatly stimulated by the intellectual
atmosphere in Antwerp, where he developed a lively interest in humanism and
church reform. He took as his tutor in Latin the noted poet and geographer
Cornelius Grapheus (Ep 1299 n24), who had just been released from confine-
ment and imprisonment at Brussels (April–November 1523) on charges of heresy. This choice indicates a religious open-mindedness that was also evident in
a visit Gois paid to Wittenberg in 1531 during one of his diplomatic journeys.
He attended a sermon by Luther and was invited to his home for dinner. While
he found Luther little to his taste, he liked Melanchthon, who became a friend
and with whom he corresponded over the next seven years (the only surviving
letter being MBW Ep 1722A). In that same year (1531) Gois enrolled as a student
at the University of Louvain, where Rutgerus Rescius and Conradus Goclenius,
professors of Greek and Latin respectively at the Collegium Trilingue and, like
Grapheus, devoted followers of Erasmus, became his friends. In the spring of

* * * * *

4 See Ep 2814:17–34.
5 For the uproar in Soest and Erasmus' mistaken identification of the Dominican
  in question, see Ep 2728:8–21 with n6.
6 There is no evidence of anyone so described doing any such thing at Frankfurt
  at this time. The only disturbance over the Eucharist at Frankfurt in the spring
  of 1533 was that caused by the publication of Luther's open letter rebuking the
  Frankfurt pastors with 'Zwinglian' views on the subject; see Ep 2806 n11. It
  may be that Erasmus had somehow misunderstood reports of Luther's letter as
  evidence of the spread of radically 'new dogmas' at Frankfurt.
7 See Ep 2798 n12.

DAMIANVS A GOES.
Thucÿdes gentis enarrat gesta Pelasgæ
Romanis claret Liuius in Decasiv
Hic, alia vt taceam serâ data scripta senectâ,
ÆTHIOPVM accepit nomen ab HISTORIA.

42

Damião de Gois
Brussels, Bibliothèque Royale Albert I

1533 (see n6 below) Gois, armed with a letter of introduction from Rutgerus
Rescius, paid the visit to Erasmus that is the background of the present letter.
Summoned back to Portugal by the king, who wanted to make him treasurer
of the Indiahouse at Lisbon, Gois, after much soul-searching, decided to
abandon royal service for humanist scholarship and returned to Louvain (Ep
2916:22–3). Erasmus, who had grown fond of Gois, invited him to be his house
guest in Freiburg. Gois arrived there in April 1534 (Ep 2924:39–40) and stayed
until August, when, bearing a letter of introduction to Pietro Bembo (Ep 2958),
he departed for Italy to continue his studies at Padua. While there he came
under the influence of the Ciceronians, and in a letter now lost he suggested to
Erasmus that he perfect his style. Erasmus sent him a lengthy reply (Ep 3043),
pointing out that pure Ciceronianism did not suit the discussion of religious
topics. By 1538 Gois was back in Louvain, where he married and fathered three
sons. In 1542, when the French attacked Louvain, Gois, who had taken part in
the defence, was captured and spent fourteen months in prison. Summoned
back to Portugal by John III, Gois and his family arrived there in 1545. He was
made royal archivist and was commissioned to write the chronicles of the reigns
of John II and Manuel I (published in 1566–7) that established his reputation as
a historian. Meanwhile, however, the Jesuits, who knew of his good relations
with Wittenberg and Erasmus, repeatedly denounced him before the high
tribunal of the Inquisition. As long as John III ruled, he was safe, but John's
successor, King Sebastian (1568), yielded to Jesuit pressure. In 1572 Gois was
found guilty of heresy and died two years later in prison.

DAMIÃO DE GOIS TO HIS FRIEND DESIDERIUS ERASMUS, GREETINGS
Through the hands of Erasmus Schets I sent you a single letter,[1] from which
I think you learned about my return to Louvain and about the arrival of
your servant in the same place.[2] I could not by any means persuade your
servant to accept any help from me. Whether his reluctance sprang from his   5
own shyness or from you and your orders I do not know.[3] But I want you
to know that you and all your servants can make use of everything that is
mine, entirely without this shyness. My friend Erasmus, since you are very
dear to me, I do not wish to hide my good fortune from you. The most serene
king of Portugal, my most estimable lord in many ways, after I had travelled   10
continually at his command for almost a decade, tending to his affairs in the

* * * * *

2826
1 Not extant
2 The servant was Quirinus Hagius; see Ep 2804 n7.
3 See Ep 2846:123–6.

provinces of Germany, Sarmatia,[4] and Dacia,[5] and had finally returned to the land of the Belgians, summoned me by letter back to Portugal, so that I could become his chief treasurer, even though I had never sought, nor even considered, such an office or anything of the kind. For such a manifestation of the king's love for me my friends can, no doubt, quite rightly congratulate me. And so I have now left Louvain and travelled to Antwerp, whence, after ten days, I shall return to Portugal. If God in his power and mercy allows me to arrive there safe and sound, I will be better able to serve both you in particular and my other friends, and I will be genuinely willing to do so.

In view of your services to me, I thought I would be transgressing what is required by the laws of friendship if I did not inform you of what I have heard about you at Louvain, especially since the case is so passionately disputed and so delicate. For they say that you approved of that notorious English divorce. When I heard that, I was completely surprised, since I knew that I had heard the opposite from your own lips at Freiburg.[6] Hence I began to disagree as strongly as I could. And finally it came to the point that through my feeble arguments I removed their suspicion about you. And so please tell me what I should respond if such foolishness ever happens to come to my ears, since I have no doubt that when I get to Portugal the conversation in the presence of the king will turn to you and your opinion against that divorce.[7]

* * * * *

4 Gois appears to mean Sarmatia Europaea, an area including parts of modern Poland and Russia.
5 The Roman province of Dacia was in the area of modern Romania, but Dacia was the medieval name for Denmark, which is the relevant meaning here; cf n14 below.
6 During his brief visit there in the spring of 1533 (cf introduction above), most probably in March. Erasmus was ill when Gois arrived (Ep 2846:13–14), but he had been well in the winter of 1532–3 until the last days of February; see Epp 2770:1, 2776:62, 2782:7–10. Gois' visit must therefore have taken place after February, but it also has to have happened before 13 April, the day on which the town of Schiltach (near Freiburg) burned to the ground, an event concerning which Gois requested, in a letter now missing, information that Erasmus supplied in Ep 2846:127–54. Erasmus invited Gois to a meal, but did not read the letter of introduction from Rescius and did not look at the book that his visitor gave him (see n8 below). Gois did not take offence at this (see lines 65–9 below), and Erasmus apologized for the cool reception in Ep 2846:8–28.
7 Ep 2846:41–97 is Erasmus' response to this request.

I remember that when I was there I gave you a little book about the
faith and morals of Prester John and his subjects.[8] At the end of it is a certain
exhortation of mine directed to the Swede[9] Johannes Magnus, archbishop of
Uppsala,[10] concerning Pilapia or Laponia,[11] a huge province in the territory   35
of Scythia,[12] much of which is located in the diocese of the aforementioned
archbishop; it has been accurately described by Jakob Ziegler in his *Schondia*
or *Scondlandia* (based on the narrative of the aforementioned archbishop).[13] In
that place there is neither any law nor any knowledge of our Saviour Christ or
his gifts – an extremely impious thing, much to be deplored by a pious heart;   40
it is something that especially moves me to compassion and great concern

* * * * *

8 Ie the Ethiopians. Since the mid-fourteenth century, Ethiopia had been the
   focus of the search for Prester John, the legendary Christian emperor whom
   the legend had otherwise located in Asia. The book, fruit of Gois' conversations
   in 1514 and 1515 with an Ethiopian emissary to King Manuel I of Portugal,
   was entitled *Legatio Magni Indorum Imperatoris Presbyteri Joannis ad Emanuelem
   Lusitaniae Regem* (Antwerp: Grapheus 1532).
9 Gois calls him 'the Goth,' a term that was used for both Swedes and Danes (who
   in those days were more difficult to distinguish from one another than they are
   today); cf n17 below.
10 Johannes Magnus (or Store, the Swedish translation of Magnus, 1488–1544),
   studied in Louvain, Cologne, and Perugia (doctor of theology 1520). In 1523 he
   was elected archbishop of Uppsala, but papal confirmation was refused, though
   Magnus was confirmed as administrator. In 1526 he left Sweden and settled in
   Gdansk, which is where he met Gois in 1527 and urged him to write on the
   subject of the Ethiopians (see n8 above) and the Lapps (see following note).
   In August 1533 Clement VII confirmed Magnus as archbishop of Uppsala, but
   by that time the Reformation in Sweden had reached the point (1531) at which
   there was a Lutheran archbishop, and Magnus was forbidden to enter Sweden.
   In 1533 he was consecrated archbishop *in absentia*, residing at Gdansk. In 1538
   he went to Italy and from 1541 lived at Rome, where he died.
11 Ie Lappland. The appended exhortation, entitled *De Pilapiis*, was an appeal for
   more humane treatment of the Lapps.
12 Scythia was the name given by Herodotus, Cicero, and Pliny to the northernmost
   part of the world known to them: the northeast of Europe and the north of Asia.
13 The work, *Quae intus continentur, Syria, ad Ptolomaici operis rationem, praeterea
   Strabone, Plinio & Antonio auctoribus locupletata, Palestina ... Arabica Petraea
   ... Aegyptus ... Schondia ... Holmiae ... Regionum superiorum singulae tabulae
   geographicae* (Strasbourg: Peter Schöffer 1532), includes a chapter on Scandanavia
   (*Schondia*) with a map that was the first to include Finland by name. On page
   lxxxv recto –verso (preface to the chapter on Scandinavia) Ziegler (for whom
   see Ep 1260) names as one of his sources 'Johannes Magnus, bishop of Uppsala.'

for this very simple people, since, when I was living among the Danes,[14] the
Prussians,[15] and the Livonians,[16] I heard from many upright merchants who
were engaged in business there that the Lapps are extremely simple and
harmless people living like animals under no sort of law, and I am convinced   45
that this is true. Hence it is to be believed that they can easily be induced to
accept the gospel of Christ if the kings and princes (I mean Christian ones)
who rule them by imposing taxes on them would remit some of those taxes,
the shameful profit they exact from them. I say this because I know for certain
that those noble rulers barely allow any truly Christian preachers to go among   50
them to proclaim the gospel. Conscious of their own tyrannical greed, they
are afraid that through the preaching of the gospel and living with Christians
these simple and brutish creatures would become wiser and would then
rightly reject the demand for such unjust taxes. Such misery is certainly not
to be tolerated by devout consciences. And so, not only for my sake but for   55
the sake of these miserable people and for the sake of Christ himself, I beg
and implore you, in the name of Christ, either to write something about this
miserable state of affairs or be willing to add a letter of commendation to that
exhortation of mine so that, when your impressive writings reach the Swedes
and the Danes,[17] and other people like them, such tyrants and murderers   60
of souls, moved by some access of piety, might awaken from such great
indifference, and the wretched souls of the Lapps might not perish through
the sinful neglect of such rulers. If you do this, you will gain the favour of
Christ and the whole Christian world, and it will bring you no small praise.[18]

To leave you a small reminder of my departure, I send you, through   65
the hands of Erasmus Schets, a little gift – hardly equal to what you deserve
– namely, a gilded silver cup, so that when you make use of it from time to
time you will think of your entirely devoted friend.[19] I too, wherever I may

* * * * *

14 Gois calls them *Dacos*, after *Dacia*, the medieval Latin name for Denmark.
15 Gois calls them *Prutenos*, residents of *Pruthenia*, the medieval Latin word for
Prussia (including Gdansk).
16 Livonia comprised the northern part of modern Latvia and the southern portion
of Estonia.
17 Gois says *Suecios Gothosque* (Swedes and Goths), making 'Danes' the only
possible meaning of 'Goths' here; cf n9 above.
18 For Erasmus' reaction to this appeal, see Ep 2846 n29.
19 The cup, the gift of which is acknowledged with thanks in Ep 2846:32–4,
appears in the inventory of Erasmus' belongings made in April 1534, with Gois
named as the donor. Next to the entry Erasmus wrote 'I sold it to Amerbach.'
See Major 41.

happen to be, will repay you in kind, that is, I will always remember you. But take in good part this little gift of mine, however inadequate it may be, 70 and make the best of it. Although it is certainly not sufficient for you, accept from this friend of yours the loving heart that is always at your disposal, this friend of yours, I say, whom you will find steadfast in friendship even to his last breath.

Whenever you want to send a letter to me in Portugal, you can send it 75 safely through Erasmus Schets; I have spoken to him about it.

As soon as I arrive in Portugal, I will send you news about myself and my circumstances. Farewell, my most genuine friend.

Antwerp, 20 June 1533

To Desiderius Erasmus of Rotterdam, his master. In Freiburg 80

2827 / To Bonifacius Amerbach   Freiburg, 21 June 1533

This letter (= AK Ep 1757) was first published by Allen. The manuscript, a copy in the hand of Bonifacius' son Basilius (1533–91), is in the Öffentliche Bibliothek of the University of Basel (MS G II 13a 42).

TO THE RENOWNED GENTLEMAN MASTER BONIFACIUS AMERBACH. AT BASEL

Cordial greetings. I was not going to answer your letter,[1] since you told me to wait until tomorrow for Trübelmann,[2] except that this old man insistently asked for something for you.[3] As soon as the weather began to grow milder, 5 the pain diminished, but it still affects the left shinbone; it is mild in the foot, even milder in the hip, variable in the knee (but always tolerable).[4]

Many are sick here, among them Zazius and Emmeus and my theologian.[5] I would long since have recuperated if I had been able to enjoy the favour of two gods, Jupiter and Bacchus.[6] If you find it convenient to come 10

* * * * *

2827
1 Not extant
2 See Ep 2554 n1.
3 Probably the same old man as mentioned in Ep 2873A:1, identified by Alfred Hartmann as the public messenger Felsenmeyer (first name unknown), who operated between Basel and Freiburg (AK Ep 1757 n1)
4 For Erasmus' illness at this time, see Ep 2818 n1.
5 Udalricus Zasius (Ep 2857), the printer Johannes Faber Emmeus (Ep 2321 n14), and 'my theologian' Ludwig Baer (Ep 2225)
6 The gods respectively of good weather and good wine

here during the approaching holidays,[7] it would be most pleasing to me, and even almost indispensable. Best wishes, my excellent friend, to you and all who are precious to you.

Freiburg, 21 June 1533

Erasmus of Rotterdam, entirely yours   15

2828 / From Nicolaus Olahus   Brussels, 21 June 1533

This letter, Olahus' answer to Ep 2792, was first published in Ipolyi pages 380–1. The manuscript is page 352 of the Olahus codex in the Hungarian National Archives at Budapest (Ep 2339 introduction). For Olahus see Ep 2813 introduction.

NICOLAUS OLAHUS, TREASURER OF SZÉKESFEHÉRVÁR,
SECRETARY AND COUNSELLOR OF QUEEN MARY,
TO ERASMUS OF ROTTERDAM, GREETINGS

In my last letter,[1] my dear Erasmus, I explained fully what I have recently done concerning your affairs, with the diligence I customarily employ in the   5
business of my friends. I promised you that I would let you know what answer we could expect from the emperor. And I was quite right to do so. For I did not want to undertake or do anything precipitously concerning your affairs. In the meantime your servant Quirinus arrived with a letter from which I easily understood your intentions.[2]   10

Everything turned out the way we wanted. There is nothing standing in the way of your returning (as we urged you to do from the beginning and as we very much wanted you to do out of the love we bear you). Although the princes also favoured you previously, nonetheless we too have done everything we could to make them yet more favourable to you because of your   15

* * * * *

7 This would have been the three–four-week holiday sanctioned by the university statutes during the *Hundstage* (the dog days of summer); see Rudolph Thomman *Geschichte der Universität Basel 1532–1632* (Basel 1889) 40.

2828
1 Ep 2785
2 Quirinus Hagius had delivered the letter on his way to London; he was currently on his return journey to Freiburg and would pass through Brussels on his way; see lines 41–3 below and cf Ep 2804 n7.

extraordinary virtues and intellectual gifts. What the emperor replied concerning you, you will learn from the copy of his letter included with this
letter from me.[3] What my queen decided afterwards at my request and in the
name of the emperor, you will learn from the letter of the lord of Palermo.[4]
The queen's sentiments and her good will towards you, you will learn from   20
her own letter.[5] The duke of Aarschot is also remarkably fond of you.[6] I have
urged all these people to love you and desire your presence here.

Thus, my friend Erasmus, there is nothing that should keep you there.
If you want everything to be provided for your comfort, quiet, health, and
tranquillity at this time of your life (which is already burdensome), and in-   25
deed in your native land, in a climate that is favourable and helpful to you,
among people close to you, friends and old associates, come back very soon;
make it your preference to reside on your native soil and to spend this period of your final years here, where both princes and all good men want you
to be, instead of there, where you have few princes on your side and many   30
ungrateful fellow citizens. You are aware that from the time when we first
laid the foundations of our friendship and intimacy in letters, I have never
treated you thoughtlessly; so much the less would I do so now concerning
your return if I thought it would not contribute to your quiet and provide
ease at this time of your life, which is now increasingly burdensome.   35

Therefore consent to come back as soon as you can. Since, however, I did
not think that everything should be included in a letter, I arranged through
the queen that Lieven should be sent to you.[7] He will tell you everything
that I have done and what he has heard and gathered from me about the
details of your affairs. I do not think I could have sent anyone more reliable   40
or more devoted to you and to me. Give credence to what he says. Your servant Quirinus, who left me here to go to England, has not yet returned. But I
expect him to arrive within hours. Farewell and love me as you always have.

Brussels, 21 June 1533

* * * * *

3 The emperor's letter, addressed to Queen Mary, is not extant; see Ep 2820
   introduction.
4 Not extant. The lord of Palermo was Jean (II) de Carondelet (Ep 2899
   introduction).
5 Ep 2820
6 See Ep 2822 introduction.
7 For Lieven Algoet and his journey to bring Erasmus back to Brabant, see Ep
   2820 introduction.

2829 / From Viglius Zuichemus   Padua, 24 June 1533

This letter was first published in Van Heussen page 114. As manuscript sources Allen lists two copies in the Bibliothèque Royale at Brussels (MS II 1040 vol 1 folio 62, MS 6919 page 123). For Viglius Zuichemus see Ep 2810 introduction.

TO ERASMUS OF ROTTERDAM

Although at the present time I had nothing worth writing about to you, my very learned friend Master Erasmus, nevertheless, since my friend Florens had received a letter from his father and wished to respond to you,[1] and since he could not conveniently send his letter without mine, I gladly assumed 5 this task, especially since for quite a while now you have been accustomed to putting up with my frivolities and vapid letters. And if I were not afraid of abusing your patience, I could tell long tales in this letter about the recent doings of the Augustinian friars who held their convocation here, as the Carmelites did last year. 10

    You would hardly believe the discussions (or rather altercations) there have been here between the Italian and the Parisian masters. And since it is the custom that once the propositions for debate have been set, the monks of different orders gather for disputation, vehement controversies and disputes have often arisen, accompanied by much shouting in favour of Scotus 15 or of Giles.[2] Most of the propositions were from the *Logic* or the *Physics*, except that the Parisians refuted some propositions of Luther, and a certain friar from Toulouse, who proposed conclusions about anything 'knowable' (as they say),[3] and even (for heaven's sake) about law, shamefully acknowledged himself beaten in the very first session: after promising an encyclo- 20 paedic knowledge of all areas, he demonstrated that he had not learned even the rudiments of particular subjects. Meanwhile, some monks spent a lot of time deliberating over their administrative organization, and when they pronounced punishment against several monks accused of *lèse majesté*, it almost came to a riot as the condemned put themselves under the protection of the 25 scholastics, by whom they were very courageously saved.

* * * * *

2829
1 The letter is not extant. For Florens van Griboval and his attempts to secure the payment of Erasmus' imperial pension, see Ep 2716:155–75 with n39, 2767:9–10, 2810:44–51.
2 The Franciscan Duns Scotus (c 1265–1308), and the Augustinian Giles of Rome (c 1243/7–1316), both of whom taught at Paris
3 The word is *scibilis*, a scholastic neologism.

For quite a while here we had a good laugh over these controversies of the monks. Logau recently passed this way, and when he had run out of money he set out for Rome.[4] Giovanni Crisostomo has been transferred to Ravenna.[5] The sermons of Ambrose are in my possession; as soon as I can conveniently do so, I will see to it that you get them.[6]

It was reported that the pope was going to set out for Nice to talk with the Frenchman about having his dignity restored.[7] But the matter has been put off. Otherwise, in Italy there is no rumour of war. The Turkish army has often tried in vain to conquer Koroni in the Peloponnese.[8] Andrea Doria has gone to the rescue with the Genoese and imperial fleet.[9] Bembo is enjoying his peace and quiet, devoting all his attention to his history of Venice, of which he has given me a sample, and which will soon be published.[10] Baïf has sought a discharge and is making efforts to return.[11]

Otherwise we have nothing here to report. Farewell.

Padua, 24 June 1533

* * * * *

4 Georg von Logau (Ep 2810 n2) had gone to Rome seeking benefices; see Ep 2854:100–5.
5 Giovanni Crisostomo Zanchi (Ep 2716 n35)
6 Concerning the *Sermones contra Arianos* of (pseudo-) Ambrose, see Ep 2716 n36.
7 'The Frenchman' was King Francis I. In the early weeks of 1532, in the midst of negotiations over the marriage of Henry, duke of Orléans, to the pope's niece Catherine de' Medici, as well as over appointments to the college of cardinals, Francis I invited Clement VII to meet with him in Nice. Clement was agreeable, but on 24 May he wrote to Francis postponing the meeting until September. The meeting finally took place in October–November, but in Marseille, where the pope himself presided at the wedding of Prince Henry and Catherine. See Pastor 10 218, 229–32.
8 Koroni in the southern Peloponnese on the Gulf of Messenia
9 In 1532 Andrea Doria, the brilliant Genoese admiral who in 1528 had entered the service of Emperor Charles V, captured the fortress of Koroni from the Turks. Despite the relief mission referred to here, the fortress was retaken by the Turks in 1534. Cf Ep 2854:108–9.
10 Since 1530 Pietro Bembo (Ep 2106) had been librarian and historian of the republic of Venice, charged with the task of writing the *Historia Veneta* in twelve books that was published by the Aldine press in 1551, four years after his death.
11 Since 1529 Lazare de Baïf (Ep 1962 introduction) had been the resident ambassador of Francis I at Venice. In 1534 he returned to France, where he became a magistrate in the Parlement of Paris.

2830 / From Charles Blount   Westminster, 26 June [1533]

> This letter, Blount's answer to Ep 2726, was first published as Ep 74 in Enthoven.
> The manuscript, in the hand of a secretary or tutor, is in the Rehdiger Collection
> of the University Library at Wrocław (ms Rehd 254 30).

In reminding me of my duty so lovingly and faithfully, most learned Erasmus,
you certainly display (to use the language of Cicero) your affection,[1] which
though well known to me is still sweet and much desired. I will try with
all diligence to follow your advice by letter. But I am very sorry that we are
separated by such a long distance that we cannot converse. For I have always   5
promised myself to derive some learning from your letters, which are so re-
plete with the highest eloquence as well as the greatest wisdom. But allow
me, my most kindly Erasmus, to beg you this one thing: if we are not often
to be given the chance to converse by the exchange of letters, deign at least to
compensate for that infrequency (should it occur) by the amplitude of your   10
pen. For I am so affected by your letters that I would be glad to pass away
as I read them.

As for the added centuries of adages, which you dedicate to me in the
preface,[2] I find no way to thank you. Nonetheless I offer you the greatest
gratitude I can muster. But, my dear Erasmus, I beg you that, since you have   15
thus far spurred on my studies so attentively, do not stop now but continue
to remind me of what I should do, if not as often as you would like, at least
as much as you can conveniently manage in the midst of your engagements
and other affairs. Nothing you can do would give me more pleasure.

Farewell, at Westminster, 26 June   20
Yours with all my heart, Charles Blount

2831 / From Thomas More   Chelsea, [June 1533]

> This letter, More's answer to two letters no longer extant, was first published in
> the epistolary appendix to Erasmus' *De praeparatione ad mortem* (Basel: Froben
> and Episcopius 1534), where the letter itself is on pages 112–15, while the Tablet
> and Epitaph (here appended to the letter, lines 74–135) precede it on pages 109–
> 11. The year-date is confirmed by the reference in line 8 to 'the present archbish-
> op of Canterbury,' Thomas Cranmer, who took office on 30 March 1533. Since

* * * * *

2830
1 A favourite expression of Cicero, frequently found in his correspondence
2 Ie in Ep 2726

Quirinus Hagius, who carried this letter, presumably also carried Epp 2824 and
2830 and was in Tournai on 9 July, having arrived there via Brussels (see Ep
2804 n7), it seems unlikely that he left England earlier than 26 June.

This is the last surviving letter in the correspondence between More and
Erasmus.

THOMAS MORE TO ERASMUS OF ROTTERDAM, GREETINGS

I have received two letters from you, one from Freiburg sent on 7 February
last year, the other brought here by Quirinus,[1] who, apart from the letter, informed me about events in those regions worthy of note. I am most grateful
to you for wanting me to know about them.   5

Concerning your affairs,[2] you can learn everything from Quirinus, who
seems to me to be both upright and diligent. I am glad for your sake (and also
for mine, since I love you) that the present archbishop of Canterbury is quite
as fond of you as was Warham, than whom no one ever lived who was more
devoted to you. If at the end he seemed somewhat remiss in his gifts, the   10
reason was inadequate means, not lack of loyalty. For when he died he was
poorer than anyone could imagine – except that there was enough to pay his
debts. He did not owe very much, but after the expenditures required for his
funeral, there was not much left. The war (or rather the skirmishes) we have
had with the Scots have undoubtedly exhausted the coffers of Tunstall, for   15
his diocese is on the border with Scotland,[3] so distant from us that now I hear
from him almost as rarely as from you. There was a rumour here that N was
here together with Melanchthon,[4] secretly protected for a long time by some
people, and that he stole away afterwards. But that rumour gradually faded
away and was discovered to be completely false. The king seems to be more   20
relentlessly opposed to the heretics than the bishops themselves.

* * * * *

2831
1 Neither letter is extant. Quirinus Hagius departed for England at the end of
   April 1533.
2 Chiefly the problems surrounding the collection of the income from the
   English livings bestowed on Erasmus by the recently deceased archbishop of
   Canterbury, William Warham; see Ep 2761 n10.
3 In February 1530 Cuthbert Tunstall (Ep 571), who had been bishop of London
   since 1522, was transferred to Durham, and in 1531 he became president of
   the king's Council of the North. During his many years of friendship and encouragement for Erasmus, Tunstall had contributed generously to his financial
   support.
4 'N' is unidentified. Philippus Melanchthon was never in England; see n6 below.

Our very own heretic Tyndale, who is in exile nowhere and everywhere,[5] recently wrote to someone here that Melanchthon was with the king of France and that he had spoken with someone who had seen Melanchthon received in Paris with a retinue of 150 horsemen.[6] Tyndale added that he was 25 afraid that if the French received the word of God through Melanchthon they would be confirmed in a teaching about the Eucharist contrary to the sect of Wyclif. How carefully they treat this matter, as if God had delegated them to instruct the whole world and imbue it with the rudiments of the faith! As for what you wrote in your earlier letter, that you had some doubts about pub- 30 lishing my letter even though there were reasons you wanted to do so,[7] there is no reason, my dear Erasmus, for you to hesitate. Some gossips have begun to spread it about among us that although I pretended otherwise, I was re- moved from office against my will.[8] But when I took care to have my tomb- stone made, I did not hesitate to let the epitaph testify to the facts, for any of 35 them to refute if he can. As soon as they copied it out, since they could not prove it to be unfounded, they attacked it as crassly boastful. But I preferred to let them hold this opinion rather than the other one, not for my own sake, since I do not care what men say as long as God gives his approval, but rath- er because I thought I should defend the integrity of my reputation for the 40 sake of the faith, because I had written books in our language against some headstrong proponents of disputed doctrines.[9] And just to let you know how boastfully I wrote, you will get a copy of my epitaph and will see with what a good conscience I make no attempt to flatter them to keep them from preach- ing anything against me. I have now waited for the period of time prescribed 45 by the syndic following the administration of an office and resignation from it, and no one has yet come forward to lodge any complaint about my

* * * * *

5 See Ep 2659 n7.
6 Except for brief journeys to other towns in Electoral Saxony, usually as an ecclesiastical visitor, Melanchthon spent the entire year 1533 in Wittenberg. It was
  the same in 1532. See MBW 10 (*Itinerar*) 401–11. Indeed, he never once travelled
  outside Germany.
7 The letter in question was Ep 2659.
8 See Ep 2659:2–38, where More pictures his resignation as the result of his poor
  health and the kind indulgence of the king, a version of events that Erasmus
  duplicated in letters to friends (Epp 2728:29–31, 2735:42–3, 2745:23–6, 2750:3–
  66). It is also reiterated in the tablet affixed to his tomb; see lines 107–13 below.
9 See Ep 2659 n8.

integrity.[10] I have either been so innocent or at least so careful that if my rivals
refuse to allow me the former, they must allow me to boast of the latter. But
concerning this matter the king himself has made pronouncements on other   50
occasions, often privately and twice in public. Although my modesty will not
allow me to recount it, when my successor (a man of exceptional worth) took
the office,[11] the king honourably enjoined a most illustrious duke, I mean the
duke of Norfolk, the high treasurer,[12] to testify that the king was most reluctant to yield to my plea to be dismissed. Not content with this, the king in   55
his extraordinary kindness later required the same message to be delivered
once more in his presence, through the mouth of my successor, during a solemn session of the lords and the commons, in the speech which is ordinarily
given at the beginning of the senate, which senate (as you know) we call
the Parliament. Therefore, if you wish, there is no reason for you to hesitate   60
about publishing the letter. Where in the epitaph I claim to have been 'harsh
against heretics,' I did so for a purpose. For I find such people so thoroughly
hateful that, if they do not repent, I want to be hated by them as their worst
enemy, since day after day I find them more and more to be such a menace
that I am extremely afraid for the whole world. To him of whom you write   65
(I will follow your advice) I will write nothing at all, although I have long

* * * * *

10 This sentence is an unsolved puzzle. More resigned from the chancellorship on
    16 May 1532. This letter was written about thirteen months later. He calls that
    period *syndici tempus* (literally 'the syndic's time'). The most likely meaning,
    as given here, is 'the time prescribed by the syndic,' but it is by no means clear
    what that means. A syndic could be an advocate or representative in a court,
    a governmental official with functions defined by local law, or the delegate or
    representative of a university, municipality, or any other corporate body. The
    implication seems to be that following More's resignation as lord chancellor
    there was a prescribed period (evidently something like a year and a day)
    within which he could have been charged with abuse of office by someone
    known as the syndic. The problem, however, is that there was no such provi-
    sion in English law, nor was there anything relevant in Roman law. It seems,
    rather, that there was some other body of custom or legislation, either real or
    fictional, known to both More and Erasmus (but which no one has yet been able
    to identify), in which there was such a prescribed period. The one thing we can
    say with some confidence is that 'I have waited for the time prescribed by the
    syndic' was More's way of saying, 'I have waited a bit more than a year.'
11 Sir Thomas Audley
12 Thomas Howard, earl of Surrey and third duke of Norfolk, uncle of Henry
    VIII's fifth wife, Katherine Howard

had a lengthy letter ready. I refrain from answering not because I attach any importance to what he or any of his accomplices thinks or writes about me, but rather because I do not want to be burdened by having to reply to foreign opponents when I am more concerned about answering domestic enemies   70
near at hand.[13] And may you, my dear Erasmus, live long happily and live forever most happily.

From my country house at Chelsea

THE TABLET AFFIXED TO THE TOMB OF THOMAS MORE
Thomas More, born in the city of London, into a family not famous but hon-   75
ourable, having devoted himself to some extent to literary matters,[14] after he had spent some years as a young man practising law and had rendered judgments as a sheriff in his native city,[15] was summoned to court by the invincible King Henry VIII (the only king who merited the unheard-of honour of being rightly called Defender of the Faith, as he proved himself to be   80
both by the sword and by the pen),[16] was chosen to be a member of the privy council, was knighted, became first the undertreasurer, then the chancellor of the duchy of Lancaster, and then, by the wonderful favour of his prince, was named the chancellor of England. In the interim he was chosen speaker of the House of Commons. Moreover, he sometimes served as ambassador of   85
the king, at various times and places. But finally at Cambrai he was the com-
panion and colleague of the head of the delegation, Cuthbert Tunstall, then the bishop of London, soon to become the bishop of Durham, than whom it would be hard to find a man more learned, prudent, virtuous.[17] There, amid the greatest monarchs of the Christian world, with great joy he saw, and as   90

* * * * *

13 This is surely a reference to Simon Grynaeus, professor of Greek at Basel and a man of Zwinglian views, who in 1531 visited England with letters of introduc-
tion from Erasmus (Epp 2459–60). More, who received Grynaeus kindly and treated him generously, was nonetheless wary of being associated in any way with him or his religious views; see Epp 2659:94–8, 2878:17–18.
14 Neither here nor in the epitaph does More make any mention of his literary works, *Utopia* and the *Life of Richard III*.
15 More was undersheriff of London from 1510 to 1519.
16 In response to Henry VIII's publication of the *Assertio septem sacramentorum* (1521), a long treatise attacking Luther's *De captivitate Babylonica ecclesiae* (1520), Pope Leo X bestowed on him the title 'Defender of the Faith.'
17 See n3 above.

an ambassador helped reestablish, treaties that restored long-desired peace to the world.[18] May heaven strengthen this peace and render it eternal.[19]

While he was so engaged in this long succession of offices or honours that the best of princes found no fault with his services, nor was the nobility incited to envy, nor was he unpopular with the people (though, on the other 95 hand, thieves, murderers, and heretics found him fierce and unrelenting), then, after some time, his father John More, a knight who was chosen by his prince to join that body of judges called the King's Bench (a statesman, urbane, genial, irreproachable, gentle, merciful, just, and upright, and though advanced in years still physically energetic beyond his age), seeing that he 100 had lived long enough to see his son become the chancellor of England and that he had spent enough time here on earth, gladly departed to heaven.[20] But the son, after the death of his father, with whom he was long afterwards compared and usually called 'young More' (and also perceived himself in that way), missing now the father he had lost, seeing the four children he had 105 produced,[21] and the eleven grandchildren, began to think of himself as old. This reflection was followed by a sudden feeling of weakness in his chest, a sign, as it were, of advancing age. And so, having had his fill of these mortal affairs, by the extraordinary kindness and indulgence of his prince he laid aside the honours of high office and finally achieved (if God favours his un- 110 dertakings) what he had almost always desired from his earliest years, that he might have some of these last years free to gradually withdraw from the affairs of this life and meditate on the eternity of the life to come; he also saw to it that this tomb was constructed for him, which would remind him every day of his death, creeping unceasingly nearer, and he had the bones of his 115 first wife moved here. In order that he might not have done this in vain when he was still alive, and that he might not have any fear at the approach of death but rather gladly wish for it out of a desire for Christ, and in order that he might find that his death is not death at all but a gateway to a happier life,

* * * * *

18 Tunstall and More were the leading members of the delegation sent hastily to Cambrai in the summer of 1529 to make a much-belated attempt to defend English interests in the negotiations leading to the Peace of Cambrai. The peace brought a welcome pause in the long string of Hapsburg-Valois wars that would last until 1536. But it also brought a reconciliation between Emperor Charles v and Pope Clement vii that proved fatal to Henry viii's hope for a papally sanctioned divorce from the emperor's niece, Catherine of Aragon. See Ep 2207 n5.
19 This sentence is a line of verse.
20 For John (1) More, see Ep 2750:72–8 with n10.
21 See following note.

I ask you, good reader, to follow him with your pious prayers while he draws   120
the breath of life and after he has died.

THE EPITAPH AFFIXED IN THAT PLACE

Here lies Jane, dear little wife of Thomas More
    I intend this tomb for Alice and also for me.
One, the wife of my young, flourishing years,   125
    Gave me this, that a boy and three girls would call me father.
The other was as kind to her stepchildren (rare praise for a stepmother)
    As any stepmother has ever been to her own children,[22]
The one lived with me once, the other lives with me still.
    It is uncertain whether the one is, or the other was, more dear to me.   130
Oh how well the three of us could have lived together
    At the same time, if fate and religion had allowed!
But I pray that the tomb and heaven may unite us.
    Thus death will give what life could not.
End of the epitaph.   135

2832 / To Ambrosius Pelargus   [Freiburg, late June 1533]

This letter and the eight that follow were all first published as a group in
Pelargus' *Bellaria* (folios H8 verso–I verso). They clearly belong together and
are presumably in chronological order. Only the last one, Ep 2840, has a year-
date. All the letters relate to Pelargus' departure from Freiburg to settle at Trier.
Like Erasmus, the Dominican Ambrosius Pelargus had left Basel for Freiburg in
1529. Since then the two had maintained a somewhat quarrelsome friendship;
see Ep 2169 introduction. The letters consist primarily of obscure and feeble
jests about Erasmus' poorly identified parting gift to Pelargus.

ERASMUS OF ROTTERDAM TO AMBROSIUS PELARGUS, GREETINGS
I am sending along a dyad, a symbol of union. Of man and woman, of matter
and form something is born. A triad is sterile. Farewell, and accept my gift.
May you have good luck with your migration.
    Yours, Erasmus of Rotterdam   5

                * * * * *

22 More's first wife, Jane Colt (d 1511) was the mother of his four children:
   Margaret, Elizabeth, Cecily, and John (III). His second wife, Dame Alice (1471–
   after 1543), whose maiden name is not known, was a well-to-do widow with a
   daughter (Alice Middleton) when More married her in 1511, a month after the
   death of Jane.

2833 / From Ambrosius Pelargus   [Freiburg, late June 1533]

See Ep 2832 introduction.

AMBROSIUS PELARGUS TO ERASMUS OF ROTTERDAM, GREETINGS
You may rest assured that I am greatly pleased to accept the dyad you sent
as a symbol of repaired friendship,[1] and that it is dearer than any triad with
the exception of that holy, uncreated one and any other one that perchance
might exist. And yet that dyad of yours does not seem to me to be an ap-   5
propriate symbol of mutual love, since it expresses almost nothing of love
itself. But if perhaps you wanted it to be a symbol of mutual love because it
is a dyad, you would have sent a pair of chickens or quails. If on the other
hand you think it is such a symbol because it is gold, I will indeed grant you
that gold is a symbol of what is dear.[2] But little images carved in gold neither 10
adequately express the action of lovers nor do they remain in one place. If
they were joined with a kiss, as it were, there would be some hope that they
would eventually come together, and in that way something would be produced from the two. But what cannot be hoped for from the dyad, namely
that the happily restored harmony might come together even more success-   15
fully and might remain firm and long-lasting between us, that is something
I wish, hope for, and await from the sacred Triad, whose goodness will keep
the well-repaired harmony from easily springing apart. In the circumstances,
therefore, the triad is not sterile, for these are the words of Isaiah concerning it: 'Shall I who make others give birth not give birth myself? Shall I who   20
give generation to others be sterile myself?'[3] But I will stop joking with you.
Sincere best wishes from the bottom of my heart.

2834 / From Ambrosius Pelargus   [Freiburg, late June 1533]

See Ep 2832 introduction.

AMBROSIUS PELARGUS TO ERASMUS OF ROTTERDAM, GREETINGS
You are wondering, my very dear friend Erasmus, what is the reason that I
do not visit you as I usually do. The reason is that I am thinking about my
departure and am much occupied in getting my baggage together. For it is
not long before I will leave here to go to Trier for good. If there is anything   5

* * * * *

2833
1 An allusion to the quarrel of 1532; see Epp 2721–5.
2 Word play on the dual meaning of the word *charitas*, 'love' and 'expensiveness'
3 Isa 66:9 (Vulgate, slightly rephrased by Pelargus)

you would like to write to the bishop of Trier,[1] you can safely send it through me. Farewell.

2835 / To Ambrosius Pelargus   [Freiburg, late June 1533]

See Ep 2832 introduction.

ERASMUS OF ROTTERDAM TO HIS FRIEND AMBROSIUS PELARGUS, GREETINGS

If you have decided to leave Freiburg – which you think will be much to your advantage – act accordingly. I will not hold you back. Go where you like, as far as I am concerned. I do not know the bishop of Trier even by sight, and I do not have anything now to write that is worthy of such a great prince.[1] Farewell.

2836 / From Ambrosius Pelargus   [Freiburg, late June 1533]

See Ep 2832 introduction.

AMBROSIUS PELARGUS TO ERASMUS OF ROTTERDAM, GREETINGS

I am Pelargus,[1] an animal with two legs, to be sure, but without feathers.[2] I can't fly, but I can fly away. Farewell.

* * * * *

2834

1 Johann von Metzenhausen (1492–1540), since March 1531 archbishop-elector of Trier, who worked to improve the training and conduct of his clergy and to reinvigorate the University of Trier. Pelargus clearly wanted a letter of recommendation from Erasmus to the archbishop, something that Erasmus was reluctant to provide; see following letter.

2835

1 Cf Ep 2834 n1. After settling in Trier, Pelargus continued to urge Erasmus to write to the archbishop, who (he said) had already shown him favour and would doubtless do so even more in response to a letter from Erasmus, however brief; see Allen Ep 2966:37–40. Erasmus did finally write a letter to the archbishop in which he commended to him the 'erudition and honesty' of 'my friend Ambrosius Pelargus'; see Allen Ep 2968:11–16.

2836

1 'Pelargus' means 'stork' in Latinized Greek.
2 According to Plato (*Politicus* 266E) the human race falls into the class of featherless creatures. Diogenes Laertius (6.40) recounts that he plucked a fowl and brought it into the lecture room saying, 'Here is Plato's man.'

2837 / To Ambrosius Pelargus   [Freiburg, late June 1533]

See Ep 2832 introduction. This letter consists of a particularly lame example of the pun on *gallus* 'rooster,' 'cock' and *Gallus* 'Gaul,' 'Frenchman' that
Erasmus used frequently in the *Colloquies* and elsewhere (see, for example, Epp
1341A:355–7, 1353:280–2). In this case, however, the contrast between the two
senses of *gallus* is disrupted by the introduction of a second contrast, namely
that between two kinds of bird, 'stork' (*pelargus*) and 'rooster' (*gallus*).

ERASMUS OF ROTTERDAM TO HIS FRIEND PELARGUS, GREETINGS
I am afraid that if you fly away from here to the half-French,[1] you will come
back to us someday not as a Pelargus but as a complete Rooster.[2] But seriously, tell me whether and when you are leaving. Farewell.

2838 / From Ambrosius Pelargus   [Freiburg, late June 1533]

See Ep 2832 introduction.

AMBROSIUS PELARGUS TO HIS FRIEND ERASMUS, GREETINGS
From time to time I have the urge to take trips, and every day I am ready to
return, because I can't bear to be torn away from such a comfortable nest, to
which for more than four years now I have become so accustomed.[1] Farewell.

2839 / To Ambrosius Pelargus   [Freiburg, late June 1533]

See Ep 2832 introduction.

ERASMUS OF ROTTERDAM TO PELARGUS, GREETINGS
Since you have made up your mind to leave, my excellent friend Pelargus,
take care that you be in the best of health and that you remain true to yourself. Farewell. But come to see me before you go.

* * * * *

2837
1 The word is *semigallos*. Trier, where Pelargus was about settle, is very close to
   the border of France and the French-speaking provinces of the Netherlands.
2 *totus Gallus*

2838
1 Pelargus had moved to Freiburg in January 1529.

2840 / From Ambrosius Pelargus [Freiburg], 1 July 1533

See Ep 2832 introduction.

AMBROSIUS PELARGUS TO HIS FRIEND ERASMUS OF ROTTERDAM,
GREETINGS

What do you mean when you say to me 'vale bis'?[1] If you are wishing me to
be well twice over, then be well three or four times over, be well a thousand
times over. If you are commanding me to be well, give what you command, 5
and then at last I will be well, but the cook will not.[2] You order me to come
greet you. I had long planned to do this unbidden. But I am afraid that I will
be coming more to sadden than to greet you; and that, when I see that it will
be our last meeting it will not be without tears. Be well as long as you live.
Live well until you die. Then die at last when a mule gives birth, that is at the 10
Greek calends.[3]

1 July 1533

2841 / From Johannes de Molendino [Tournai], 9 July 1533

This letter was first published as Ep 110 in Enthoven. The autograph is in the
Rehdiger Collection of the University Library at Wrocław (MS Rehd 254 108).
The letter was presumably carried by Quirinus Hagius, along with Epp 2826
and 2842–4, on his return journey from England. For Johannes de Molendino,
canon of Tournai and close friend of Pierre Barbier, dean of Tournai, see Ep 371
introduction.

Cordial greetings. If you are well, all is well. I humbly beg the saints above
that this may be so for years and years to come, most learned master. For
why should I not be permitted to honour you with the same epithet that the
poet applied to Cicero, 'the most learned of the descendants of Romulus?'[1]

* * * * *

2840
1 This expression does not occur in any of the surviving letters. Pelargus writes
  it as two words, in which case it means 'be well twice.' Written as one word
  (*valebis*) however, it means 'you will be well.'
2 As Allen observes, the language is obscure, but Pelargus may mean that if he is
  in good health he will have a good appetite and the cook will suffer. There may
  have been a joke here that Erasmus was uniquely in a position to understand.
3 Ie never; mules are sterile, and the Greeks had no calends (*Adagia* I v 84).

2841
1 Catullus 49.1

But I would not hesitate to say (meaning no offence) that in eloquence you   5
surpass not only the Romans, but all other nations. How so? This is testified by your innumerable writings, suitable for both boys and old men, and
indeed for those of any age. I would not say this out of any desire to flatter,
but rather because it is permissible to declare the truth candidly as long as it
hurts no one. And as for myself, I most eagerly pass time in your works as in   10
a lovely garden, where there is no lack of the sweetest fruit. I am hardly ever
without one of your books, either just published or revised or translated,[2]
except those that were published this year – the reason being a sickness that
afflicted me so badly that I could not go to Antwerp, where I usually go every
year at the time of the fair to buy books,[3] and especially yours. But perhaps   15
I have said too much about these matters, if too much can ever be said
about choice merchandise.

To come finally to the point, Quirinus gave me your letter,[4] which I
read and reread most eagerly, as I do whatever you have written. But as for
your hardly being able to keep from laughing at me when I exhorted you to   20
return, I do not know how you took it, most kind Master Erasmus, but I want
you to rest assured that I wrote it with friendly and kind intentions. For I
was considering how fierce the Germans are, and I think they are thoroughly
outraged because you do not support their sects or agree with their opinions
and for that reason it is to be feared that they will devise some plot against   25
you. And indeed I feel very sorry for you when I read either your apologias or your letters. In them I clearly see the huge number of your adversaries, some of whom in France have been punished by exile.[5] These and many

* * * * *

2 According to a letter of Levinus Ammonius to Nicolaus Olahus dated 29 May
  1534, Molendino had an 'absolutely magnificent library' (*splendidissima biblio-
  theca*); see Ipolyi page 500.
3 Antwerp had no fair devoted specifically to books, but as a great commercial
  centre it had fairs.
4 Not extant. Perhaps an answer to the letter that Molendino had written to
  Erasmus in early March 1533 (see Ep 2763:4–7). Erasmus appears to have written to both Molendino and Pierre Barbier at the end of March, though in writing to Erasmus Schets at the same time he mentions only the letter to Barbier
  (Ep 2781 n8), which Schets forwarded to him via Molendino (see line 35 below).
5 This is clearly a reference to Noël Béda, syndic of the Paris faculty of theology
  and Erasmus' most dogged critic in France. In May 1533 King Francis I ordered
  the exile of Béda and three others who had preached against Gérard Roussel
  (Ep 2810 n52), the confessor and favourite preacher of Margaret of Angoulême,
  Francis' sister. Back in Paris after his brief exile to Montargis, Béda continued
  to alienate the king in ways that led to months of imprisonment (1534), public

other things impelled me to give that advice at the time. But I most certainly
implore you, be so kind as to take my ignorance in good part.   30

But, so far as Dean Barbier is concerned, I could not go to see him
because my illness kept me at home, especially at the time when Erasmus
Schets wrote that he would stand as surety and give a quittance to Barbier
himself in your name if he wanted to send any money to you. He also sent
me your letter to Barbier, which I immediately sent to Barbier together with   35
the letter of Erasmus Schets.[6] But Barbier promised to come visit me, which
he has not yet done. Still, I am confident I will soon meet him and I will look
after your interests more carefully than if they were my own. May God preserve you and long keep you safe for all the devotees of learning. Farewell,
most renowned Master Erasmus.   40

7 July 1533
Sincerely yours forever, Johannes Molendino
To the most renowned gentleman Desiderius Erasmus of Rotterdam.
At Freiburg

2842 / From Pierre Barbier   Tournai, 9 July 1533

This letter was first published as Ep 189 in Förstemann / Günther. The autograph was in the Burscher Collection of the University Library at Leipzig
(Ep 1254 introduction). For Pierre Barbier, dean of Tournai, whom Erasmus
suspected of cheating him of the income from his Courtrai pension, see Epp
2404, 2407. The best account of the complicated business of that pension and
Barbier's role in its payment is still CEBR I 94. This particular letter is Barbier's
response to one, not extant, that was written in March 1533 (see Ep 2781:17–19
with n8). In the absence of Erasmus' letter, some of the references in this letter
are obscure.

Cordial greetings, most learned Master Erasmus. The main reason I did
not send the money is that until now I did not have it. I excused myself on
the grounds that you had not sent the quittance (or, if you prefer, the 'letter
of receipt'), not that this was the principal and basic reason that I did not

* * * * *

degradation (31 January 1535), and subsequent exile to Mont-Saint-Michel. In
addition to CEBR I 117–18, see *Registre des procès-verbaux de la Faculté de théologie
de l'Université de Paris de janvier 1524 à novembre 1533* ed and ann James K. Farge
(Paris 1990) 293–4 (no 388A).
6 Cf n4 above, and see Ep 2842.

immediately pay out the sum that was sought, but that the lack of the quit- 5
tance could keep me from sending the money even if I had the resources to
do so. For who ever paid out money without getting a receipt?[1] Nor was that
the only thing necessary: he who pays something must acknowledge that he
owes it, and that he has the resources to do so. I have thus far had nothing
that compelled me to acknowledge that I owed it or had the means from 10
which to pay it.[2] Moreover, the necessary quittance or letter of receipt was
lacking. On this last point you have now made a satisfactory arrangement, so
that when I want to pay it, I have Laurinus or Schets or even Quirinus from
whom I can get such a quittance.[3] I do not mention the other two points as
if I do not intend to pay, when I get the opportunity or the resources, but so 15
that no one can accuse Barbier of not keeping his promises. But I hope that I
will soon receive from Spain the wherewithal to pay a good part of what you
want,[4] which, in fact, should have been paid a year and a half ago; the judgments[5] were seen by both Petrus Vulcanius and Quirinus himself, the one an
old disciple of yours, the other still your servant now.[6] 20

I do not know of anyone who knows me as well or better than you
who might think that Barbier is making fun of Erasmus.[7] For I know of no

* * * * *

2842
1 On this strange business of wanting a quittance in advance of payment, cf Ep
  2781:1–5.
2 The combination of Barbier's meagre income and his heavy expenses had over
  the years led to frequent delays in the payment of what he owed out of the
  Courtrai pension (see, for example, n14 below), but never to a denial of his obligation to pay. His statement here that nothing compelled him to acknowledge
  that he 'owed it' presumably refers to the demand for a specific payment.
3 For Erasmus Schets see Ep 2896, and for Quirinus Hagius see Ep 2804 n7.
  Marcus Laurinus (Ep 2810 n19), had frequently played a role in the complicated
  arrangements for the payment of Erasmus' Courtrai pension (Ep 1695 n6) and
  was evidently still doing so; cf Ep 2781 n3.
4 In 1519, thanks to the patronage of the imperial chancellor Jean Le Sauvage,
  Barbier was given a benefice in the Spanish Indies, but it does not seem to have
  yielded much income. Indeed, his friends treated his 'rich benefice' as a joke
  (see Ep 913:6n). If this reference to money from Spain is not just empty talk,
  then the reference may be to the long-delayed delivery of a sum that had accumulated over the years. Otherwise one has to speculate that during his residence in Spain in the service of Le Sauvage and then the future Pope Adrian vi
  (1517–22) Barbier had acquired some other, entirely unknown reason to expect
  income from that country.
5 The word is *iudicium*, which usually refers to the judgment of a court.
6 For Petrus Vulcanius, see Ep 2460 introduction.
7 Cf Ep 2763:4–6.

one who could truly say this. Nor am I bringing a legal action against you
(as God is my witness, and my conscience) in the way they imagine or you
yourself report.[8] Rather, I have never said a word about this matter to either 25
Latomus or Aleandro that might prompt them to persuade or dissuade anyone from gratifying you in this matter.[9] Quite the contrary: when Aleandro
himself was here a year and a half ago,[10] he often spoke of you in honorific
terms. And he also spoke so about Lefèvre, whose reputation has for some
years now been besmirched (falsely, I trust);[11] he is a man I have always re- 30
vered as a father.

What I have been able to manage with your servant Quirinus,[12] he can
report to you orally better than I can present in a letter. Believe me, there is
nothing I can do until that money from Spain is paid.[13] If you persist in dealing harshly with me, please reflect on these matters and choose what is just. 35

I returned from Italy full of affection for you,[14] and here too I will remain true to myself; no one has transformed me or driven me out of my
mind with the cups of Circe or anyone else.[15] And I do not know what Hezius
or others are plotting or fomenting against you.[16] One thing I do know (and
you know it too) is that whenever something in your books has offended me, 40
I did not scoff and revile but rather, as a son to his father, or a young man to
his elder (in so far as it was just), I brought it to your attention, pleaded, and
begged. If we were face to face, if you were here, I could say more that would
give ample testimony that I never had the intention or the inclination to treat
my elders in any but a proper way. But this is not the place to commend 45

* * * * *

8 We are unable to document a report.
9 Erasmus suspected that Jacobus Latomus and Girolamo Aleandro had plotted
   Barbier's withholding of his pension; see Ep 2799:27–30.
10 Aleandro was in Tournai on 3 December 1531; see *Lettres familières de Jérôme
   Aléandre, 1510–1540* ed Jules Paquier (Paris 1909) 142.
11 Jacques Lefèvre d'Etaples (Ep 315), the French humanist who, like Erasmus and
   for similar reasons, incurred the wrath of the Paris theologians (Ep 2362 n15)
12 See n3 above.
13 See n4 above.
14 Barbier was in Rome in 1524–5 in connection with his suit to win the deanship
   of Tournai. He used the income from the Courtrai pension to cover his legal
   expenses; see Epp 2404 n8, 2781:14–16.
15 Cf *Adagia* IV ix 42. In classical mythology the sorceress Circe used magic potions
   to turn men into pigs.
16 In 1530 Theodoricus Hezius (Ep 1339), inquisitor of the diocese of Liège, had
   ordered the removal of all of Erasmus' books from the library of the school of
   the Brethren of the Common Life in that city; see Ep 2566 n40.

myself; God is my witness either to my guilt in this matter, or rather to my innocence. I leave everything in his hands. Whether there are any errors in your books let others judge; I will not presume that I am able to pass judgment. But this one thing I can say, that I was often grieved that you had so many critics and detractors, against whom I sometimes stood up. Zúñiga, 50 who showed himself carried away against you not by reason but by a sort of madness, will be able to testify to that.[17]

Farewell, from Tournai, 9 July 1533

Always your obedient servant, Pierre Barbier

To the most learned and renowned gentleman Master Desiderius 55 Erasmus of Rotterdam, professor of sacred theology.[18] At Freiburg im Breisgau

2843 / From Jacob Hessele   Ghent, 12 July 1533

This letter was first published as Ep 111 in Enthoven. The autograph is in the Rehdiger Collection of the University Library at Wrocław (MS Rehd 90).

Jakob Hessele (1506–78) of Nieuwkerke-les Bailleul in Flanders (now Département du Nord in France) was lord of Ter Caemere in West Flanders and a knight of the Golden Fleece. In 1527 he matriculated at the University of Louvain and at some point seems to have studied law (see lines 18–19 below). From 1546 he was a member of the council of Flanders in Ghent, becoming proctor-general in 1554. In 1577 he was taken prisoner by Dutch rebels at Ghent and was hanged the following year. If this letter of self-introduction elicited a reply or led to any further contact with Erasmus, there is no trace of it in the surviving correspondence.

JACOB HESSELE SENDS CORDIAL GREETINGS TO MASTER ERASMUS OF ROTTERDAM

Although your most devoted friends have frequently urged me in their letters to write to you, I have thus far been reluctant to do so, most learned Erasmus, but my reticence was overcome by the arrival of your man Quirinus.[1] When 5 I told the count of Egmond (a young man who is greatly devoted to you)

* * * * *

17 Diego López Zúñiga (Ep 2873 n1) had died in 1531.
18 On the title of professor, see Ep 2855 introduction.

2843
1 Quirinus Hagius, on his way back to Freiburg from England via the Netherlands (Ep 2804 n7)

of his arrival, he begged insistently to see him and talk to him.[2] I promised
I would arrange it. I went to the house of Uutenhove together with Omaar
van Edingen, our clerk,[3] and after dinner we went to the court house.[4] I took
Quirinus with me. The count was quite pleased to see the servant of Erasmus,   10
and he asked what Erasmus was doing at Freiburg and whether he intended
to return to Flanders. He praised the invitation, indicating that money had
been sent for the journey. Quirinus pretended he knew nothing about it, and
asked whether a letter should be written to Erasmus about it. Promising he
would send a letter, the count detained Quirinus until the day agreed upon,   15
and since he was writing, availing himself of the opportunity I gave him and
wishing to make up for my idleness, he demanded that I in turn should write
you a letter. I pleaded that I knew more about Accorsio and Bartolo than
about Cicero.[5] 'Plead as you like in the council,' he said, 'but here deeds, not
words, are what is needed.' Quirinus also spurred me on, drawing attention   20
to the kindness with which you treat those who love you. And so it happens
that I am writing a letter to you, at the same time begging and pleading by
all that is holy that you take it in good part. For I do not lay claim to being
worthy of writing to you; but I know well enough that I can venerate and
cherish you for as long as I live.   25

Daniël Tayspil, bishop of Byblos,[6] who was greatly devoted to you,
died on 20 June, deeply mourned by his confrères.[7] He was highly learned
in both Greek and Latin, and was also a patron to many. I commend his soul
to Christ, who I pray will keep you and yours well until you have lived as
long as Nestor.[8]   30

Ghent, 12 July 1533
Your true and most devoted servant, Jacob Hessele
To Erasmus of Rotterdam, the prince of theologians, at Freiburg

* * * * *

2 Probably either Maximiliaan van Egmond (Ep 1018 introduction) or his cousin
  Joris van Egmond (Ep 1322 n3)
3 For Karel Uutenhove see Ep 2001 n7; for his kinsman, Omaar van Edingen,
  clerk of the council of Flanders, see Ep 2060.
4 Ghent was the seat of the council of Flanders, a court of law that met in an old
  castle called the Gravensteen.
5 Francesco Accorsio (1182–1260) and Bartolo da Sassoferrato (1313–56) were renowned medieval jurists who did not write elegant Ciceronian Latin.
6 Ep 1221 introduction
7 The brother mentioned in the introduction to Ep 1221, Pieter, was president of
  the council of Flanders in 1527 and of the privy council in 1531.
8 Ie to a great age; see *Adagia* I vi 66.

2844 / From Joost Sasbout   The Hague, 14 July 1533

> The autograph of this letter, first published as Ep 112 in Enthoven, is in the
> Rehdiger Collection of the University of Wrocław (MS Rehd 254 133). For Joost
> Sasbout, member of the council of Holland, see Ep 2645 introduction.

Cordial greetings. Your servant Quirinus Hagius delivered on 12 July just
passed your letter written to me on 24 April at Freiburg.[1] I am extraordinarily grateful to you for remembering me and also for not hesitating to tell
me so in a letter. I only wish that I had some opportunity that would allow
me (without any inconvenience to you) to reciprocate your kindness and to   5
demonstrate the favourable opinion I have of you.

Our Holland is besieged by many evils. First of all, Neptune has either
subjected all our territories to his dominion or has entered into a treaty with
them that will require, it seems, perpetual tribute.[2] And then Lübeck with its
allies has declared war on Holland alone and has deprived it this year of the   10
gains of seafaring,[3] whereas the other neighbouring provinces, also subject
to the emperor, are in the meantime sailing, as if they did not have the same
prince. Worst of all, moreover, is that the people are divided into sects, which
are somehow being held in check with fire and sword to prevent them from
burgeoning and exceeding all bounds. Everything is truly in flux and there   15
seems no way for prosperity and tranquillity to be restored. Nothing is left
except for our Lord to deign to look mercifully upon us.

I pray that you may have a peaceful old age, so as to furnish even more
abundant fruit for the cultured and the learned. Farewell to you and to all
who wish you well.   20

From The Hague, 14 July 1533

Yours truly, Joost Sasbout

To the most excellent professor of Holy Scripture Desiderius Erasmus
of Rotterdam, at Freiburg im Breisgau

* * * * *

2844
1 Not extant
2 In December 1532 there were terrible floods in Holland, Zeeland, and on
  the coast of Flanders; see Alexandre Henne *Histoire de la règne de Charles v en
  Belgique* 6 (Brussels and Leipzig 1859) 48.
3 See Ep 2798 n12.

2845 / To Johann von Vlatten   Freiburg, 25 July 1533

This letter, Erasmus' reply to Ep 2804, was first published in LB III/2 1758E–
1759E *Appendix epistolarum* no 373. Two contemporary manuscript copies, both
in the same hand, survive: one in the Bibliothèque Royale at Brussels (MS II 3750
folio 27) and one in the British Library (MS Add 38512 folio 82). Many of Allen's
readings were taken from the manuscripts.

Cordial greetings. It is very difficult, my most distinguished friend Vlatten,
in this most turbulent state of human affairs, to give fruitful advice, and for
me it is not without danger. For if something should be reformed at my instigation, the superstitious theologians who have now stirred up great com-
motions at Paris would immediately cry out that Erasmus has fathered a   5
new sect known as 'the moderates.' But if my advice has a fruitful outcome,
it is to be attributed more to the skill of an excellent prince than to my good
judgment. I do not disdain the generosity of the prince, however little I have
earned it. He will not long be burdened by my pension:[1] for this caterpillar is
thinking about becoming a butterfly.   10

Concerning the Lord's Prayer there is no controversy.[2] Even Luther has
written piously about it;[3] and there is my paraphrase of it dedicated to Justus
Decius.[4]

I have written carefully about the Apostles' Creed, and also about the
commandments of the Decalogue.[5] The book came out at the spring fair.[6] I   15
will send a copy by this messenger if I can get one, for there are none left here.
Hieronymus says that he sold all of them within three hours at Frankfurt.[7]

I have read the ordinance of the most illustrious duke.[8] I only hope that
the people will follow his pious admonitions, instead of listening to some

* * * * *

2845
1 For the annual pension of thirty gold florins awarded to Erasmus for his advice
and counsel on the new church order in Jülich-Cleves, see Ep 2804:1–13.
2 For the request to Erasmus for instruction on the Lord's Prayer, the Creed, and
the Decalogue, see Ep 2804:14–19.
3 Luther had written about the Lord's Prayer in several works, most recently in
his *Small Catechism* and *Large Catechism*, both published in 1529.
4 See Ep 2804 n3. Erasmus here refers to Decius as 'Iudocus.'
5 Both subjects in *Explanatio symboli*; see Ep 2804 nn4–5.
6 The book fair at Frankfurt
7 Hieronymus Froben, the publisher of the volume
8 See Ep 2804 introduction.

vagabonds who are promoting themselves, not Jesus Christ. They want to be   20
safe themselves and to prevail, to the misfortune of the people.

How many opinions there are about the sacrament of the Eucharist!
Someone at Frankfurt has begun spreading a new dogma that completely
undermines the sacrament. I hear he has been thrown into prison, but he deserves worse than that.[9] Some ill-omened men have almost turned the sacra-   25
ment, which is the unique delight of pious souls, into something disgusting
with their absurd opinions; but if they are in doubt, as is clearly the case, how
much better it would be to persist in what the Catholic church has handed
down to us and what the usage of so many centuries has approved. I am now
engaged in a book *On the Concord of the Church* against schisms and heresies,   30
which will come out at the next fair.[10] I have been ill this whole summer, and
my strength has not yet returned.[11] I pray that Christ may graciously deign
to favour the pious undertakings of the most excellent duke; would that I
were able to offer as much help as I wish I could. The first thing that should
be done is to silence or restrain seditious preachers. After that is done, if there   35
are things about which the people have reason to complain, it will be possible to correct them gradually, with no uproar.

The city of Augsburg is in extreme danger, so great is the tumult.
Anton Fugger, because he supported the Catholics with more bravery than
prudence, was declared guilty of inciting sedition and was completely dis-   40
graced in the eyes of the city council. He is preparing to emigrate to a town
of which he is the lord and will be followed by a good part of the people, for
the council is almost entirely Zwinglian. The people are, for the most part,
Catholic and could easily be set straight, except that the preachers daily blow
wartrumpets.[12] I very much fear that this famous city will be destroyed. You   45
will learn the story more fully from Karl Harst.[13]

Convey my respectful thanks to both princes, the elder and the
younger,[14] and give them my affectionate greetings. I have been called back
to Brabant, and I am thinking about leaving here, as long as I can do so without danger to my life.[15] From you, most honourable friend Vlatten, I will ask   50
nothing except that you remain true to yourself. Farewell.

* * * * *

9 See Ep 2806 n11.
10 See Ep 2859.
11 See Ep 2818 n1.
12 See Ep 2818:29–43 with n12.
13 Who had delivered Ep 2804
14 John III and William V
15 See Ep 2820 introduction.

Freiburg, the feast of St James, 1533

Erasmus of Rotterdam, in my own hand

To the most honourable gentleman Lord Johann von Vlatten, councillor
to the most renowned prince of Jülich   55

2846 / To Damião de Gois   Freiburg, 25 July 1533

> This letter, Erasmus' reply to Ep 2826, was first published in the epistolary
> appendix to De praeparatione ad mortem (Basel: Froben and Episcopius 1534)
> pages 144–52.

DESIDERIUS ERASMUS OF ROTTERDAM TO THE HIGHLY RENOWNED
GENTLEMAN DAMIÃO DE GOIS, CHIEF TREASURER TO THE MOST
INVINCIBLE KING OF PORTUGAL

The reason my servant brought you nothing more than my greetings,[1] my
distinguished friend Damião, is that I did not suspect that you would have   5
completed such a long trip so soon and had already returned to Brabant (for,
if I remember correctly, you said that you intended to make a long circuit
through Germany and France). When you left me, I was angry with myself
for a long time because I had received such a sincere friend so coolly.[2] First,
I was confused about your name, remembering as if in a dream that that   10
name had come up in letters I had received from certain people. Hardly a
day passes on which I do not receive letters, sometimes more than twenty in
a single day.[3] Added to this was an illness that for several months now has
been nagging me.[4] These are the reasons that, my memory finally having returned during the night, I could enjoy only a single conversation and a single   15
dinner with such a friendly guest. And in the book you left behind,[5] I did not
know there was anything of you until I actually examined at leisure who you
were. And in this respect I assigned part of the blame to your modesty. From
the conversation at dinner I knew that you were a good man, as the Romans
of old used to say: frank, a lover of what is right and pious.[6] In my letter to   20

* * * * *

2846
1 The servant was Quirinus Hagius; see Ep 2826:2–4.
2 See Ep 2826 n6.
3 For Erasmus' difficulties dealing with the volume of his correspondence, cf Epp
  2295:1–4 with n2, 2451:11–13, 2716:148–50, 2800:6–7, 2847:7–8.
4 See Ep 2818 n1.
5 See Ep 2826 n8.
6 Vir bonus in the sense of a man of good moral character is a favourite expression
  of Cicero. See for example Tusculanae disputationes 5.10.28, Academicae quaestiones 2.8.23, De officiis 3.15.64.

Amerbach there was no mention of you, for it had been written and sealed
before you came.[7] But he was more perceptive than I and immediately recognized your intellectual endowments: he thanked me for sending such a man
to him. He added that he saw in you a good and honourable man.[8] How easily kindred spirits are drawn to each other! Now and then people come to me   25
who seem to all appearances benevolent, but sometime I discover that their
minds are much different from their faces. That is the reason that sometimes
I am rather cold in accepting greetings from travellers.

But while I was ashamed of my conduct towards you and angry with
myself, I was comforted by the two letters in which you console me and   30
reconcile me to myself, even giving me thanks (if it please the gods!) for my
extraordinary kindness.[9] Not content with that, you left with Erasmus Schets
a token and memento of your kindness, which I have not yet had a chance to
see, but those who have seen it proclaim that it is worthy of a king.[10] But the
more abundantly you reveal your kindness, the more you make me ashamed   35
of my unkindness. What is left then except that we, by following the Greek
proverb,[11] repair with services the gap created by what has so far been left
undone? And that, my renowned young friend, will be taken care of in such
a way that you will understand that all else may be lacking in me but not zeal
and good will.   40

As for what you say about certain people bruiting it about at Louvain
that I supported those who approve of the royal divorce,[12] asking how you
should answer them,[13] how should you reply, my excellent friend Damião,
but with that text from the Psalms, 'their teeth are like weapons and arrows,

* * * * *

7 This does not respond to anything said in Ep 2826, but may respond to something said in the missing letter that preceded it (see n9 below). In Ep 2805:7–9
   Erasmus refers to an unnamed Portuguese whom Bonifacius had found troublesome but was nonetheless a man of good character and education. Either
   Erasmus is referring to some other letter that is no longer extant, or he is denying that the reference in question was to Gois. It is not clear how Gois could
   have known about Ep 2805.
8 There is no surviving record of these comments. On the other hand, AK IV contains thirteen letters from the friendly correspondence between Bonifacius and
   Gois that lasted from May 1533 until December 1536.
9 Ep 2826 and the missing letter that preceded it; see Ep 2826:2.
10 See Ep 2826:65–9 with n19.
11 'Better the second time' (Zenobius 315), cited in *Adagia* I iii 38
12 In this paragraph, *royal divorce* and several other terms are given in Greek (or
   Latinized Greek) in order to provide a defensive cover for the discussion of
   sensitive matters.
13 Ep 2826:21–31

and their tongue is a sharp sword'?[14] But I am quite sure you never heard 45
this from a man of consequence, but rather from some babbler, some reckless gossip, and everywhere now the world is full of this pestilent breed. No
mortal ever heard me utter a single syllable either approving or disapprov-
ing of this deed.[15] With everyone I clearly affirmed that it troubled me greatly
that a prince, otherwise most fortunate, had fallen into that labyrinth,[16] a 50
prince who I hoped would be of one mind with the emperor because I understood that this would contribute significantly to the public tranquillity
of the world. It would have been not so much temerity, I will say, as insan-
ity on my part to make a pronouncement, when I was neither required nor
asked to do so, concerning a matter about which so many learned bishops in 55
that country and even the apostolic legate Lorenzo Campeggi, a man highly
skilled in both civil and canon law, hesitated to give their opinion.[17] I rightly
love the monarch whose support and favour I have always enjoyed. But from
the time when this business was first dealt with, I have received no favours
from him except expressions of good will. Together with all good people, if 60
I am not mistaken, I loved and for many good reasons continue to love his
consort, and I think she is not disliked by the king himself. I would be either
completely stupid or remarkably ungrateful if I did not acknowledge that I
owe everything to my prince, the emperor, of whom I am a sworn councillor and to whom I am extraordinarily indebted for myself and my studies.[18] 65
Where could I have got the foolish idea of involving myself, on my own initiative, in such an odious business, which, even if I had been asked or summoned, I would have refused to do with all my might?[19]

No prince has ever asked my opinion about this matter, except that
two years ago two nobles from the court of the emperor came to me, and in 70
some conversation or other they urged me to reveal what I thought about

* * * * *

14 Ps 56:5 (Vulgate)
15 For the views on divorce in general that Erasmus expressed in his published
works, see Anton G. Weiler 'Desiderius Erasmus of Rotterdam on Marriage and
Divorce' *Nederlands archief voor kerkgeschiedenis / Dutch Review of Church History*
84 (2004) 149–97. Erasmus' views on the delicate subject of Henry VIII's divorce
from Queen Catherine (a matter in which he did not want to become involved)
were confined to letters to trusted friends that he either left unpublished or in
which he expressed himself with great caution. See Epp 1803:313–15, 2040:45–9,
2256:39–63, 2267:46–142, 2271:1–2, 2810:13–26, 3001.
16 Cf Ep 2271:2.
17 See Ep 2256 n22.
18 For Erasmus' appointment (1516) as councillor to the future Charles V, see Ep
370:18n. Charles V was also the nephew of Queen Catherine.
19 Literally 'with hands and feet,' ie with the greatest effort; see *Adagia* I iv 15.

this case.[20] I answered (and it was the truth) that I had never turned my attention to this question, about which I saw that men of the greatest authority
and learning had been in doubt for so many years. I said that it would be
easy indeed to declare what I would wish for, but that to declare what the   75
laws of God or of men allowed or forbade would require not only many
days of consideration but also a knowledge of the circumstances of the case.
They acknowledged that they had not undertaken anything at the command
of the emperor and departed. After that no mortal has ever disturbed me
about this matter. Therefore, though it was a thoroughly shameless lie that   80
was reported to you by some jokester, whoever he was, I think I know the
occasion that prompted him, according to the proverb 'Evil men lack nothing
but the occasion for perpetrating some audacious crime.'[21] Some years ago
I dedicated *Psalm* 22 to the man whom the king is said to recognize as his
father-in-law,[22] doing so in compliance with a request from him.[23] For he is a   85
man who is universally praised and stands almost alone among nobles for
his learning and for his distinctly philosophic mind. He accepted this service
from me with great gratitude and asked me to publish something on the
Apostle's Creed, as it is called. I did as he wished,[24] and all the more willingly
because it seemed to be something that would be useful to a wide audience.   90
In this work not a word was said about the matter of the divorce, of which,
I hear, that gentleman was neither the instigator nor the promoter, since he
is far more inclined to peace and quiet than to wealth or honour. While the
emperor and King Francis of France were at war with one another,[25] I dedicated writings to each of them,[26] and there was no one who claimed that I   95
supported the enemy of the emperor. How much less propriety did the man
possess who fashioned this calumny?

But enough of this nonsense! I come now to that place in your letter
where with devout sentiments you deplore the fate of the Lapplanders, who

* * * * *

20 The agents cannot be identified. As Allen observes, it is conceivable that (if
   one does not take 'two years' too literally) it was in the wake of this visit that
   Erasmus requested from Bonifacius Amerbach his view of the divorce; see Ep
   2356:39–56.
21 *Adagia* II i 68
22 Thomas Boleyn (Ep 2266), father of Anne Boleyn, Henry VIII's chosen replacement for Queen Catherine
23 See Ep 2232:7–12.
24 See Ep 2772.
25 In the series of wars that preceded the Peace of Cambrai in 1529
26 The Paraphrase on Matthew was dedicated to the emperor (Ep 1255), and that
   on Mark to King Francis (Ep 1400).

are being stripped of their external goods by Christian princes but not al-   100
lowed to grow rich with interior goods; they are burdened with a human
yoke and are not taught to submit their necks to the sweet yoke of Christ.²⁷
For those princes measure victories by booty and prefer to rule over beasts
rather than human beings. That is the reason why so few peoples who do
not know of Christ join the fellowship of the church: they see that they are   105
sought after not for the purpose of bringing them to Christianity but rather
for the sake of plunder and miserable servitude and whatever conspicuous
depravity there is in the lives of Christians. It is one thing to do business and
quite another to do the business of piety. And so when I read about the victories of that famous captain, so illustrious and blessed by fortune to be sure,   110
who plundered so many coastal cities, throwing into the ocean whatever the
ships could not carry, I was, to tell you the truth, full of grief.²⁸ But it would
be better for me not to make any pronouncements about military matters,
especially since I am unfamiliar with their character and circumstances. In
general I will say this: greed and the desire for power are not the least rea-   115
sons why Christianity is reduced to these straits. Wild animals are tamed and
even eat out of your hand if they are treated with gentleness and kindness;
those that are gentle by nature are made wild by cruelty and mistreatment.

In this matter I will gladly undertake what you want me to do.²⁹ But I
am afraid I will not be able to do so in time for this coming fair.³⁰ My servant   120
was late in coming back from England,³¹ and the only printer here has been

* * * * *

27 See Ep 2826:32–64.
28 There is no reference to this in Ep 2826, but it was perhaps in the letter that
   preceded it; cf n7 above. We have no idea who the 'famous captain' was.
29 Ie write something about the exploitation of the Lapps; see Ep 2826:56–64.
   Erasmus had German translations made of Gois' *Legatio* and *De Pilapiis* but
   encountered difficulties with the printer, Faber Emmeus; see Ep 2914:30–4.
   In his *Deploratio Lappianae gentis* (1540) Gois reports that following his initial
   correspondence with Erasmus concerning the Lapps, he returned to the subject the next time he visited Erasmus in Freiburg (1534). Erasmus agreed to
   publish an appropriate work, but died before he managed to do so, though
   he was not silent [*non obticuit*] on the subject in the *Ecclesiastes*. See Tom Earle
   'Damião de Góis, *Deploratio Lapiannae gentis*. Text and Translation' *Humanitas*
   (Universidade de Coimbra) 58 (2006) 347–67, here 360–1). The reference to the
   Lapps in *Ecclesiastes* I is actually very brief (see CWE 67 359–60, but it occurs in
   the context of a longer section (pages 357–63) chastising Christians for treating
   the 'barbarian races' as objects of exploitation rather than as brethren in need of
   the gospel, which some of the 'myriads' of Franciscans and Dominicans might
   well be sent to preach to them.
30 The autumn book fair at Frankfurt
31 Quirinus Hagius: see Ep 2804 n7.

ill like me throughout the whole summer.[32] But I will do my best. As for
your failure to induce my servant to make use of either your help or your
money,[33] I had not given him any instructions except that he should everywhere avoid any appearance of looking for handouts and should remember   125
that old proverb, 'not everything, not everywhere, nor from everyone.'[34] But
I had taken care that he would not lack anything. The town about which you
heard the story is called Schiltach by the Germans, about eight long German
miles from Freiburg.[35] I would not dare to affirm that everything which is
commonly gossiped about it is true. This much is certainly true: it was com-   130
pletely burned to the ground and a woman confessed and was executed.
The fire happened on 10 April, which was the Thursday before Easter, in this
year of Christ 1533. Some citizens of that town told the city council here that
it had definitely happened in the following way, as Henricus Glareanus told
me,[36] so far as I can remember. A demon signalled by whistling from some   135
part of the house. Suspecting it was a thief, the innkeeper went upstairs. He
didn't find anyone. The same signal was given again from a dining room on a
higher floor. The innkeeper went up there looking for the thief. When no one
appeared there either, the whistling was heard from the top of the chimney.
Immediately it came to the innkeeper that this was something diabolical. He   140
told his people to be alert. Two priests were summoned. An exorcism was
performed. He responded that he was a demon. When they asked what he
was doing there, he said that he wanted to burn down the town. When the
priests threatened him, he answered that he cared nothing for their threats
because one was an whoremonger and both were thieves. A little after that,   145
the demon lifted up into the air a worthless woman with whom he had con-
sorted for fourteen years and who had all that time confessed and received
the Eucharist. He placed her on top of the chimney. He handed her a pot
and told her to turn it upside down. She did, and within an hour the whole
town was burned down. I did not learn for certain whether the demon took   150
offence because the innkeeper's son had become his rival, and thus both destroyed the town and betrayed the woman, but it is not unlikely. This story
was so consistently reported in the neighbourhood that it seems impossible

* * * * *

32 On the illness of the printer Johann Faber Emmeus, cf Ep 2827 n5.
33 See Ep 2826:4–5.
34 Cited in Greek. 'The lesson of this adage is that in accepting gifts we should be
   selective as well as moderate' (*Adagia* II iv 16).
35 This is yet another matter not mentioned in Ep 2826 (cf nn7, 28 above); cf Ep
   2799:16–18 with n8. Schiltach is roughly 65 km from Freiburg; the German mile
   referred to here was approximately 7.5 km in length.
36 For Glareanus see n38 below.

to believe that it was made up. Other things of this sort are passed around
but I shouldn't detain your ears with such tales of the rabble.   155

Bonifacius Amerbach has your letter.[37] I promise you that he is a steadfast and constant friend, and also a faithful and careful agent, if there is ever
something you want him to do for you. As I said to you when you were here,
this one man and no other is for Germany a piece of true gold, a gem, or
whatever else may be more precious. But there is nothing, however rich and   160
precious, to which such a talent may be compared. I do not know, however, if
he should be counted as a German; certainly Glareanus would not allow it.[38]
Basel belongs to the Rauraci,[39] and the city has some noteworthy vestiges of
urbanity left over from the general council that is said to have lasted sixteen
years there.[40] I will see to it that Damião will be known and loved by even   165
more people – which will be a good and advantageous thing for me because
in doing so I will gain a great deal for my own reputation. I heartily congratulate you because the most invincible king of Portugal has, on his own initiative, bestowed such a splendid office upon you,[41] and I pray that it may prove
both fortunate and successful for you. If the occasion presents itself, I beg   170
you to make my excuses for my preface to the Chrysostom.[42] I was informed
meticulously and at length by a certain Portuguese, but erroneously.[43] This
incident turned out badly for me, but perhaps it can be remedied by the
friendly attention of someone else. If you write something to Hieronymus
Froben, it can safely come through me. I was getting things ready to return   175

*****

37 AK Ep 1750
38 Henricus Glareanus (Ep 440) was a Swiss patriot and champion of Swiss national consciousness.
39 In classical times the Rauraci, mentioned in Caesar's *Bellum Gallicum*, were
   Gauls living along the Rhine around Basel.
40 The Council of Basel, 1436–49
41 The king had called him home to Portugal to become treasurer of the Indiahouse
   at Lisbon, but in the end Gois opted to pursue humanist studies at Louvain (cf
   Ep 2826 introduction).
42 In 1527 Erasmus had dedicated his edition of *Chrysostomi lucubrationes* to
   John III of Portugal (Ep 1800), but, as he learned in 1530 from an unidentified
   Portuguese visitor, the references to monopolies and profiteering in the dedicatory letter had caused the king's advisers to withhold the gift copy from him,
   believing that he would take offence; see Ep 2370:7–11.
43 Not the Portuguese visitor mentioned in the preceding note, but rather the
   Portuguese doctor in Antwerp who sent Erasmus detailed information about
   King John III and the history of his family; see Ep 1783:20–4. In Ep 2370:9–10
   Erasmus reports that he was 'misinformed about the genealogy of the king.'

to Brabant, but unending overcast skies and many other problems, together with my health, which cannot cope with harsh weather, forced me to stay here until the west wind blows.[44] Farewell.

Given at Freiburg im Breisgau, 25 July 1533

2847 / To Fridericus Nausea   Freiburg, 25 July 1533

This letter was first published in the *Epistolae ad Nauseam* pages 116–17. For Nausea and the circumstances of this letter, see Ep 2823 introduction and n1.

ERASMUS OF ROTTERDAM SENDS GREETINGS TO THE
DISTINGUISHED GENTLEMAN MASTER FRIDERICUS NAUSEA
I have never felt any anger towards you, my excellent and very dear friend Nausea, but rather I have always maintained my kindly feelings towards you. In excusing your silence so meticulously, you were simply wasting your effort. I do not measure friendship by the courtesy of sending me letters.[1] Those who are not very friendly write and write again, to the point that I am almost buried in letters.[2] I merely suspected that you were not pleased by my advice, which did not come to mind without good reason. But if you do not approve of the advice, at least it gave proof that I have your interests at heart; otherwise I would not have given it. For why should I care about what everybody writes?[3]

I have learned from much evidence that the cardinal of Trent is just as you proclaim him to be.[4] I am glad you have enough recommendations to him not to need any from me. I congratulate you on being summoned to the court of such a splendid prince,[5] and I hope that his affairs will some day prosper, for one can scarcely imagine a spirit happier than his. A while ago

* * * * *

44 See Ep 2820 introduction.

2847
1 None of Nausea's letters to Erasmus have survived.
2 Cf Ep 2846 n3.
3 The language suggests that Erasmus had advised Nausea to be cautious about defending him against his detractors.
4 Bernhard von Cles, cardinal-bishop of Trent and chancellor to Ferdinand of Austria (Ep 2821 introduction)
5 Through the patronage of Cles, Nausea had been appointed preacher at the court of King Ferdinand in Vienna; cf Ep 2823 n1.

I dedicated the Irenaeus to the cardinal.[6] If something comes to fruition that would be suitable for him, I will not hesitate to do what you ask.[7] For me this summer has been barren; I have been continually ill.[8] Through the kindness   20 of the cardinal, your book, together with the letter,[9] has been delivered to me from Vienna.

Farewell, Nausea, very dear in the Lord. Freiburg, on the feast of St James in the year 1533

2848 / From Nicolaus Olahus   Brussels, 25 July [1533]

This letter was first published in Ipolyi page 144, where the year-date is errone-ously given as 1531. Quirinus Hagius (line 3) made no trip to England in 1531, but he did go there in 1533, which was also the year in which Lieven Algoet (line 6) and Pieter van Montfoort (lines 7–8) were sent on missions to Erasmus at Freiburg.

NICOLAUS OLAHUS, THE TREASURER OF SZÉKSFEHÉRVÁR,
TO ERASMUS OF ROTTERDAM
Your servant Quirinus returned here from England two days ago, having tak-en care of all your matters there, as he told me. I did not send you a longer let-ter through him, for I had informed you previously about everything through   5 Lieven,[1] both by letter and by oral message. I am looking forward to your re-turn – may it go happily and well. I am now attending to the business of Pieter van Montfoort as well as I can.[2] Concerning the commandership, it seems that it is more prudent and less troublesome for him to come to terms with the

* * * * *

6 See Ep 1738 introduction.
7 Ie insert a recommendation of Nausea into the introduction; see Ep 2906:27–9.
8 See Ep 2818 n1.
9 The letter that was delivered with Ep 2823. The book was probably a copy of Nausea's *Tres Evangelicae veritatis homiliarum centuriae* (Cologne: Peter Quentell 1532).

2848
1 Lieven Algoet, who in June 1533 had been sent to Erasmus to arrange for his return to Brabant; see Ep 2820 introduction.
2 In May 1533 Pieter van Montfoort (Ep 2812 introduction) was sent to Erasmus at Freiburg to deliver an honorarium granted him by the Estates of Holland. Following a stay of six weeks, Montfoort returned home with two laudatory letters in support of his candidacy for the provostship of Haarlem and the com-mandership of St John at Utrecht (Epp 2812–13).

other man, who in his absence set about getting himself elected as the succes-   10
sor of the present commander. Now the question is about the provostship of
Haarlem; concerning it and some other benefices, I do not know what wheels
the emperor has set in motion, as they say,[3] to have the vacancies filled by
certain designated persons. Unless something gets in the way, the hope is that
in this matter the chubby man most dear to both of us will have his wishes   15
fulfilled.[4] On the day after tomorrow the queen will set out to make a journey
of inspection through Flanders, where I think she will stay for two or three
months. If it should happen that you return there, send Lieven ahead of you.

 Farewell, from Brussels, 25 July 1531[5]

2849 / From Jakob Jespersen   Brussels, 25 July 1533

The autograph of this letter, which was first published as Ep 190 in Förstemann/
Günther, was in the Burscher Collection of the University Library at Leipzig
(Ep 1254 introduction). For Jakob Jespersen see Ep 2570 introduction.

Cordial greetings. I wrote to you very recently, my dearest Erasmus, through
Lieven,[1] a friend to both of us, and so I do not think it will be necessary for
me to deal with you now by means of long circumlocutions. Master Pieter
van Montfoort, the chubby one,[2] says that you are still somewhat angry with
me for showing a letter to Aleandro.[3] But already a year ago now my master   5
wrote you that I did not show your letter to Aleandro;[4] and I myself wrote

* * * * *

3 Cf *Adagia* IV iv 9.
4 On the description (in Greek) of Montfoort as 'chubby,' cf Ep 2849:3–4.
5 The year-date is incorrect; see introduction above.

2849
1 The letter is not extant, but given that it was carried by Lieven Algoet, it was
 presumably written late in June and delivered with Epp 2820, 2822, 2828.
2 Montfoort had recently visited Erasmus at Freiburg (Ep 2848 n2). On the description of him (in Greek) as 'chubby,' cf Ep 2848:15.
3 Erasmus' complaint was that Jespersen had offended Johannes Dantiscus by
 showing one of Erasmus' letters to him to Girolamo Aleandro; see Ep 2644:25–6
 with n17.
4 No extant letter of Olahus to Erasmus says this. In Ep 2693:146–7 (6 July 1532)
 Olahus reports that both he and Dantiscus were 'more than a little irritated' by
 Jespersen's having circulated Erasmus' letter. But he does not say that it had

the same.⁵ May I die the worst of deaths, even by lightning or the gibbet, if
I ever showed that letter to Aleandro or gave it to him to read, as I wrote to
you at length a while ago. Whoever said this to you or wrote to you about
it, my best friend Erasmus, is the worst sort of liar. But all good men here   10
and all your friends are eagerly awaiting your arrival in these parts. So do
not allow their expectations of your arrival to be disappointed any longer.
And farewell.

Brussels, on the very feast day of St James the Apostle, in the year 1533

Your Jakob Jespersen, Dane from Aarhus, at the residence of Nicolaus   15
Olahus

To the most distinguished gentleman Master Desiderius Erasmus of
Rotterdam, his dearest friend by far. At Freiburg

2850 / To Bonifacius Amerbach   [Freiburg], 26 July 1533

This letter (= AK Ep 1759) was first published in the *Epistolae familiares*. The
autograph is in the Öffentliche Bibliothek of the University of Basel (MS AN III
15 50).

Greetings. I am absolutely of two minds. The emperor, the queen, and the
whole court call me back to Brabant, and have also sent travel expenses.¹ If
you were to send a covered carriage from Neuenburg, I would immediately
fly away from here to see whether my body would tolerate the change of
weather. Do not be concerned about the price; I have more than enough mon-   5
ey. I would like to have it done as soon as possible, and not at your expense.
I am shamelessly imposing on your generosity.

But you should come first,² by horse, to announce that the carriage is
coming, so that we can have ready a flagon of Burgundian wine. But if that is
not convenient, let me know. Time is pressing. Today I sent off someone who   10

* * * * *

been shown to Aleandro. Any contact between Jespersen and Aleandro would
have had to take place no later than January 1532, when Aleandro left Brussels
to become papal legate in Venice.
5 The letter is not extant.

2850
1 See Ep 2820 introduction. For the problems connected with the travel money,
see Ep 2860:14–18.
2 Bonifacius came quickly, and wrote to his brother Basilius from Freiburg on
3 August (AK Ep 1767). But Erasmus was too ill to travel.

is going to Sadoleto. He seemed to be a good fellow, if only for the reason that
he refused to take any money.

Farewell, the day after the feast of St James 1533

Erasmus, from his dining room

To the most renowned Master Bonifacius Amerbach. At Basel   15

2851 / From Conradus Goclenius   Louvain, 26 July 1533

This letter was first published by Allen on the basis of the autograph in the
Öffentliche Bibliothek of the University of Basel (MS Goclenii epistolae folio 6).
For Goclenius, professor of Latin at the Collegium Trilingue in Louvain and one
of Erasmus' closest friends, see Epp 1209, 1994.

Cordial greetings. The queen of Hungary enjoyed herself during all of last
week by riding to the hunt in the Sonian Forest.[1] Meanwhile I spent my time
every day with Master Olahus. He told me nothing that brought more joy to
my ears than when he confirmed the hope that you would return and told me
that Lieven Algoet had been sent there for no other reason than to bring you   5
back.[2] I hope that it all turns out favourably and fortunately. And I have no
reason to suspect any difficulty, since almost all those who were consumed
with an incurable hatred of you and who had any responsibility for stirring
up the minds of the ignorant masses against a good cause have been brought
under control.   10

Titelmans is coldly received outside his own walls.[3] What you heard
about Hermannus Buschius is mere fiction.[4] For one thing, he has never come
here; for another, his name is so celebrated among the raging leaders of the
sects that he could not come to the land of the Belgians with impunity. And
so I have held back your letter to him until you arrive.[5] But there is someone   15
else, a certain Petrus Busconius, a lawyer who is madder than Folly herself,
whom you used to call a versifier when he showed you his poems, as he

* * * * *

2851
1 Known in French as the Forêt de Soigne, a wooded area at the southeastern
  edge of Brussels
2 See Ep 2820 introduction.
3 For the Franciscan of Louvain Frans Titelmans, see Ep 1823 introduction.
4 For Buschius see Ep 830.
5 The letter, evidently one of complaint about 'Buschius,' is not extant.

often did.[6] When he grew tired of his profession, he began to poetize and to write apologias; he began with Turnhout, in whose book he discovered some heresy or other.[7] Right after that, congratulating himself, he wrote some sort   20
of comment on one of your letters, saying that some things could have been expressed more briefly and more circumspectly. His comments were such that you yourself, I know for certain, could not have read them without amusement. And this, I think, is why that completely unsubstantiated rumour came to your ears. He was next heard from in some epigrams, but they   25
were a failure. He neither understands nor provides wit. I am sending you a poem in his own handwriting that he recently sent to the queen, one that you would not judge to be a lion by its claws but to be a Cumaean donkey by its ears.[8] Here he is laughed at just as the common crowd customarily laughs at freaks.   30

Damião de Gois has been recalled to Portugal by his king to preside over the treasury. He promised that he would soon send you some token of his good will towards you.[9]

As for investing your wealth, I said nothing except at your instigation and I did not think that a satisfactory way of protecting your interests would   35
be lacking.[10] But as soon as I learned from your letter how many people you

* * * * *

6 Pieter Gherinx, whose surname in Latin was Busconius (documented c 1521–34), attended lectures at the Collegium Trilingue in the 1520s and appears to have had contact with Erasmus before the latter left Louvain in 1521. He was a prolific but bad poet who also took an interest in theological questions and was given to finding errors in the works of others. In the lines that follow Goclenius indicates that in his letter (see preceding note) Erasmus had erroneously attributed to Buschius criticisms of him made by Busconius.

7 Jan Driedo of Turnhout (Ep 1127A n11) was professor of theology at Louvain, a noted biblical scholar, and a warm supporter of the Collegium Trilingue for whom Erasmus had considerable respect. The work in question was presumably *De ecclesiasticis scripturis et dogmatibus* (Louvain: R. Rescius and B. Gravius 1533), a careful and moderated defence of the use of the Vulgate in theology and liturgy.

8 For the lion and its claws, see *Adagia* I ix 34; for the Cumaean donkey and its ears see *Adagia* I iii 66.

9 For the recall to Portugal, see Ep 2826:9–15; for the token of good will, see Ep 2826:65–74.

10 Erasmus had deposited considerable sums of money with Goclenius with the intention that it be distributed for charitable purposes in Brabant following his death; see the introductions to Epp 2855, 2863. It appears that Erasmus had at some point asked Goclenius to suggest an investment that would after his death yield a steady income for the intended charitable purposes.

complained about for handling your affairs in bad faith,[11] I did not want to suggest anyone whom you should trust, since you had found men to be unreliable whom I would have thought to be thoroughly trustworthy. For the moment I will not present the plan I had decided to undertake, since I 40 would not attempt anything in your absence, and the situation cannot be explained to you in a few words. When you are present here it can be discussed if you wish.

I am sending you a letter from Hector van Hoxwier so that if you think the matter deserves some attention, you can either take care of it when the 45 occasion arises or else you can instruct me how to deal with it.[12] I have added the letters of Kan, Lips, Cammingha,[13] and the one that Sasbout wrote to you at the last fair;[14] but since it happened that I wrote to you from Brussels at that time, they remained with me for quite a while. I know that you are aware of what happened to Béda in Paris,[15] but I have nevertheless sent what 50 was written to me about it from there. I hope that I will soon see the day when Erasmus has overcome the envy of all these monsters and is celebrated in the mouths of everyone, although in fact (except for a few people whose minds are incapable of learning what is right) you have already achieved that as no other mortal has. 55

I hope that your prediction about the outcome of my suit at Antwerp will turn out to be wrong.[16] The matter has come to the turning point. And my enemies can no longer be evasive. They have changed their shapes so often that compared to them Proteus would no longer be Proteus.[17] They want to come to a settlement with me, and the sum they offer is not inconsiderable. 60

* * * * *

11 The letter is not extant, but letters to others are full of Erasmus' complaints about the alleged mishandling of his Courtrai pension by Pierre Barbier and others; see especially Epp 2404, 2527 n8, and Ep 2896:9–11.
12 The letter from Hoxwier (for whom see Ep 2586), as well as all the others mentioned in this paragraph, are lost.
13 See Epp 1832 (Nicolaas Kan), 2566 (Maarten Lips), 2073 (Haio Cammingha).
14 Since the 'last fair' at Frankfurt was in the spring, Ep 2844, written in mid-July, cannot be the letter referred to here.
15 See Ep 2841 n5.
16 For Goclenius' suit to acquire a canonry at Antwerp, see Ep 1994A n17. Erasmus' surviving letters to Goclenius reflect his anxiety on the subject but sustain an air of optimism and do not predict failure; see Epp 2587:40–6, 2644:6–8.
17 In Greek mythology Proteus was a sea god who could foretell the future but would constantly change his shape in order to avoid having to do so.

But my mind is fixed on pursuing it to the end that I be 'a king or an ass,' according to the proverb.[18]

Lambert de Briaerde is still acting as the emperor's ambassador to Ferdinand, negotiating about convening a council; he is not expected to be at Mechelen before winter or next spring. He wanted to have your interpreta- 65 tion of Psalm 50, according to what your host Maarten Davidts says.[19] I hear of a marvellous riddle here, which needs not an Oedipus but an Erasmus to interpret. When your servant Quirinus came back from Holland, he said that no honorarium had been sent to you from there. But when Pieter van Montfoort came back from Germany a few days ago, he said that he himself 70 had delivered it to you and did so at the same time that King Ferdinand sent a gift of two hundred golden coins. I myself would prefer to believe an eyewitness rather than hearsay, especially when the witness says he himself performed the deed.[20] As for other matters, I hope that we will soon discuss them in person. I pray that God will favour all your undertakings and that he 75 will restore you to us hale and hearty. In the meantime, farewell, O one and only ornament of the whole world!

Louvain, 26 July in the year of our Lord 1533
Yours, however little he may amount to, Conradus Goclenius.
To the prince of all learning, Master Erasmus of Rotterdam. At Freiburg 80

2852 / To Julius Pflug   Freiburg, 31 July 1533

For Julius Pflug see Ep 2806 introduction.

This is the preface to the *Liber de sarcienda ecclesiae concordia* (Basel: Froben 1533). A translation of the letter by Emily Kearns has already appeared in CWE 65 134. A number of readings from her text have been incorporated into the one below.

Erasmus wrote the work in response to friendly admonitions from both sides of the confessional divide. In the autumn of 1532, Philippus Melanchthon had urged Erasmus to use his influence to promote religious peace and dissuade

* * * * *

18 Ie 'either victor or vanquished' (*Adagia* III v 41); cf Ep 2876:3.
19 For Lambert de Briaerde, president of the grand council of Mechelen, and his desire that Erasmus should write a commentary on Psalm 50 (Vulgate numbering), see Ep 2571:5–14. For Maarten Davidts, canon of the collegiate church at Brussels, in whose home Erasmus had stayed in 1516, see Ep 1997A introduction.
20 Montfoort's version of events was the accurate one. For the honorarium from the Estates of Holland, see Epp 2818:15–17, 2819:1–19; for the gift from King Ferdinand (and Bernard von Cles), see Epp 2801, 2808:1–11.

DES· ERASMI

ROTERODAMI LIBER DE SARCIEN/
da ecclesiæ concordia deǵ sedandis opi/
nionum dissidijs, cum alijs non/
nullis lectu dignis.

Omnia recens nata, & nunc primum typis excusa.

FRO BEN·

BASILEAE EX OFFICINA FROBENIANA
ANNO M. D· XXXIII.

Cum gratia & priuilegio Cæsareo ad sex annos.

Title-page of Erasmus' *Liber de sarcienda ecclesiae concordia*
(Basel: Froben 1533)
Centre for Reformation and Renaissance Studies
Victoria College, University of Toronto

'those in power' from resorting to war (Ep 2732:14–16). Pflug had already addressed essentially the same appeal to Erasmus in the spring of 1531. Harbouring the false hope that Melanchthon might be moved to 'intervene and persuade his followers to agree to many things that in themselves are not acceptable but must be tolerated in the circumstances,' Pflug exhorted Erasmus to persuade the princes that 'controversy can be removed from religion,' and that 'certain prescriptions of the church can be changed,' so as to make them less severe (Ep 2492:38–52). When Pflug repeated his request a year later (Ep 2806:4–42), Erasmus responded with *De sarcienda ecclesiae concordia*. It was in print by the end of August or soon thereafter; see Epp 2865:20–2, 2868:36–7. Six reprints followed rapidly (three in Antwerp, one each in Cologne, Leipzig, and Paris) before Froben's publication of a lightly revised version early in 1534 (CWE 65 131). Within a year two German translations had been published, one at Strasbourg (M. Apiarius) and one at Erfurt (M. Maler).

The treatise was a manifesto of what was already called 'the middle way' (*via media*), and was in essence an elaboration of the principles embodied in the church order of Duke John III of Jülich-Cleves (1532–3), which had been prepared in consultation with Erasmus and given his seal of approval, though privately, lest the Paris theologians have a pretext for accusing him of being the founder of a new sect known as 'the moderates' (Epp 2728 n24, 2804 introduction, 2845:1–6). In *De concordia* Erasmus called for agreement based on the use of language vague enough to satisfy all parties except Anabaptists and other radicals; the subordination of interim agreements to the decision of a general council; the recognition that some questions can be left to individual judgment; the maintenance of the status quo in cases of doubt; and the practice of mutual accommodation. Examples of the kind of accommodation on controversial subjects that Erasmus favoured can be found in Ep 2853, which is essentially a summary of the final section of the treatise.

The work received mixed reviews in both religious camps. Catholic irenicists like Pflug were delighted, but some cardinals in Rome, favouring harsher measures, were not pleased (see Ep 2906:5–6). Some of Luther's followers joined Melanchthon in welcoming Erasmus' efforts to keep peace and avoid war (without necessarily endorsing his doctrinal views), but Luther himself, though willing to admit that Erasmus and his disciples were 'perhaps' well intentioned in their desire for peace, was firmly convinced that there was no middle way between scriptural truth and 'popish' error and that needy souls could not find peace in the 'doubtful and uncertain doctrines' espoused by Erasmus (*Purgatio adversus epistolam Lutheri* introductory note CWE 78 399). Indeed he was already planning to 'slay Erasmus with the pen.' For his attempt to do so, see Ep 2918 introduction.

DESIDERIUS ERASMUS OF ROTTERDAM SENDS GREETINGS
TO THE MOST RENOWNED GENTLEMAN JULIUS PFLUG

How much you are displeased by these continually worsening conflicts and
how ardently you sigh and yearn for that ecclesiastical concord that all devout men hope for is made sufficiently clear, my most distinguished friend 5
Julius, from your many letters to me, which always sing the same tune, demanding with great insistence that I step forward to calm the present storm.
Although you do this with no less shame than if you were to ask a pigmy to
take the place of Atlas in holding up the sky, you still will not allow me to
make any excuse.[1]   10

    You are very much mistaken, my friend Julius, because you do not
know me. But such a grave error as this reveals all the more clearly your
extraordinary loyalty to the house of God, where you hold high office,[2] and
hold it most deservedly because of your outstanding virtues. Your distinguished status is all the more fitting in that you do not exhibit any pride, 15
but you recognize in it the munificence of God. If Christendom had many
such men, either there would not have been such tumults or they would
long since have been laid to rest. But because I am caught between the knife
and the altar, as they say,[3] since you will not let me make any excuse for not
doing what you demand, and I on my part am unable to do it, I have found 20
a middle course, by which I hope to render you more indulgent in the future.
I have expounded Psalm 83, in which the Divine Spirit marvellously recom-
mends to us the concord of the church. One who exhorts assists to no small
degree in this kind of situation, where a good part of the deed consists of a
ready will, and to that the protection of divine beneficence will not be want- 25
ing. If Christ should deign to grant that a love of peace in the church, with
which you so obviously burn, would seize the hearts of everyone, then it
would not be long before neither of us would need to waste our time, you by
demanding and I by refusing, yet we would congratulate one another. But I
will not keep you any longer from the Psalm.   30

    Given at Freiburg, 31 July 1533

* * * * *

2852
1 See Ep 2806:17–37.
2 See Ep 2806 n1.
3 Literally 'between the shrine and the stone' (*Adagia* I i 15)

2853 / To ?   [Freiburg, August 1533]

First published in the *Vita Erasmi*, this fragment of a letter has no beginning,
no end, and no address. The addressee is clearly someone living in a city
where support for the Reformation was rife. As Allen notes, that could indicate
Christoph von Stadion, bishop of Augsburg, in which case this letter would be
that referred to in Ep 2856:15. But it could also indicate a number of other people
in other places. There are, however, some useful clues to the approximate date.
The letter is little more than a summary of the final pages of the *Liber de sarcienda eccclesiae concordia* (cf CWE 65 201–16), suggesting that it was written while
that project (Ep 2852) was still fresh in Erasmus' mind. Similarly, the reference
in lines 65–6 to the duke of Jülich-Cleves and his adoption of Erasmus' counsel
of moderation also points to a date in or near the summer of 1533 (cf Epp 2804,
2845). So the letter is as well placed here as it is possible for it to be.

FRAGMENT OF ANOTHER LETTER
... Both sides pull so hard on the rope that it breaks,[1] to the injury of both
sides, and from that comes this worldwide tumult. They take down all the
images, though they are both exceptionally beautiful and useful. Let superstitious worship be done away with; let images that are unseemly or extrava-   5
gant be removed, but let it be done gradually and without tumult. They want
to drive out priests. Let them make an effort to have priests who are learned
and devout, and let them not easily admit just anyone to this honour but only
those who are upright and deserving. There will be fewer of them. What then?
It is better to have three good priests than three hundred useless ones. They   10
do not like the church's liturgy. Much that is sung and enacted in churches is
not fitting. Let faults be corrected, and let it be done gradually; let the liturgy
remain. They execrate masses, out of hatred for corrupt priestlings who have
learned nothing else but to say mass and are otherwise more profane than
the laity.[2] Get rid of these hirelings, and in the manner of the ancients let only 15
one mass be celebrated in church, or two on feast days: a private mass for the
family and guests and another at about ten o'clock. Indulgences have now
been discredited; they were inflicted on the world for several centuries, with

* * * * *

2853
1 Cf *Adagia* I v 67.
2 The reference is to 'mass priests' (*Messpriester* in German), ie priests with no
  parish and no fixed income who earned money by saying mass for a fee. They
  were numerous, and would be hired to say masses for the repose of the soul of
  someone in one's family or confraternity, for example.

the help of monks and the connivance of theologians. If some think masses
and parentalia[3] do no good for the dead, let them spend on the poor who are   20
alive what the common crowd ordered to be done for the dead. And let no
trouble be made for those who are convinced that the dead reap benefit from
the works which, while they were alive, they arranged to have done for them
once they were dead. Let those who think that the saints have no influence
with Christ invoke with good faith the Father, the Son, and the Holy Spirit.   25
Let them honour the saints and venerate them by imitating them, and let
them not revile those who honour and invoke the saints with pious feelings.
Superstition should be condemned, but devotion, which I think is not displeasing to Christ even it if is in error, should be approved. The saints do not
understand your prayers? But Christ understands and on their behalf grants   30
what we ask. Those who are convinced that confession is not part of the sacrament and was not instituted by Christ should still preserve it as a salutary
practice introduced by the Fathers and approved by the consent of many
centuries, until the church decrees otherwise. And in confession let there be
sincerity; let there be no superstition. No one will be burdened by confession   35
if he chooses a suitable priest, if he confesses nothing except manifestly mortal
sins, and if he is careful not to commit any capital sin. As for purgatory, let
everyone abide in his own understanding; there is no reason that Christian
charity should be torn apart because of such things. Let the theologians of
the Sorbonne dispute free will; let lay people walk in simplicity and confi-   40
dence. Whether good works justify or not does not matter as long as there is
agreement that faith without works does not suffice for salvation. As for baptism, let us preserve what the church has preserved for so many centuries.
Nevertheless, every parent could be left free to decide whether he should
have his child baptized immediately or whether that should be delayed until   45
adolescence, as long as in the meantime the child is carefully instructed in
orthodox doctrine and pious behaviour.[4] The Anabaptists can by no means
be tolerated.[5] The Apostles command us to obey magistrates,[6] but they refuse
to obey Christian princes. Let the community of goods be a matter of charity;

* * * * *

3 Erasmus uses the word for the Roman nine-day festival in remembrance of the
  dead. The Christian version of it was a novena (nine-day observance) of mourning for the dead, with a daily mass.
4 This had been a bone of contention in *Declarationes ad censuras Lutetiae vulgatas*:
  see CWE 82 16–21.
5 Not because of their rejection of infant baptism, but (as the next two sentences
  show) because of their perceived threat to government and public peace
6 The classic texts on this point were Rom 13:1–6 and 1 Pet 2:13–14.

let property and the right to dispose of it remain in the hands of the owner. If   50
there is so much uncertainty nowadays about the Eucharist that they invent
new and absurd opinions every day,[7] how much more judicious it would be
to hold to the old opinion until either a general council or a divine revelation
makes known something more certain. The scruple concerning the adoration
of the Eucharist is easily resolved. No one adores it unless Christ is complete-   55
ly present. And no one is so insane as to adore the human nature of Christ
instead of the divine nature.[8] But the divine nature is always present. The
abuses of this sacrament could be corrected. In the past it was not displayed
but was shut up in a purified place. It was not carried about in celebrations or
across the fields by a priest riding a horse.[9] It was given to those who wanted   60
to receive it. Now in England, there is no house, no inn, I had almost said no
brothel, where mass is not celebrated. Courtesans traffic in these things.

Likewise in other matters, if both sides acted with moderation these
tumults might perhaps gradually be reduced to some state of tranquillity.
This advice was followed by the duke of Jülich, and he acknowledges that   65
it is going well.[10] I have no doubt that your city would do the same if the
preachers would allow it. I am afraid that they look after their own interests,
so as to remain safe ...

2854 / From Viglius Zuichemus   Padua, 2 August 1533

This letter, Viglius' answer to Ep 2810, was first published as Ep 45 in VZE.

I have always considered it to be an example of great kindness that you,
Master Erasmus, a patron to be honoured above all others, were not reluctant
to write to me. But now that you have deigned to write to me, time after time,
letters that are so long, so honorific, so generous, I owe you an enormous
debt of gratitude. For I am so incapable of doing my part in our correspon-   5
dence that it seems to me that a letter of mine has abundantly fulfilled its

* * * * *

7 Cf Epp 2806:107–15, 2845:22–9.
8 Cf *De sarcienda ecclesiae concordia* CWE 65 210.
9 This may be a reference to Corpus Christi processions, popular since the thir-
   teenth century, when the Eucharist was carried through a town and the surrounding area (cf *Ecclesiastes* I CWE 67 425 with n1203), and/or to the Rogation
   Days, an ancient ritual given official recognition in the reign of Pope Leo III
   (795–816), when priests led the faithful out into the countryside to celebrate
   mass, bless the newly planted crops, and pray for a good harvest.
10 See Epp 2728 n24, 2804 introduction, 2845:1–6.

duty if it has not offended you and has offered you some sort of opportunity
to continue this kindness to me in the future as well. But if heaven answers
my prayers – that is, keeps you alive and well for us for a long time and
provides me with somewhat more prosperous circumstances – I will in fact   10
manifest my gratitude to you in such a way that you will in no wise regret
your kindness to me.

I have told you before that, at the advice of friends, I want to change
the course of my studies and direct them one day at a more accessible target.[1] For almost all of us, it is a question of demonstrating that our discipline   15
is of some use in law courts or in government. For I have already more or
less mastered civil law, that is, in so far as our courts require it. And this
Italian training has helped me a good deal and will shelter me from the attacks of people who accuse those who have cultivated humanistic literature
of being unskilled in the law and fling at us the conventional insult of being   20
mere grammarians.

I have sent the Greek text of *The Institutes of Civil Law* to Hieronymus
Froben to be printed.[2] I wrote a slightly verbose preface to it, in order to encourage students to investigate the commentaries of the Greeks. And I hope
that if men of our profession begin to cultivate the Greek language they will   25
also devote more care to Latin. To lend authority to this work, and for some
other reasons, I dedicated it to the emperor, following the advice and urging
of the vicechancellor, Matthias Held.[3] And so that I could do this with the
kind indulgence of Bembo, I showed him the preface, in which I included
honourable mention of him for his generous assistance. In return, I got from   30
him a most correct and complete copy of the *Novellae*;[4] actually, an edition of
them was issued hastily at Nürnberg.[5] I hope that my edition of the *Institutes*,
long desired by scholars, will be issued with favourable prospects. For your
recommendation, I think, has already aroused a certain expectation about
me,[6] and although I may not immediately live up to it in this first production,   35
which belongs to another in any case,[7] I will nevertheless make every effort

* * * * *

2854
1 See Ep 2767:26–7.
2 See n4 below.
3 For Held and his efforts to promote the career of Viglius, see Ep 2767:27–31 with
  n13.
4 See Ep 2791:57–63 with n22.
5 See Ep 2791 n23.
6 Presumably a reference to Ep 2681, Erasmus' letter to Bembo recommending
  Viglius
7 Theophilus Antecessor; see n4 above.

to produce, at some time or other, some provision from my storehouse that is not altogether unworthy of your praise.

But for the moment I will tend to follow the advice of Aristotle, who urges a poor man to pursue riches rather than philosophy.[8] Still, when I have 40 acquired moderate resources, enough to provide free time for study and to cover expenses, I have decided to take up again all the studies I interrupted. But I will explain my plan to you more fully, and I know you will be both willing and able to further it in no small way. I have great and powerful patrons in Germany. They all urge me to go to Speyer, and they promise that 45 when I have lived there for a while, some honourable position will be provided for me.[9] And in that matter Master Matthias has promised that he will also help me with the emperor.[10] I will gladly follow such sponsors. And so I have decided go revisit my native land at the beginning of winter, there to provide myself with enough travelling money to maintain myself in Speyer 50 until some occasion of carrying out their promise presents itself to my patrons. And that delay will not be disadvantageous to me, since I will use it to gain some familiarity with the language and the procedures of the court, sitting first on the lawyers' lower benches and from there (God willing) moving up the prescribed steps to higher levels. 55

I have one scruple about it, and if I could remove that I would hope for a successful outcome. I have some prominent friends in Lower Germany to whom I was recommended a while ago by my uncle.[11] Since they judge everything by profit, they will not be pleased, I know, if I look for a more remunerative position in Germany, given that there is more money to be made in 60 our own courts. For that reason they will suspect that there is another reason why I am considering Germany. But, when I see them in person, I will try to dissipate whatever suspicion there is.

This is the gist of my plans. I was also greatly pleased by your most kind offer of help.[12] In the past I have owed you a great deal, since your 65 recommendations of me, both private and public, have gained me a highly

* * * * *

8 *Politics* 5 1308a1
9 Speyer was the seat of the *Reichskammergericht*, the imperial supreme court.
10 See n3 above.
11 Lower Germany = The Netherlands (see Ep 2812 n1). The uncle was Bernard Bucho van Aytta (Ep 1237 introduction), whom Charles v had appointed president of the council of Friesland (1515) and member of the council of Holland (1519), offices that he held until his death in 1528. He left his library and a considerable sum of money to Viglius, who always remembered him with gratitude.
12 See Ep 2810:127–9.

honourable status among the learned and the studious.[13] For surely what
I gain from you is by far the greatest fruit of my studies, and I hope it will
be everlasting, for, by heaven, I would rather die than lose your kindness
through some fault of my own. My efforts rely heavily on the favour of 70
Master Anton Fugger,[14] and I think that I am leaning on a solid wall. But
since your authority means a great deal to him and he attributes a great deal
to your judgment, your would be doing me no small favour if, when you
have an occasion to write to him, you would encourage his liking for me by
your recommendation.[15] I think he will be here very soon, for that is what 75
I heard from Mariangelo Accursio, who passed through here yesterday on
his way to his home city. I think he is known to you by reputation: for he
recently published Cassiodorus and some books of Ammianus Marcellinus,
and he spent all of this year with Master Anton.[16] It seemed to me that he
was well provided for as he returned from Germany, and that it was not for 80
nothing that he praised her. Also last year a certain mathematician named
Gaurico came back from Germany with his pockets full. But his ears were
not plugged when he sailed past the Sirens,[17] for he often spoke of Luther
and Melanchthon.[18] The reason Anton is getting ready to come here is to look
out for his health, following the advice of his doctors. 85

* * * * *

13 Besides the letter of recommendation to Bembo mentioned above (see n6),
   Erasmus had recommended Viglius to Andrea Alciati for study with him at
   Bourges (Ep 2329:41–2), and he wrote again in support of Alciati's attempt
   to get Viglius appointed as the successor of Udalricus Zasius at Freiburg (Ep
   2418).
14 On a visit to Augsburg in the autumn of 1531, following visits to Bonifacius
   Amerbach at Basel and Erasmus at Freiburg, Viglius had stayed with Fugger
   before setting off on his journey to Padua.
15 If Erasmus wrote such a letter of recommendation, it did not survive. His last
   extant letter to Anton Fugger is Ep 2525.
16 See Ep 2814 n15.
17 In Greek mythology the Sirens were dangerous creatures whose enchanting
   songs would cause sailors to venture too close to their rocky island and suffer
   shipwreck. To avoid this fate, Odysseus had his sailors plug their ears with
   beeswax, tie him to the mast, and not release him for any reason until he signalled that the ship was safely out of earshot of the Sirens' song. See Homer
   Odyssey 12.155–200.
18 Luca Gaurico of Gauro (1475–1558), is best known for his numerous works on
   astrology, the most famous of which was his *Tractatus astrologicus* (1552). His
   accurate predictions (1529 and 1532) that Cardinal Alessandro Farnese would
   be elected to the papacy earned him the favour of the pope, who took the name
   Paul III. Gaurico moved to Rome (1534), received a papal knighthood, and was

2854 FROM VIGLIUS ZUICHEMUS 1533

The son of the treasurer has gone away to Rome, has seen the city, and will soon return to his country.[19] I think that he will meet you and greet you in person and that he will explain his feelings and plans more fully to you.

As for me, I certainly thought that the matter of your pension could have been settled by the father.[20] Hence I encouraged the young man, who is favourably disposed on his own, to give effect to this praiseworthy desire. You will judge for yourself about Ricci's book.[21] Hieronymus requested it from Ephorinus,[22] if I am not mistaken, and Bebel carried it to Basel.[23] If I could have persuaded him to do the same for me, I would gladly have given him a second copy to be carried to you. Girolamo Vida is a canon regular. But as soon as he had gained some reputation for learning, he acquired patrons and left the monastery. At Bologna recently, as I wrote to you, he was appointed to a bishopric because of the dedication of his *Christiad* to the pope.[24] His poems, and those of a certain Fracastoro,[25] receive the highest acclaim in Italy. On one occasion I sent books by each of them to Glareanus.[26] Alogos is in Rome busily seeking to gain benefices,[27] but I am afraid he is hunting without the favour of Diana.[28] You know the saying 'the Roman curia does not want a sheep without wool.'[29] Someone wrote me from there that Logau

90

95

100

* * * * *

made bishop of Giffoni (c 1539) and then (1545) bishop of Civitate. The details of his trip to Germany and his acquaintance with Luther and Melanchthon are not known, but two letters to him from Melanchthon survive: MBW Epp 1223 (February 1532) and 3330 (1 October 1543).

19 Florens van Griboval; see Ep 2810 n18.
20 Ie the treasurer; see preceding note.
21 See Ep 2791 n19.
22 Anselmus Ephorinus (Ep 2539)
23 The Basel printer Johann Bebel visited Italy frequently in the years 1533–6.
24 See Ep 2791 n17.
25 Girolamo Fracastoro of Verona (1479–1553) was a renowned physician but also a poet of considerable fame in Italy. His most famous work was *Syphilis sive morbus gallicus* (Syphilis, or the French Disease). Published in 1530, it was the work that gave the name of a fictional Greek shepherd to the terrible disease; cf Ep 2209 n40.
26 Henricus Glareanus (Ep 440)
27 Alogos (here given in Greek characters) = Georg von Logau; see Ep 2810 n3. On his penury and search for benefices, cf Ep 2829:28–9.
28 Diana was the goddess of the hunt.
29 Ie a sheep that cannot be shorn (a petitioner with no money); see *Thesaurus proverbiorum medii aevi: Lexikon der Sprichwörter des romanisch-germanischen Mittelalters* 13 (Berlin / New York) 2001, item 4.2 under 'Wolle.'

is suffering from a grave illness, both in body and in purse, and yet here he
was all decked out in silk.   105

At Rome an admonition has been promulgated against the king of
England: if he does not take his wife back before 1 September he will be
excommunicated.[30] The inhabitants of Koroni are still being besieged by the
Turk. It is said that Andrea Doria has set sail to relieve them.[31] I am glad
that the counts of Rennenberg are with you.[32] I was often in the company of 110
Kaspar in France. I have never seen anyone more modest and sincere than
he. And although these virtues are sufficiently illustrious because of their
inherent splendour, he strove tirelessly to enhance them with indefatigable
literary studies. I owe you a great deal, my friend Erasmus, worthy of the
greatest respect as you are, but I want to owe you something in his name   115
also. And I will owe you that if you will not be unwilling to extend your
kindness to one who greatly desires it. I have given your letter to Vincenzo
Maggi.[33] He lives here and is professor of philosophy. He is especially learned
in Greek literature and is commended very highly by those who have heard
him. Baer's letter has not reached me.[34] Perhaps I will soon be writing you   120
something about G.A.,[35] for I have decided to go to Venice a few days from
now. Anselmus has just now added a letter by a certain monk to my letter
to you.[36] I do not know who he is and I wonder why he didn't write to you
directly. Farewell, Erasmus, luminary of all literature and the patron whom
I cherish most highly.   125

Padua, 2 August 1533

* * * * *

30 See Scarisbrick 317–18.
31 For Andrea Doria and the relief of the siege of Koroni, see Ep 2829:34–6 with
   nn8–9.
32 See Ep 2810 n54. Allen's note quotes from the manuscript of a letter of Viglius
   to Kaspar von Rennenberg (not in VZE) that was written on the same day as
   the present letter: 'For why are you still seeking Italy for the sake of literary
   pursuits when you had the good fortune of being admitted into the household
   of Erasmus, who can be the equivalent not only of Italy as it is today but as it
   was a thousand years ago? And what single individuals provide for you here
   you can see gathered all together in Erasmus as in a cornucopia. What part of
   literary studies is there that he does not know to perfection? What is there that
   can be learned anywhere from anyone that he cannot teach without the slightest difficulty?'
33 For Maggi see Ep 2154 n2. Erasmus' letter is not extant.
34 For Ludwig Baer, see Ep 2225.
35 Girolamo Aleandro, who was currently papal legate at Venice (Ep 2810 n22)
36 Anselmus Ephorinus; see n22 above. The unknown monk's letter is not extant.

2855 / From Bonifacius Amerbach   Basel, [c 6 August 1533]

This letter (= AK Ep 1768, dated 'after' 6 August) was first published by Allen. The manuscript, an autograph rough draft, is in the Öffentliche Bibliothek of the University of Basel (MS C VIa 73 295 verso). Also in the Öffentliche Bibliothek (MS C VIa 71 100) is the manuscript of the quittance (receipt) accompanying the letter (lines 9–21 below), signed by Bonifacius on 6 August. On the day before, 5 August 1533, Erasmus had executed a signed deed in his own hand attesting to the deposit with Bonifacius of sixteen hundred gold florins and indicating the purpose for which they were intended. The document (MS C VIa 71 98 in the Öffentliche Bibliothek) reads as follows:

I, Desiderius Erasmus of Rotterdam, professor of theology, of sound mind and of my own volition, have delivered to the most excellent gentleman Doctor Bonafacius Amerbach sixteen hundred gold florins in cash, with this provision and intention, that if I should have rendered the debt of human mortality and if I should not have specifically decided anything different concerning this money, he should distribute it as he sees fit for pious purposes: that is, to support promising young men, to arrange marriages for virgins whose virtue seemed to be endangered by poverty, or for any other persons whomsoever that are deserving of support. He himself [Amerbach], in return for his services (as is just), should take two hundred florins. To testify to my good faith in this matter, I have written this with my own hand and have sealed it with my own Terminus signet ring, at Freiburg im Breisgau, 5 August in the year 1533 after the redemption of the world.

Erasmus was able to refer to himself as 'professor of theology' because, on the same day that he made this deed, he matriculated at the University of Freiburg as 'theologiae professor.' See *Die Matrikel der Universität Freiburg i. Br.* 2 vols in 3 (Freiburg im Breisgau 1907–10; repr Nendeln, Liechtenstein 1976) I/1 285. As for the deposit and the money to be paid to Amerbach, both were substantial sums: sixteen hundred Rhenish florins were equivalent to £393 6s 8d groot Flemish or forty-five years' wages of an Antwerp master mason/carpenter; Amerbach's honorarium of two hundred florins (£49 3s 4d groot Flemish) to more than five years' wages (CWE 12 650 Table 3, 691 Table 13). For the 'Terminus signet ring,' with which Erasmus customarily signed important documents, see Ep 2018 n2.

On 8 April 1534 Erasmus drew up a new deed in his own hand regarding the same sixteen hundred gold florins, apparently after having received a new quittance for them from Bonifacius (see Ep 2901:1). The document (MS C VIa 71 97 in the Öffentliche Bibliothek) reads as follows:

I, Desiderius Erasmus of Rotterdam, professor of theology, have deposited sixteen hundred gold florins in cash with the extraordinary gentleman Master Bonifacius Amerbach, citizen of Basel, under the conditions that he describes in his quittance. If I have not decided anything new concerning this sum before my last day, I want a third part of it to be possessed free and clear by the said Bonifacius, and the rest to be dispensed for pious purposes according to the discretion of the said trustee and the executors. To testify to my complete good faith in this matter I have written this document with my own hand and sealed it with my own Terminus signet ring. And I want this document to be as valid as if it had been inserted into my will. From my house at Freiburg im Breisgau, 8 April in the year of our Lord 1534.

Cordial greetings, most illustrious Erasmus. I send the quittance according to the instructions I had received about how to draw it up. If you approve it and are satisfied with it, I will be quite pleased. If not, please be kind enough to formulate for me how it should be written. I will take great care to send you as soon as possible a copy, in my own handwriting, of whatever formulation 5 you come up with. Take care of yourself, I beg you, and enjoy good health for as long as possible, incomparable master and patron.
    At Basel

I, Bonifacius Amerbach, doctor of law, citizen of Basel, profess that Master Erasmus of Rotterdam, my patron, most estimable in all manner of ways, 10 has placed at my disposal sixteen hundred gold florins, which I will faithfully return at his request (or if he himself does not request them, then to those to whom he commanded them to be returned in his will or according to his last wishes). If it should happen that he makes no decision concerning this money, I promise that I will most carefully disburse it, as should be 15 done among good men, to be used as he himself prescribed to me in his own handwriting. To testify to my complete good faith in all these things I have written this quittance in my own hand and have impressed it with my own family seal or sign.
    Executed at Freiburg im Breisgau, 6 August in the year 1533 after the 20 birth of Christ

2856 / From Christoph von Stadion   Dillingen, 8 August 1533

This letter was first published as Ep 191 in Enthoven. The autograph was in the Burscher Collection of the University Library at Leipzig (Ep 1254 introduction). For Christoph von Stadion, bishop of Augsburg, see Ep 2029 introduction.

I send you cordial greetings. Most learned Erasmus, I am sending you two horses, an ambler and a trotter. Choose whichever of the two is suitable for you. Among my own horses and those of my family none was found that could adequately serve your purpose. I wrested these from certain great nobles by means of much begging and the payment of a high price; in such 5 a short time I could not find any better ones, as Lieven himself will attest.[1] Therefore, if the one you choose turns out to have the virtues of a good confessor,[2] do not attribute it to me but rather to those who sold them to me. Do not take it ill that the horses come to you without the proper harnesses; they could not be fitted out because the time was short. Nevertheless, so 10 that you will not think they were omitted for any other reason, I am sending you through Lieven forty crowns,[3] with which you can get them fitted out at your discretion.

It seems that nothing is preventing religious conflict from being settled by the means you mention in your letter,[4] except (in my judgment) that those 15 who are dealing with it are more concerned with their own interests than with God's. Would that God might grant us the grace finally to recognize our own blindness!

As for the Bédaican tragedy, I wonder why the Sorbonne theologians have fallen into such blindness that they do not allow any of the old obser- 20 vances to be discontinued. Now at last they will realize that Christ still lives, when being sent into exile renders them infamous.[5] Everyone who has read your explanation of the Creed commends it.[6] Hence there is no need for you to expect any verdict from me. That which judges itself has no need to be judged by another. 25

* * * * *

2856
1 Lieven Algoet had come from Brussels in July to arrange for Erasmus' return to the Netherlands (Ep 2820 introduction) and had evidently been sent by Erasmus on an errand to Augsburg.
2 This is clearly a jest, meaning perhaps that the horse might prove to be patient and deliberate rather than quick and lively.
3 Almost certainly the French écu au soleil (also called 'crown' or 'sun crown'), which was officially valued at 76d groot Flemish in 1533. Forty sun crowns were equivalent to £12 13s 4d or eighteen months' wages of an Antwerp master mason/carpenter (CWE 12 650 Table 3, 691 Table 13).
4 Possibly Ep 2853
5 See Ep 2841 n5.
6 The *Explanatio symboli* (Ep 2772). Stadion had acknowledged receipt of the work in Ep 2787:1–3, deferring until later any expression of opinion.

A letter has arrived saying that a peace between King Ferdinand and the Turk has been put into effect; but it says nothing about its conditions.[7]

The citizens of Augsburg, so far as religion is concerned, still waver, although they seem to be more inclined to the Zwinglian rather than the Lutheran sect.[8] May God bring everything to a good end, and may he long keep you safe for us. 30

Given at Dillingen, 8 August in the year, etc 33

Your bishop of Augsburg, written by my own hand

To his friend, the most learned theologian Erasmus of Rotterdam. At Freiburg 35

2857 / From Udalricus Zasius [Freiburg], 11 August 1533

This letter was first published as Ep 192 in Enthoven. The autograph was in the Burscher Collection of the University Library at Leipzig (Ep 1254 introduction). For Udalricus Zasius, renowned jurist and professor of law at Freiburg, see Ep 303.

With his commendations. I was bathing, O great Erasmus, divine hero, when your letter was presented to me,[1] together with the pears, which were most welcome. Concerning Alexander of Hales, I divined beforehand that he would be of little use to you, since he is a man who belongs to the old barbarism. But I sent it for this reason, that you could see that, since I can- 5 not accommodate you by sending better works, I can at least try to do so with discarded and insipid authors.[2] But I am glad to hear that you are occupied in working on the Psalms. For next to your most felicitous translation of the gospel (in which I take great pleasure, wholeheartedly and every day) there is nothing you could work on that would be more useful to the 10 Christian world than to unravel the obscurities of the Psalms. For apart from

* * * * *

7 See Epp 2699 n5, 2780 n9.
8 See Ep 2814 n8.

2857
1 Not extant
2 It is not known in what connection Zasius had sent a volume by the thirteenth-century Franciscan and Paris theologian Alexander of Hales (d 1245), whose *Summa theologica* had first been printed at Venice in 1475 and then at Nürnberg in 1481 and 1502. He was not known as an authority on the Psalms.

the Psalter, there is no other prayer (to use your own expression)[3] with which I occupy myself, though there are many places that I do not understand. Therefore, if you intend also to explain the other psalms (as you have done for the first, second, and twenty-eighth),[4] may the Lord support you with strength and genius, so that you can proceed not only eloquently but fruitfully.[5]

But alas you complain of the weather, which is always adverse, and of the year, which is always ill-omened. As for the troubles that afflict your studies, whether this is brought about by the malice of the heavens or of men, what can it be but the threat of shipwreck for all literature? An *actio popularis* (which occurs frequently with us jurists) would have to be brought against the weather, the earth, men, and whatever has breath, in order to ensure your tranquillity.[6] But do not resign yourself, godlike hero, to allowing exterior tumult to disturb the tranquillity of your mind in any way. We are all sailing in the same ship, on this vast, wide sea that stretches its arms far apart, as the Psalm says.[7] It is no wonder that all of us are sometimes shaken by the same storms. But this is more than enough! Please lay down for us, not for the theologians you are familiar with but for us semipagans, precepts about what we should do in times like these.

From the bottom of my heart I commiserate with you about your servants,[8] but go boldly against such fates as this.[9] Farewell, and love me, as you do, being confident that for your sake and for your wellbeing I would expend, if it were necessary, all that I have. The learned gentleman Wilhelm

* * * * *

3 Zasius follows Erasmus in using the word *precatio*, which is rarer than *preces*, for 'prayer.'
4 Erasmus had in fact already published (in the period 1515–32) commentaries on Psalms 1, 2, 3, 4, 14, 22, 33, 38 (not 28), 85, and he had just published his commentary on Psalm 83 under the title *De sarcienda ecclesiae concordia* (Ep 2852).
5 Zasius plays on the words *facunde* 'eloquently' and *fecunde* 'fruitfully.'
6 In Roman law an *actio popularis* was a legal proceeding initiated by a member of the public in the interest of the citizenry. The term is still used in many places to designate public-interest litigation initiated by third parties in the general interest of society.
7 Ps 103:25 (Vulgate)
8 Erasmus had had troubles with his disreputable servant Jacobus (Ep 2652 n4), but he was now worried that he might lose the services of Gilbert Cousin (Epp 2872:3–4, 2889 introduction), and he may already have become suspicious that Quirinus Hagius had embezzled money from him (Ep 2896:21–2).
9 Virgil *Aeneid* 6.95 (the words of the Sibyl urging Aeneas to pursue his destiny)

Gamshorn,[10] a doctor of law who was here recently, wrote me that the king of 35
France has yielded to destiny – at least that is what he heard.[11] And so it was
not for no reason that in the space of one year two comets appeared.[12]

Once more, farewell. 11 August, in the year, etc 1533

Take in good part a letter written in the bath.

Yours from the bottom of my heart, Udalricus Zasius, doctor of laws 40

To the great Desiderius Erasmus, a godlike hero, prince of all refined
writings, human and divine, a most authoritative preceptor

2858 / To Bonifacius Amerbach [Freiburg], 17 August 1533

This letter (= AK Ep 1772) was first published in the *Epistolae familiares*. The
autograph is in the Öffentliche Bibliothek of the University of Basel (MS AN III
15 51).

Greetings. I cannot promise anything certain concerning this miserable state
of my health.[1] The north wind, which arose during the night, has made me
suddenly take a very bad turn for the worse. If you can, hire a boat with
a good roof covering for fifteen florins;[2] but if I were forced to change my
mind before the twelfth day of September, the sailors would receive gratis a 5
third part of the fare, and they could rent their ship to whomever they might
wish. Farewell.

Your unfortunate Erasmus

On the Sunday after the Assumption of the Virgin 1533

To the outstanding gentleman Master Bonifacius Amerbach, doctor of 10
laws. At Basel

* * * * *

10 Unidentified
11 The rumour was false; Francis I died in 1547.
12 There had been particularly bright comets in 1531 and 1532, and another one
   appeared in June 1533; see Wolfgang Kokott 'The Comet of 1533' *Journal of the
   History of Astronomy* 12 (1981) 95–112.

2858
1 See Ep 2818 n1.
2 For the trip to Cologne, on his way back to Brabant; cf Ep 2859:16–20. Almost
   certainly Rhenish florins; the sum was equivalent to £3 13s 9d groot Flemish,
   about half a year's wage of an Antwerp master mason/carpenter (CWE 12 650
   Table 3, 691 Table 13).

2859 / From Bonifacius Amerbach   Basel, [August 1533]

This letter (= AK Ep 1769), Bonifacius' answer to Ep 2858, was first published
by Allen. The manuscript, an autograph rough draft with no date, is in the
Öffentliche Bibliothek of the University of Basel. Alfred Hartmann's argument
(see his introductory note in AK) that this letter predates Ep 2858 is not strong
enough to overturn the sequence assigned by Allen.

Cordial greetings. Although your kindnesses to me are without number, my
most renowned friend Erasmus, and you never cease to heap up more and
more of them, this is certainly an instance of your characteristic goodness,
from which all manner of kindnesses flow as from an inexhaustible fountain. And so, in return for the generosity that you very recently manifested   5
towards me,[1] I would be obliged to thank you and make requital, if I were
equal to doing so, either in words or in deeds. But since neither of these is
possible, given the limits of my mind and of my resources, and since you
are beyond the heights to which my efforts can aspire, I will do what is left
for me to do – that is, I will be grateful, and will console myself with those   10
sayings of the ancients who teach that he who has conducted himself honourably is seen to have given thanks,[2] and that even in great matters a good
intention is sufficient.[3] I will always make every effort to keep from seeming
to have been at all ungrateful. And on your part, I both beg and beseech you
not to refuse my humble efforts but to make use of them however you wish.   15
    Our sailors, in leasing their services, ordinarily furnish a boat that is
both covered as well as fitted out according to the wishes of the passenger. As
fare to Cologne they ask as much as twenty gold coins;[4] they add, however,
that if they understand it to be a serious matter, they will lower the price for
a good customer.   20

* * * * *

2859
1 The deposit with him of sixteen hundred florins, a substantial portion of which
  was to accrue to him as a fee; see Ep 2855 introduction.
2 The Latin of this passage is obscure. We follow Gerlo's suggestion that *recte
  habere* can be understood to mean 'conduct oneself honourably,' the point being
  that Bonifacius would so conduct himself as the trustee of the monies deposited
  with him and that this would constitute a demonstration of his thanks. We cannot identify the 'sayings of the ancients.'
3 *Adagia* II viii 55
4 Probably Rhenish florins; if so, the fare to Cologne was £4 18s 4d groot Flemish,
  just under a year's wage of an Antwerp master mason/carpenter (CWE 12 650
  Table 3, 691 Table 13). Cf Ep 2858:3–7 with n2.

I am sending along Sadoleto's book *On the Proper Education of Boys*.[5] I hope you will like it, if for no other reason than that it is new.

Take care of your health, my dear Erasmus.[6] And you should know that no news can be more agreeable or pleasant to me than that your health has improved.   25

Farewell. At Basel

2860 / To Nicolaus Olahus   Freiburg, 23 August 1533

This letter was first published in Ipolyi page 399. The manuscript is page 354 of the Olahus codex in the Hungarian National Archives at Budapest (Ep 2339 introduction). For Nicolaus Olahus, secretary to Queen Mary, regent of the Netherlands, see Ep 2813.

ERASMUS OF ROTTERDAM TO NICOLAUS OLAHUS,
SECRETARY OF HER MOST SERENE MAJESTY

I am grateful to everyone for having taken care of my business so lovingly, but especially to you, my dear Olahus. I have prepared clothing and horses, I have chartered a ship and hired a crew and I await only the opportunity   5 to leave here safely.[1] But so far the weather has been such that I can barely keep alive. February treated me very roughly and then turned me over to March, the deadly enemy of all old people. And the whole summer was no different from March, which was followed by a very stormy August. What the coming weather will be I do not know.[2] And so I have thought it better   10 to return somewhat later than I very much wanted to, instead of rushing this little body, battered and weakened as it is, into clearly lifethreatening danger.

I sent Lieven ahead to prepare for me there, with the help of certain friends, a nest where I may immediately settle in.[3] I wonder whose idea it was that Lieven should get the money at Dole. It could have been paid in   15 cash to the Fuggers or Schets, and I could have received it here by letter of

* * * * *

5 *De pueris recte instituendis* (Venice: Io. Antonius et Fratres de Sabio 1533)
6 See Ep 2818 n1.

2860
1 See Epp 2858–9.
2 See Ep 2818 n1.
3 Lieven Algoet had been sent to Freiburg, with travel money, to bring Erasmus back to Brabant (Ep 2820 introduction).

credit.[4] As it is, of the three hundred florins I will lose more than sixty, for the crown is valued there at thirty-seven, but in Dole at forty-seven.[5] But even though he was afraid of the dangers of the trip, Lieven travelled six days from Dole, on a road that was not at all safe.   20

Lady Margaret summoned me under more generous terms than the ones now offered.[6] But if there were nothing else there more inviting than the generosity of the court, I would not lift a foot. Love of my native land draws me. But if something happens that makes me spend the winter here, expect me to come with the west wind and the first swallow,[7] and in a healthier   25 condition, I hope. The chief cause of my illness was a Burgundian wine that induced vomiting and strongly disagreed with my stomach. Now they will send me one that is mellower. But if necessity, with whom even the gods do not fight, as the saying goes,[8] does not allow me to strike camp, I will return the travel money so that no one will suspect me of even the tiniest bit of   30 monetary fraud, though in fact I am now owed from the imperial pension three thousand and three hundred French pounds,[9] and even more than that. For many reasons it is complicated to get it paid here without making a will,

* * * * *

4 The Latin term that Erasmus uses is *syngrapha*; in the present context he is probably referring to a bill of exchange, the most common method for transferring
   large sums.
5 The travel allowance was generous: three hundred Rhenish florins were equivalent to £73 15s 0d groot Flemish or eight and a half years' wages of an Antwerp
   master mason/carpenter (CWE 12 650 Table 3, 691 Table 13). Because of rising
   gold prices in this period, a discrepancy like the one Erasmus mentions between
   the value of the 'crown' (presumaby the écu au soleil) 'there' (probably Brussels)
   and Dole in the Jura is not impossible. If, however, the numbers '37' and '47'
   refer to d groot Flemish, the passage is confusing, since the *official* value of the
   écu was 76d groot Flemish, around which exchange rates would fluctuate.
6 Margaret of Austria, Mary of Hungary's predecessor as regent of the Netherlands, who had made the payment of Erasmus' imperial pension contingent upon
   his return to his native land. The details of the terms she offered are not known.
7 Ie in the spring
8 *Adagia* II iii 41
9 Presumably livres tournois (a money of account) and therefore equivalent
   to 1,650 écus au soleil or £522 10s 0d groot Flemish, that is, just over the annual wage income of sixty Antwerp master masons/carpenters (CWE 12 648,
   650 Table 3, 691 Table 13).

which is extremely difficult for outsiders in this town.[10] I have had my hands
full with this for a long time but I have not brought it to completion.[11]   35

I beg you, my friend Olahus, continue doing what you have begun,
that is, go on supporting our Lieven until he has something like a stable
situation. He already owes you a great deal, and so do I on his behalf.[12] Fulfil
your generous offices. I am not writing now to her most serene Majesty, although Lieven has importuned me to do so.[13] I am distracted by other mat-   40
ters. Farewell to an unparalleled advocate.

Freiburg, 23 August 1533

2861 / From Piotr Tomicki   Cracow, 25 August 1533

This letter, Tomicki's answer to Ep 2776, was first published in Wierzbowski
I 327. The manuscript, a rough draft by a secretary, is in the Zamoyski Collection
of the National Library of Poland at Warsaw (MS BN BOZ 2053 vol 16 no 1925).
For Tomicki, bishop of Cracow, see Epp 1919, 1953.

TO THE MOST RENOWNED AND DISTINGUISHED GENTLEMAN
DESIDERIUS ERASMUS OF ROTTERDAM, MY VERY DEAR FRIEND
Cordial greetings. When you were reproached, most learned sir, by our friend
Justus Decius for neglecting to write to me, even though you had written to
other friends of yours here in Poland,[1] he did so out of his special fondness   5
for me, since he was not unaware of how fond I am of you and how much
pleasure I always take in your letters. But since I am also guilty of the same
fault, for the same reason that you are, namely, the exceptionally burdensome tasks that occupy me, I take your silence in good part and I pray that

* * * * *

10 In May 1530 Erasmus had procured letters from King Ferdinand and Emperor
   Charles (Epp 2317–18) urging the town council of Freiburg to eliminate any
   obstacles in the path of Erasmus' making a will.
11 Erasmus drew up and signed a will at his home in Freiburg on 26 November
   1533 (AK Ep 1775 n1), but no copy of it survives. His final will, the one that was
   actually executed, was made on 12 February 1536 (Allen XI 362); cf Ep 2754 n7.
12 Cf Ep 2865:8, where Erasmus calls Lieven a good-for-nothing that he would
   like to be rid of.
13 This may indicate that Lieven carried the present letter.

   2861
 1 See Ep 2776:3–6.

you, in turn, forgive me for my failure to write. For I would not wish to im- 10
portune you by either by fulfilling or requiring these ordinary obligations (as
you call them),[2] and thus interrupt your studies, which are profitable to the
whole world, especially when no other subject matter presents itself except
the renewal of friendship, which I do not consider to be full and firm if it
requires this kind of renewal. 15

But I am deeply grieved that fate has taken your friends from you, especially those whose patronage and extraordinary services you found useful.[3]
But you still have me, whose services you can make use of as you wish, and
you can grieve for me in turn because this year has also deprived me of not
a few friends. One of them was Krzysztof Szydłowiecki, castellan of Cracow, 20
whose death causes me great sorrow,[4] which I believe you share. But when I
think of the necessity of the human condition in which we are all born, and
since there is no room to complain of it – in fact, there are those who number
death among the good things – I refrain from grief and yield with equanim-
ity to the common condition and necessity. But I was even more frightened 25
when you write that ruin threatens the dwelling place of your body,[5] for I
think it is very important, and I desire that it should long be safe, not only for
the sake of private friendship, but also because of the spirit it contains, which
was born to ennoble literary studies and to support and pacify the church.

I am pleased that Germany is quiet, since the Turks, as you write, have 30
fortunately been driven away.[6] May they too think, as we do, that they have
been driven off! For us also, by the kindness of God, everything is peaceful,
and because of the treaty we made with the Turks, the armed incursions of
the Tartars and Wallachians have ceased.[7] As for the condition of the church,
it is disturbed by so many perverse opinions that I do not know what we 35
ought to hope for. But I am confident that she will be pacified through the

* * * * *

2 Ep 2776:8–9
3 In Ep 2776:26–53 Erasmus mentions only William Warham by name, but alludes to 'three others' unknown to Tomicki.
4 Szydłowiecki, grand chancellor of Poland (Ep 1593), died 30 December 1532.
5 The Latin is *domicilium corporis tui ruinam minari*. This is a slightly garbled reference to Ep 2776:67, where Erasmus says: *Domicilium hoc minitatur ruinam*, which
  we understood to mean: '[Given the danger of religious war in Germany], my
  [continued] residence here [in Freiburg] threatens ruin [and that is why I have
  made plans to leave].' Cf Ep 2776 n11.
6 Ep 2776:71–2
7 On 1 May 1533 Sigismund I and Suleiman I concluded a peace that, despite
  difficulties, proved to be durable.

protection of him who promised that he would be with her until the end of
the time.[8] Finally, my excellent friend, from the bottom of my heart I wish
you the best of health and a very long life. As for my health (about which you
inquire),[9] by the grace of God it is good.   40

Cracow, 25 August 1533

2862 / From Jan (II) Łaski   [Cracow, c 25 August 1533]

This letter was first published as Ep 28 in Hermann Dalton *Lasciana [Denk-
schriften und Briefe], nebst den ältesten evangelischen Synodal-protokollen Polens,
1555–1561* (Berlin 1898; repr Nieuwkoop 1973). The manuscript, a copy (end
missing) in the hand of a professional scribe, was in the same ill-fated collection
at Warsaw as that of Ep 1954. Since the letter answers Ep 2780 and is in turn
answered by Ep 2911, it falls somewhere between March 1533 and March 1534.
The only other extant letters to Erasmus from Poland in that period are Ep 2811
of 15 May 1533 and Ep 2861 of 25 August 1533. Allen, judging it probable that
this letter was delivered by the carrier of one or the other of those two letters,
placed it with Ep 2861 because both make reference to Poland's troubles with
the Wallachians.

On Jan (II) Łaski, canon of Cracow, provost of Gniezno, royal secretary,
prominent Erasmian, and (in the end) Protestant reformer, see Epp 1593 n18,
1821 introduction.

COPY OF AN EPISTOLARY RESPONSE OF THE LORD PROVOST
I cannot, and do not wish, my dear Erasmus, to blame Fortune, since she
has long since satisfied my wishes. Rather I truly and sincerely congratulate
my native land because it has many who deserve its recognition more than
I do, and who, in the judgment of the prince, are more worthy to receive   5
those honours which, because of your affection for me, you attribute to me
for some slight of merits of mine.[1] Certainly I am not so hard to please that
if something fell to my lot I would not accept it. But to tell you the truth, I
have so little ambition that, although the prince himself not long ago gave me

* * * * *

8 Matt 28:20
9 Ep 2776:78–9

2862
1 Cf Ep 2780:2–3.

some substantial hope of being promoted,[2] nevertheless I did not betake my- 10
self to the court until all the preferments that were available at that time had
been distributed, and I had written letters time after time to my friends who
at that time supported my interests at court, instructing them not to trouble
the prince in any way on my account.[3] Moreover, in France, too, nothing
would have been denied me if I had asked for it.[4] And I refused a bishopric in 15
Hungary that had been offered me without my asking.[5] In fact, I also yielded
to my brothers a sizeable sum that I had inherited at the death of my uncle,[6]
an amount not at all to be reckoned lightly, and I remained quite content with
only the income from my benefices. Clearly I would now have been as rich
as Croesus if this Hungarian tragedy, in which my brother somehow or other 20
involved me,[7] had not consumed amounts of money I am ashamed to mention, so much so that I almost had to start all over again. My paternal uncle
expressed his feelings for you on his deathbed;[8] besides his extremely honorific praise of you, he bequeathed to you, leaving the rest to my judgment, the
ring that he always used to wear and that I am sending to you.[9] And I think 25
there was no other cause of his long silence than my absence,[10] since I left
here and joined my brother four years ago and finally went to Hungary,[11] and
after that, I was too preoccupied with affairs to be able to enjoy my uncle's
company. He died while I was gone, and certainly I could not wish to have a

* * * * *

2 The prince was King Sigismund I (Ep 1819).
3 The hopes of Jan (I) Łaski, who died in May 1531, that his nephew, Jan (II)
  would succeed him as archbishop of Gniezno and primate of Poland, had been
  disappointed; see Ep 2780:3–4.
4 In 1524–5 Łaski had spent nearly a year in France, mostly at Paris, and formed
  close ties to Margaret of Angoulême (Ep 1615 introduction), sister of Francis I,
  with whom he remained in correspondence; see Ep 1615:56–7 with n3.
5 The bishopric of Veszprém, in the Turkish-controlled portion of Hungary. John
  Zápolyai, whose service Łaski entered as a diplomat in 1529, offered him the
  revenues of the see, but he never collected them.
6 See Ep 2780 n1. Allen's text has *a patris morte* 'after the death of my father,'
  a mistake for *a patrui morte* 'after the death of my father's brother,' as in the
  Lasciana text.
7 For Jan's brother Hieronim and his embrace of the cause of John Zápolyai,
  Ferdinand of Austria's rival for the kingship of Hungary, see Ep 2780 n10.
8 Jan (I); see n3 above.
9 A golden sapphire ring; see Major 38–9 with n8.
10 A reference to the elder Łaski's failure to send Erasmus a note of thanks for the
   dedication of his edition of Ambrose; see Ep 2780:5–7.
11 In 1529; see n5 above.

IOHANNES A LASCE

Jan (II) Łaski
University of Warsaw Library
Collection of King Stanisław August Poniatowski
Photo Maria Piwowarska

happier death than his. But it would take too long now to tell what he did as   30
he died.[12] It will be easier to do that later at our leisure.

As for the library, the contract is so far from displeasing to me, my dear
Erasmus, that I consider myself altogether happy because I will have such
precious furnishings, which I will always think of as my greatest treasure.[13]
As for what you write concerning the two hundred ducats to be paid for the   35
dedication of the Ambrose, and concerning my praiseworthy generosity,[14] I
certainly understand that nothing more honorific could befall me than to be
praised by a man so great that he will always be admired by posterity, and
nothing in the end more pleasing than to be esteemed by a man who is the
most commended by everyone, even his rivals, as long as I see in myself   40
something especially worthy of your praise. But there is no hope that my
name or my kindness will be praised, nor is there any quality of mine worthy
of the kindness with which you always treated me, both when I was with
you and afterwards,[15] so that it seems that I could hardly ever do enough to
live up to it. Your kindness has so utterly carried me away with affection for   45
you that I will always most steadfastly execute whatever I once promised
you in writing. You could do nothing that would please me more than if you
used me, my possessions, and my resources no differently than if they were
yours. And so, my dear Erasmus, as concerns those two hundred florins, let
it be done as you decide, so that you can do with them whatever you wish.   50

* * * * *

12 In his last years Jan (I) was much troubled by poor health as well as by the con-
    sequences of his support for the claims of John Zápolyai in Hungary. In January
    1530 Pope Clement VII, acting at the request of the imperial court, summoned
    him to Rome to answer charges of complicity with the Turks. King Sigismund
    rejected the summons of his archbishop, but the incident may well have pre-
    cipitated the elder Łaski's death.
13 In 1526 Łaski had arranged to purchase Erasmus' library on terms that granted
    Erasmus the use of it for the rest of his life. The agreed price was '400 gold
    pieces,' 200 of which were paid at the time, while the balance was to be paid
    upon delivery after Erasmus' death; cf Ep 2780 n3.
14 In Ep 2780:12–16 Erasmus suggested that if Łaski wanted to cancel his contract
    for the purchase of Erasmus' library, he would gladly return the 200 ducats
    already paid. Alternatively Łaski could, as an act of generosity, let Erasmus
    keep the 200 ducats as a substitute for the reward that Łaski's uncle (Jan I) had
    not sent in return for the dedication of the edition of Ambrose (see Ep 2780:5–7
    with n2).
15 In May 1524, on his way to France, Łaski had visited Erasmus at Basel; returning
    to Basel in the spring of 1525, he was a guest in Erasmus' house for six months.

I ask only one thing, that you receive them from me willingly and that you be persuaded that I have nothing at all that I would not gladly share with you and that all I want from you is that you continue to treat me with your customary affection. For it is enough for me if you alone know the feelings I have towards you. There is nothing which you do not have the absolute right 55 to demand of me. I beg you, do not change your mind about the contract; for even though at the present time, apart from those Hungarian expenses, I had to pay out a good deal to cover the debts of my uncle, who transferred all of them to me when he was dying, so that I myself was also forced to borrow money, I will nevertheless make sure to send without delay, through our 60 friend Justus,[16] either the whole price or a good part of it.

I would hope that what you write about the Turks being put to flight is true. But they boast that they have never seen an enemy confronting them whom they would not only have sought out in their own territory after a long journey of two days but also would have waited for them for a long 65 time, to say nothing of the thousands of people that they either killed or carried away into perpetual servitude. The fact is that the Grand Turk himself, to whom one in ten captives is normally given, has received seven thousand as his portion. Guess how many others there were. That is the way we triumph over the Turks. As for the fight between these two emperors, 70 if it should be called a fight, I am sending you an elegant epigram, recently brought here from Italy, in which the palm is elegantly assigned to each of them.[17] True, there are discussions about bringing peace to Hungary,[18] but in such a way that neither side trusts the other, and it seems that nothing else is ever done except to put the matter off to another time, until forces are regath- 75 ered and war breaks out again; what I am terribly afraid of is that, while each struggles to gain the throne for himself, in the end both of them will lose it, with as much danger to Christendom as to themselves. Now the Grand Turk has sent out a fleet of five hundred sails, as they say, to regain the forts taken from them by Andrea Doria.[19] Hungary too is full of Turks. All this, I think, 80 seems to promise anything but peace, which the Grand Turk will never agree to unless John remains king,[20] not so much to have John rule as to prevent

* * * * *

16 Justus Ludovicus Decius, secretary to King Sigismund I (Ep 1341A n210)
17 No one has succeeded in finding this epigram.
18 See Ep 2780:19–21 with n9.
19 See Ep 2829 n9.
20 John Zápolyai

Ferdinand from also becoming rooted there; he considers Ferdinand an untrustworthy neighbour because of the power of his brother Charles.

As for me, I have completely renounced the whole Hungarian affair,   85
and there is nothing more I can expect to get from it, even if peace is established. In fact, I would gladly withdraw my brother from it if I could. I thoroughly praise the decision of More,[21] and for that reason, to be sure, I offer
him my fullest congratulations. For in fulfilling such offices, apart from having to turn a blind eye to many abuses, or even agree with opinions you do   90
not hold, you cannot easily do anything without danger. Here we have nothing to fear from those evangelicals, at least for the moment.[22] But even now
we seem to have among us seedbeds, as it were, of internal dissension, and
if they spread any farther, there is a danger that they will produce tumults
more violent than those of the evangelicals. I do not see anything that will   95
hold some of them back except the authority of an elderly prince, whom everyone everywhere will consider to be acting not so much as a prince but as a
father.[23] He has now set out for Lithuania, to look after his dominions there,[24]
against which the Wallachian is said to be plotting.[25] There is a rumour here
that before long the pope will be meeting the kings of France and England.   100
I do not know whether it is true.[26] If it is, I am afraid that this meeting will
beget new disturbances.

                    * * * * *

21 Ie the decision of Thomas More to resign as lord chancellor; see Ep 2780:21–7.
22 Cf Ep 2780:28–31.
23 From c 1530 Sigismund I (born in 1467) was known as Sigismund the Old, in
   contrast to his son and designated heir, Sigismund II Augustus. Although the
   elder Sigismund was unsympathetic to Lutheranism, he had been unable to
   prevent the transformation (1525) of the territory of the Knights of the Teutonic
   Order into the secular duchy of Prussia (under Polish suzerainty), in which the
   last grand master of the order, Albert (I) of Brandenburg-Ansbach, who had
   converted to Lutheranism, became the first hereditary duke. On the other hand,
   Sigismund's armed suppression (1525–6) of a Lutheran uprising in the city of
   Gdansk postponed the reformation of that city by a quarter century. Outside
   Prussia and some of the Germanized cities on the Baltic, Lutheranism remained
   a marginal phenomenon in Poland. Later in the century Calvinism would strike
   deeper roots.
24 Several weeks before being elected king of Poland, Sigismund was acclaimed
   grand duke of Lithuania.
25 This is probably a reference to Wallachians in general rather than to an individual Wallachian. The Polish-Ottoman peace of 1533 had reportedly resulted
   in a diminution of the threat from Wallachia, which was a vassal state of the
   Ottomans; see Ep 2861:32–4.
26 It was not.

2863 / To Conradus Goclenius   Freiburg, 28 August 1533

First published by Allen, this letter was found among the papers of Goclenius
(Ep 2851) in the Collegium Trilingue at Louvain following his sudden death in
1539. A notarized copy of it, sent to Bonifacius Amerbach by the University of
Louvain, is preserved in the Öffentliche Bibliothek of the University of Basel
(MS Goclenii epistolae folio 34). On the reverse side of the same folio is a copy
of the memorandum of 8 April 1534 (see item A2 on pages 310–11 below) be-
stowing on Goclenius the monies Erasmus had deposited with him. Two other
copies of the letter, one of them notarized, are preserved among the accounts of
Erasmus' bequest kept by Bonifacius Amerbach and his son Basilius (MS C VIa
71 109 verso, 114).

Because the letter, read in isolation from other relevant documents, could
be read as a deed of gift rather than as a deed establishing a trust, it became
the principal basis of the claim of Goclenius' heirs, his seven brothers, that
they were entitled to inherit the monies that Erasmus had deposited with him.
But the University of Louvain, assisted by Bonifacius Amerbach, the trustee
of Erasmus' last will, successfully contested the relatives' claim by presenting
solid evidence that both Erasmus and Goclenius had understood the deposited
money to be a trust, disbursements from which had to be made for charitable
purposes as Erasmus had directed. See 'The Donation to Goclenius (Ep 2863)'
303–33 below.

DESIDERIUS ERASMUS OF ROTTERDAM SENDS GREETINGS
TO MASTER CONRADUS GOCLENIUS

So that you may have from me a memorial of our truly genuine friendship,
my dearest Conradus, and also some recompense for the services you have
rendered me in private as well as for the efforts you have expended publicly   5
to promote scholarship, I wish you to have, with full authority, all the money
that I have heretofore deposited with you, to do with it whatever you wish,
whether I am living or dead. I have enough money otherwise. I know that
you will make better use of it than I. In short, I consider whatever is possessed by such a friend as you to be mine. But lest anyone cause you any dif-   10
ficulty concerning this matter, I want this letter in my own handwriting to be
considered a written bond, which I have also sealed with the special image
of my ring.[1] At Freiburg im Breisgau, 28 August in the year of our Lord 1533

* * * * *

2863
1 The Terminus ring; see Ep 2018 n2.

2864 / To Paolo Sadoleto   Freiburg, 30 August 1533

This letter, the answer to one not extant, was first published in the epistolary
appendix to Erasmus' *De praeparatione ad mortem* (Basel: Froben and Episcopius
1534) pages 154–5. Born at Modena, Paolo Sadoleto (1508–72) was the son of
Cardinal Jacopo Sadoleto's cousin. In 1527, after studies at Ferrara, he went
to Rome to join the household of his kinsman, whom he addressed as 'uncle'
and whose indispensable confidant and assistant he quickly became. Later that
same year he accompanied the cardinal on his journey to Provence to take up
residence in his diocese of Carpentras, where he was the cardinal's trusted coadjutor, able spokesman and defender, and eventual successor as bishop (1547).
By the time of the cardinal's death, Paolo was already a distinguished figure
in his own right. He was twice a candidate for the secretariat of the Council of
Trent, and he spent two periods (1552–4, 1561–4) as a papal diplomat before
returning for the last time to Carpentras. Despite his early promise as a classical scholar and poet, his literary accomplishments were no match for those of
his elder kinsman. Indeed, he is known only through his letters and those of the
cardinal, for the first publication of which (1550) he was responsible (see Ep
2816 introduction). This is Erasmus' only known letter to Paolo.

DESIDERIUS ERASMUS OF ROTTERDAM TO PAOLO SADOLETO,
GREETINGS

Why should I not rejoice in having been enriched with a splendid treasure,
my most accomplished young man, since in your letter to me you bring before
me the extraordinary intellectual gifts of your uncle, the most reverend Lord   5
Jacopo Sadoleto – gifts that I have long not only loved but also looked up to
and revered: his admirable eloquence, joined to singular wisdom, piety, and
modesty – in such a way that he himself seems to regain his own youth in you.

Thus far, therefore, I have reason to rejoice. But I am also grateful to
you, my dear Paolo, because at the same time you enhance my reputation   10
by your praise, however much, in your modesty, you make light of this service. Through Bonifacius Amerbach I had received *A Dialogue on the Correct
Ordering of Studies* before you sent it,[1] and though I was overwhelmed by
labours and difficulties, I nevertheless from time to time relieved my mental
weariness by reading it, until a sea of engagements forced me to put it aside.   15
But I will soon return to it, and I will have no peace until I have devoured
all of it. In the meantime I will enjoy your presence as much as I can, and

* * * * *

2864
1 See Ep 2859:21–2.

also that of your uncle, since the Fates have kept me from enjoying it in any
other way. But keep in mind that the most reverend lord your uncle holds
the chief place among my most genuine friends, and rightly so. The very next   20
place belongs to you, who are quite like him. You have this letter in my own
handwriting, written extempore, with revisions and additions – which you
will take as a sign of familiarity rather than negligence. Farewell.

At Freiburg im Breisgau, 30 August 1533

2865 / To Bonifacius Amerbach   [Freiburg], 31 August 1533

> This letter (= AK Ep 1775) was first published in the *Epistolae familiares*. The
> autograph is in the Öffentliche Bibliothek of the University of Basel (MS AN III
> 15 52).

Greetings. I have put off my return to Brabant until next spring. Necessity demanded it, and I think it is to my advantage.[1] For when I changed the wine,
my stomach began to revive. Till then I was drinking not wine but poison.[2]

My servant Lieven, who has never done what I want him to do,[3] brought
me two horses from the bishop, from which I chose one.[4] But in the morning,   5
when the messenger was prepared to return, he said that the ambler limps.
After the messenger set out, the other horse also limped, and is now just a
burden to me. Would that God would free me from that good-for-nothing![5]

As for the will, the more I try to extricate myself, the more entangled I
become. But still I will make sure that nothing falls into the hands of brigands   10

* * * * *

2865
1 See Ep 2820 introduction.
2 See Ep 2818 n2.
3 This appears to be an expression of Erasmus' lingering disappointment at
   Lieven's hasty marriage to a woman with no fortune and his determination to
   seek a career in the imperial administration rather than enter one of the learned
   professions and devote himself to 'intellectual pursuits'; see Epp 2693 n13,
   2792:46–56.
4 For the gift of the horses from Christoph von Stadion, bishop of Augsburg, see
   Epp 2856:1–13, 2868:35–6.
5 'That good-for-nothing' (*ille nugo*) is presumably not the horse, nor is it likely
   the messenger. The reference is, rather, to Lieven and his tendency not to conduct his life as Erasmus had hoped (cf n3 above). His disappointment in Lieven
   notwithstanding, Erasmus continued to urge Nicolaus Olahus to promote his
   fortunes at the imperial court; see Ep 2860:36–9.

if something happens to me.[6] I will write you about it if I send my man Gilbert there,[7] which I have not yet decided to do.

Sadoleto has sent me his private messenger with the book he wants me to correct.[8] I have read through it and done what he wanted. He also wants you to read it. You will be able to sample and examine it. A letter of his to   15 you was enclosed.[9] The messenger thought you live here. Sadoleto seems to believe the same thing. Basel has a bad reputation.[10] So I told him you were detained there by family obligations but that you are free of all contagion from the sects, for I am confident that that is so.

I am surprised that nothing is being sent from Basel. If the book *On the*   20 *Concord of the Church* has been printed,[11] send it to Sadoleto. If it is almost finished, send what has been printed.

If you want the messenger to stay there for a day or two more, until you write and acquaint yourself with the book,[12] that is all right with Sadoleto.

I have told this messenger to go by way of Neuenburg,[13] just in case you   25 are there. I hope this is not a mistake.

I am sending you the epitaph that Thomas More had engraved on his tomb.[14] I was going to publish it with some letters, but Emmeus deceived

* * * * *

6 Erasmus second will, of which no copy survives, was made and signed at his home in Freiburg on 26 November 1533; see AK Ep 1775 n1 (citing the certificate of the notary). The reference to 'brigands' may well be, as Alfred Hartmann says (AK Ep 1755 n1) an expression of Erasmus' lingering fear that, because he was still legally a member of the Augustinian canons, the prior of his home monastery at Steyn would lay claim to his property. To allay that fear he had in 1525 procured from Pope Clement VII a dispensation (Ep 1588) granting him full power to dispose of his property in a will. He kept the document confidential, but carefully preserved among his papers.

7 Gilbert Cousin (Ep 2381 n1)

8 His commentary on Romans; see Ep 2816 n3. The private messenger may well have been Jean Morel (Ep 2872 n1).

9 AK Ep 1770; see Ep 2816 n7.

10 Ie as a place that had fallen to the Evangelical reformers

11 See Ep 2852 introduction.

12 That's what Erasmus says, though one would expect Bonifacius first to examine the book and then write about it.

13 Neuenburg am Rhein, halfway between Basel and Freiburg, where Bonifacius' father-in-law was the burgomaster

14 See Ep 2831:122–35.

me.[15] If you want, copy it for yourself and send my copy to Sadoleto. I have
mentioned it in a letter.[16]   30

    At Lyon Hilarius Bertolph perished utterly from the plague – that is,
he himself, his wife, and three children.[17] The rest I will write by means of
my servant Gilbert, or I will keep it in store for a private talk. Take good care
of yourself.

    31 August 1533   35
    Yours truly, Erasmus of Rotterdam
    To the most famous gentleman Master Bonifacius Amerbach. At Basel

2866 / From Haio Cammingha   Leeuwarden, 2 September 1533

> This letter was first published as Ep 193 in Förstemann / Günther. The auto-
> graph, address sheet missing, was in the Burscher Collection of the University
> Library at Leipzig (Ep 1254 introduction). For Haio Cammingha see Ep 2766
> introduction.

Cordial greetings. Salutations, my most learned and loving father and patron, singularly dear to me. I am at a complete loss for words to express
how much joy the last letter of Master Rutgerus Rescius brought me.[1] For a
long time I had heard nothing certain about how you are doing and for that
reason I had decided to send my servant to Goclenius,[2] when, lo and behold, 5
Rescius himself informed me that you are enjoying good fortune as well as
good health and that her serene Majesty and all of Brabant are expecting
your return.[3] I was thoroughly comforted by this message: partly because it
reported that a man singularly dear to me and a most delightful patron was
enjoying the prosperity I had so long wished for him (and I considered that   10

* * * * *

15 It was in due course published, not by Johann Faber Emmeus, the Freiburg
   printer, but by Froben; see Ep 2831 introduction.
16 Not extant
17 Following Erasmus' advice (Ep 2581:14–20), his former famulus Hilarius
   Bertholf (Ep 1712) had settled at Lyon, where he could tutor students and work
   for the printers. He seemed to be doing well, and was on friendly terms with,
   among others, François Rabelais (Ep 2743:22–6), when the plague took him and
   his entire family.

2866
1 For Rescius, first professor of Greek at the Collegium Trilingue, see Ep 546.
2 Conradus Goclenius (Ep 2851)
3 See Ep 2820 introduction.

I shared your happiness, since among friends all things are common,[4] and partly because you will ennoble our region by your presence.

Therefore, though I was uncertain whether you were still staying in Freiburg or had entered upon the journey to your native land, I wanted this letter to testify to our friendship and mutual love and to show that a genuine friendship is not at all weakened by long absence or great distances. No one can doubt how much I owe to your affection and to your great kindnesses to me, since everyone readily understands that, and I freely proclaim my gratitude. And there is no better way for me to declare my love for you than by requesting a favour from you with the highest confidence befitting a friend, namely that you love me and forgive my former fault.[5] After all, Seneca thinks that a friend who requests an honourable service is no less a friend than the one who renders it.[6] Bestow on me that favour, namely your love for me, not grudgingly, I beg you), but as soon as possible, as you have always done, so that others may see it. I shall also grant you exactly the same right to what is mine, so that you can use, or even abuse, my good offices in any service whatsoever.

Farewell, my dearest patron. Wherever on earth you are settled, I want to join you, so that, following whatever advice your Benevolence gives me, I may either stay where you are or travel to Italy. Therefore, before setting out I sent my servant with this letter to Antwerp in Brabant to inquire about you and the details of your arrival. For unless I am completely informed about these matters, I would set out without a plan, not knowing where in the world I might meet you. Farewell once again, my best and greatest friend. Greetings from my brothers and from Master Willem Zagare, an imperial councillor here.[7]

* * * * *

4 *Adagia* i i 1
5 His 'fault' was leaving Erasmus' service owing him money and taking a long time to pay it back; see Ep 2552 n6.
6 This does not appear to be a direct quotation from Seneca. For the notion that the receiving of a favour is an important part of friendship see Seneca *De beneficiis* 2.22.
7 Willem Janszoon Zagare of Goes (d December 1538), who had studied at Louvain (where he may have known Erasmus) and Orléans, became pensionary of Zierikzee in 1521 and was the first recorded rector of its Latin school. In 1533 he moved to Leeuwarden and was appointed to the council of Friesland.

2 September 1533, at Leeuwarden, from my house, the use and enjoy-
ment of which, together with the gardens, I gladly grant to you, as I have
often signified, if your Excellency should deign to abide there.[8]

Yours whether you wish it or not, Haio Cammingha, your slave   40

2867 / To Franciscus Rupilius   Freiburg, 8 September 1533

This letter was first published in the epistolary appendix to *De praeparatione
ad mortem* (Basel: Froben and Episcopius 1534) pages 153–4. It answers one,
not extant, in which Rupilius, prompted by Johann Koler (see below and cf Ep
2868), had supplied Erasmus with information about the Paumgartner family.
Erasmus made use of this information, with additions from Koler, in Ep 2879.
For Franciscus Rupilius, tutor to the sons of Johann (II) Paumgartner (Ep 2603)
and, it seems, in Padua at this time, see Ep 2682 n21.

ERASMUS OF ROTTERDAM TO FRANCISCUS RUPILIUS,
DOCTOR OF LAW, GREETINGS

To be sure, my dear friend Rupilius, I am obliged to our friend Koler in many
important ways, and I profess, both gladly and heartily, that I am indebted
to him because his insistence overcame your shyness and compelled you to   5
write to me and to add your name to the list of my friends. Far be it from
me that I should shift any fault from myself, as you suggest, by throwing
on Koler the blame and the offence of having changed you, as you write,
from being diffident to being impudent, and from being modest to being
presumptuous. As it happens, I have already written a letter to thank him.   10
But what you freely promise by the laws of the Graces, I promise in good
faith to you in turn, if anything should arise in which you seek my services,
or, even if you do not ask, if the circumstances themselves will require the
good offices of a friend.[1]

I am already too longlived, and death has taken away many of my   15
friends, not only in Rome, but also in England, France, Germany, and also in
Poland. I would be greatly pleased if you would deign to let me know what

* * * * *

8 Cf Ep 2766:100–6.

2867
1 One law of the Graces, according to Seneca *De beneficiis* 1.3, is that in the unbroken regular order of doing good deeds one does a good deed, another receives
   it, and a third repays it.

is happening at Rome, as long as it is something of such a nature that it can safely be committed to a letter. I took great pleasure in what you write concerning your most generous Maecenas Paumgartner,[2] not only because I am just as delighted by the success of a man I like very much as I am by my own, but also because you suggest that I write a memoir, as it were, to illustrate his glory. I know that owing to his modesty he does not in fact seek any glory at all, but it contributes publicly to the advancement of good morals that the virtues of outstanding men should not be concealed but be set forth for imitation in the theatre of the world. I only wish that my rhetorical abilities were sufficient to carry that out in a way which his merits demand or that they were as great as you, perhaps, believe them to be. However that may be, I will try my best, and do so soon, with the help of Christ. But note well that in this matter you must lend me your assistance, so that you make sure my zeal does not offend the modesty of this thoroughly judicious man. I am emboldened to undertake this task by the encouragement of many people, but especially of Zasius,[3] whose authority in all matters I regularly follow as if it were that of an oracle. I certainly would have liked to write more to you in this letter, but I did not have the time. Farewell, and give my personal greetings to Logau if he is there.[4]

Given at Freiburg im Breisgau, 8 September 1533

If *autography* pleases you, do not be offended by *cacography*. That is the way I am. But your *macrography* will never offend me.[5]

2868 / To Johann Koler   Freiburg, 9 September 1533

This letter was first published in *Pentas epistolarum clarorum virorum hactenus nondum editarum* (Ulm: Wagner, 24 June 1798) pages 3–4, where the text is said to be 'Ex Autographo Coleri' (from the autograph in Koler's papers). The Allen editors, on the other hand, citing no manuscript source, state that 'the original was not Erasmus' autograph, but a copy made by Choler and afterwards

* * * * *

2 See Ep 2815 n6.
3 Udalricus Zasius, who had initiated the contact between Erasmus and Paumgartner; see Ep 2602.
4 The most recent news of Georg von Logau (Ep 2810 n2) was that he had left Padua for Rome in search of benefices (Ep 2829 n4).
5 The italicized words are Greek in the text (*autographia, kakographia, makrographia*), and at least the last two are inventions of Erasmus. Autography is writing in one's own hand. Cacography is writing in a bad hand (but punning on Greek *kakos-* 'bad' and Dutch/German *kak- / kack-* 'shitty'). Macrography is writing a great deal (ie a long letter).

annotated by Conrad Peutinger.' Peutinger (Ep 318:3n), a scholar of Erasmian
sympathies who resigned as town clerk of Augsburg in 1534 (when it became
a Protestant city) and thereafter devoted himself to private studies, might well
have acquired the letter or a copy of it. There was indeed a comment in his hand
in the margin of the manuscript used for *Pentas epistolarum* (see n2 below), but
it is not clear why that comment could not have been made on the autograph.

ERASMUS TO JOHANN KOLER, PROVOST OF CHUR
Cordial greetings. I am greatly pleased that by your insistence you overcame
the shyness of Rupilius and persuaded him to write to me,[1] for he seems to be
a learned, modest, and judicious man. He provided me with much material to
enhance the reputation of an outstanding man,[2] but more briefly than I would   5
have desired, so I would like you to supplement it. I want to know the origins
of Paumgartner's nobility, and in what circumstances the wealth of his family diminished, and what princes he served, whether through necessity or by
right, and whatever else it would be useful to know. How many children does
he have, and by whom they were educated? – for I know only Georg.[3] I would   10
also like you to do this as soon as possible. For when the printers return from
Frankfurt,[4] there may perhaps be an occasion to publish something.

The Paris theologians have gone back to their madness.[5] A certain office of sworn bookseller fell vacant, and the whole university was consulted about it.[6] The rector,[7] instructed by some monks and theologians, began   15

* * * * *

2868
1 See Ep 2867:3–6.
2 Johann (II) Paumgartner (cf line 7 below). In the margin in the hand of Konrad
  Peutinger: 'Ioann. scilicet P[aumgartner].' See note b in the *Pentas epistolarum*
  text and line 4n in Allen's text.
3 Johann Georg Paumgartner (Ep 2809)
4 From the autumn book fair
5 The text says *furcas* ('gallows' or 'racks'), which makes no sense. We follow
  Gerlo in reading it as a mistake for *furias* (as in line 31 below), and have translated 'madness' in both cases.
6 The word *librariatus*, translated as 'sworn bookseller,' is otherwise unknown
  and doubtless never existed. We take it to be a scrambled version of *librarius
  juratus* (*libraire juré* in French). At any given time, there were twenty-four Paris
  bookseller-printers who enjoyed the status of *librarius juratus* of the University
  of Paris. One of them was Josse Bade, who at one time had been Erasmus' favourite printer; see Ep 2021 n4. It seems that a vacancy had now occurred and
  that the university had inaugurated steps to fill it (result unknown).
7 The rector of the University of Paris from 23 June to 10 October 1533 was the
  Portuguese scholar Andrea Govea, principal of the Collège de Sainte-Barbe; see
  César-Egasse du Boulay *Historia universitatis parisiensis* 6 (Paris 1673) 977.

to complain loudly that there were booksellers who secretly print and sell books in French. Then there was some consultation about the office, but after that there was no mention at all of the complaint. Immediately after lunch the presiding theologians sent a commissioner with a huge retinue to the workshops of the booksellers, and with one stroke they ordered all the shops to be closed, took away the keys, and closed up everything with the royal seal. Seeing such a sudden commotion, the printers were afraid. At length the commissioners returned to inspect the shops, and they also seized my books, especially the *Colloquies*, the translation of the New Testament, the *Folly*, the *Praise of Matrimony*, the book about eating meat, just about everything all the way to the *Copia* and *On the Writing of Letters*.[8] None of this was any longer done in the name of the theologians but in that of the rector. Béda and his minions were not there,[9] but he did more in his absence than if he had been there. They took unjust advantage of the king's absence.[10] My books were handed over to the Franciscans to be examined. They will find thousands of heresies. Can anything be more insane than this madness?[11] I see clearly what will happen: if Lutheranism declines, the monks will become so tyrannical that we will miss Luther. And these are the monsters against whom I fight, to my own destruction.

I wrote recently via the man through whom I sent the horse back to the bishop.[12] By the same man I sent my book *On the Concord of the Church* to Paumgartner.[13] I suspect that Hieronymus printed it secretly out of fear of the

* * * * *

8 The standard titles of the works mentioned are, in order: *Colloquia, Novum Testamentum, Moriae encomium, Encomium matrimoniae, De esu carnium, De copia verborum, De conscribendis epistolis.*
9 Béda had been sent into exile and had not yet been called back to Paris; see Ep 2841 n5.
10 In the late spring, summer, and autumn of 1533 King Francis was away in the south of France, where in October–November he held a meeting with Pope Clement VII; see Knecht 228–9.
11 Efforts by the faculty of theology and the Parlement of Paris to prevent the publication and sale of heretical books were a fairly frequent occurrence, but we have been unable to find in the sources known to us any trace of an incident that fits the description offered here. Ep 2906:42–5 may indicate that Erasmus himself eventually came to doubt the story.
12 For the gift of a horse to Erasmus by Christoph von Stadion, bishop of Augsburg, see Ep 2865. Lieven Algoet, who fetched the horse from Augsburg and brought it to Freiburg, cannot be the one who took it back: he had already returned to Brabant; see Ep 2860.
13 For the book, *De sarcienda ecclesiae concordia*, see Ep 2852.

preachers.[14] For he sent me only three copies, and none to anyone else. It will be easy to take care of the will, and there is no need of any great sponsors.[15]

You tell me to stop worrying; if worries could have killed me, I would 40 long since have been dead. I can pretty well endure the clamours of the theologians, the yapping of the monks and others. But there is one crime committed in my own house a year ago by a thieving scoundrel and a thoroughly degenerate whore who broke all the locks, took away all the most beautiful pieces of my furnishings, and made off with a considerable sum from my 45 chests.[16] This indignity I can neither forget nor digest. It grieves me all the more because it cannot be avenged. The thief is a woman who is a native of this place and has many relatives and acquaintances here, all of them remarkably wicked. All leisure for study had to be set aside. But I tell you this in confidence, lest we somehow stir up sleeping Camarina.[17] Take the best 50 care of yourself, sincerest of friends.

At Freiburg, 9 September 1533
Erasmus of Rotterdam, in my own hand

2869 / From Celio Calcagnini   Ferrara, 17 September 1533

This letter was first published in *Caelii Calcagnini opera aliquot* (Basel: Froben 1544) 166–7. Calcagnini (1479–1541), whom Erasmus had met at Ferrara in 1508, was a distinguished member of the humanist circle in that city and a lifelong admirer of Erasmus. His *Libellus elegans de libero arbitrio* (1525), which Erasmus arranged to have published by Froben and for which he supplied the preface (Ep 1578), was inspired by Erasmus' *De libero arbitrio*. This is the last of the three surviving letters in Erasmus' correspondence with Calcagnini (the other two being Epp 1576 and 1587).

CELIO CALCAGNINI TO ERASMUS OF ROTTERDAM, GREETINGS
I acknowledge that even in writing there are certain decisive moments which can be neither avoided nor disregarded; I myself have had that experience. For on many occasions, when I had taken it upon myself to write to my

* * * * *

14 Ie the Evangelical preachers in Basel
15 On the will, see Ep 2754 n7. As sponsors or patrons in the making of his will, Erasmus already had King Ferdinand and Emperor Charles; see Epp 2317–18.
16 The 'scoundrel' was apparently the servant Jacobus (Ep 2652 n4), who had joined forces with a young housekeeper (the 'whore') to commit the theft first mentioned in Ep 2735:52–6. Cf Ep 2897:25–31.
17 Ie stir up unnecessary trouble (*Adagia* I i 64)

friend Erasmus and was already holding the pen in my hand, somehow, all   5
of a sudden, other thoughts and diversions occurred to me that struck the
pen from my hand and, as I was writing, put it off to another day. Certainly
I was greatly disturbed about this because I knew that no small part of my
reputation consists in writing to you. For it was my responsibility especially
to protect the friendship struck up between us, to do so not only out of cour-   10
tesy but even as a duty. Moreover, there was the disadvantage I suffered
because by my silence I was deprived of a pleasant experience, namely the
sweetness of a letter from you, since by not writing I deprived you of an
occasion to write in return. For how else could I get a letter from someone so
occupied except by writing?   15

To be sure, this part of the accusation is so important for me that there
is no argument by which it can easily be refuted. Otherwise I could easily
make amends for this complete idleness with the plea that in the meantime
nothing especially important had happened, either for me to write or for
you to know. And indeed, would that instead certain things worthy of be-   20
ing suppressed in everlasting oblivion had not occurred. On the other hand,
as is the proper duty of love, which cannot be neglected without expiation,
the memory of our mutual friendship, which in any case will never perish,
has remained unimpaired with me. And I have never ceased to compensate
fully and abundantly for whatever could be found lacking in my correspon-   25
dence by my unceasing praise of your virtues and the frequent mention of
our friendship.

And thus far you have the argument in defence of my indolence. But
now that the time of silence ordained by destiny has passed away, and having been advised by a friend that a reliable messenger who is travelling your   30
way is available, even though there was nothing at hand to write about, I
have nevertheless written this, such as it is, and have broken that ironclad
constraint. Now that I have been offered the opportunity to write, I will also
not neglect to express my thanks to you and to give testimony of my undying gratitude for inviting me so often to share in your glory and giving me   35
honourable mention in your book of *Adages* and your *Ciceronianus*.[1] So far am
I from taking offence at your denial that I am skilled in Ciceronian rhetoric
that of my own accord I confess that you attributed more to me than I would
ever have dared to hope for, even if I were excessively ambitious. For you
conceded to me wide knowledge and an acceptable style. You even ranked   40

* * * * *

2869
1 See *Adagia* II 1 34, II iv 91; for the *Ciceronianus* see the following note.

me higher than a most learned man,[2] to whom on my own initiative I regularly yield precedence in talent,[3] even though, if the matter were weighed in the scales of truth, I can rightly claim nothing except persistent study and an insatiable desire for higher learning.

Therefore whatever you grant me in minerals and timber, as a gener-   45
ous landowner might,[4] I must attribute entirely to your kindness. In other respects I entirely agree with you when you judge in that book that after Cicero no one has fulfilled all the requirements of eloquence. Some lack the right choice of words; others, gravity; others, charm; some this and some that; certainly all writers are deficient in arrangement and rhythm. For these   50
are two Ciceronian features, among others, that some will censure rather than imitate.[5] Still, I would not deny that there are some remarkable masters in this list of imitators who have come rather close to this goal, but 'rather close' is nonetheless a great distance. I think those did well who expressed some feature of Cicero, just as once the disciples of Apelles thought they had   55
made great progress in their art if they sought to achieve some brushstrokes of their master – for they thought that to aspire to all of them was immoderate and far beyond their grasp.[6] Farewell.

17 September, my birthday, 1533. From Ferrara

2870 / To Désiré Morel   Freiburg, 12 October 1533

This letter was first published in the *Epistolae universae* page 1111. Désiré Morel, canon of Besançon and, from 1529, official of the archdeacon (ie chief judge of the archidiaconal court), was one of Erasmus' friends in that city (see Ep 1534 n11) as well as the great uncle of Gilbert Cousin (line 11 below). He had already died (23 July 1533) when this letter was written.

* * * * *

2 See CWE 28 420. The 'most learned man' was Lodovico Ricchieri (identified in n666).
3 Literally 'lower the fasces' (*fasces summittere*) in acknowledgment of superior rank; see *Adagia* I viii 69.
4 In the sale of a property, already cut timber and stones that had been quarried were commonly excluded, but generous vendors were wont nevertheless to grant to the buyer some portion of the excluded timber and minerals. See *Adagia* IV iv 38, citing *Digest* 19.1.17.2, and Cicero *Topica* 26.100.
5 The concluding phrase is in Greek. The words translated as 'censure' (*momesetai*) and 'imitate' (*mimesetai*) play on the words 'Momus' (Greek god of carping criticism) and 'mimus' (mimic).
6 This story is not found in Pliny, the most abundant source for information about Apelles, the foremost painter of antiquity. Nor have we found it anywhere else.

ERASMUS OF ROTTERDAM SENDS GREETINGS TO DÉSIRÉ MOREL

I congratulate your commonwealth, my dearest Désiré, on being freed from
the dissension that I heard had arisen there. It was unquestionably fear of
that disturbance that kept me from moving there in order to avoid a too frequent shortage of wine.[1] For from the end of February to September I have   5
been continually ailing from the deterioration of my stomach, which will
not keep anything down. And I discovered that the cause of the ailment was
nothing but a lack of a suitable wine. For when I changed the wine my stomach immediately revived. This disastrous condition of my little body must be
tolerated until God destroys both stomach and food. But to keep that from   10
happening to me again this winter, I have sent my servant Gilbert Cousin,
who is indeed extremely dear to me on many counts, but even dearer because he is closely related to you, to get two or three casks of wine.[2]

I think that the official has not yet returned from his embassy, for he
recently wrote me most affectionately from Lucerne.[3] And I hear that Master   15
Bonvalot has retired from all human affairs.[4] That is all the more reason for
me to ask you to give your advice to our Gilbert so that he may place his
money wisely and return to us as soon as possible. It may be that someone
will laugh at me for being so concerned about wine. I would laugh myself
if I had not so often learned better from actual experience. I have been re-   20
called to my native land by Queen Mary, the emperor, the high chancellor,[5]
and the duke of Aarschot;[6] I have also been sent three hundred florins for

* * * * *

2870
1 For the importance of Besançon in the supply of the Burgundy wine that
  Erasmus considered essential to his health, and for the dissension between the
  city council and the canons in that city that made moving there problematic, see
  Epp 2759 n3, 2895.
2 For Cousin, see Ep 2381 n1, and for other traces of his activities on this trip see
  Epp 2878:45–6, 2880:9–10, 2881.
3 Léonard de Gruyères (Ep 1534), canon at Besançon and official (chief judge) of
  the archiepiscopal court. He was a capable diplomat who represented Charles v
  on missions among the Swiss cantons in the years 1533–6. The letter referred to
  here and again in Ep 2880:2–5 is not extant.
4 This report was false: François Bonvalot (Ep 1534 n10) did not die until 1560. By
  December Erasmus knew that Bonvalot was still alive and addressed Ep 2890
  to him.
5 See Ep 2820 introduction.
6 Philippe de Croy (Ep 2822)

travel expenses, and arrangements have been made for an annual grant of
that amount.[7] The horses were ready and I was girded up for the trip. But
weakness forces me to wait for spring.   25
     You will learn the rest from Cousin, who is yours in two ways and mine
in only one. For some time now we sigh rather than hope for the concord of
the church. I have certainly encouraged it strongly; I think Gilbert will show
you the book.[8] I hope that you are in excellent health.
     Given at Freiburg im Breisgau, 12 October in the year of our Lord 1533   30

2871 / From Giambattista Egnazio   Venice, 13 October 1533

This letter, the answer to one now lost, was first published as Ep 194 in
Förstemann / Günther. The autograph, in a hand that Allen found difficult to
decipher, and with the address sheet missing, was in the Burscher Collection
of the University Library at Leipzig (Ep 1254 introduction). For Egnazio, one
of the few consistent admirers of Erasmus among the Italian humanists, see
Ep 2105 introduction.

JESUS + CHRIST

I did not allow Viglius[1] – your friend, should I say, or mine? – to return to you
without a letter from me signifying that I find nothing more important or more
pleasant than to hear that everything is going extremely well with you.[2] For
quite some time ago some unreliable people spread vague rumours saying   5
that you had yielded to nature and the Fates. But though I believed that such
rumours originated with detractors hostile to you, I nevertheless knew that
such a fate could have befallen you, physically weak as you are and harassed

* * * * *

7 Cf Ep 2820 introduction. On the travel allowance, see Ep 2860 n5. The annual
  pension was equally generous.
8 *De sarcienda ecclesiae concordia* (Ep 2852)

2871
1 Viglius Zuichemus (Ep 2810). Egnazio writes 'Villius,' which corresponds to the
  way an Italian would pronounce the 'gl' in 'Viglius.'
2 Viglius commenced his homeward journey from Padua on 16 October 1533.
  See *Vita Viglii Zuichemi* 13. He visited Erasmus at Freiburg in early November;
  see Ep 2875 n1.

by such great labours that press upon you from all sides, especially since death
has long been accustomed to claiming the most distinguished men;[3] but all 10
these deep anxieties that afflicted me were completely swept from my mind
by Viglius, who gave firm testimony that you are doing well and are entirely
absorbed in your writing. I embraced him heartily, both because of his outstanding intelligence and because I knew that he was one of your best friends,
and (as an Attic messenger could testify) I have never refused him any kind of 15
service.[4] I only wish that people like him would come to me more often. For
I would never fail them as long as they came from you.

For the exceptionally kind deed of sending the Basil printed in Greek
I offer my deepest thanks.[5] I hope to return the favour in like measure or better if ever I am able to do so. But you should know that apart from the letter 20
no Basil was delivered to me by Cyprius.[6]

Our friends the Asulani,[7] who are working very hard at the restoration
of literary texts, send you most cheerful greetings. They have undertaken the
Themistius in Greek; as soon as it is finished I will send it to you. Farewell,
my most kind friend Erasmus, and give my best wishes to your learned boon 25
companions there.

From Venice, at the Aldine Press, written hastily because Viglius is
standing by, wearing his travelling cap. 13 October 1533
Egnazio

2872 / To Bonifacius Amerbach [Freiburg], 19 October 1533

This letter (= AK Ep 1785) was first published in the *Epistolae familiares*. The
autograph is in the Öffentliche Bibliothek of the University of Basel (MS AN III
15 53).

* * * * *

3 Cf Cicero *Philippicae* 14.12.32: 'In truth, Mars himself seems to select all the
bravest men from the battle array.'
4 An Attic messenger is a completely trustworthy one; cf *Adagia* I viii 25.
5 For the Froben edition of St Basil in Greek, published in March 1532, see Ep
2611 introduction.
6 Petrus Cyprius, who c 10 March 1532 had been entrusted with a copy of Ep 2604
for delivery to Padua; see Ep 2657:5–7. At that time, the Froben Basil would
have been hot off the press. Cyprius presumably also carried the letter to which
this is the answer.
7 Ie the Aldine Press, now run by Gianfrancesco Torresani and his brother
Frederico, often referred to by the Latin surname Asulanus, after the birthplace
of their father, Andrea Torresani of Asola.

Greetings. If Morel is the squint-eyed fellow whom Sadoleto recommended to me, the one who lived with Hieronymus, I have no need of the likes
of him.[1] I would want someone fluent in German and with some degree of
Latin, who could take Gilbert's place.[2] As long as he is not from this region.
One taste of that is enough.[3]   5

I will give him a month on trial. If he is unsatisfactory to either one of
us I will give him the travel money to go back.

The rest when we see one another, as you promise.[4] Be well, together
with all those dear to you.

19 October 1533   10

Yours, Erasmus of Rotterdam

To the renowned gentleman Master Bonifacius Amerbach. At Basel

* * * * *

2872
1 Apparently Jean Morel of Embrun, sieur de Grigny (1511–81). He may have
   been the messenger who in August 1533 brought Erasmus a manuscript of
   Sadoleto's commentary on Romans (Ep 2865:13–14). He had matriculated at
   Basel, made the acquaintance of Bonifacius Amerbach, and was living with
   Hieronymus Froben when Bonifacius passed along Sadoleto's letter of recommendation and suggested Morel as a suitable famulus for Erasmus. He was
   still, or once again, at Basel in 1537, and it is possible that he was present when
   Erasmus died in Froben's house in 1536. During these years Morel appears
   to have been connected in some way with the efforts of Guillaume du Bellay,
   Francis I's most able diplomat, to establish a network of agents aimed at allying
   France with Protestant princes and cities, promoting alliance as a step towards
   reconciliation of the old faith and the new. From 1543 he is documented at Paris,
   where he became maréchal des logis to Queen Catherine de' Medici and friend of
   her chancellor, Michel de l'Hospital. In 1556 he engaged Karel Uutenhove (Ep
   2093) as the tutor of his three daughters, and he himself supervised the education of one of the natural sons of Henry II.
2 Gilbert Cousin (Ep 2381 n1), who was currently hunting for a benefice in his
   native Burgundy and whose continued service to Erasmus was consequently
   in doubt; see Epp 2889–90.
3 See Ep 2868:42–8 with n16.
4 See Ep 2878:42–4, written on 18 November, where Erasmus complains that
   thirty days have passed since Bonifacius promised to visit him within two
   weeks. Because the undated Ep 2873A contains precisely such a promise, AK
   and CWE have dated that letter at 'mid-October 1533.' Bonifacius did indeed
   have good reasons for wanting to visit Freiburg at this time: he had business
   to conduct on behalf of his father-in-law; he wanted to discuss with Erasmus
   the offer of employment that he had received from the city of Strasbourg; and
   Erasmus wanted to discuss the preparation of his new will; see Epp 2873A:5–8
   with nn1–3. On 30 November Erasmus informs Bonifacius that 'this business
   [of the will]' has been taken care of – it had been signed on 26 November – and
   that he not need make the trip for Erasmus' sake (Ep 2883:2–4). Ten days later,

2873 / From Juan Ginés de Sepúlveda   Rome, 23 October 1533

This letter was first published in the *Sepulvedae epistolae* folios A5 verso–A8 verso. Erasmus' answer is Ep 2905.

JUAN GINÉS DE SEPÚLVEDA SENDS GREETINGS
TO DESIDERIUS ERASMUS OF ROTTERDAM
For quite some time I did not know what you were doing, and I did not even know for sure whether Zúñiga's book against your observations on the New Testament,[1] which I recently sent to you from the city of Bologna, had actu- 5
ally reached your hands.[2] But since I have no doubt that it has been delivered to you, and I suspect that because of his strictures you are engaged in more carefully revising the scholarly results of your nightly vigils, I thought that it would be contrary to my duty, and even my loyalty, to conceal from you what I have often considered to be relevant to this matter. You should know 10
that the Greek copies you followed in your New Testament have been cor-
rupted in many places, sometimes in single words, sometimes in the omis-
sion or repetition of whole sentences. I think this is the fault of the copyists, who were led to make mistakes because of some comments ineptly added, as often happens, in the margins of the text by some scholars. And so, once 15

* * * * *

however, Erasmus tells Bonifacius that 'we are expecting you for the holidays,' though the visit did not finally take place until 7 January (Ep 2887:5–6 with n4). One assumes that he and Erasmus will have discussed the terms of the offer from Strasbourg. At all events, it was not until 25 January 1535 that Bonifacius wrote the letter declining the offer (AK Ep 1898).

2873
1 At the time of his death in 1531 the old foe of Erasmus' New Testament scholar-
ship, Diego López Zúñiga (Ep 1260 n36), had accumulated a set of unpublished notes or observations on Erasmus' edition of Jerome and his Annotations on the New Testament and stipulated that they were to be given to Erasmus for his use; see Ep 2637:24–36 with n4.
2 It appears that two different copies of Zúñiga's notes had been sent to Erasmus. The first was sent from Rome in August 1532 by Cardinal Iñigo López de Mendoza y Zúñiga (see Ep 2705). Subsequently, when Mendoza and Sepúlveda were to-
gether at Bologna for the meeting between Clement VII and Charles V (December 1532–February 1533), Mendoza gave Sepúlveda a copy of Zúñiga's notes on the Annotations, which Sepúlveda then forwarded to Erasmus (cf Ep 2938:1–5). In mid-February 1534 the copy sent from Bologna by Sepúlveda had still not arrived (Ep 2905:3, 11), but already in mid-May 1533 Erasmus had received the copy sent from Rome by Mendoza; see Ep 2810:87–91, and cf Ep 2905:3–10.

such a corruption was wrongly accepted by some, it became so widespread, as I see it, that not only are all printed books circulating with such errors but even some manuscript copies are not free of them.

Thus no one should think it surprising that while you are following the blind you should stumble in the same rough places. For there is an ex- 20 tremely old Greek copy in the Vatican library that contains both Testaments conscientiously and carefully written in capital letters and much different from the usual copies.[3] When I learned about it from Zúñiga,[4] I took care to look into the matter and to compare texts. That this copy is the most correct of all is evident from both its antiquity and the carefulness of the scribe, and 25 also because it agrees closely with our old translation,[5] which undoubtedly also must have been translated from the most correct copy and handed down to us by our ancestors. Therefore, since other texts ought to be guided and corrected by being faithful to this text as a norm (so to speak), you yourself should also consider what needs to be done. This is how things stand: rarely 30 does the common Greek edition differ from our old translation (though, as you know, it often does) without differing also from the Vatican copy. And not to detain you, I have noted 365 places where this text is different.[6]

Likewise, the same feeling that impelled me to give you a general warning about these differences – since I promote your praise all the more gladly 35 when I see that it contributes to the common good – does not allow me to

* * * * *

3 The reference is to the famous Codex Vaticanus B 1209, now recognized as the oldest extant manuscript (first half of the fourth century) of the Bible. It consists of the Greek (Septuagint) translation of the Old Testament together with the New Testament. Erasmus learned of its existence in 1521, in a letter from Paolo Bombace (Ep 210), an old friend at the papal court who had evidently undertaken to consult Vatican manuscripts for him; see Ep 1213:74–94 with nn14–17). In that same year he mentions it in the *Apologia de loco 'Omnes quidem'* (CWE 73 48) and in the *Apologia ad annotationes Stunicae* (LB IX 353A). In the 1527 edition of the New Testament he quotes it in the annotation to 1 John 5:7 (ASD VI-10 548:353–8).

4 The codex appears to have been added to the Vatican collection c 1480. When Zúñiga found out about it is not clear, but it was not used for the Complutensian Polyglot (text printed, but not yet circulated, in 1515), in the preparation of which he had been actively involved.

5 The Vulgate

6 It is not clear from this letter or from Erasmus' reply to it (Ep 2905) whether Sepúlveda enclosed a list of the 365 variants referred to here. What is clear from Erasmus' reply (and other sources there cited) is that he did not understand or acknowledge the importance of the Codex Vaticanus.

remain silent about what for a long time now I have noticed concerning the
fourth chapter of Paul's Epistle to the Galatians.⁷ I was reading the Epistles
of Paul, as I frequently do – sometimes in Greek or sometimes in Latin, in
whichever text may be at hand – not (to be sure) to test my ability to arouse   40
someone's envy by comparing the Latin with the Greek, but in order that the
meaning of the texts become more fixed in my memory. And so, when I had
come to the passage where the old translation says, 'Sinai is a mountain in
Arabia which is said to be joined to the one that is now in Jerusalem,' examining the matter carefully, I could not but be surprised that its actual location   45
differs so much from Paul's words. For it is a fact that the mountain which is
said to be joined to Jerusalem is distant from that city by a journey of many
days. My perplexity was also much increased by the explanation of Thomas,
who first says that these places were twenty days' journey apart but gives
the explanation that they are said to be joined because of the uninterrupted   50
journey of the Jews.⁸

     And so at that time, suspecting what was really meant, I decided to
consult the Greek text. That easily removed all doubt. For the text is τὸ γὰρ
Ἅγαρ Σινᾶ ὄρος ἐστὶ<ν> ἐν τῇ Ἀραβίᾳ συστοιχεῖ δὲ τῇ νῦν Ἰερουσαλήμ.⁹ Unless I am
in error, the true understanding of these words is much different from that   55
in both the old translation as well as yours, which I had no hesitation about
examining at the same time. For the verb συστοιχεῖ means neither 'is joined
to' [conjunctus est] nor 'borders on' [confinis est], as I was surprised that you
translated it.¹⁰ For σύστοιχα, as Aristotle shows in many places, are things that
have in common a certain proportion or relation. And such a relation is ev-   60
erywhere called by the same philosopher συστοιχία, as in the first and third

* * * * *

7 Ie Gal 4:25
8 See Thomas Aquinas *Super Epistolam B. Pauli ad Galatas lectura* chapter 4
   lecture 8.
9 'Hagar is Mount Sinai in Arabia; it corresponds to (συστοιχεῖ) present-day
   Jerusalem.' In the Vulgate the Greek verb is translated as *coniunctus est*, which
   could mean 'is joined to.' As Sepúlveda points out, however, that could not be
   literally true of two places so far apart. Hence the difficulty of understanding
   the passage and translating it correctly.
10 *Confinis est* means both 'has common borders with' and 'is closely related to.'
   Sepúlveda is here being more literal-minded than Erasmus. There was no fundamental disagreement between them over the metaphorical nature of the
   passage in Galatians; cf n13 below.

books concerning the physiology of hearing, and likewise in the first book of the *Nicomachaean Ethics*,[11] and in many other places.

Although it seems to me that no one uses this word more frequently than Aristotle, still Suidas makes its meaning very clear. 'ούστοιχα is a word applied   65 to things that are like one another in certain respects,' he says, 'which also may be according to analogy, etc,'[12] so that it seems to me that this passage could be more appropriately translated in this way: 'For Hagar is Mount Sinai in Arabia. It has the same proportions as what is now Jerusalem.' The meaning is: Sinai, which is figuratively applied to Hagar, is a mountain in Arabia, which   70 has the same proportions as the one in the city of Jerusalem, which we now see with our bodily eyes; for like this city it is also earthly, and both are related in the same manner to the one on high, that is, the heavenly Jerusalem.[13]

I have been led to write these things to you by the nature of my duty and by my devotion to you. It will be up to you in turn to write back to me what   75 you think, what you have done, what you are planning to write. Farewell.

From Rome, 23 October in the year 1533 after the birth of Christ

2873A / From Bonifacius Amerbach   [Basel, mid-October 1533]

This letter (= AK Ep 1783) was first published by Allen. The manuscript, a hasty rough draft, is in the Öffentliche Bibliothek of the University of Basel (MS C VIA 73 425). Noting that a precise date was not possible, Allen saw 'the matters you raised recently' in line 7 as quite possibly a reference to Erasmus' request for Bonifacius' opinion on the royal divorce in England, a request to which Bonifacius responded at length in Ep 2267. On this basis he assigned the conjectural date '? January 1530' and published the letter as Ep 2259 in his volume VIII. As the AK editor Alfred Hartmann points out, however, the draft of the letter is on the recto of a page, the verso of which contains a letter clearly dated in October 1533. In his letter to Bonifacius of 30 November, moreover (Ep 2883:5), Erasmus makes reference to 'a post that has been offered' (cf line 8 below), and in a letter to Viglius Zuichemus of 18 November (Ep 2878:42) he writes that 'Amerbach promised he would be here within a fortnight' (cf lines 5–6 below).

* * * * *

11 The subject of hearing is treated at length in the *Physics*. We could not find the word in the *Nicomachean Ethics*.
12 Greek in the text. See *Suidas lexicon* ed A. Adler 5 vols (Stuttgart 1971) under σύστοιχα.
13 For Erasmus' response to Sepúlveda on this matter see Ep 2905:18–33. For his treatment of the subject in his Paraphrase on Galatians see CWE 42 119, with nn21–2 on pages 166–7.

All this points to a date in mid-October 1533. We have placed the letter at the end of the letters for that month.

Cordial greetings. This old man is asking me if there is anything I wish to convey to you. Since nothing occurs to me at present, I have nothing to write, and so I write this: as I never cease to urge you, and as I think you have long been convinced, you can make use of my services always and everywhere according to your wishes. Within ten days, or fourteen at the most, 5 unless something else turns up, I have to go to Freiburg on business for my father-in-law.[1] Then we can talk about the matters you raised recently.[2] But I shall need your advice also on the terms that are now being offered to me.[3] Farewell, Erasmus, my most distinguished friend.

2874 / To Justus Ludovicus Decius   Freiburg, 1 November 1533

This letter was first published in the epistolary appendix to De praeparatione ad mortem (Basel: Froben and Episcopius 1534) pages 115–25. The manuscript, an autograph rough draft, is in the Royal Library at Copenhagen (MS GKS 95 Fol, folio 164 verso). Justus Decius (Ep 1341A n210) was secretary to King Sigismund I of Poland and a patron of humanist scholars.

ERASMUS OF ROTTERDAM SENDS GREETINGS TO JUSTUS DECIUS, SECRETARY TO THE KING OF POLAND
I have long been beholden to you in many ways, my dearest friend Justus, but day after day you make me even more indebted to you by heaping up your services to me. Please know that what is most pleasing to me among 5 them is that you give me careful and reliable information about what is happening, both publicly and privately, in Poland, and that you take care that the letters of my friends to me and mine to them arrive safely, even though we are separated by such an immense distance.

* * * * *

2873A
1 Leonhard Fuchs, burgomaster of Neuenburg am Rhein, a small town halfway between Freiburg and Basel
2 Doubtless the question of a new will. On 26 November 1533 Erasmus made and signed a new will in his home at Freiburg; see Ep 2754 n7, and cf Ep 2883:2–3.
3 By the city council of Strasbourg, which at least since 1531 had considered Bonifacius a suitable candidate for the post of legal adviser (AK Ep 1549). An offer had now been made (AK Ep 1784), and negotiations by correspondence continued until 25 January 1535, when Bonifacius sent a letter (AK Ep 1898) rejecting the offer. Cf Ep 2883:5–6.

In these past two years we have suffered the grievous loss of friends,   10
especially William Warham, the archbishop of Canterbury, who to me was
one equal to many.[1] And so I am all the more eager to enjoy the ones who are
left. One must also endeavour to make up the loss of old friends by gaining
new ones. And in that regard I could not even hope for anyone more fitting
than you, who offer yourself to me spontaneously.   15

I have sometimes had it in mind to warn you about something, but
because it seemed somewhat petty to do so, I have thus far preferred to conceal my thoughts. But now, since the shamelessness of some people increases
daily, I am forced to warn my special friends not to allow themselves to be
imposed upon any longer. You know that in our times there are certain vag-   20
abonds, not to say swindlers, flitting around, whose resources are as thin
as a snake's sloughed-off skin and who find nothing sweeter than idleness
and other people's food.[2] This (if it please the gods above) they call freedom.
Some of them have devised a new trick: either from my writings or from
what others say, they find out who are my close friends and where they are.   25
They approach them, boasting that they are my servants or disciples and
that they are such fierce defenders of my reputation (if it please the gods)
that they are prepared not only to fight singlehanded for Erasmus but also to
die for him. They make up things about me that they think will be welcome
to the ears of my friends: that Erasmus is a champion in combat,[3] that he   30
hammers out divine lucubrations. What more? that he is completely trium-
phant. In the meantime they are received hospitably for several days, sometimes for months, and are sent away with provisions for their journey. For
however many of these tricksters there are and wherever they arrive, they do
so having been robbed by thieves.   35

But it is even more amusing how some of them hunt out this lucre from
those who they think are enemies of Erasmus. To them they tell incredible
tales: some say that Erasmus fell from his horse and broke his neck; some that
he is lying in his sickbed suffering from an incurable disease; some that he
has been buried. And to dispel any doubts, they add the place, the year, the   40
month, the day, and the hour; finally they say they were present at his burial
and trampled on his grave. Nor was there any lack of those who spread the
rumour that Erasmus, together with Oecolampadius,[4] was beaten with rods

* * * * *

2874
1 See Epp 2726:35–62, 2758:35–79, 2776:28–51.
2 Cf Ep 2798:42–63.
3 Literally 'in the pancratium,' a contest that includes both wrestling and boxing
4 Johannes Oecolampadius (d 1531), leader of the Reformation at Basel

and driven from Basel. And these actors are applauded in their theatre. And
although the facts so often convict them of their mendacity, they are still so   45
unashamed to go on making up similar stories. Those who tell such tales
must have lost all shame. There is actually a danger that because of these
tricksters no one will believe I have died when I really reach my last day. And
in fact that cannot be far off, since I am old, sickly, worn out by so much work
and so many troubles. But I take pity on these people and I pray for nothing   50
more than that they be given sounder minds.

      I return to my eulogists, whose wiles could be overlooked except that
some of them defraud my friends quite shamelessly, extorting considerable
sums from rich men and princes, so that through their conduct I am rendered beholden and am forced to give thanks for the sake of people I either   55
do not know or know only well enough to consider completely undeserving
of consideration. From many examples I will recount a few, to give you a
laugh. Almost ten years ago in Basel a certain young man was arrested during a fight because he would not sheathe his sword after peace had been in-
voked – which is almost a capital crime there – and was thrown into prison.[5]   60
I did not know him even by sight. I suspect that at some time or other he had
been employed in printshops. My friends urged me to ask pardon for him,
through the good offices of the ambassador of the king of England, a most
benevolent gentleman, who happened to be there at the time.[6] On the previous day the ambassador had paid a courtesy call on me because he had heard   65
that, in addition to the burden of my occupations, my health was not very
good. Nevertheless, the importunate demands of such people had so much
influence over me that I came before the royal ambassador, acting as an ambassador myself for a morally depraved scoundrel. In the evening I met the
ambassador, who was extremely busy; I briefly explained the matter, and on   70
the following day that 'warrior' was released. The city council thought that
they had done me a great favour, and I was obliged to render them elaborate
thanks for it. Do you think that at this point the released man thanked me?
On the very same day he was released, he got drunk in a printshop on the
printer's wine and gave Erasmus such a tonguelashing that he would have   75
threatened to dispatch me with his drawn sword if I had been present. Asked

        * * * * *

    5 The young man was Benoît Vaugris; for him and this incident, see Ep 1395
      introduction.
    6 Presumably Richard Pace (Ep 350) whom Henry VIII had sent on a mission to
      Switzerland in 1523; see *Letters and Papers, Foreign and Domestic, of the Reign of
      Henry VIII* ed J.S. Brewer et al 36 vols (London 1862–1932) vol 3/2 1223 item 2901.

on the next day if he really meant what he had said, he gave drunkenness
as an excuse – a sufficient justification in this tribunal! I suspect he had conceived this anger against me because I seemed not to approve of the 'gospel'
which at that time they had dug up from some grave or other. At that time I   80
said nothing about all this. He departed without saying goodbye. He went
to Constance. There he boasted to Botzheim,[7] a singularly honourable friend
of mine, that he was my servant and that, after I had dismissed him with
great gratitude, he had set out for some place or other. He was treated most
kindly for several weeks and then sent away, not without a gift. I learned   85
this afterwards by chance, when Botzheim told me about it. I have no doubt
that he planned similar deceits against others, especially Melanchthon, with
whom he knew I was exceptionally friendly and who even so was still much
favoured by important people who at that time were inclined to the teachings of Luther. He is familiar with such people and embraces this gospel. I   90
know someone else who is also well known to you,[8] for he has frequently
gone to Poland. There, among the powerful and generous lovers of Erasmus,
he proclaimed that he was a servant of Erasmus, who had sent him to greet
all his friends (whereas, in fact, at Basel I hardly knew him even by sight, and
he venerated me so much that he did not even tip his hat when we passed   95
by each other). Nevertheless, by this trick he scraped together quite a few
gold coins, so that he now lives at leisure, very evangelically, and is no more
fair to me than if I had stripped him of all his resources. Another one came
to me who had never seen me nor I him.[9] He was returning from Rome, on
his way back to Bruges, where he lived. He did not conceal that he had been   100
a Franciscan, though I had not asked him about it. When I saw that he was
shabbily dressed, I asked him where he got his travel money. He frankly
said that he lived on what he got by begging. When I said I hardly believed
that people would be that generous, he added that in Germany he feigned
that Erasmus was his master. When I expressed surprise that my name was   105
so well received in Germany, he replied that everyone gave gladly to a servant of Erasmus, except for two priests in the town of Laufenburg,[10] who
did give him something, but grumbling because he had mentioned Erasmus.
In Germany at least he found the name of Erasmus holier for him than that
of Francis. What did I do? you ask. What else could I do? I laughed at the   110

* * * * *

7 Johann von Botzheim (Ep 1285)
8 Unidentified
9 Unidentified
10 A town on the Rhine, 46 kilometres east of Basel

barefaced shamelessness of the man, and for the honour paid to me gave him
some coins as travel money. Some of them have a set speech that they have
learned by heart. They use it on many people, with a few minor changes in
the wording. If not accorded an interview, they send it in writing. If asked
where they come from and where they are going, they say different things   115
to different people, whatever is suited to extorting something. Some of them
are afraid that servants will keep them from speaking to their masters unless
they bring letters from friends; so they lie, saying that they have them but
that they are such that they can only be delivered person to person. If they
get a chance to speak, the gist of their speech is this: they want to be assisted   120
at least by some advice. 'For what purpose?' 'To complete my journey.' 'What
is holding you back?' 'The lack of travel money.' 'What need drove you to
undertake this expedition?' 'To see learned men, and you in particular.' 'By
what advice do you think to acquire travel money? ' 'If you give it.' 'Easy
advice! But that is to ask for help, not advice.' Others reply that they are   125
looking for a job. 'What kind of job? Do you want to be a servant to someone
or to work in a printer's shop?' 'By no means.' 'What then?' 'I want to have
time for literature.' 'But what kind of literature?' 'Good literature.' (For he
is ashamed to confess that he is possessed by a love of new dogmas.) 'But is
there travel money at hand to support studies?' 'Not at all.' 'Then what hope   130
do you have?' 'That someone will supply it.' Such charming fellows! From
people they do not know and who are even of different religion they seek the
means to live at leisure, at their own whim and in their own comfort. I know
such things seem ridiculous and foolish, but such foolishness has serious
consequences. If magistrates would consider how harmful it is to the com-   135
monwealth to have young people grow accustomed to idleness and for the
world to become gradually full of meddlesome and lazy vagabonds, they
would soon look for ways to obviate such a danger. Little boys are learning
the same thing, begging under the pretext of going to school and doing nothing but playing. If they are offered a job as a servant to someone, they reject it.   140
As for learning to write so as to earn something, they don't want to. So sweet
is that miserable and squalid leisure. And then what is to become of them
when they reach adolescence? They have no command of reading and writing, they despise the religious life, and they have not learned any trade. What
can they do except run off to war and under the cover of military service   145
learn brigandage? Germany produces talents that are by no means unfruit-
ful, if they were properly brought up from their youngest years. But worse
than these are the ones who have grown up, are educated, and are burdened
with religious instruction, but who nevertheless wander about idly, looking
like soldiers, shamelessly abusing not only my name but that of great kings   150

and princes, when in fact they serve no one but Comus and his wife Methe,[11] as if they had been born for nothing but the gullet and the belly.

But I will not now recount their stratagems. For they are an Iliad of evils.[12] I will just warn you so that you yourself will be wary of such people and can warn our friends to be wary of them. 'How shall I be wary?' you will ask. By not believing any of their stories unless they produce letters signed by my own hand in which they are recommended by name. They will say that they ran into robbers and were stripped of all their belongings, and that the letters were also taken from them. Don't believe them. You are experienced enough to read the deception in their faces. And don't too easily put your faith in letters. At Siena I had a pupil, titular archbishop of St Andrew, illegitimate son of the king of Scotland, a young man of exceptional intelligence and upright character.[13] In the margins of a codex I had never seen, he imitated my handwriting so well that I myself would have been deceived if I had not known for certain that I had never seen or read the codex. He pressed me, saying I had forgotten it. 'Otherwise,' he said, 'where would this handwriting of yours have come from?' 'I recognize the handwriting,' I said, 'but before this I have never laid eyes on this book or any book like it.' Finally he laughed and admitted his trick. To these stories I will add just one more little tale, and I will not burden you with any more of them. Almost twelve years ago, Christophe de Longueil, a man of great literary skill (which would have been the very greatest if the Fates had granted him a longer life) visited us at Louvain, on his way back to Italy.[14] After we had been at one or two dinner parties, he asked for a private conversation. I agreed. He asked if I was acquainted with anyone named Sylvius. I said I knew the poems of a certain Ambosianus. He shook his head. Moreover, I had seen François Dubois at Louvain.[15] 'Both of them,' Longueil said, 'are advanced in years. The one I am asking about was

* * * * *

11 Comus was the god of revelry, Methe the goddess of drunkenness, but in ancient mythology they were not married.
12 Ie a long tale featuring every kind of evil (*Adagia* I iii 26)
13 Alexander Stewart, illegitimate son of James IV of Scotland (Ep 604:4n)
14 Longueil (Ep 914 introduction) had spent two or three days with Erasmus at Louvain in October 1519; see Ep 1011 n1. Cf Ep 2798:53–63, where Erasmus tells this same story.
15 *Ambosianus* is probably Erasmus' mistake for *Ambianus* ('from Amiens') the name used by Jacques Dubois of Amiens (Jacobus Sylvius Ambianus), the younger brother of François Dubois (Sylvius), also of Amiens. For both, and their connection with Erasmus, see Epp 1407 n26, 1600.

seventeen or eighteen years old.' When he saw that I did not know any other
Sylvius, he told a tale of quite amusing audacity, as the comic poet says.[16] A
teenager calling himself by the name Sylvius (which I imagine was fictitious),   180
who had run away, as Longueil said, from a Benedictine monastery came to
Rome. He had heard that I was a close friend of Paulo Bombace, who (in my
experience) was the brightest talent in Italy.[17] He had learned about the favour bestowed on me by Leo x, which I wish I had used more skilfully.[18] This
Sylvius had fabricated two letters of recommendation I had allegedly written   185
for him, one to Bombace and one to Leo. He easily deceived Bombace, a man
not at all suspicious, who was also such a good friend to me that if someone
brought greetings from Erasmus, Bombace would embrace him most heartily.
The young man's audacity was so exceptional that, perfectly conscious of his
impudent deceitfulness, he did not fear to approach the prince of the whole   190
world, the supreme pontiff Leo. 'I have a letter from Erasmus,' he said. He
was admitted. He submitted the forged letter. Who would have ever suspected that such an audacious crime could have entered into the head of a man
so young? In his kindness Leo embraced him, lifting him up from his prostra-
tion with both arms and promising him everything. So great was the power   195
of a forged recommendation from Erasmus. When, however, Sylvius delayed
in returning to the supreme pontiff, Leo himself, on his own initiative, asked
where the young man was who was recommended by Erasmus. But Sylvius,
seized by a fever, died while he was on the road, before he had reached the
pontiff, who was at that time residing at Ostia. And so the comedy was inter-   200
rupted; otherwise it would have had many other acts. If a similar bird flies
into your Poland, warn my friends about him, especially the more kind and
generous among them, such as the reverend lord bishop Piotr of Cracow,[19]
Krzycki, bishop of Płock,[20] Johannes Dantiscus, bishop of Chełmno,[21] Erazm,

* * * * *

16 Terence *Phormio* 1.2.84
17 Ep 210
18 This does not appear to be a reference to a specific favour bestowed by Pope
    Leo. It is more likely a reference to the great kindness of Cardinal Giovanni de'
    Medici (the future Pope Leo) to Erasmus during his visit to Rome in 1509; see
    Epp 296:107–111, 335:8–15.
19 Piotr Tomicki (Ep 2861)
20 Andrzej Krzycki (Ep 1629)
21 Ep 2163 n34

abbot of Mogila,[22] Jan Łaski, provost of Gniezno,[23] Seweryn Boner,[24] Antonin   205
the physician,[25] and whoever else greatly esteems me – not that I would hin-
der them from giving of their wealth to whomever they wish, but because I
would not like to have my friends cheated by panderers using my name and
because I don't want myself to be put under such false obligations. I hope that
you and all who are dear to you are in the best of health.   210

Given at Freiburg im Breisgau, 1 November 1533

2875 / To Bonifacius Amerbach   Freiburg, 6 November 1533

This letter (= AK Ep 1788) was first published in the *Epistolae familiares*. The
autograph is in the Öffentliche Bibliothek of the University of Basel (MS AN III
15 54).

Greetings. If this man Viglius encounters you in Basel,[1] I beg that you redou-
ble for him your inborn generosity, which you customarily extend to all good
and learned men, since nowhere will you find a man more upright than he.
I will not add anything more, lest I waste the effort. We are waiting for you.[2]
Farewell. Cordial greetings to Basilius.[3]   5

Freiburg, 6 November 1533
Your Erasmus of Rotterdam
To Master Bonifacius Amerbach. At Basel

* * * * *

22 Erazm Ciołek (Ep 2811 n1)
23 Ep 2862
24 Ep 2533
25 Jan Antonin (Ep 1602)

2875
1 While still in Padua, Viglius Zuichemus had sent to the Froben press the manuscript of his edition of Theophilus Antecessor's Greek translation of the *Institutes*;
see Ep 2791 n22. Now, having visited Erasmus at Freiburg, Viglius was going
to Basel to see the work through the press (Epp 2878 n2, 2885:1–6, 2888:10–13,
2925:1–5). During his stay there, which lasted until February 1534, Viglius did in
fact encounter Bonifacius, whose friend and correspondent he remained in the
years that followed.
2 See Ep 2878:42–4.
3 Bonifacius' older brother

2876 / To Conradus Goclenius   Freiburg, 7 November 1533

This letter was first published in the *Vita Erasmi*. For Goclenius see Ep 2851
introduction.

ERASMUS OF ROTTERDAM TO MASTER CONRADUS GOCLENIUS,
GREETINGS
How shall I greet you? As an ass or a king?[1] I am terrified by what is por-
tended by the church that burned down in Antwerp, if the rumour that flew
here is true.[2] Bishop Johannes Dantiscus writes that the city of which he was   5
lord and where he owned the central castle burned down so completely that
nothing was left except rubble and the city walls. Before that Chełmno, his
metropolitan city, burned down.[3] In various places there are stories of various and prodigious fires. I do not know what this means, except that, as was
once true about Africa, this gospel now brings us something new every day.[4]   10
    Jan van Campen has, I think, already left Poland, making his way, with
detours, to visit Venice in order to talk with a certain Jew, a meeting with whom
has been promised to him by Aleandro, who now lives there in an openly

＊ ＊ ＊ ＊ ＊

2876
  1 Ie 'either victor or vanquished' (*Adagia* III v 41). See Ep 2851:61–2, where
    Goclenius cites this adage in connection with his lawsuit to acquire a canonry
    at the Cathedral of Our Lady in Antwerp (cf following note).
  2 Cf Epp 2877:11, 2906:87–8. On the night of 5–6 October 1533 the cathedral at
    Antwerp was severely damaged by fire, but the building was not destroyed.
  3 Cf Ep 2877:16–18. Apart from Ep 2563A, no letter to Erasmus from Johannes
    Dantiscus (Ep 2163 n4) has survived. As bishop of Chełmno, Dantiscus' main
    residence was a castle at Lubawa, a little over 100 kilometres to the east of
    Chełmno. There was a disastrous fire in that town on 20 June 1533, though the
    castle itself was spared. Erasmus' report of the earlier burning of the city of
    Chełmno, however, rests on a misunderstanding of Dantiscus' letter. Erasmus
    refers to the town that burned as *Culmum*. There is no record of a fire at Chełmno
    (*Culma*) in this period. But there was a fire in 1531 at Chełmża (*Culmense*), an
    important town in the diocese of Chełmno about 26 kilometres north and a
    bit west of Chełmno. Both fires are referred to in a letter of 17 July 1533 from
    Dantiscus to Piotr Tomicki; see *Acta Tomiciana ... Epistolarum, legationum, respon-*
    sorum, actionum et rerum gestarum Serenissimi Principis Sigismundi Primi Regis
    Poloniae ... vol 15, ed Władysław Pociecha (Wrocław / Kraków 1957) 490–1.
    (Thanks are due to Dr Anna Skolimowska of the University of Warsaw for sup-
    plying the information on which this note is based.)
  4 See *Adagia* III vii 10: *Semper Africa novi aliquid apportat* 'Africa always produces
    something novel.'

Epicurean style, though not without dignity.[5] In my last letter to Dantiscus I made honourable mention of Campen. For that he thanked me profusely, not 15 concealing that he had suspected I was possessed by an implacable hatred of him, because I had not sent him any greetings for five whole years.[6] I had a good laugh at this because I had never so much as dreamed of any hatred for him. I understand that at Paris there is a brotherhood of Germans presided over by Carinus, who proclaims how in Christian charity he has forgiven me 20 for the horrible crimes I have committed.[7] Guinterius of Andernach is there;[8] from a letter of his I understand that Paschasius often writes to him.[9] You do not need any prudent guide. In the end, after all, they will overwhelm you if you write to them often.

* * * * *

5 In the autumn of 1531 Jan van Campen resigned his post as professor of Hebrew at the Collegium Trilingue at Louvain and entered the service of Johannes Dantiscus, then Polish ambassador to the imperial court; see Ep 2570 n30. In the autumn of 1532 he accompanied Dantiscus to Poland, where he quickly established contact with Erasmus' Polish friends and continued his scholarly work. He lectured briefly at the University of Cracow in January 1534, which means that at this point he had not yet left Poland, though his plans for doing so were evidently well known. He departed in the winter or spring of 1534, making his way to Venice in pursuit of his ambition to meet the celebrated Hebrew scholar Elias Levita (for whom see Ep 2447 n4). On his arrival in Venice (25 May 1534) Campen joined the household of Girolamo Aleandro, who was living there as papal legate (Ep 2810 n22).

6 Neither Erasmus' letter to Dantiscus nor Campen's to Erasmus is extant.

7 For Ludovicus Carinus and the enmity between him and Erasmus, see Epp 2111 n2, 2779:37–60. Carinus was currently living at Paris, where he was tutor to the sons of Eucharis Holzach of Basel; see AK Ep 1780:18–23.

8 Johannes Guinterius of Andernach, also known as Johann Winter von Andernach (d 1574), studied and taught Greek at Louvain before proceeding to Paris (1526) to study medicine (doctorate in October 1532). In November 1534 he became one of the two professors of medicine at the University of Paris and by the following year he was one of the royal physicians. He used his knowledge of Greek in a long series of translations of Greek medical authors. Possibly because of his evangelical faith, Guinterius left Paris in about 1538 for Metz and Strasbourg, where in 1544, with the support of Martin Bucer, he was appointed to teach Greek and medicine at the Gymnasium.

9 For Paschasius Berselius of Liège, who shared Guinterius' interest in Greek, see Ep 674.

Melanchthon has been summoned to Poland. I learned this through a   25
letter from the bishop of Płock, who summoned him.[10] And Melanchthon
himself, in his commentary on the Epistle to the Romans and in a private letter to me, makes it sufficiently clear that he is displeased by his own people.[11]
Towards the end of the month of September, I received a letter from Dilft,[12]
written in Spain in the month of May, together with a letter from Juan de   30
Vergara.[13] Both promise money from the archbishop of Toledo.[14] But neither
mentions the amount.[15] Not so much as the shadow of any money has come
to me. Dilft said nothing to my servant Quirinus when he was there,[16] and
he sent no written word through him. Indeed he dismissed him, promising
that he would send a letter to you through a servant of his own. Here we get   35
help from the saying in the tragedy: the gods have many shapes.[17] I think that
what I wrote through Lieven has been delivered to you faithfully.[18] I have
not abandoned the plan to return.[19] That rumour was spread about, much
against my wishes. It is easy to read the minds of some people. I am sorry

* * * * *

10 Cf Ep 2911:21–6. The letter of Andrzej Krzycki, bishop of Płock, is not extant.
    Neither is the original letter of invitation from Krzycki to Melanchthon, but in
    a letter of 10 January 1535 he reiterated his offer of support for the quiet pur-
    suit of Melanchthon's humanistic studies if he would dissociate himself from
    heretics and come to Poland (MBW Ep 1526).
11 The private letter is perhaps Ep 2732, in which Melanchthon complains that
    'neither side' in the religious controversy is interested in moderation, and urges
    Erasmus to continue his efforts in support of peace. See especially n2 in that
    letter. As for the commentary on Romans (Ep 2818 n19) the reference may be
    to the dedicatory letter to Albert, cardinal-archbishop-elector of Mainz (MSA
    5 28:25–29:9) where Melanchthon diplomatically expresses his distaste for all
    manner of religious controversy. In both cases, Erasmus gives a tendentious
    reading to what was actually said.
12 Frans van der Dilft (Ep 2904 introduction)
13 Ep 2879
14 Alonso de Fonseca (Ep 1748)
15 Neither letter is extant.
16 'There' being Antwerp, to which Dilft had returned by July 1533, when Quirinus
    Hagius was on his way home to Freiburg from London via the Low Countries
    (Ep 2804 n7)
17 Cited in Greek: Euripides *Andromache* 1284 and *Helen* 1688
18 Probably Ep 2863. Lieven Algoet, who had been sent to Freiburg to bring
    Erasmus back to Brabant (see following note) had departed Freiburg towards
    the end of August 1533.
19 Ie the plan to return to Brabant, which had been postponed but not abandoned;
    see Ep 2820 introduction.

that the Collegium has languished so quickly,[20] and I see that it will perish 40
unless the president and the trustees take care that they have diligent professors.[21] Campen is gone.[22] You litigate (even though you are unmarried).[23]
Rescius supports many people.[24] I have written this through Viglius, who
will take the place of a long letter from me.[25]

    Farewell. Freiburg, 7 November 1533 45
    Erasmus of Rotterdam, in my own hand

2877 / To Nicolaus Olahus   Freiburg, 7 November 1533

> This letter was first published in Ipolyi page 424. The manuscript is page 358
> of the Olahus codex in the Hungarian National Archives at Budapest (Ep 2339
> introduction). For Nicolaus Olahus, secretary to Queen Mary, regent of the
> Netherlands, see Ep 2813.

ERASMUS OF ROTTERDAM TO NICOLAUS OLAHUS,
TREASURER OF SZÉKESFEHÉRVÁR, ETC
How I wish that your court would welcome the likes of Viglius Zuichemus,[1]
who is delivering this letter,[2] a young man of spotless character, a doctor of
law, who taught publicly at Padua, not without a struggle but also not with- 5
out glory. And he is up to his own high standards in humane studies. No

* * * * *

20 The Collegium Trilingue at Louvain, which had commenced operations in 1518
21 From December 1529 until his death in July 1536, Joost van der Hoeven was
    president of the Collegium Trilingue at Louvain. His long experience as beadle
    and notary of the faculty of theology and his acquaintance with the trustees of
    the college and its faculty enabled him to be a successful and well-liked man-
    ager of the college.
22 See n5 above.
23 Another reference to Goclenius' suit to acquire a canonry at Antwerp. See *Adagia*
    IV ii 35: *Qui non litigat caelebs est* 'If he has no disputes, he is a bachelor.' (*Litigare*
    means both 'go to law' and 'to dispute, quarrel.')
24 For Rutgerus Rescius, professor of Greek at the Trilingue, his marriage, and his
    family, see Ep 2644 n19.
25 Erasmus appears to have given this letter and Ep 2877 to Viglius Zuichemus
    on his departure for Basel; see Ep 2875 n1. But Viglius returned to Freiburg in
    February 1534 on his journey north; see Ep 2878 n2. So the letters were doubt-
    less entrusted to some other messenger.

2877
1 Ep 2810
2 See Ep 2876 n25.

gem is clearer than his mind. Those who do not deserve recommendations manage to extort a great many. This young man did not ask for a single word of recommendation. For my own part I ask only this: that you become acquainted with a young man of such remarkable talents.   10

They write that the principal church at Antwerp has burned down.[3] What is the meaning of all these fires? They write that some little towns around Cologne have been destroyed by fire. According to a persistent rumour, a town that is a day's journey from here was consumed by a fire set by a demon.[4] They also say that some villages in Switzerland have burned   15 down. Johannes Dantiscus, the bishop of Chełmno, writes that the cathedral city of Chełmno has burned down, and also that another town where he has a castle was so consumed by fire that nothing remains but the city walls.[5] It seems to me that these things are not happening just by chance. There is a rumour here that the king of England is living with his wife Catherine as he   20 did before. Though this seems hardly credible, I wish it were absolutely true.[6] Concerning my proposed return,[7] nothing has changed, unless something new happens there in the meantime. I beg that you preserve your feelings for me and that you promote the favour of the queen. Greetings to the Dane and Lieven.[8]   25

Farewell. Freiburg, 7 November 1533

2878 / To Viglius Zuichemus   Freiburg, 18 November 1533

This letter was first published in LB III/2 1759–60 *Appendix epistolarum* no 374. The autograph, address sheet missing and date obliterated, is in the University Library at Leiden (MS Papenbroeck 2). Allen took the date from LB. Viglius' reply is Ep 2888. For Viglius Zuichemus see Ep 2810 introduction.

* * * * *

3 See Ep 2876:3–5.
4 See Ep 2846:127–55.
5 See Ep 2876 n3.
6 The rumour was not true; in mid-January 1533 Henry VIII secretly married the already pregnant Anne Boleyn, and on 1 June Anne was crowned in Westminster Abbey. It was presumably knowledge of the latter event that made the rumour seem 'hardly credible' to Erasmus.
7 Ie the proposed return to Brabant (Ep 2820 introduction)
8 Jakob Jespersen (Ep 2849) and Lieven Algoet (Ep 2820 introduction)

For your eyes only[1]

Cordial greetings. You wanted others to know more about you than I do. You told me you would delay there for a few days, but from what I understand through others, your intention seems to be to spend the whole winter there.[2] And I pray that everything will be propitious and fortunate for you. 5
I am glad to have you nearby for a while. The one thing I advise and beg you, out of my devotion to you, is to avoid completely the contamination of the sects and not to give them any opportunity to spread it about that Zuichemus is one of them. Even when you agree with their dogmas, do not let them see it. But I do not want you to argue with them. It is sufficient for a lawyer to 10
elude them as a dying man eluded the devil. The devil tempted the man by asking him what believed. He said, 'What the church believes.' The devil said, 'What does the church believe.' 'What I believe.' 'What do you believe?' 'What the church believes.'[3] I hope this warning is superfluous. But if we could speak to one another in person, I would make you understand that I 15
am not warning you without reason.

I know that Thomas More, Tunstall,[4] and other learned men have an extremely low opinion of Grynaeus.[5] When he went to England, he wrung recommendations out of me. I gave recommendations to a few people, but reluctantly. I advised him that if he had any attraction to the sects in England, 20
he should not let it be known. He ignored this advice so thoroughly that in many letters sent while he was there he defended the opinions of Zwingli. He did not even hesitate to write frequently to More concerning such matters. Finally he decided to dedicate to More his Plato,[6] which he had corrupted in many places, and he would have done so if I had not persuaded him 25

* * * * *

2878
1 Greek in the text
2 Viglius had gone to Basel to see his edition of the *Institutes* through the Froben press, and would remain there until 7 January 1534, when he paid another visit to Erasmus in Freiburg on his way home to the Netherlands; see Epp 2871 n2, 2875 n1, 2887 n4. Erasmus had hoped to retain Viglius as a permanent resident of his household and offered to make Viglius his heir if he would stay; see *Vita Viglii Zuichemi* 13.
3 Erasmus gives the same advice in *De praeparatione ad mortem* (Ep 2884 introduction), the writing of which was under way at this point; see CWE 70 441–2.
4 Cuthbert Tunstall, bishop of London
5 For More's views, see Ep 2831 n13.
6 An edition published by Froben at Basel in 1531

not to. For that, More was most grateful to me. But without my knowledge he dedicated his Euclid to Tunstall.[7] But I know for certain that More and Tunstall hate those sectarians more than the serpent. I recently advised Grynaeus not to write with familiarity to those who completely detest the dogmas that he defends. Now he is doing so, in order to obtain an annual pension from the archbishop of Canterbury.[8] And what is even more amusing, in one of his letters he included these words: 'You would do well, if, like a leech that has sucked itself full,[9] you would yield the Canterbury pension to a hungry man like me.' When he calls me a leech, he judges me by his own temperament. And this man of different religious beliefs, someone who has never deserved anything at all from me, asks me to provide him with two hundred florins a year – something a brother would never dare to ask even from a brother who liked him.[10] Judge from this how shameless he is, though he manages to look as if he were the very soul of respectability.

In person, between the two of us, I would have said more about these and other matters – if that were allowed by a pair of theologians and doctors![11]

Amerbach promised he would be here within a fortnight. Thirty days have gone by.[12] I would like to know whether he has set out for somewhere, or whether he is not well.

My servant Gilbert has not returned.[13] I suspect that the rascal has spent some days in Basel, carousing with his drinking companions.

* * * * *

7 The *editio princeps* of the Greek text (Basel: Johann Herwagen 1533)

8 Thomas Cranmer, who had succeeded William Warham in March 1533. Erasmus is the only source for this report of Grynaeus seeking a pension from Cranmer, but it is surely relevant here that Grynaeus' Latin translation of Plutarch's *Sitne rationis aliqua in bestiis vis*, dedicated to the archbishop, had been published by Johann Bebel at Basel in March1534; cf Diarmaid MacCulloch *Thomas Cranmer: A Life* (New Haven and London 1996) 67.

9 The proverbial image, taken from Horace *Ars poetica* 476, of 'the leech that won't let go till full of blood' (cf *Adagia* II iv 84)

10 If Erasmus is thinking of Rhenish florins, the value of the annual pension Grynaeus wished him to cede was £49 3s 4d groot Flemish, equivalent to five and a half years' wages of an Antwerp master mason/carpenter (CWE 12 650 Table 3, 691 Table 13).

11 The reference is unclear, doubtless deliberately so.

12 Cf Epp 2873A:5–6, 2875:4.

13 Gilbert Cousin had gone home to Burgundy in search of a benefice, and his return to Erasmus' service at Freiburg was currently in doubt; see Epp 2889–90.

I hope that you have found Hieronymus there.[14] I would like to know whether he is ready.[15]

Farewell. Freiburg, 18 November 1533

Your friend Erasmus, in my own hand   50

2879 / To Juan de Vergara   Freiburg, 19 November 1533

This letter, Erasmus' reply to one no longer extant, was first published in the epistolary appendix to *De praeparatione ad mortem* (Basel: Froben and Episcopius 1534) pages 81–92. The manuscript, an autograph rough draft, is in the Royal Library at Copenhagen (MS GKS 95 Fol, folio 107 verso). For Juan de Vergara, secretary to Alonso de Fonseca, archbishop of Toledo, and a faithful friend and champion of Erasmus in Spain, see Epp 1277, 1814. This is Erasmus' last known letter to Vergara. In May 1534 Erasmus would receive from Juan Luis Vives the news of Vergara's arrest in Spain on charges of heresy (Ep 2932:30–1).

The main purpose of this letter is to supply a panegyric of Johann (II) Paumgartner (Ep 2603 introduction), the Augsburg merchant of whom Erasmus had high expectations as a patron; see Epp 2867:19–28, 2868:2–12. Paumgartner's friend Johann Koler (Ep 2195), who carefully guarded his interests, was embarrassed by the letter, thinking it incomprehensible that Erasmus would advertise a German to the world by means of a letter to a Spaniard; see Ep 2936:7–23.

DESIDERIUS ERASMUS OF ROTTERDAM SENDS GREETINGS TO
THE OUTSTANDING THEOLOGIAN MASTER JUAN DE VERGARA

Perhaps it seemed to you that I bear the death of William Warham, the archbishop of Canterbury, with too little restraint, since I poured out my grief 5 in your bosom in such a sorrowful and griefstricken letter.[1] I imagine it also seemed so to your patron, the archbishop.[2] For I received almost the same response from Bernard, the reverend lord bishop and cardinal of Trent, and

* * * * *

14 Ep 2888:3–5 indicates that Hieronymus Froben had been in Freiburg at some point before 10 December, perhaps on the way home to Basel from one of his journeys. Erasmus seems to have worried that Viglius had arrived in Basel while Froben was absent.

15 Presumably ready to publish Viglius' edition of the *Institutes*; see n2 above.

2879

1 Not extant; but for Erasmus' sorrow at the death of Warham, cf Ep 2874 n1.

2 Alonso de Fonseca (Ep 1748)

from Christoph, the bishop of Augsburg.[3] Indeed, in similar circumstances (as you write) I am accustomed to alleviating the sorrow of others, but I have learned by experience that what the writer of comedies says is true: 'If you were here you would feel otherwise.'[4] Nevertheless, to tell you the truth, I myself was somewhat dissatisfied by such severe and prolonged mental distress, and I often said to myself what I would say to others: 'He was mortal; he had reached almost the limits of old age; he lived with the greatest dignity; he was extraordinarily devout; he left behind an honourable memory of himself; from this unhappy exile he moved on to eternal tranquillity; there he is waiting for you, who will soon follow him. If you really love the man, you should congratulate him, not mourn him.' Such admonitions, and many others, I said to my mind, but I was deaf to them all. Nor was there any occasion for what the satirist says: 'Real tears are shed for the loss of money.'[5] If you judge by what in his kindness he offered me, it was huge; if you judge by what I received, it was a tiny amount. But in his friendship I could rest so assured that I considered myself abundantly rich, since I had a patron whom I could ask for anything at all if there happened to be any need for it. No such need befell me, nor is it likely to befall anyone who lives frugally and is content with what bodily necessities demand.

My grief was redoubled by the death of Krzysztof Szydłowiecki, a man of the highest authority in Poland and a most loving friend of mine.[6] The Lord in his mercy has assuaged these wounds with many consolations, and with the trial he has provided a fortunate outcome, so that I can bear it.[7] For the dead archbishop has been succeeded, in rank and position, by the reverend lord Thomas Cranmer, a theologian by profession and a thoroughly upright gentleman with the most spotless morals, who of his own accord promised that he would by no means withdraw the favour and generosity formerly accorded me, and what he spontaneously began he has spontaneously fulfilled, so that it could seem to me that Warham has not been snatched away from me but has been reborn in Cranmer.[8] Augsburg has also provided some generous friends who have come forward voluntarily. Of these the first, both in

* * * * *

3 The letter from Bernhard von Cles was perhaps Ep 2797; that from Christoph von Stadion is not extant.
4 Terence *Andria* 310
5 Juvenal 13.134
6 See Ep 2776 n4.
7 1 Cor 10:13
8 Thomas Cranmer, Warham's replacement as archbishop of Canterbury. Erasmus calls him 'Cronmar.'

time and in generosity, is the reverend lord Christoph von Stadion, the bishop
of Augsburg,[9] a gentleman who is both illustrious in the armorial bearings of 40
his ancestors, and also hardly second to anyone in these regions in prudence,
good judgment, the love of piety, and munificence. Besides him, Augsburg
provides a gentleman more renowned for his mental endowments than for
armorial bearings and richer in virtue than in wealth, Anton Fugger.[10] A close
friend of his is Johann Koler, provost of Chur, a man of spotless integrity.[11] But 45
Johann Paumgartner of Paumgarten and Erbach,[12] a gentleman of ancient nobility and golden character, the most recent of my benefactors in time, yields
to none in the munificent gifts he has bestowed not only on me but on all who
are praised and recommended for their learning and piety. For many years
now Udalricus Zasius, an illustrious ornament of this age, has had him for a 50
friend; now, since Zasius is a most generous soul, he is greatly pleased that he
has him as a friend in common with me.[13]

   The name Fugger is well known and famous among Spaniards, I think,
but I do not know if you have heard of Johann Paumgartner. So I will give a
brief description of him, so that, just as you grieved with my grief, you may 55
now rejoice with my joy, and just as by your consolation you manifested your
good will towards me, so now by congratulating me you may manifest that
among true friends both sadness and joy are shared. Therefore, in that Johann
Paumgartner is extremely rich, he has something in common with others; but
what he shares with very few is that he possesses his wealth but is not pos- 60
sessed by it, and that his money serves him but he does not serve it. For he
possesses those gifts that are called the goods of fortune, not only through
ownership, but also philosophically: he is fully persuaded that goods which
fall indiscriminately to both the good and the bad cannot properly be called
human, and he does not think it so outstanding to have riches as to despise 65
them. One despises them if, according to the advice of the sage, he pays no
attention to them when they are abundant, if he does not fatten on such lucre
or waste away without it, if he also considers that these things also are given
by the king of heaven not to be loved but rather to be rightly and prudently

* * * * *

9 Ep 2856
10 Ep 2145
11 Ep 2814
12 Paumgarten and Erbach (which Erasmus spells 'Ernbach') are the names of
   palaces in the possession of the Paumgartner family; cf lines 192–7 with nn28–9
   below.
13 It was Zasius who mediated the first contact between Paumgartner and Erasmus;
   see Ep 2602.

distributed. The Lord urges the rich to use unjust mammon to make friends 70
for themselves who will receive them into eternal dwellings.[14] Paumgartner
does more, for with marvellous generosity he uses justly acquired gains to fill
the stomachs of the poor, considering that what has been spent on the members of Christ is well invested. According to the Stoics, having riches is no part
of happiness. But in my judgment, to possess wealth as Paumgartner does is 75
a large part of happiness. Thus Abraham, who possessed great wealth, was
dear to God as a teacher and an example of hospitality.[15]

Moreover, the nobility of his family descends from far back in time. For
extant documents attest that three hundred years ago his family was numbered among the renowned. It sprang from a people in Eastern Franconia, an 80
ancient source of noble gentlemen; from that region are descended those now
called *francs* among the French.[16] His ancestors formerly had a seat there. In
that region there is still a monastery that through their generosity was both
magnificently established and generously endowed with income.[17] But to
keep from going too far back in the past, the father of the man I am now 85
discussing was endowed with such extraordinary intelligence, such integrity of character, such wisdom in giving counsel, such trustworthiness and
dexterity in business matters, such loyalty to his native land, that he received
the highest favour and the highest positions of authority from the greatest
monarchs in the world, Matthias the king of Hungary, a man of far-reaching 90
judgment, the emperor Frederick – the mere mention of whom is sufficient
praise – and his son Maximilian.[18] To all of them he often provided excellent

* * * * *

14 Luke 16:9, omitting the words 'when you fail' (ie when your mammon is gone)
   in the phrase 'who, when you fail, will receive ...'
15 Gen 13:2 and 18:2–8
16 In modern parlance 'Franconia' (*Franken*) refers to the area of Germany in
   which the East Franconian dialect is spoken. In the sixteenth century the greater part of that area was included in the Franconian Imperial Circle, which in
   turn corresponded roughly to the eastern portion of the early-medieval 'stem
   duchy' of Franconia. (There was no longer a duchy of Franconia, but the bishop
   of Würzburg claimed the title 'duke of Franconia.') Today the area is divided
   between the states of Bavaria and Baden-Württemberg (with bits and pieces
   scattered elsewhere). Its east-west axis, along the Main river, includes the cities of Würzburg, Bamberg, and Bayreuth; further south it includes Schwäbisch
   Hall, Ansbach, Nürnberg, and the bishopric of Eichstätt.
17 Unidentified
18 Johann (1) Paumgartner (1455–1527) was born in Nürnberg, settled in Augsburg
   in 1485, and prospered from the sale of silver and copper mined in the Tirol.
   He repeatedly lent money to Emperor Maximilian I, who ennobled him in 1499

and loyal service in warfare and in domestic affairs. To have pleased great
men is not the lowest praise,[19] especially great men who are praised for their
laudable deeds. Meanwhile he was no less pleasing to both the aristocracy   95
and the populace, because of the amiable affability of his character and his
constant readiness to render service to everyone.

But such are the tumultuous fluctuations in human affairs that the
wealth of this renowned family, though in itself most ample, had substan-
tially decreased under his ancestors, partly because of the flood-tides of war,   100
partly because of many daughters who had been splendidly furnished with
very large dowries, thus transferring sizeable portions of wealth to other
families. And though wealth is only a very small part of true nobility, nevertheless Johann Paumgartner did not allow whatever distinction it contributes to be lost to his family; rather, with remarkable prudence and vigilance,   105
he remedied the losses borne by his ancestors and filled in all the gaps so
well that nowhere was there any trace left of the reduction in resources. Not
even in his friendship with princes has he been – or is he now – at all inferior to his parent. Princes have hitherto favoured him and valued him most
highly, and still do so today for his exceptional mental dexterity and his ex-   110
traordinary prudence; he is very dear to the nobles and the common people
because of the generosity he displays to everyone, especially the poor, so
that he can quite rightly be called the delight of his native land. Called upon
by Emperor Charles for the expedition against the Turks, he supported him
generously with his wealth, faithfully with his advice, bravely with his as-   115
sistance; he shared all his perils, ready to lay down his life for his native land
and his emperor.[20] In fact before that time and for that same war he had sent
at his own expense thirtytwo soldiers decked out in mailed armour and well
trained, not a huge number (by Hercules!) but carefully chosen men, many of
whom could take the role of extraordinary commanders. Moreover, the loy-   120
alty, commitment, and service that he provided for Emperor Charles he now
provides for his brother Ferdinand, to whom he is especially dear because of
his exceptional mental endowments.

* * * * *

and named him councillor in 1502, entrusting him with the financial administration of the Tirol. We have no information concerning his services to Matthias
Corvinus of Hungary or to Emperor Frederick III.

19 Horace *Epistles* 1.17.35, cited in *Adagia* I iv 1

20 The immediate reference would appear to be to the efforts undertaken in 1532
to defend the Empire and the Austrian lands against the renewed attempt of
the Turks to capture Vienna; see Ep 2654.

Now you know of his devotion to his native land and his prince. Now hear with what piety he devotes himself to his children. He has four sons and the same number of daughters, all of them highly talented. Perhaps you will say this is a matter not of his piety but of his good luck. But wait and you will learn of his extraordinary piety. He has seen to it that all of them were educated with such care, such holiness and wisdom, that he can quite rightly be called the parent not only of their bodies but also of their minds. He did not destine any of the sons for business or any other lowly skill. He educated them all for learning, for piety, for fulfilling the grand offices of princes and of the commonwealth, which often fall to unsuitable people who have grown old with books and studies (for accustomed to shadows, they seem somehow dazed and, like those whose eyes have been overcome by glaucoma, they suffer from a kind of dizziness of mind when they are summoned into the dust and sunlight, that is, to public offices). In their tender years children are taught honesty and integrity. They are provided with teachers, not from the highways or byways but men of proved morals and no ordinary knowledge of letters. When they reach adolescence are they immediately sent far away from their paternal dwelling, to Italy or France, so that they will become accustomed to foreign languages and customs. This is a kind of grafting of mental powers by which they become milder in disposition and cast off their wild nature, if they have one. (For almost none are more difficult to please than those who have grown old in their home country: they hate foreigners and condemn anything different from their homegrown customs). Some of them he allows to have a taste of princely courts, but select ones. For there is no small difference between one court and another, although in all of them there are not only various experiences but also no lack of allurements that corrupt young people, who are more inclined to what is pleasant than to what is wholesome. But no state in life is free from such dangers, even if you betake yourself to a Carthusian monastery. Against these Sirens we are not rendered safe by the place but rather by carefully blocking our minds rather than our ears, not with wax as Homer's Odysseus did,[21] but with the precepts of philosophy.

And so the eldest son Johann, bearing the Christian and family names of his father as well as his character, was with great success trained in literary culture, first in France and then in Italy, and is now active at the court of Lady Mary, formerly the queen of Hungary, who is among the holiest and wisest

* * * * *

21 See Ep 2854 n17.

women of our times.[22] The next son, Georg, is destined for the law and has   160
already advanced beyond his years in literary studies and in the wisdom of
the law.[23] The third son, Anton, lives in Venice, the most splendid theatre in
all of Italy, proficient in various languages and honed to the sharpest edge in
manners.[24] The youngest son, Daniel,[25] still at home, where his character is
being shaped to be blameless,[26] is soon to be dedicated to whatever training   165
to which he seems naturally disposed. Certainly anyone of acute insight understands that it is essential for everyone to be directed from his most tender
years to the training to which he seems to be naturally disposed. Is this not

* * * * *

22 Johann (III) Paumgartner, 1513–41, the eldest and most talented son, studied
    law at Bourges and then in 1533 joined the court of Queen Mary of Hungary,
    regent of the Netherlands. In 1536 he returned to Germany to become active in
    his father's business but died before his father.
23 In 1532 Johann Georg Paumgartner visited Erasmus on his way to study law
    at Padua, where he remained until sometime after December 1535; see Ep 2683
    introduction. Returning to Augsburg, he became active in the family firm.
    After the death of his elder brother (see preceding note), and the exclusion
    of his brother Anton from his inheritance (see following note), Johann Georg
    and his brother David (see n25 below) shared responsibility for the firm. Like
    David, he enjoyed an influential position at the court of Ferdinand I. When
    David encountered financial difficulties, Johann Georg refused to pay his debts
    but could not escape liability for them. In August 1565 he ended up in debtors'
    prison, from which he was not released until May 1570, shortly after which he
    died from an illness that he had contracted while in prison.
24 Anton Paumgartner, c 1518–1581, was sent to France and Italy to study and by
    1533 was the representative of his father's firm in Venice. After he returned to
    Augsburg, his spendthrift ways and mismanagement of his affairs caused his
    father to exclude him from his inheritance (1543), buying him off with an annuity.
    Subsequently, however, he became more careful with his money and managed to
    avoid involvement in the financial ruin that befell his brothers in 1563 and 1565.
25 A mistake for David, 1521–67, who studied briefly at Padua before being sum-
    moned home by his father in 1538. Meanwhile, in 1535, Erasmus had dedicated
    to David his *Precationes aliquot novae* (Epp 2994–5). After the death of Johann
    (see n22 above) and the exclusion of Anton from their father's will (see n24
    above), he and Johann Georg jointly administered the family's commercial in-
    terests. For some time David enjoyed prosperity and an influential position at
    the court of Ferdinand I, but in the 1560s a series of unwise loans to several
    nobles resulted in financial difficulties from which he did not manage to extri-
    cate himself, and he lost most of his estates. He died on the scaffold after having
    joined the Franconian knight Wilhelm von Grumbach in his private war against
    the city of Würzburg.
26 All the sons were tutored at home by Franciscus Rupilius; see Ep 2867
    introduction.

precisely what it means to be a father? Why should anyone be called a father if he begets nothing but a body and then relinquishes all care of his children, or (if he cares about anything) cares about nothing beyond the body, paying no attention to the mind, which is the principal part of a human being? But it is worse yet to hold back boys who seem to be made by nature for an honourable career and to be mentally inclined to it by restricting them to illiberal pursuits. Certainly that is not to educate them but to leave them helplessly exposed. And in my judgment it is more criminal to expose a mind to vices than to expose a body to uncertain fortunes. It may be some part of happiness to be born of wealthy parents, to be descended from illustrious and renowned ancestors; but the greatest, and indeed the rarest, happiness is to be born of such a parent as Johann Paumgartner showed himself to be to his children.

What should I now say about the devoted and vigilant solicitude with which he brings up his daughters, the courtesy with which he guides his wife, the fondness with which he cherishes the old age of an excellent mother? You would say he is a man born to virtue, who never fails in his duty. Who could be happier than this man, if there is any such thing as happiness in this life. He has ancient noble ancestry, wealth suitable to his armorial bearings. He has a wife who is the best he could wish for, also renowned for her noble ancestry.[27] He has children who live up to the extraordinary character of their parents in every way. As for himself, he is blessed with a good physique and he is in sound and vigorous youth, but he has the wisdom of old age, a mind provided with such extraordinary endowments that in the scale of happiness they are far above wealth and noble birth. He has two castles. One, called Paumgarten,[28] had been neglected by his predecessors, but he restored it magnificently and extended it beautifully. The other, named Ernbach (a name hitherto corrupted in the vernacular to 'Erbach'), is located on the Danube a little above Ulm, on a very pleasant site with extensive grounds; beneath it lies a town of the same name.[29] Happy are the people who have such a lord! Under his auspices everything flourishes. Such is his skill in commerce that you would say that he alone is enough to make a small city large or an obscure one famous.

* * * * *

27 His wife was Regina Fugger, a sister of Anton Fugger.
28 Paumgarten (Baumgarten/Aislingen), on the Danube, about 16 kilometres from Dillingen, in the present state of Bavaria
29 Erbach (Erbach an der Donau) is a town on the Danube between Ulm and Ehlingen, in the present state of Baden-Württemberg. Its most prominent site, Erbach Castle, dates from the early sixteenth century.

Germany has an abundance of great and outstanding men, but I only wish that it had a great many more who are the equal of Paumgartner. Consider also this: although extraordinary virtue and great happiness are always open to envy, everyone applauds the successes of Paumgartner; no one envies him. That is because of his affable temperament, his candour, his cour- 205 teous bearing towards all people, and, as the Greeks say more expressively, his goodness of heart. How much wealth this nation possesses in this one man alone: for emperors, he is always a trustworthy and wise counsellor in civic government, and in warfare a strong and ready leader (and this he does at no cost); for his country, a peaceful and helpful citizen; for his household, 210 a comfortable and watchful caretaker; for the upright and lovers of good let-ters, a generous Maecenas;[30] for friends, a pleasant companion; for the poor, a generous provider or, more truly, a parent! Happy is Germany in such a hero!

Happy am I to have such a friend, with whom I have all things in com-mon.[31] This right, to be sure, is not found in the laws of the emperors, but 215 it is written on the tablets of the Graces, and by it I consider all the goods of Paumgartner to be mine. Not that I would want to diminish his fortune (which neither my character nor ordinary circumstances would require) but because I live all the more tranquilly in that I consider whatever is possessed by a genuine friend to belong to my world. Accordingly, I will never think 220 myself to be poor or destitute as long as I have such friends, not necessarily many but rather extraordinary, so that any one of them could be worth many others.[32] No possession is more priceless than a true friend. In this I have peace of mind and I comfort myself against the croaking of the frogs.[33] But since in this world nothing is truly owned or lasting, it is best, according to 225 the advice of St Paul, to have this possession also as if we did not have it.[34] Mortal minds are inconstant, and even if no such thing happens, no one is safe from death.[35] But far from us be baleful omens! Give my greetings to our common patron, the archbishop of Toledo, whenever the opportunity arises.

* * * * *

30 See Ep 2815 n6.
31 *Adagia* I i 1
32 *Adagia* I viii 13, citing Homer *Iliad* 11.514
33 Ie the noise of his critics, the newest of whom was the Franciscan Nikolaus Ferber; see Epp 2896:12–15 with n8, 2898:12–21, 2899:10–56.
34 1 Cor 7:30–1
35 The meaning here appears to be that one can lose one's friends because, being human, they prove inconstant or, even if they remain faithful, they die. Hence the wisdom of following Paul's advice by not counting too heavily on one's attachments in this world.

It is many years ago that he deigned to number me among his friends, but, as   230
every one proclaims, his benevolence is still in full vigour. Farewell.

Given at Freiburg im Breisgau, 19 November 1533

A few days ago I wrote via the imperial ambassador, a commander, a
man of good character it seems, and a supporter of mine; he told me a great
deal that I was glad to hear about the bishop of Toledo's continuing favour   235
towards me.[36]

2880 / To Pierre Richardot   Freiburg, 19 November 1533

This letter was first published in the *Epistolae universae* pages 1112–13. Pierre
Richardot of Morey (c 1503–41), who held a doctorate in law, was a member of
the household of Erasmus' friend Léonard de Gruyères, official (chief judge)
of the archiepiscopal court at Besançon (Ep 1534). In July 1533 Richardot succeeded Désiré Morel (Ep 2870) as official of the archidiaconal court, and in the
following year was appointed to a canonry at Besançon, a position he held until
his early death. A close friend of Erasmus' famulus Gilbert Cousin (Ep 2381 n1),
Richardot also endeared himself to Erasmus by playing his part in the efforts of
his friends in Besançon to keep him supplied with his favourite Burgundy wine.

ERASMUS OF ROTTERDAM TO PIERRE RICHARDOT, GREETINGS
It is almost a month now since the patron we have in common sent me from
Lucerne a letter full of kindness and good wishes.[1] I answered it,[2] but briefly because someone had indicated that he would have to be in Besançon,
though that did not seem likely to me. Through the same messenger I had   5
written to the bishop of Veroli, but he had already flown back to Italy to

* * * * *

36 If, as the Allen editors say, this is a reference to the imperial ambassador to
   the papal court, the person in question is either Fernando de Silva, count of
   Cifuentes and ambassador in Rome, or Miguel Mai, who succeeded him in
   April 1533. But we have no evidence whatever that either man ever visited
   Erasmus at Freiburg. It seems, rather, that the ambassador conveyed his news
   in a letter, and that Erasmus' earlier letter to Vergara was sent to the ambassador for forwarding.

2880
1 The patron was Léonard de Gruyères; for his letter see Ep 2870 n3.
2 The answer is not extant.

await the commands of the pope in Milan.³ There is no reason for you to be
concerned about the letter that I sent through my servant,⁴ for it was nothing
but a thank-you note and the return of greetings. My servant Gilbert brought
more of the old wine than I wanted. I will procure the new wine in Lent. But   10
to let you know how much of a drunkard I am, two casks will last me up to
ten months, if I am the only drinker. But I prefer to have some extra so that
the hard drinkers, servants, gluttons, and ne'erdowells can have their share
of flat and acerbic wine. I am grateful that you instruct me how to remedy
wine that is going flat with after-wines.⁵   15

But seriously, I would like you to be persuaded, my dear Richardot,
that the affection that you display more than express in your letter gives me
great pleasure. I laughed, but I did not understand what you meant by calling me the third light of eloquence. You make too much of me if you think
that in our times there are only two who are more eloquent than Erasmus.   20
Indeed I think I would hardly consider myself to be the thousandth, except
that I think that I, like the Megarians, should not receive any place at all in
the list.⁶ I only wish that in these times Christian piety had flourished as
much as eloquence has.

Listen to a story that annoys me, but will give you a good laugh. Apart   25
from other troubles that have afflicted me during this summer and fall, my
house was infested with such a swarm of pestilential fleas that I could not
sleep, read, or write. And this affliction has not yet been alleviated. As a joke I
say to my friends that they are not fleas but demons. But this turned out to be
not a joke but a prophecy. For in fact several days ago a woman was burned   30
who had a husband but who for eighteen years was having secret intercourse
with a demonic rival to her husband. And among the other crimes to which

* * * * *

3 Ennio Filonardi, who as papal legate to the Swiss cantons resided at Lucerne in
   the years 1532–3; see Ep 2712 introduction.
4 Presumably Gilbert Cousin (Ep 2381 n1); cf the following sentence. The letter,
   presumably one of thanks for the latest shipment of wine, is not extant.
5 The word for 'after-wines' is *vinacei*, the plural of *vinaceum*, which can refer to
   either the residue of the pressing of grapes (skin, pips, etc) or to poor-quality
   wine produced from the last pressing. The second meaning appears to be the
   one relevant here.
6 See *Adagia* II i 79: *Megarenses neque tertii neque quarti* 'The Megarians are neither
   the third nor the fourth.' Asked by the Megarians, who had just won a battle, who
   was first among the Greeks, the Pythian Apollo replied that 'you ... are neither
   third nor fourth / Nor twelfth nor of any reckoning or account.'

she confessed was this: through her lover she sent into this town some large
sacks of fleas. The village where she was burned is called 'Kylchove'; it is
about two leagues from here.[7] I am standing here writing and they are biting   35
inside my boots and in my shirt around my neck. They bite in a strange way
and are so tiny you can't pinch them. Is so much freedom allowed to harmful
creatures?[8] Farewell.

Freiburg im Breisgau, 19 November in the year of our Lord 1533

2881 / To Simon Lagnier   Freiburg, 19 November 1533

This letter was first published in the *Epistolae universae* page 1112. Simon
Lagnier is documented as a notary and citizen of Besançon in 1531. This is a letter of thanks to him for an unexpected gift of wine. A few months later Erasmus
expressed his sorrow at Lagnier's 'misfortunes' (Allen Ep 3104:12), which appear to have consisted of a serious illness that afflicted him and his wife (Allen
Ep 3115:58–9).

It was indeed most kind of you, my excellent friend, to offer the wine unbidden, but it was hardly prudent of Gilbert Cousin to accept it. Still, to me
your kindness was all the more pleasing because it was spontaneous and
unexpected. I will diligently follow your instructions about your sons, and
if I can accommodate them in any other way, I will do what is proper for a   5
grateful and mindful recipient.[1] I am not unaware of how much I owe to the
illustrious city council of Besançon, and the perpetually foggy and cloudy
weather here is hard on me. The emperor is summoning me back to Brabant,
and if the infirmity of this little body prevents me from going there, I will
try to crawl away to Besançon.[2] May the Lord grant that I find all my friends   10
there safe and sound.

Farewell to you and to all those most dear to you.
Freiburg, 19 November 1533

* * * * *

7 Kirchhofen, a town about 10 kilometres south of Freiburg
8 For an earlier plague of fleas, see Epp 2329:76–7, 2362:8–9 (where the translation
  reads 'lice'), 2394:139–40 (where the translation reads 'bedbugs').

2881
1 Lagnier had two sons, Hugues and Ferry, who were soon to matriculate at
  Freiburg.
2 For the intended return to Brabant see Ep 2820 introduction; for the earlier consideration given to moving to Besançon, see CWE 19 xv.

2882 / From Johann (II) Paumgartner   Augsburg, 28 November 1533

This letter was first published as Ep 195 in Förstemann / Günther. The manu-
script, in a secretary's hand but signed by Paumgartner, was in the Burscher
Collection of the University Library at Leipzig (Ep 1254 introduction). For the
Augsburg merchant Johann (II) Paumgartner, see Ep 2603 introduction.

Greetings. With incredible pleasure, my excellent and delightful master
Erasmus, I have received the letter that you sent me on the 26th of October;[1]
it was especially agreeable to me because it emitted the aura of your most
learned and polished talent (which not even the hastiness of your pen could
dispel), and because I could clearly recognize in it your longstanding affec-   5
tion and your special good will towards me. I extend to you all possible gratitude for congratulating me in the opening and introduction of your letter
on my acquisition of the castle of Ernbach and for hoping and praying that
its name may be an omen of my happiness and prosperity.[2] I will return the
favour if an occasion ever arises. But whatever honours I gain from that ti-   10
tle we will have in common and will share quite equally between us.[3] May
the gods grant that it will bring us much honour and advantage!
     And then, as for what you say about the king of England, that he has
taken his wife back (according to a letter written to you by Koler), I was glad
to read it, but on that point I nevertheless agree with your belief and opinion,[4]   15
although I have not heard anything about it. But this much is clearly being
written about it: that the emperor is planning to wage war against the king of
England, and that the French king has demanded for his eldest son (whom
they call the dauphin) the daughter whom the English king had by his first
wife,[5] and that he has offered to expel the English king from his realm if the   20

* * * * *

2882
1 Not extant, presumably the letter referred to by Erasmus in Ep 2906:106–7
2 The castle in question, then and now, was known as 'Erbach,' but Erasmus
   insisted that this was a corruption of 'Ernbach' (Ep 2879:194–7 with n29).
   'Ernbach' (Ehrenbach in modern spelling) means 'stream of honours,' a meaning that Erasmus had evidently exploited in his letter. Paumgartner does the
   same thing in the sentences that follow.
3 Because friends have all things in common (*Adagia* I i 1)
4 The letter from Koler is not extant, but for the false rumour that Henry VIII was
   once again living with his first wife, Catherine of Aragon, and Erasmus' refusal
   to believe it, cf Ep 2877:19–21.
5 In 1520 the eldest son of Francis I, also called Francis (1518–36), had been
   formally betrothed to Princess Mary, Henry VIII's daughter by Catherine of
   Aragon, and the prospect was still alive in 1527 (Knecht 214).

emperor agrees to it. But I do not know whether he has been given permission or not.[6] May the gods make it turn out for the best!

But I am eternally grateful to you for giving me such friendly advice about my son.[7] Although I do not want to bother you, and I hesitate to put you under any obligation – not because I have any doubts about your friendly intentions (since I know that you are always far more ready to gratify me than I could ever have deserved) but rather because in my own mind I could hardly escape being branded as shameless if I should continue to burden you (since you are laden and overwhelmed with so much business and so many tasks) – nevertheless, since I know that you are so kind, I cannot refrain from also asking you now to expend some effort in this matter, and I beg you, most renowned Master Erasmus, to explain more clearly what I ought to decide about this. Obliged as I am to you for so many reasons, you would bind me yet once more by doing this. I would take care to repay you someday, in so far as I can, for these immense and extremely important services you have done for me, and if I do not rise to what they deserve, my intention to do so will never fail, and in important matters good intentions are enough.[8] In the meantime, I pray that everything will come out according to your wishes and that God will long preserve and protect you, keeping you safe and sound for us.

Augsburg, 28 November in the year after the Virgin birth 1533
Johann Paumgartner, yours as much as his own

To the renowned and most excellent gentleman Master Erasmus of Rotterdam, the best and greatest professor of true theology, the restorer of the language of Rome, his most venerable Master. At Freiburg im Breisgau

2883 / To Bonifacius Amerbach   Freiburg, 30 November 1533

This letter (= AK Ep 1791) was first published in the *Epistolae familiares*. It answers Ep 2873A. The autograph is in the Öffentliche Bibliothek of the University of Basel (MS AN III 15 55).

* * * * *

6 There is no substance to this report of hostility between Henry VIII on the one hand and Francis I in collusion with Charles V on the other. Henry and Francis were in fact on fairly good terms at this point, while Francis' relations with Charles were as bad as ever; see Knecht 213–14, 225–8.
7 Johann Georg Paumgartner (Ep 2683 introduction)
8 *Adagia* II viii 55

Cordial greetings. If things go well with Bonifacius, there is nothing more I could ask from him. This business, with which we have had our hands full for a long time, we have finally taken care of,[1] and there is no reason why you should make the trip for my sake.[2]

You wrote something about a post that has been offered. I still do not 5
know what this is.[3]

I want to know whether the chick your Juno delivered is a rooster or a hen.[4] Farewell, my closest friend. Freiburg, on the feast of St Andrew 1533

Erasmus of Rotterdam

To the most renowned gentleman Master Bonifacius Amerbach. At Basel 10

2884 / To Thomas Boleyn   Freiburg, 1 December 1533

This is the prefatory letter to *De praeparatione ad mortem* (Basel: Froben and Episcopius, c January 1534). The autograph of the letter (followed by the original manuscript of the treatise in Erasmus' hand) is in the Royal Library at Copenhagen (MS GKS 95 Fol, folio 58). *De praeparatione* turned out to be one of Erasmus' most enduringly popular works, with twenty Latin editions and eight vernacular translations (four in French, two each in Dutch and Spanish, one each in German and English) in the space of six years; see CWE 70 xxvi–xxvii. Appended to the original Basel edition, and constituting slightly more than half the content of the volume, were sixteen previously unpublished letters (*Epistolae aliquot de rebus cognitu dignis, quarum nulla fuit antehac excusa typis*), the first such collection since the *Epistolae palaeonaeoi* of 1532, and the penultimate collection of letters to be published by Erasmus himself. The final collection would be appended to *De puritate tabernaculi* of 1536 (Ep 3086).

DESIDERIUS ERASMUS OF ROTTERDAM SENDS GREETINGS
TO THE MOST RENOWNED GENTLEMAN LORD THOMAS,
EARL OF WILTSHIRE AND ORMOND

You urge me on to the colophon of Christian philosophy,[1] most renowned gentleman (more famous as you are for piety than for the trappings of 5

* * * * *

2883
1 See Ep 2873A n2.
2 The Latin says literally 'move your foot for my sake.'
3 Doubtless the offer from the city council of Strasbourg; see Ep 2873A n3.
4 Bonifacius' only son, Basilius, was born on 1 December 1533. Cf Ep 2887.

2884
1 See *Adagia* II iii 45: 'He added the colophon,' ie he added the finishing touch, without which a bit of business cannot be concluded.

Thomas Boleyn
From a drawing by Holbein

fortune), when you urge me to add to my earlier writings at least a brief explanation of how everyone should prepare himself for death. For this is the last act of human life, like the last act of a play, on which depends either one's eternal happiness or eternal doom. This is the last battle with the enemy, from which the soldier of Christ expects either everlasting triumph if he conquers or everlasting ignominy if he is conquered. Actually I was already completely occupied with this theme when your exhortation came to me; it was like spurring on a galloping horse, but at the time I was, to be sure, philosophizing for myself alone. In your piety, however, you want this fruit also to be shared through us with many people. I only wish that the Lord in his goodness will grant a happy outcome to your most holy desire and my attempt. Certainly I will not be lax in following his will, since I think it was at his prompting that you requested this service from me.

Farewell. At Freiburg im Breisgau, 1 December 1533

2885 / From Viglius Zuichemus   Basel, 5 December 1533

This letter was first published as Ep 50 in VZE. For Viglius, see Ep 2810 introduction.

When I arrived in Basel,[1] my most learned friend Erasmus, I found a good part of the Greek *Institutes* already printed by Froben in elegant type, just as I wanted, and that was a great pleasure for me. And then, while I was staying with him for a few days to see how the work was going and to compare it with a second copy lent to me by Giambattista Egnazio (which I had brought with me from Italy),[2] I happened to show to Bonifacius Amerbach some of the commentaries that I had drawn up this year in Padua concerning those sections about which I had lectured publicly there.[3] Amerbach liked them so much that he thought I should publish them, and I did not object, since I had prepared them for that purpose, and Froben was happy to undertake the task.[4] And so I decided to stay with him for a while, until the work was finished and to help Gelenius in correcting it,[5] since he was not sufficiently

* * * * *

2885
1 For Viglius' itinerary since leaving Padua in October 1533, see Epp 2871 n2, 2875 n1.
2 For Viglius' edition of the Greek *Institutes* and both of the manuscripts that he used, see Ep 2791 n22.
3 Ie the sections (*tituli*) of the *Institutes*
4 See Ep 2888 n4.
5 Sigismundus Gelenius (Ep 1702 n1), editor and proofreader at the Froben Press

acquainted with our rules for superscripts and references in law texts. I wanted you to know this so that you would excuse me for holding back your letters somewhat longer, but I will deliver them faithfully as soon as I free 15 myself from my business here.[6] And if there is any other task you wish to assign to me, I will be free to do it.

When I was there I forgot to deliver to you the *Sermons against the Arians* of Ambrose, but I am sending them now. A secretary of mine copied them in Italy, and I compared his copy with the archetype, which itself has some 20 errors that will shock you. But I did not want to change anything, so that I could leave the revision and correction to you, if you should be willing to do it. Zanchi, the canon who lent me this little work, has moved from Padua to Ravenna. But the life of Cyprian that he gave me is the same as the one that you lent to Froben a while ago, and so I thought there was no need to send 25 it to you.[7]

Moreover, my most learned friend Erasmus, you are not unaware that whatever reputation for learning I have gained thus far, and whatever literary accomplishment I have achieved, I attribute to your recommendations and exhortations. Certainly that is the main reason I have finally dared to 30 seek the publication of some specimen of my studies. Now it is your part not to abandon the one whom you have thus far promoted, but rather to support him with your favour so that he will not be shamefully hissed off the stage on which he is beginning to tread. I am not asking you to adorn me with new recommendations, but rather, when there is a favourable oc- 35 casion to ensure that scholars retain your long-standing judgment of me. This is also important to Froben, so that he not suffer any losses from my commentaries. Farewell.

Basel, 5 December 1533

2886 / To James v, king of Scotland   Freiburg, 8 December 1533

For King James v see Ep 2283 n5.

This letter was first published by Allen. The manuscript, a contemporary copy, is in the Caprington Royal Letter Book at the National Records of Scotland in Edinburgh (GD 149 264 folio 26 verso). Preceding it in the Letter Book is a letter of Ferdinand of Austria to King James, commending Johannes Cochlaeus (for whom see Ep 1863). Following it is the king's reply to this letter, Ep 2950.

* * * * *

6 Epp 2876–7, which were finally entrusted to a messenger; see Ep 2876 n25.
7 For the contents of this paragraph, see Ep 2716 nn35–6.

And following that is the king's letter to Cochlaeus thanking him for his book against Alexander Alesius (see below).

Like King Ferdinand, Erasmus writes in commendation of Cochlaeus, who had become embroiled in a controversy with the Scottish reformer Alexander Alesius (c 1500–65), for whom see OER I 18–19. Living in exile at Wittenberg, Alesius had published, in the form of a long letter to King James, a book denouncing a decree of the Scottish bishops against the reading of the New Testament in vernacular translations: *Alexandri Alesii Epistola contra decretum quoddam Episcoporum in Scotia, quod prohibet legere Novi Testamenti libros lingua vernacula* (Wittenberg: J. Klug 1533) Cochlaeus' reply, also in the form of a letter to the king, was entitled *An expediat laicis legere Novi Testamenti libros lingua vernacula* (Dresden 1533). The controversy between Alesius and Cochlaeus continued into the following year, with a further treatise from each. For details, see Allen's introduction to this letter. It may seem surprising to find Erasmus, who in the *Paraclesis* had pleaded so eloquently for the provision of vernacular Bibles to ordinary laymen, indeed even women (see CWE 41 410–12), lending his support to a vituperative campaign against doing so. On the other hand, his description of the matter as 'of overwhelming importance to the tranquillity of your kingdom' suggests that he had accepted Cochlaeus' view that the matter was one of dealing with heretics and subversives rather than pious Bible readers.

Cordial greetings. I would rightly seem to be shameless, most serene King, if I wrote to your Majesty as someone unknown to you. But I think the name Erasmus is not unknown to you, since I taught your brother Alexander,[1] the archbishop of St Andrews, at Siena, and was extraordinarily fond of him because of his outstanding character – at that time James was also there,[2] a boy of remarkable talent – and I was no less fond of your father,[3] who had been amply furnished with all the virtues of a king. To be sure, my work called *Adagia* makes it clear how bitterly I mourned the death of both of them by name in the adage 'Sparta is your portion,' where I grieve for them in a lengthy and not at all feigned discourse.[4] Accordingly, I think I am writing to a prince who is friendly and wishes me well, even though I am unknown to him by sight. But I am persuaded that what I ask now is of overwhelming

* * * * *

2886
1 See Ep 2283 n6.
2 James Stewart; see Ep 2283 n7.
3 James IV (Ep 2283 n4)
4 *Adagia* II v 1 CWE 33 241–2

importance to the tranquillity of your kingdom. What this is, your Majesty will deign to learn from this young man Franciscus and from the letter he is delivering, or else he will entrust to some learned and devout gentleman 15 the task of conveying its content.[5] For he has been sent by Master Johannes Cochlaeus, counsellor of George, the most illustrious duke of Saxony, not only a remarkable scholar but also a most diligent supporter of the Christian religion. If in future Erasmus is able to please your most serene Majesty in any way, you will find him eminently prepared to serve you in every 20 way. May the Lord keep you and make you prosper and flourish in all good endeavours.

Given at Freiburg im Breisgau, 8 December 1533

His Majesty's humble servant, Erasmus. I have written it with my own hand. 25

To the most serene king of Scotland James, fifth of that name, in the royal palace of Scotland

2887 / To Bonifacius Amerbach [Freiburg], 10 December 1533

This letter (= AK Ep 1793) was first published in the *Epistolae familiares*. The autograph is in the Öffentliche Bibliothek of the University of Basel (MS AN III 15 56).

Cordial greetings. Rejoice, but do so silently, so that Nemesis does not hear you.[1] Commit the tiny infant to God and to his mother.[2] There are very few children alive who are tenderly loved by their parents, and among us mothers commonly believe that a father's gaze at his infants has the power to bewitch them.[3] We are expecting you for the holidays; may Viglius come 5 with you.[4]

* * * * *

5 'The letter' was presumably Cochlaeus' treatise against Alesius (see introduction above). Franciscus was one of several nephews of Cochlaeus, the son of one of his sisters. Nothing else is known of him.

2887
1 Nemesis was the goddess who punished excessive hopes or happiness; cf *Adagia* II vi 38.
2 See Ep 2883 n4.
3 'Among us' (*apud nos*) presumably means 'here in Freiburg.'
4 The visit did not actually take place until 7 January, see *Vita Viglii Zuichemi* 13.

I rejoice greatly for Alciati.⁵ As for me, I can barely stay alive in this fog.
Farewell to you and those dearest to you. 10 December 1533
Your Erasmus of Rotterdam
To Doctor Amerbach. At Basel   10

2888 / From Viglius Zuichemus   Basel, 10 December 1533

This letter, Viglius' reply to Ep 2878, was first published as Ep 49 in vze. The
surviving manuscript, in the Bibliothèque Royale at Brussels (ms 6919–20 page
133), is 'an inferior eighteenth-century copy.'

TO ERASMUS OF ROTTERDAM

Before I received your letter,¹ I had indicated to you briefly what I was doing
and what the reason is for my delay.² But I understand from Hieronymus
that my letter was not delivered to you in good faith,³ or certainly delivered
later than I wished. But what you previously wrote to me was as pleasing to   5
me as are all the things that Erasmus bestows on Viglius, which, though they
are many and great, I nonetheless always value all the more highly because
I do not deserve them and because you strive to increase this spontaneous
benevolence of yours by daily additions to it.

I had not at all decided to spend the winter here, and I have not yet   10
made up my mind, but my plan in coming to Basel was to see what was being done with my Greek *Institutes* and to collate the second copy with the
first, which I thought I could complete in a few days, as I told you. But I had
brought with me from Italy some of my commentaries on our civil law, and
I was not at all averse to having some of them printed, but I did not think   15
Froben would consider them worthy of his press. When, however, I gave
Amerbach a sample of them, he recommended them so strongly to Froben
that he for his part asked for them. And that was the reason I stayed here,
so that the work would be published more correctly and according to my

* * * * *

5 In 1533 Andrea Alciati (Ep 1250), who had been teaching law at Bourges while
  seeking an appointment at Padua, was summoned back to Italy by Duke
  Francesco II Sforza to teach law at Pavia.

  2888
1 Ep 2878
2 Ep 2885
3 Hieronymus Froben

wishes.[4] I told you this in my last letter, and I begged your pardon for be-   20
ing somewhat late in taking care of your letters,[5] and once more I beg your
forgiveness. If you want your letters to be returned to you or if you want to
write or have me do something else, I will send my own courier to you before
my departure.

Concerning the dogmas of this city I will follow your advice, and I   25
thank you for it.[6] In fact my attitude towards religion has always been such
that, however little inclined I may be to superstition, I also do not easily yield
to new opinions and dogmas. In this I not only follow your authority but
have always taken you as my master, so that I can embrace whatever you
approve and consider as anathema whatever you reject. I have now fixed   30
this attitude in my mind so firmly that I have no fear that anyone can use
magic spells to make me change my mind. I have nothing to do with the
dogmatists, certainly not with the one whom you specifically advised me
to shun.[7] And I will also do this with all the more caution because I see that
you yourself quite rightly have that attitude towards him. At the same time,   35
Amerbach, a thoroughly learned and honourable man linked to me by virtue
of our studies and our profession, does not allow me to be lonely or bored.
And at home I have Froben and Sigismundus Gelenius,[8] whose company
I enjoy whenever I want to take a break from reading. Farewell.

At Basel, 10 December 1533   40

2889 / To Louis de Vers   Freiburg, 11 December 1533

This letter was first published in the *Epistolae universae* page 1112. Little is
known of Louis de Vers (d 1553), abbot of two Cistercian monasteries in the
Franche-Comté. He was a member of the noble family of Vers-en-Montagne,
as was Erasmus' famulus Gilbert Cousin (Ep 2381 n1), who regarded him as a
patron and dedicated his *Oἰκέτης* to him (Basel: Froben and Episcopius 1535). In
October–November 1533 Cousin paid a visit to Burgundy, where he received either a benefice or the promise of one from De Vers and brought back some wine

* * * * *

4 Froben published the volume in 1534 under the title *Commentaria Viglii Zuichemi
  Phrysii in decem titulos Institutionum*. The preface states that the work consists
  essentially of the content of the course of lectures given at Padua in the preceding year.
5 Ep 2885:1–17
6 See Ep 2878:6–16.
7 Simon Grynaeus; see Ep 2878:17–39.
8 For Gelenius, see Ep 2885 n5.

for Erasmus (Epp 2878:45, 2880:9–10, 2881:1–2). Eager to retain Cousin's services, Erasmus sent him back to Burgundy with this letter and Ep 2890, pleading
that Cousin be permitted to keep the benefice while continuing to reside with
Erasmus at Freiburg. Cousin did in fact manage to remain with Erasmus until
the latter's return to Basel in the summer of 1535.

ERASMUS OF ROTTERDAM SENDS GREETINGS TO LOUIS,
ABBOT OF MONT-SAINTE-MARIE AND LA CHARITÉ
Reverend lord and father, for many reasons the object of my esteem, for
more than three years now Gilbert Cousin has been a faithful and devoted
servant to me – though in fact, because of his gentlemanly behaviour, I have   5
considered him to be not so much a servant as a fellow lodger and a partner
in my literary labours. Accordingly I congratulate your reverend Lordship
on having such a kinsman,[1] and him even more on having such a friend
and kindly patron. For that reason, just as he owes you a great deal, so I too
am grateful to you. For my fortunes are such that it is much easier for me   10
to share literary learning with him than to bestow riches or benefices. But I
hope that he will not regret the time he has spent with me. For apart from
the fruits of learning that he has gained from my company, which there is no
reason to regret, you in your good judgment know by how many pleasures
young people are tempted to moral corruption if they are left to their own   15
judgment. In other places he could have contracted some contagion from the
sectarians. But with me, even if any such contagion attracted him, he could
be purged. And then our manner of life is such that there is no free time to
indulge in pleasures, even if one should seek them. In the ranking of rewards, I consider this fruit to be far from the least valuable. But he deserved   20
so much from me that we always held my meagre resources in common, and
beyond that, he had whatever services I could perform for him. Now I find
his absence most distressing, and I would be immensely pleased if he would
come back to us as soon as possible. But I beg you earnestly to continue to
favour him as you always have. Believe me, you would be right to bestow   25
your kindness on him, even if he were not related to you by blood. But if you
would deign to include Erasmus in the list of your clients, you would have
two instead of one.
    Best wishes to your reverend Lordship.
    11 December, in the year of our Lord 1533   30

        * * * * *

2889
1 Punning on the Latin form of Cousin's name, *Cognatus*, meaning 'blood relative,' 'kinsman'

2890 / To François Bonvalot   Freiburg, 11 December 1533

This letter was first published in the *Epistolae universae* page 1112. For François
Bonvalot, canon and treasurer of the chapter at Besançon, see Ep 2142 introduction.

ERASMUS OF ROTTERDAM SENDS GREETINGS
TO FRANÇOIS BONVALOT, TREASURER
I am grateful for your efforts on my behalf, my very renowned friend; they
are nothing new; but I am still unable to do any more than be grateful.
Reverend Lord Louis de Vers, abbot of Mont-Sainte-Marie and La Charité,   5
has bestowed a certain benefice on Gilbert Cousin, his relative and my servant.[1] If there should be any need for your support in this matter, I beseech
you earnestly not to fail to lend it to him, because he himself is quite worthy
of it, for he is a young man of honourable and upright character who also has
no lack of learning – certainly he was a great help to me for several years in   10
my scholarly endeavours. For that reason I will consider whatever service
you bestow on him as bestowed on me.
    I hear that through you many priestly offices have been conferred, and
your Prudence knows that a large part of the Christian religion depends
on pastors. In Paris I have a certain friend, Philippus Montanus,[2] who once   15
helped me in my studies, a most learned man, even in theology, but I have
never seen anyone who surpassed him in holy or devout living. He does not
lack financial resources, but in his heart he would like to be a good pastor, if
he should receive the call. He is a Frenchman, about thirtyfive years old. If
you deign to keep him in mind, you would be doing something that would   20
be extremely pleasing not only to me but also to Christ himself – whom I beg
to keep you safe.[3]
    Freiburg, 11 December 1533

2891 / From Viglius Zuichemus   Basel, 14 December 1533

This letter, which responds to one no longer extant, was first published in Van
Heussen page 114. For Viglius, see Ep 2810 introduction.

* * * * *

2890
1 See Ep 2889.
2 For Montanus, see Ep 2065 introduction.
3 There is nothing to indicate that Bonvalot responded in any way to this request.

TO ERASMUS OF ROTTERDAM

I was greatly pleased indeed when you removed the little difficulty that had
arisen between us (which was much more troublesome to me than to you),
so that after this each of us will afterwards be all the more deeply fond of
the other.[1] For after you learned that I was not to blame, and through this   5
very suspicion you recognized the manifestation of my feelings about you,
from now on you will, I hope, consider Viglius more worthy of your good
will. Certainly I will never intentionally do anything that would make me
less deserving of your favour. In this matter I also noted how fair you are,
since you did not immediately condemn me when this suspicion first arose   10
but rather gave me an opportunity to clear myself, and then you were not
reluctant to believe my earnest entreaty. Heaven forbid that any whisperer
should draw me away from my love and veneration for you,[2] whom I value
above all other mortals. Heaven forbid that I should ever think that he could
turn me away from my allegiance to you. Heaven forbid that I should give   15
credence to anyone who thinks that Desiderius Erasmus, with no offence on
my part, could ever bring himself to have a less friendly opinion of me, since
he has honoured me with such high praises, which I have not at all deserved,
and has always treated me with such great affection. For my part, I will make
every effort to revisit you, and if I can free myself from here, I will be there   20
with Bonifacius.[3]

     I am stepping out to the front of the stage with very little confidence.[4]
But in the end, anyone who deigns to read what I have written will be fair-
er to me if he compares it, not with the writings of Alciati or Zasius,[5] the

* * * * *

2891
 1 The 'little difficulty' was evidently the unforeseen prolongation of Viglius' visit
   to Basel, where Froben was publishing both his edition of the Greek *Institutes*
   and a volume of his lectures on the *Institutes*. This resulted in a major delay in
   the delivery of the letters that Erasmus had entrusted to him for delivery in the
   Netherlands. Viglius had twice explained the situation in letters to Erasmus;
   see Epp 2885:13–16, 2888:20–4.
 2 On the basis of Epp 2878:17–18, 2888:32–5 Allen suggests that 'the whisperer'
   might have been Simon Grynaeus (for whom see Ep 2659 n5), but it is difficult to imagine what motive Grynaeus would have for wanting to undermine
   Viglius' esteem for Erasmus.
 3 The visit took place on 7 January 1534, on Viglius' homeward journey to the
   Netherlands; see Ep 2887 n4.
 4 This applies particularly to the volume of his lectures on the *Institutes*; see n1
   above.
 5 Andrea Alciati (Ep 1250) and Udalricus Zasius (Ep 2857)

Coryphaeuses of our profession,[6] but rather with what is published by the   25
crowd of Bartolophiles.[7] Farewell, and continue to love and support Viglius.

At Basel, 14 December 1533

2892 / To Pero and Cristóbal Mexía   Freiburg, 12 December 1533

This letter was first published in the epistolary appendix to *De praeparatione ad mortem* (Basel: Froben and Episcopius 1534) 155–67. For the Spanish Erasmian Pero Mexía and his brother Cristóbal, see Epp 2299–2300 introductions. This is the last surviving letter in Erasmus' correspondence with Spain.

DESIDERIUS ERASMUS OF ROTTERDAM SENDS GREETINGS
TO THE MOST DISTINGUISHED GENTLEMEN PERO
AND CRISTÓBAL MEXÍA, BROTHERS

For the sake of brevity, most noble sirs, I will send a single letter in reply to several letters from both of you.[1] A while ago I received a letter from the two   5
of you expostulating (or rather lamenting, such is your courtesy) because I had not replied to your letters. I found that highly gratifying, because it revealed that your affection for me is far from ordinary. To an intense desire any delay is long and even quickness is slow. But from now on I would like you, in your wisdom, to consider how many mountains, plains, and oceans   10
separate us, and by how many roundabout ways letters make their way from Freiburg im Breisgau to Seville in Spain, though it is good luck if they are finally delivered at all, however unsealed and tattered. But if it should happen that I do not reply to some letters, you will be kind enough to forgive my advanced age, which, even if it were not burdened by scholarly labours   15
or worn out by illness, grows weary by its own nature, especially since I am inundated by bundles of letters from all sides, and that almost every day, so that there is hardly time to read them, much less any leisure to respond to

* * * * *

6 The name Coryphaeus, the leader of the chorus in Greek drama, was used to describe the leader of any company or enterprise.
7 Ie lovers of Bartolo da Sassoferrato (1313–55), who was the most famous of the medieval commentators on Roman law. For humanists his name was synonymous with barbarous legal Latin; cf Ep 2604 n8.

2892
1 None of the letters are extant.

each of them.[2] But you can be assured that, whether I write back or remain
silent, your favour towards me is most gratifying, and your letters are not   20
only pleasing but also delightful.

In your last letter, which I received a few days ago, you indicated that
through a bookseller you had received my letters, which was no less pleasant
to me than to you.[3]

That being said, I shall get to the point, but laconically. It would be   25
discourteous of me not to embrace your support, and I do not distrust your
wisdom. For it could be that in this matter you have deeper insight than I.
As for me, I still stick to my previous opinion: I think it is more advisable to
imitate that noble Cunctator who preferred to conquer by remaining in place
rather than by fighting,[4] especially since it is not a single fight of one against   30
one, nor is it a matter of one against two (although we learn that Hercules
admitted that he was no match for two),[5] but a battle of one against so many
anthills, so many wasp nests, so many phalanxes of frogs, so many mag-
pies, such swarms of grasshoppers, such flocks of starlings and jackdaws,
that though they have no stings or beaks or claws, they can still exhaust a   35
man, no matter how steadfast, just with their chattering. How often have I
refuted their manifest and shameless slanders? And yet, to this very day, as
if I had done nothing at all, they croak their old lies at me, and they do so
even in published books: 'Erasmus makes confession optional, he condemns
all ceremonies, he mocks veneration of the saints, he mocks ecclesiastical cer-   40
emonies, he rejects Christian fasting, he condemns abstinence from food, he
dissolves the celibacy of priests, he eliminates the vows and ceremonies of
monks, he condemns human regulations. Why say more? He paved the way
for Luther.' Now those who pretend to be modest – so that they may gain
more credence for their slanders – say that they think I am a good man and   45
did not write such things in order to promote these uproars; they even praise
me for writing differently now.

* * * * *

2 On the volume of Erasmus' correspondence cf Ep 2846 n3.
3 Apart from this letter, the only extant letters from Erasmus to the brothers are
   Epp 2299–2300.
4 'Cunctator' (Slowcoach) was the nickname given to Quintius Fabius Maximus,
   whose slow, deliberate tactics against the Carthaginians under Hannibal succeeded in saving the Roman state and led to the proverb 'Rome wins by sitting
   still' (*Adagia* i x 29).
5 See *Adagia* i v 39: 'Not even Hercules can take on two.'

This is in fact the juice of the black cuttlefish, that is, pure venom.[6] Let them defend others with this colouring; I do not want to be defended in that way. I frankly confess, and I will continue to confess, that if I had known be- 50 forehand that this age would occur, I would not have written much of what I wrote, or I would have written it differently; and I would also not have done some things that I did. 'But a prudent man' they say, 'should have divined the future.' To be sure, but not all of it. Nevertheless, I acknowledge, to some degree, that I was naive and thoughtless. But the things they are always 55 yapping about are nowhere to be found in my writings, provided that the interpreter is not malicious. And in my *Clarifications*,[7] to which they give the polite title of *Palinodes*,[8] I don't express anything differently than I intended when I wrote it or than what I expressed in the words; but I exclude an unfair reader, for whom nothing can be written with sufficient circumspection. 60 I wrote brief notes and commentaries for scholars and good men; I did not think that I was writing warranties or court documents.

But they are growing milder, as you write. It doesn't make much difference, most renowned gentlemen, how mild they have grown towards me; I am just surprised they are not yet worn out. I only wish they would truly 65 grow mild in the image of him who said, 'Learn from me because I am mild and humble of heart, and you will find rest for your souls.'[9] I think there are such people, even among my enemies, but I do not know why I am so unlucky that among those I encounter I find some so ferocious and so implacable that it would be safer to contend with any cardinal than with them, 70 and I could sooner placate any offended prince or pope than one of these people, who boast that they are dead to the world, although in fact there is hardly any other sort of mortals in which the world lives and reigns more than in them. For a few I want to make an exception; I wish I could say that of many more. 75

Very recently a new one has arisen, to whom I had courteously given advice that was not only useful to him but even necessary;[10] he responded as if I had thrown rocks at him.[11] I thought I was dealing with a calm and

* * * * *

6 The line is from Horace *Satires* 1.4.100–1. It is cited in *Adagia* III v 74, which explains, citing Aristotle, that a frightened cuttlefish ejects a black fluid to darken the water and thus keep itself from being caught.
7 *Declarationes ad censuras Lutetiae vulgatas*, 1532 (Ep 2552 n10)
8 Ie 'retractions' (see *Adagia* I ix 59)
9 Matt 11:29
10 Agostino Steuco; see Ep 2465.
11 Ep 2513

philosophic temperament, but I seem to have bumped into a Citeria that missed no opportunity to blare against me.[12] For, to say nothing about the   80
usual old stories about me with which they customarily enliven their drinking bouts, he accuses me of claiming to be the leading authority in the field of letters – no, as he says, 'in the entire human race,' and not the best but the 'only' one.[13] Although this is a shameless lie and an outrageous slander, still I could hardly read it without laughing. I do not claim for myself any other   85
place than the Megarians got from the oracle.[14] But to say nothing about the leading men of letters, to none of whom I have ever equated myself, I see and rejoice that all over the world young men flourish who outstrip me by many miles. He also accuses me of jealousy,[15] but he gives no evidence, he just throws the dart. I confess that by nature I am susceptible to many vices.   90
But if I know well enough what envy is, I have never felt that I was assaulted by this feeling – thanks be to Christ. For I think that envy is the burning pain a person feels at the success of someone else, even though it causes him no harm. For if someone is distressed by the promotion of his enemy because he will have more power to hurt him, that feeling is fear, not envy.   95
But I have even rejoiced when a deadly enemy of mine was promoted to a high position,[16] because it often happens that accession to greater authority puts an end to the contention, either because the one promoted simply scorns his inferior or because he has no time to bother with him. They say that this happened to Hadrian: after he had become emperor, when he met   100
a man for whom he had felt the bitterest enmity he said nothing more than 'you have escaped.'[17] He adds another absolutely capital crime, but by all odds the flimsiest of all. He says he has seen with his own eyes and read a letter of mine in which I openly write that 'no greater evil could be found in the Christian religion than the invention of those religious orders.'[18] Such   105

* * * * *

12 Citeria was an 'an amusing and loquacious figure, carried along in procession to raise a laugh, making a great noise and racket all the time.' The word became a term of abuse for people who talk too much. See *Adagia* IV viii 44, and cf II vii 44.
13 Ep 2513:708–10
14 See Ep 2880 n6.
15 Ep 2513:710–12
16 Perhaps a reference to Edward Lee (Ep 765), who in 1531 had been made archbishop of York, or perhaps Girolamo Aleandro (Ep 2810 n22), long since a leading papal diplomat and member of the college of cardinals
17 See the life of Hadrian by Aelius Spartianus in *Scriptores Historiae Augustae* 17.1.
18 See Ep 2513:439–42.

words never entered my mind nor were they ever expressed by either my
pen or my tongue. What more outrageous accusation could be imagined to
stir up all the bands of monks to seek to destroy me? He adds, 'You will say
the letter is not yours. Please God that it was not!'[19] If the letter has the words
he recites, let him know for certain that it is not mine but was made up by   110
some filthy wretch possessed by a devil – and in our times there is no lack of
those who devise such tricks. But if it is the letter sent to Servatius,[20] he will
find nothing like that written there. It speaks only of a certain person who
at a tender age was forced into a religious order by tutors and other people.
This is essentially what it says: though he was unhappy in many ways, no   115
unhappiness in all his life was worse than that he was forced into this kind
of life, to which he was suited neither in mind nor in body.[21] I do not think
there is anything here to which one can rightly object. But if he thought the
letter was fictitious, why did he publish to the whole world something that
was doubtful and unknown? If, on the other hand, he didn't remember very   120
well what he had read, how responsible was it of him to be so thoughtless
as to hurl such a deadly slander? I don't want to pursue this any further.
And someone who swallows these things so often and turns neither pen nor
tongue against them is thought to be irascible! But these very people, if they
had been drenched with such vinegar, how furious would they be?   125

For my part, in this great tumult of insults, I easily find consolation in
what St Paul says: 'Whom the Lord loves, he chastises, and he scourges every
son whom he receives.'[22] And I am happy to employ the most Christian saying of St Augustine: 'Lord, cut here, burn here, so that you will spare me in
eternity.'[23] It is something to conform to the image of Christ even in this way.   130
While that lamb, purer than purity itself, was alive was there any insult he

* * * * *

19 Ep 2513:442–3
20 Ie Ep 296 to Servatius Rogerus. Cf Ep 2513 n59.
21 See Ep 296:12–34. Steuco was perhaps judging Erasmus in the light of the un-
   flattering account of the rise of monasticism that follows in lines 73–85 and ends
   with the words 'What is more corrupt and impious than such easy obligations
   as these?'
22 Heb 12:6
23 This quotation, which Allen was not able to trace, recurs in two of Erasmus'
   last letters; see Allen Epp 3077:9–10, 3108:7. In neither place is it attributed to
   Augustine. A search of Augustine's writings in the *Patrologia Latina* does not
   turn up these exact words, though in his *Enarrationes in Psalmos* (section 3 on Ps
   6:2) he says *[U]bi enim sanitas est, nec mors metuenda est, nec urentis aut secantis
   manus* 'Where there is sanity, neither death nor the hand of one who burns and
   cuts must be feared' (PL 36 92). *Hic seca, hic ure* 'cut here, burn here' occurs in

did not hear from the Pharisees? Drunkard, seducer of the people, demonic, blasphemous.[24] Was there any sort of mockery he did not suffer? Spat upon by the soldiers, struck with a rod, crowned with thorns, struck and slapped.[25] Why should I, who deserve worse, refuse to be scourged, spit upon, and 135 struck by the insults of insolent assailants, and to be purged by this merciful medicine? My mind is also consoled by what holy men have said and what men just as holy have experienced: the judgments of God are one thing, the judgments of men something quite different. And if they are so determined that they will not relent until they drive me to the cross, I will pray to the 140 Lord to grant me patience and them a better understanding. In the meantime I have decided neither to quarrel with people of this kind nor to be close friends with them. In other respects I want to keep a Christian peace with everyone, and I will do everything that I can to maintain it. And I would also like everyone who comes to my defence to have the same attitude. 145

Finally, even if you imagine that I am fighting one on one, wouldn't it be perfectly fair for an old man to leave the field to a young man? The ancient custom was to throw any man over sixty off of the bridge.[26] And so, since I am almost seventy,[27] isn't it time for me to withdraw from the assemblies of scholars and leave voting rights to others? It is more fitting that I should 150 abstain from the fierce disputes of young men. The human temperament is amazingly stubborn, and everyone is beautiful in his own eyes.[28] Ultimately, with whatever plumage we deck ourselves out, we are all men, not angels. I grant that without letters life is no life,[29] but he does not live without letters who delights in perusing the books of pious men. 155

But now I am engaged in a serious matter. You will be able to determine what it is from the book that you will receive with this letter. Its title is *On the Preparation for Death.*[30]

* * * * *

Peter Lombard's *In totum Psalterium commentarii* (Ps 6:1) and is followed almost immediately by the sentence just cited, which is identified as coming from Augustine (PL 190 105A).

24 Matt 11:19, 27:63, Mark 3:22, Luke 11:15, Matt 9:3, Mark 2:7
25 Matt 27:28–31, Mark 14:65, 15:17–19, Luke 22:63, John 19:1–3
26 In ancient Rome sexagenarians, no longer eligible to vote, were driven from the bridge leading to the voting place; see *Adagia* I v 37.
27 If one accepts 1467 as the most likely date of Erasmus' birth (rather than 1466 or 1469), he would have turned sixty-six in October 1533.
28 *Adagia* I ii 15 (CWE 31 160:84)
29 Plato *Apology* 38A
30 See Ep 2884 introduction.

I have also received the letter of Christophorus Fontanus,[31] which is marvellously clever and witty. How much he accomplishes in a few words! I greatly admired the man's intelligence, but I would wish that he had expended his energy on a more worthwhile topic. And so I am glad that this document was not published.[32] He gave the Franciscan's book greater honour than I did;[33] it seems he devoured the whole thing. I sampled some pages of it, but only in snatches, and I soon sent the little book to Alfonso de Valdés,[34] a most honourable friend whom the envy of the Fates, it seems, took from me.[35] If my letter that the two of you were thinking of publishing is not already in circulation, I would prefer that it be suppressed. You say, 'They expect more moderation from you; this letter will shut their mouths because it is written with great moderation.'[36] How can you deal with the fickle and peevish judgments of these men? With no provocation, they sometimes tear a man to pieces with false and outrageous slanders and with insane insults, and then they claim Christian moderation for themselves and complain that he who defends his innocence from the accusation of impious wickedness is lacking in moderation. What kind of moderation, I ask you, do they want?

160

165

170

175

* * * * *

31 Quite possibly Constantino Ponce de la Fuente (1502–59), Spanish theologian, preacher, and reformer deeply influenced by Erasmian ideals, who not only admired his scholarship but also possessed a similar sense of humour and sarcasm and aimed his barbs at similar targets, including the regular clergy. After completing his studies at Seville in 1534, he was ordained the following year and appointed preacher at the cathedral. In the 1540s he published several books promoting an Erasmian style of piety. Called to serve Charles v as court preacher, he twice accompanied the court on journeys through the Low Countries and to Germany (1548–50, 1553–5). Back in Seville, he associated with local 'Lutherans,' ran afoul of the Jesuits, and in 1558 was found guilty of heresy by the Inquisition. He died in prison while awaiting his sentence. See OER III 294–5.

32 The words 'this document' (*scriptum hoc*) indicate that the 'letter' (*epistolam*) of line 159 was not really a letter to Erasmus but some sort of pamphlet.

33 The Franciscan was Luis de Carvajal (Ep 2110 n10), who is named in this connection in Ep 2932:21–3.

34 The book sent to Valdés was Carvajal's *Apologia monasticae religionis diluens nugas Erasmi*, which had been published in two editions, one at Salamanca in 1528, and one at Paris in 1529; see Epp 2126, 2198.

35 Valdés died in 1532.

36 Bataillon (page 532) surmises that Erasmus had written a conciliatory letter to Carvajal, that he subsequently received a similar letter from Carvajal via the Mexías (see lines 194–7 below), and that he wanted both letters to remain unpublished.

That he should thank them for abuse and slanders and that to please them he should confess to wicked impiety, of which he knows he is innocent? They do not care at all that this situation created a serious stumbling block to weak people, so careful are they that their honour be taken into account. I do not understand very well what they mean by moderation. But there are some people – and they are not unlearned or frivolous – who accuse me of excessive moderation in my apologias, thinking that a tough knot needs a sharp axe; and if they want a specimen of my moderation they should read my *Clarifications*.[37] Furthermore, fair judges admit that I have never forgotten moderation or courtesy, except in the apologia in which I replied to Cousturier.[38] As for him, he had no case, and he was arguing about matters in which he had no judgment, but he still raged against me with unbridled impudence – a theologian and a Carthusian, no less! What then? Would one letter be enough for them to register me immediately in the approved list of the moderate? I don't think so. Rather, some will say I am just wearing a false mask; others will accuse me of doing what cockerels do when they are defeated – flee from the fight with drooping feathers – and instead of calling me moderate they will boast that I am cowardly.

Furthermore, I predict what will happen: one letter will generate another. If that letter you mention is published, the person to whom it is written will not allow his own letter to be suppressed. For that letter was also delivered to me together with your letter. With what spirit it was written, God only knows. But I take it in good part, for Christian charity ought not to be suspicious. Give the man my most loving wishes and at the same time persuade him that my failure to respond did not spring from any ill will. Indeed the very reason I did not answer is that I want our mutual good will to be permanent. What the Greeks commonly say is true: in many cases friendship is destroyed by silence.[39] On the other hand, it is also true, as I have discovered from experience, that friendship between some people is better nourished by silence than by conversation or epistolary exchanges. In writing I am often somewhat frank, judging the temperament of others by my own. But not infrequently that has turned out badly for me. Moreover, the two of you will be acting in accord with your kindness if you do not impede the momentum of an enthusiastic young man. Perhaps it will turn out for him the way it does for a noble wine: when the wine is new, it is somewhat

180

185

190

195

200

205

210

* * * * *

37 See n7 above.
38 *Apologia adversus debacchationes Petri Sutoris* (Ep 1591)
39 *Adagia* ii i 26

sharp; but when it has aged and ceased to ferment, it becomes more mellow. Some leeway should be granted to youth because self-love, as long as it is not excessive, can stimulate young people to be industrious and to work hard at honourable tasks.

I am grateful to you for the care you took to send me the letter of   215
Luis Vives. If he really means what he writes, he seems to suspect that my friendship for him had grown chilly because in his letters he praised the Franciscan.[40] And that suspicion seems to have also made its way into your minds. But I will not allow it to be rooted there any more deeply. Therefore I want you to take it to be as certain and indubitable as if it were delivered   220
from an oracle that not even the slightest notion of such a thing entered my mind. Indeed I read only one of those laudatory letters, a very short one. It contained a recommendation, but such a moderate one that it was easy to see that Vives was merely complying with someone who had asked this little favour from him. But why should I have been alienated from Vives because   225
he was friendly with someone with whom I had a quarrel, since I never demanded such a thing even from my servantpupils, as long as their friendship did me no harm? At Louvain, when I was engaged in deadly combat with a Briton,[41] Vives was not only friendly with him but was his close companion, and there were those who claimed that he lent his aid to the Briton. But that   230
did not make me the least bit less fond of Vives, and with every fibre of my being I avoided accusing that learned gentleman of anything. On my own initiative I usually advise some of my friends not to withdraw for my sake from their friendship with those who happen to be engaged in polemics with

* * * * *

40 It appears that the Mexías had forwarded to Erasmus a letter from Vives (not extant) in which he expressed his suspicion that Erasmus' friendship for him had grown cool because of the praise for Carvajal found in some of his (Vives') letters. He goes on to specify (lines 222–5) that he had read 'only one of those laudatory letters,' which he describes as brief and perfunctory letter of commendation. This would be the letter to Charles de Croy that Carvajal published in his *Dulcoratio* of 1530 (folio 18 verso). It is indeed a non-committal letter of introduction rather than a commendation. From Ep 2932:2 it appears that on 5 January 1534 Erasmus, having read Vives' letter to the Mexías, wrote directly to Vives (as promised in line 242 below) a letter explaining that he had not grown cold in friendship on account of Carvajal or for any other reason. Erasmus' letter is not extant, but Vives' answer to it (Ep 2932) indicates that he had written to Carvajal complaining of the use of his letter of introduction in the *Dulcoratio* and asking Carvajal not to make use of his (Vives') name in any future publications against Erasmus.
41 Edward Lee; see n16 above.

me, since I am aware that they may be of assistance in ending the quarrels.   235
But I wonder how Vives came to suspect me, unless perhaps it was because
I do not write to him very often. But I do not write without reason, even to
old and tested friends, unless there is some special occasion for it. There is
no region where I do not have some friends, but if when I wrote to one I
had to write to all of them, I would certainly be subjected to an extremely   240
burdensome obligation. Accordingly, if I have removed this source of uneasi-
ness from you, I will also relieve the suspicions of Vives as soon as possible.
All that is left, most renowned gentlemen, is to thank you for your favour
towards me. Cordial greetings to Christophorus Fontanus.[42]
    Given at Freiburg im Breisgau, on the eve of Christmas in the year 1533   245

2893 / From Bernardus Gravius   Cologne, 24 December 1533

This letter was first published as Ep 196 in Förstemann / Günther. The autograph was in the Burscher Collection of the University Library at Leipzig (Ep
1254 introduction).
    Little is known of Bernardus Gravius (documented 1533–44?), one of the
eight children of Tielmannus Gravius (Ep 2894). In the spring or summer of
1533 he was briefly a servant-pupil of Erasmus before going on to study for
a time at Basel. More given to drinking than to studying, he had to borrow
money from the Freiburg publisher Johannes Faber Emmeus to pay his debts.
After Erasmus wrote to complain of his conduct, Tielmannus called Bernardus
home and made him write this letter of apology. Bernardus wrote again in the
spring (Ep 2910) asking for Erasmus' support in his attempt to persuade his
father to give him another chance and to let him study at Louvain, but there is
no record of him in the Louvain matriculation register. In the summer of 1535
the incensed Faber Emmeus had still not been paid the money owed him (Ep
3040). Bernardus may be the Bernardus Gravius a Fossa who matriculated at
Cologne in 1544 to study law. The translation faithfully reflects the clumsiness
of Bernardus' Latin.

Cordial greetings. I beg you, distinguished sir, to accept in good part the limi-
tations of my time as the excuse for the interruption of my correspondence.
For I was hindered from writing letters partly by the storms of tumultuous
business transactions that fell to my lot, partly by the lack of a letter bearer.
But I will try as hard as I can not to incur the same bad marks for not writing,   5

* * * * *

42 See n31 above.

providing that access to reliable people is made available to me and that I
notice that my eagerness in writing letters does not displease you.

I reached Cologne, where I was expected and was received quite happily,
but not without being attacked by the fiercest of robbers, who are swarming on
the roads because of the wars in Lower Germany,[1] so that you would think   10
it was a confused chaos of the most rabid dogs. And now, my most honourable preceptor, nothing remains, I think, but for me to offer your Excellency
eternal gratitude for your extraordinary kindnesses towards me, to which I
will almost never be able to make myself equal. But I will make every effort
never to seem to lack good will and good intentions, whatever my meagre   15
resources allow. I beg you, by your immense kindness to me, to forget what
is past and not to open the wound that has healed over.[2] Let the confession
be the medicine for the sin, and deign to dash fresh water on your Bernardus,
who is ranked at the very lowest level of your clients. I cannot dare to entice
you, most excellent gentleman that you are, to write back. But if you do so of   20
your own accord, Bernardus will be overjoyed and you will suffuse my heart
with pleasure. I would write you at greater length if the urgency of the letter
bearer did not prevent me or if you, in your kindness, would be pleased with
a longer composition. For I am afraid that I would sin against the common
good, as the poet says,[3] by taking up time that you should devote to more   25
suitable studies. And so, farewell, my patron and incomparable preceptor,
and take in good part this monstrous mass of scribbling. Finally, continue to
maintain our mutual affection.

In haste, from my father's house, on the eve of Christmas, etc 1533
Bernard, prostrate at your feet   30
To the high priest of learning, Erasmus of Rotterdam, a preceptor ever
to be honoured

2894 / From Tielmannus Gravius   Cologne, 26 December 1533

This letter was first published as Ep 197 in Förstemann / Günther. The autograph
was in the Burscher Collection of the University Library at Leipzig (Ep 1254
introduction). For Tielmannus Gravius of Cologne, see Ep 1829 introduction.

* * * * *

2893
1 Ie the Netherlands (see Ep 2812 n1). This reference is puzzling. The only warfare in the Netherlands at the moment was a maritime war between Holland
  and Lübeck (Ep 2798 n12), and it is not clear how that would affect the numbers
  of robbers on the roads in nearby Germany.
2 Ie his bad behaviour in Basel; see introduction.
3 Horace *Epistles* 2.1.3–4

Cordial greetings. Perhaps I shall seem to have utterly renounced any affection for you, my most renowned master and patron, most respected of mortals, for not having answered your letter,[1] which was in the highest degree
both learned and affectionate. Please ascribe my failure to do so not to any
pride or contempt or negligence but to the numberless tasks and engage-   5
ments in which I have been detained for quite some time, especially in arranging the coadjutorship for our archbishop. Because of his advanced age
and the many other troubles that princes daily encounter by the hundreds in
this most violent and gangrenous age of ours,[2] he has chosen Count Adolf
von Schaumburg (a young man, to be sure, but nevertheless gifted with the   10
prudence beyond that of old age and with wonderful learning) as his bishop
coadjutor, to be appointed and confirmed by apostolic authority.[3] If you had
seen the labours that I have endured in this matter, composing letters and
writing documents that are even more prolix than papal diplomas, I would
not need any justification in the eyes of your Worship.   15
     As for what you have so faithfully revealed to me concerning all the
circumstances of the life led there by my son Bernardus, I hardly know (so
help me God!) any good deed that could have bound you any more closely
to me than that. Before this I had seen his temperament, his life, and his behaviour as if through a fog and in an enigma, but now I see them clearly as if 20
in a mirror held up before my eyes.[4] The fawning indulgence of parents and
the blindness of their love for their children is sometimes so great that they
cannot see what would contribute most to their welfare. Although I have
never sinned in that regard (for when they were at home as well as when
they were abroad with others I myself took care that my sons be restrained   25
by rigorous discipline), I would nonetheless be foolish and stupid twice over
if I did not agree with what you wrote about Bernardus as the judgment of a
great man whose faith has always been sacrosanct to me and will always be
so as long as I live.
     When he came flying back to me, I did not receive him at all courteous- 30
ly or with a happy face. But I nevertheless cleverly pretended not to know
many things that he did not yet know I knew, but would know soon enough
when paternal kindness was withdrawn and he was left to his own fate and

* * * * *

2894
1 Not extant
2 The archbishop, Hermann von Wied (Ep 1976), was 57.
3 Schaumburg (1511–56), canon of the Cologne cathedral since 1529, was elected
   coadjutor to the archbishop on 17 December 1533 and confirmed in that office
   by the pope on 27 August 1535. He succeeded Wied as archbishop in 1547.
4 Cf 1 Cor 13:12.

could live as he wished. I would not have recalled him if I had not known about his ungrateful conduct from your letter. For who would want such a worthless son to live in your household if all you got from him was trouble and disdain? No one, I say, except someone completely ignorant of how ungrateful and intolerable a thing it is to disrupt the studies of learned men and disturb the quietness of their lives by associating with insolent rowdies. You urged that he be sent to France or Italy. Who would dare attempt this, to the loss of his resources? For what hope of future progress could there be if he were in the hands of less learned men, after he has produced such a lamentable outcome when he was with the very highest proponent of learning in the whole Christian world? Whose rule will he obey if he has refused to lower his neck under your yoke, for nothing could be lighter, more bearable, sweeter than that to an eager student? To sum it all up in a few words, one would certainly have to have a disagreeable, rude, illiberal, vulgar, hard, shameless, obstinate, and stubborn character in order to scorn your authority and do just as he likes, to be swept away, not where judgment leads him but where he is driven by stupidity and disorderly passions. He is still living with me, but ignored and as if he were not my offspring. For I cannot forget the story of his past life, the ugly role he played there under an ignorant director.[5] Something different will be set up for him in the coming summer, which I know he may perhaps not find very pleasant. From the accounting he rendered to me I understand that your Worship allotted thirty-four florins for expenses incurred by him.[6] If this amount is not sufficient, I will be more than happy to add to it whatever you wish.

Together with a letter, Agrippa sent me his apologia written against certain theologasters, to be delivered there when the occasion arises.[7] A few days ago I also received two bundles of letters from Antwerp, which I am now sending along as well. If you have anything that needs to be taken care of among us here or in Brabant, or in the duchy of Jülich or Cleves or anywhere else, let me know, and I will be, as I always have been, most obedient and ready to do whatever you wish.

* * * * *

5 During his stay in Freiburg Bernardus had evidently been accompanied by a supervisor in the employ of his father.
6 If Rhenish florins, the expense allowance was £8 7s 2d groot Flemish, equivalent to a year's wage of an Antwerp master mason/carpenter (CWE 12 650 Table 3, 691 Table 13).
7 Henricus Cornelius Agrippa von Nettesheim *Apologia contra theologistas Lovanienses* (Ep 2790 n2)

Farewell from Cologne, on the day after Christmas 1533   65
Your Worship's most dutiful servant Tielmannus Gravius
To the great high priest of sacred and human learning, Desiderius
Erasmus of Rotterdam, my ever venerable master and patron

2895 / From Etienne Desprez   Besançon, 4 January 1534

This letter was first published as Ep 199 in Förstemmann / Günther. The autograph was in the Burscher Collection of the University Library at Leipzig
(Ep 1254 introduction). For Etienne Desprez, rector of the school at Besançon,
who played an important role in supplying Erasmus with Burgundy wine, see
Ep 2140 introduction. The translation attempts to duplicate the strain and the
awkwardness of Desprez's Latin.

Cordial greetings. O most rare and extraordinary divine spirit, most absolute
in piety, possessed of an authority accepted everywhere and a wisdom that is
consummate, if your last two letters had come from the heavenly empyrean
to me, completely devoted to your Humanity as I am, they could not have
been more longed for or received with more love or pleasure, entrusted as   5
they were to Gilbert, a distinguished young man, who is most promising in
every way, a servant most dear to you, bright and gifted with many talents,
whose loyalty is absolutely clear to you from numerous proofs.[1] I did not
respond to the first of the letters because I had that same Gilbert as a living
letter worthy of your divine ears, and (what counted for more) because I am   10
impeded in responding by a lowly and completely disjointed mode of expression. If my eloquence were measured by my wishes, it would certainly
surpass that of Nestor.[2] But at the present moment this monstrous stammer-
ing of mine has been conquered by my enormous respect for you, which
would convict me of extraordinary ingratitude if I made no reply to the sec-   15
ond letter. I would very much like to be able to give you some special token
of how great that respect is and to pour out all of my feelings of benevolence
upon you, who deserve to be revered in every possible way.

* * * * *

2895
1 The two letters from Erasmus are not extant. They were evidently delivered by
  Gilbert Cousin during one of his visits to Besançon in the autumn of 1533 to
  procure wine for Erasmus; see Ep 2889 introduction.
2 Nestor was renowned not only for having lived to a great age but also for his
  'more than honeyed eloquence' (*Adagia* I ii 56).

In truth, you could secure any service – however great, without exception – that you could request throughout your whole life, if there were any   20
way I could gratify you. The last time was in the matter of wine, and I was
happy to do everything I could to provide it. But what torments me most of
all is that you have deigned to thank me seriously for it, since I am in fact
obliged to you more than I or anyone could ever repay, even someone most
capable of giving thanks and most eager to do so. And perhaps if you had   25
entrusted this little task (which has been executed not very carefully) of seeking out, buying, and transporting by wagon a wine more suited to your pal-
ate, less sour or sharp to the taste, to high-ranking people here, they would
have embraced it with all the enthusiasm at their command and would have
executed it with greater resources but not with more affection. If it had been   30
a domestic transaction, you would not have paid a cent for it. And though I
did not provide that, I still rejoice everlastingly that you did not refuse to entrust me with this task, which will be an honour to my whole family. I have,
moreover, instructed your servant Gilbert about how to manage the special
character of our old wine, which should never be opened except to enjoy the   35
wine. Otherwise the old wine immediately loses its taste because it does not
bear up, I would imagine, under transport or any lengthy slushing around.
If it is drained over a long period, it generates head colds, stomach cramps,
and gout, with which I hear you are well acquainted. About that I am deeply
sorry because I hate my own health if it is not joined with yours. And I do not   40
see how remaining any longer in Freiburg contributes to your health (which
may God in his power and mercy propitiously keep intact for us). It would
be more advisable for you to come down this coming Easter with fortunate
foot[3] to Besançon, which is yours on many counts, which your extraordinary
and incomparable language has gained as a friend, which will have all the   45
Muses residing within her bounds when you arrive.[4]

O Besançon, three and four times blessed if it should ever happen that
Desiderius Erasmus, the most devout, learned, and blameless of theologians,
should slip quietly into it, a city whose gifts we now marvel at and appreciate
all the more on closer contact. Here you will find the fountain of rejuvenes-   50
cence, far different from the Clitorian fountain,[5] for it offers all manner of

* * * * *

3 Allusion to Horace *Epistles* 2.1.37
4 For Erasmus' contemplation of leaving Freiburg to settle in Besançon, and for
   the importance of suitable wine as a motive for it, see Ep 2870 n1.
5 Ovid *Metamorphoses* 15.322–3: 'Whoever slakes his thirst at Clitor's fountain /
   shuns wine and enjoys only pure water.' (Clitor was a town in Arcadia.)

most noble wines, wines suitable to your taste, wines to which you attribute
half your life. I only wish that my powers of persuasion were as great as the
sincere regard I have for you! Certainly we would today be enjoying such
a great guest, in whose fame the entourage of Mercury and all the Muses   55
takes delight.[6] And do not (if you love yourself) refuse to say goodbye soon
to the houses and stoves of Germany.[7] Believe me when I give you salutary
admonitions (although you are the most sensible man on whom the sun
shines here): everyone in both ruling orders here in Besançon welcomes with
incredible enthusiasm, everyone venerates the most sacred lucubrations of   60
Master Erasmus.[8] On my word I promise you, I swear it by my life, that everything you encounter here will be much better than what I am telling you.
In fact, everyone here sings with one voice that the special glory of Erasmus
is unique, since it is not increased by anyone's recommendation; it is a glory
that surpasses all praise and grows day by day, based on a love that was   65
conceived long ago and marvellously increased by the death of Guillaume
Guérard, who was once official of the archdeacon,[9] and who shamelessly
took it upon himself with supreme impudence to dishonour the brilliant
Erasmus in the eyes of the official Désiré.[10]

Désiré himself had recently become one of your most avid promoters   70
and had the very highest opinion of you before he passed to a happier life.
This Guérard had forcefully inculcated in Désiré's mind that you were a only
a lukewarm papist, whereas no theologian had expressed the life of the gospel more truly than Erasmus, and that you were a familiar friend and adviser
of Luther, whose enslaved will is far removed from the free will espoused by   75
Erasmus; and this same Guérard made up some other outrageous foolishness

* * * * *

6 Mercury was, among other things, god of eloquence and poetry.
7 For Erasmus' aversion to German stoves, see Epp 1248 n5, 1258 n18, 1399:4–7,
  2055 n7, 2112:4 and 23–4, 2118:45–6.
8 The two 'ruling orders' were the municipal government and the cathedral clergy, but Erasmus had reason to doubt the unanimity of the two orders on wanting him to settle in their city; see Ep 2870 n1.
9 Guillaume Guérard (d January 1529), canon of the cathedral and official (chief
  judge) of the archdeacon, played host to Erasmus when he visited Besançon
  in 1524 (Ep 1534 n9). He was one of those whom Erasmus consulted in 1529
  when contemplating the possibility of moving to Besançon, only to be told that
  it would be inappropriate because of 'some sort of disagreement between the
  clergy and the authorities.' See Ep 2112:5–11 with n2.
10 Désiré Morel (d 23 July 1533) was Guérard's successor as official to the
   archdeacon; see Ep 2870 introduction.

about a little prayer and the blessed womb.[11] But these empty rumours have
been completely dissipated, replaced by a unanimous vote of approval, far
removed from what had been spread about by Guérard, the source and author of this tragedy (or rather, comedy).[12] Not long ago you would have had a 80
complete explanation of all this if an untimely death had not taken away the
official Désiré and deprived you of his kindness. You would have received
a token of his kindness (if he had lived), an expression of his reconciliation.
For not long before he was removed from all human affairs, he had intended
to give you two casks of a noble wine, but his generosity was prevented, cut 85
off by an intervening plague. All the canons habitually press to their breasts
and continually read that book of yours *On Concord*,[13] together with all
your other writings. And so as soon as your health permits, get ready for
the journey. Here there are many handsome residences open to you, and
among those innumerable ones mine also, which you can more truly claim 90
as your own. Finally, there is nothing new here that can give you pleasure
while you are absent, except that I implore you to continue the favour of loving your Etienne,[14] who in return will always strive mightily to outdo himself
every day in in his absolute commitment to Master Erasmus. I pray for what
is best for this best of men, including complete health of body and soul be- 95
yond the time allotted by the Fates, and I pray that he may consent to return
to Besançon, where he will be able to enjoy the knowledge of a life well lived
and the most pleasant memory of many wonderful accomplishments.

At Besançon, 4 January in the year 1534 after the virgin birth

Yours with his whole heart, Étienne Desprez, who is unconditionally de- 100
voted to you, and from whom may you deign to expect everything promised

To Master Desiderius Erasmus, remarkably extraordinary paraphraser,
defender, and vindicator of Holy Scripture, marvellous theologian, worthy
to be celebrated through all ages, the most learned restorer of humane learning, living in the proud city Freiburg im Breisgau 105

* * * * *

11 For Erasmus' own account of the incident in which a jesting remark about a
   too-long prayer of thanksgiving after a meal resulted in his being accused of
   shocking irreverence towards the Virgin Mary, see Ep 1956:26–46.
12 Even if one accepts at face value these assurances that the death of Guérard
   had yielded an atmosphere of universally friendly welcome for Erasmus at
   Besançon, the fact remains that those assurances came too late to alter Erasmus'
   decision to return to Brabant.
13 *De sarcienda ecclesiae concordia* (Ep 2852)
14 The Latin of this passage is obscure. This is our attempt to rescue some meaning
   from it.

2896 / To Erasmus Schets   Freiburg, 23 January 1534

This letter, written in answer to one no longer extant, was first published by Allen on the basis of the autograph in the British Library (MS Add 38512 folio 84). For Erasmus Schets, the Antwerp banker who looked after the collection and transmission of the income from Erasmus' livings in England and the Netherlands, see Ep 1541 introduction.

Cordial greetings. Would that the bundle you sent to Tielmannus had come a little more promptly.[1] For it was delivered on 22 January, when I had already written, through Viglius the Frisian,[2] to Vincent Cornelissen and Arnoldus van der Goes concerning the grant from Holland.[3] I find it easy to believe what you wrote concerning the sixty florins for travel expenses. But I suspect 5 that all the money is in the hands of Montfoort.[4] He is hunting for large prey with empty hands.[5] But as for me, I will not allow the hundred florins to be taken away from me, now that they have been granted to me.[6]

P. Barbier is laughing at me from on high. And that Molendino was the first one to show him how to intercept the pension.[7] For my part, I am think- 10 ing of how I can make some trouble for Barbier.

Hillen has printed a book of sermons by some Franciscan that is absolutely asinine. He did so, apparently, for no other reason than to mix in his

* * * * *

2896
1 Presumably one of the bundles mentioned in Ep 2894:59–61
2 Viglius Zuichemus (Ep 2810), who visited Erasmus at Freiburg on 7 January 1534; see Ep 2878 n2. The letters he carried are not extant.
3 For Vincent Cornelissen see Ep 2819 introduction. For Aert (not 'Arnoldus') van der Goes see Ep 2819 n5. For the grant from Holland see Ep 2819 n2.
4 For Pieter van Montfoort, who had delivered the honorarium from the Estates of Holland, see Ep 2812 introduction. For the misunderstanding about the amount of the grant that destroyed Erasmus' good opinion of Montfoort, see the following lines and n6.
5 Not in the *Adagia*. There were many versions in the Germanic and romance languages of the proverb 'You can't snare a bird with empty hands.' More to the point here was the Latin proverb *Non facile vacuis manibus occiditur ursus* 'A bear is not easily killed with empty hands.' See *Philosophia patrum, versibus praesertim leoninis, rhythmis germanicis adiectis, iuventuti studiosae hilariter tradita* ed Julius Wegeler (Confluentibus [Koblenz]: Rudolph Friedrich Hergt 1869) 57 no 738.
6 See Ep 2819:7–16 with n6.
7 Cf Ep 2763:4–6, and see Ep 2851 n11.

own poisons.[8] The world is forced not only to put up with such rascals but to
nourish them as well.   15

I have written asking you to send the cup of Damião, to which you
should join the gift of your wife; I do not know how I can show my gratitude
to her.[9]

I have written this through the messenger from Cologne. I will write
about the rest through Hieronymus.[10]   20

If Quirinus Hagius, formerly my servant, comes to you, do not treat
him with any courtesy. He is a two-faced talebearer.[11]

Farewell, from Freiburg, 23 January in the year 1534 after the birth of
Christ

Erasmus of Rotterdam   25

Concerning the English diploma[12] I have written via Viglius to Master
Gillis, the cantor.[13] You will be able to talk to him.

To the outstanding gentleman Erasmus Schets. At Antwerp

* * * * *

8 In 1533 the Antwerp printer Michaël Hillen published the *Enarrationes evan-
geliorum per sacrum quadragesimae tempus occurrentium* of Nikolaus Ferber of
Herborn, a Franciscan Observant of Cologne, who from 1532 was commissary-
general for all provinces of the order outside Italy. By the time of this letter,
Erasmus had received from the Netherlands a few pages of Ferber's work,
which attacked him as a source of the heresies of the Protestant reformers; see
Epp 2899:10–38, 2906:49–69. Erasmus appealed unsuccessfully to the imperial court at Brussels to punish Hillen (Epp 2899:54–6, 2912:18–36, 2915:40–8,
2922:16–17, and Allen Epp 2948:7–9, 2981:25–7, 3053:1–4, 3100:77–83). Erasmus
also called for action against Ferber (Epp 2898:11–21, 2899:51–6), who, however,
died before any such action could be taken (Allen Ep 3053:4). Erasmus toyed
briefly with the idea of writing a public letter in reply to Ferber's charges (Allen
Ep 2961:135–40), but in the end did not do so.

9 For the gift cup from Damião de Gois, see Ep 2826:65–9 with n19. For the gift
from Schets' wife, of household linens, see Epp 2897:14–20, 2924:1–2.

10 Hieronymus Froben

11 For Quirinus Hagius and Erasmus' conviction that he was an embezzler and a
hostile gossip, see Ep 2704 n6.

12 Schets was engaged in the drafting of a legal instrument concerning the redemption of the pensions that Erasmus had received from archbishop William
Warham in England; see Epp 2512, 2924:18–23, and cf Allen Ep 2997:49–50.

13 On 4 February 1535 Jan van Campen, writing from Venice to Johannes Dantiscus
in Cracow, informed him that 'Pieter Gillis and his brother, the canon and cantor
at Antwerp,' had both died 'the previous year.' Pieter Gillis died in November
1533, so the brother presumably died at some point in 1534. Allen's identification of him with Pieter's brother Frans cannot be correct, for Frans, who is
mentioned several times in the letters of 1526, was a merchant, not a canon and

2897 / To Gaspar Schets   Freiburg, 23 January 1534

This letter was first published by Allen. The surviving manuscript is a sixteenth-century copy in the Bodleian Library at Oxford (Lat Misc c 20 folio 50). It bears the date 12 June 1533, which Allen rejected as an obvious error. In Ep 2913:1–5 (11 March) Erasmus acknowledges the receipt of two bundles of letters, the first of which, received on 22 January (see Ep 2896:1–2), contained a letter from Erasmus Schets and one from his son Gaspar Schets, both of which Erasmus says he has answered. If the present letter was actually dated in June, one would have to assume that Gaspar Schets had written twice. But Erasmus' comments in Ep 2913 appear to be directed at a letter received in January, which he praised highly to the boy's father. If there had been an earlier letter, one would expect Erasmus to mention it in his reply to Gaspar.

Gaspar Schets (1513–80), the eldest son of Erasmus Schets (Ep 2896), matriculated at the University of Louvain in February 1531. Although he was gifted in the liberal arts, composed Latin poems, and throughout his life maintained contacts with humanist scholars, he became a successful financier like his father and an even more important figure in the political life of the country. In 1555 he was appointed Philip II's factor in charge of the Antwerp exchange, and in 1564 he was promoted to the office of treasurer-general for the Netherlands, serving until 1577, when in the initial phase of the Dutch revolt his castle at Grobbendonck, which included his splendid library, was besieged and burned. For further details see Allen's introduction to this letter and de Vocht CTL III 358–61.

ERASMUS OF ROTTERDAM SENDS GREETINGS TO GASPAR SCHETS
I was extremely pleased, my very dear young man, that you wanted to send me a sample of your talent and your learning. For your letter makes it clear

* * * * *

cantor. Henry de Vocht has identified the cantor as another brother named Gillis (= Giles in English and Aegedius in Latin), the entry for whom in CEBR II 99 is entitled 'Gillis Gillis.' Canon and cantor at the church of Our Lady in Antwerp from 1510, Gillis took his father's given name (Nicolaas) as his surname and called himself Aegidius Nicolai (= Giles Nicholas). See de Vocht CTL II 66–7 and see also de Vocht *John Dantiscus and His Netherlandish Friends as Revealed by Their Correspondence, 1522–1546* (Louvain 1961) 234. Both works include the passage of the letter of Jan van Campen cited above. None of this explains why Erasmus would have written to the cantor about a legal document related to his (Erasmus') English pensions. From Epp 2924:22–3, 2933:11–12, however, it can be inferred that it was through the cantor that Erasmus hoped to secure a document from the papers of his late brother Pieter Gillis that was relevant to one of his (Erasmus') English pensions.

that you have a very sharp mind (in which you resemble both your parents)
and a considerable acquaintance with literature in both languages. Your ac-   5
complishments are all the more pleasing to me in that my friendship with
your excellent parents is neither new nor slight, so that I rejoice no less in
their good fortune than I do in my own. For what can make anyone happier
than to have children who educate themselves in studies that render them
profitable and distinguished, both privately to their relatives and publicly to   10
their country. Hence, my dear Gaspar, to spur on the galloping steed (as they
say),[1] I urge you again and again always to outdo yourself in this splendid
race you are running until you reach the finish line.

     Your mother has no obligation to me, since I have never done her any
favours or served her in any way, or if I have, she has already repaid me. And   15
so, since you have provided her with an occasion to think that she should
give me a splendid gift, it is only right that you should do the same for me
with regard to her and should thank her very much in my words, as best
you can, promising that I will see to it that her gift will not seem to have
been bestowed on an ingrate.[2] But I only wish that, just as she has sent clean   20
linens, she could also send a clean maidservant! For nothing could be dirtier
than these women! If you give them some elegant piece to wash, it will be destroyed by the third washing. Such is the way they twist, pound, and shake
the things they wash.

     I have an old housekeeper, ugly, lazy, loquacious, voracious, abusive.   25
I wouldn't hesitate to match her, all by herself, against fifteen other women!
But she has lived with me for almost twelve years. No one urges me to get a
new one, who might well be worse. I tried that once. I threw her out and got
a young girl, but she was a complete criminal – she would have thrown my
house into total confusion if I had not caught on to her in time. And so I took   30
my old woman back into favour.[3]

     The filth here is piled high. An artificially diverted stream runs through
the whole town. It collects the bloody gobbets of the butcher and the meat
market, and also the rotten waste from the kitchens, the filth from individual
homes, everyone's vomit and piss, and even the excrement of those who do   35
not have latrines at home. This is the water in which they wash linens, clean

* * * * *

2897
1 *Adagia* I ii 47
2 For the gift, see Ep 2896 n9.
3 For this story of Erasmus' ferocious housekeeper and his failed attempt to re-
   place her, see Ep 2735:56–7 with nn24–5, and cf Ep 2868:42–9.

wine casks and even kitchen pots and pans.⁴ These things could be tolerated
if there were anything to eat. All year long I eat young chickens. There are
no delicacies here, or if there are, they are carried off to the nobles. That is
why I am thinking of Brabant, if the unfavourable gods allow it.⁵ But I will   40
stop belabouring you with these trifles. Take care of yourself, and conclude
diligently what you have undertaken.

Given at Freiburg, 23 January in the year 1534 after the birth of Christ
Erasmus Rotterdam, in my own hand

2898 / To Nicolaus Olahus   Freiburg, 23 January 1534

This letter was first published in Ipolyi page 448. The manuscript is page 355 of
the Olahus codex in the Hungarian National Archives at Budapest (Ep 2339 introduction). Olahus' reply is Ep 2915. For Nicolaus Olahus, secretary to Queen
Mary, regent of the Netherlands, see Ep 2813.

ERASMUS OF ROTTERDAM TO NICOLAUS OLAHUS, THE TREASURER
OF SZÉKESFEHÉRVÁR, SECRETARY AND COUNSELLOR OF HER MOST
SERENE MAJESTY MARY, ETC, GREETINGS
The severe pain in my limbs returns so often that I do not know if there is
anything to be hoped for from this fragile little body of mine. From Christmas   5
on I have been most grievously afflicted, and I am miserable and afraid of
what will happen to me when the ice melts.¹ Therefore I have made a will,²
and my book on the preparation for death is being printed.³ Everything else
is in the hands of the Lord, and if he grants me even moderately good health
I have decided to come back to see you at the end of April.⁴   10

* * * * *

4 Water from the Dreisam river was diverted through Freiburg in runnels known
   as *Bächle* 'little brooks,' remnants of which are still functioning today in the old
   part of town. On its way though town to the fields it irrigated the water was
   subject to the use and abuse described here.
5 Virgil *Georgics* 4.7. For the ill-fated attempt to return to Brabant, see Ep 2820
   introduction.

2898
1 See Ep 2818 n1.
2 See Ep 2873A n2.
3 See Ep 2884.
4 See Ep 2820 introduction.

A book has been printed at Antwerp written by some ignorant, witless, arrogant, insane buffoon who vomits up astounding slanders against me.[5] And it seems that the only reason he published his sermons was to mix some poison into his insults – in the whole book there is not a spark of devout sensibility. But if such monsters can do whatever they want there, I do not know whether it would make any sense for me to go back there, though for many reasons I very much want to. You will get a better idea of the matter from the pages that I attach to this letter. Show them, if you wish, to our friends and to anyone else who you think might be able to restrain such bawlers. I only wish that the emperor had not granted so much leeway to such men – if they can be called men.[6] Since Lieven left here,[7] nothing from you has been delivered; perhaps some letters will come from the Frankfurt fair.[8] In the meantime give my best wishes to the most illustrious Duke of Aarschot.[9] Greetings to the Dane,[10] to whom I have not replied because I did not have the time.

Farewell. At Freiburg, 23 January 1534

2899 / To Jean (II) de Carondelet   Freiburg, [23 January] 1534

This letter was first published in Ipolyi pages 449–51. The manuscript is page 356 of the Olahus codex in the Hungarian National Archives at Budapest (Ep 2339 introduction). Jean (II) de Carondelet (Ep 1276), principal counsellor of Queen Mary, regent of the Netherlands, had conveyed to Erasmus the queen's formal invitation to return to the Netherlands (Ep 2784). Carondelet's reply to this letter is Ep 2912, line 6 of which indicates its month-date.

ERASMUS OF ROTTEDAM TO JEAN, ARCHBISHOP OF PALERMO, CHANCELLOR OF THE EMPEROR IN BRABANT, GREETINGS
My desire to return to my native land grows day by day and hour by hour. But final choice in the whole matter is in the hands of God, to whose will it is right that we submit our will. I am afflicted all too often by this torture,

* * * * *

5 See Ep 2896 n8.
6 On the emperor's alleged favour to the Franciscans, cf Ep 2906:46.
7 Lieven Algoet had been sent to Freiburg to bring Erasmus back to Brabant; see n4 above.
8 Ie the spring book fair at Frankfurt
9 Philippe de Croy (Ep 2822)
10 Jakob Jespersen, whose most recent letter was Ep 2849

the appropriate name for which I have not yet determined, and day by day
my bodily strength declines. Ever since Christmas I have been grievously
afflicted, and now I am very much afraid of the breakup of winter, but not
without some good hope.[1]

Her serene Majesty, your Highness, and other friends at court promise 10
that they will defend my person. But Michaël Hillen is publishing at Antwerp
(or rather has already published, I think) a book by a certain Franciscan,
Nikolaus Ferber, the commissary-general for the order north of the Alps,[2] a
man who is ignorant and intemperate (as his book shows) and who has no
ability except an inept loquacity, which he seems, however, to have absorbed 15
from my writings. In this book he rages more than scurrilously against my
reputation, lying prodigiously.[3] On the verso of page 285 he writes that in
my *Colloquies* I write not only wicked but also manifest lies against the religious orders (which he there calls 'families'), even though in all my books
there is nothing that attacks any nation or religious order. Thus far no mortal 20
has been able to show this. On the verso of page 322 he lists me among the
heretics who harass the church of God and then goes on to call me a 'soldier
of Pilate.' He adds that Luther has drawn to himself one part of the church,
and Oecolampadius and Zwingli a considerable part, but that Erasmus has
drawn away the largest part.[4] This ignorant buffoon, this shameless drunk- 25
ard vomits out such stuff, though no one has yet been able to indicate clearly
any place where I agree with the Lutherans and the Zwinglians. I have never
censured anything but human superstition and abuses. I only wish that I
could drag the universal church to where I was struggling to lead it, so that,
throwing off superstition, hypocrisy, worldly attachments, and frivolous lit- 30
tle questions, we would all serve the Lord with pure hearts, each in his own
vocation. This commissary seems to be angry at my *Colloquies* because I make
fun there of the superstition of some people who think themselves safe from
hell and purgatory if they are buried in a Franciscan habit, a deception with

* * * * *

2899
1 Cf Ep 2898:4–10.
2 See Ep 2896 n8.
3 For the summary that follows, cf Ep 2906:49–69.
4 We have been able to verify the accuracy of the first reference (to the verso of
   page 285) in the digitized version of a copy from which the last fifty pages of the
   work are missing.

which they have tricked the whole world for ages.[5] And they cannot fling   35
this at this or that group of Franciscans: they carry these dogmas around,
adding them to the rule. And I have no doubt that this whole work is littered
with such insults. But if it is licit there for such rogues to use printers to distribute whatever they like among the mob, and if it is not to be permitted to
print anything except what has been approved by such judges, what can we   40
expect but that good authors will be excluded and nothing will be worn out
in people's hands except their ignorant and witless nonsense? As for me, I
approve of the Franciscans from the bottom of my heart, and according to my
meagre resources I help them with a few coins. But if they were all like this
commissary, I would declare it right for them to be fed hay instead of wheat.[6]   45
For this cisalpine commissary is not a fit pastor even for a herd of pigs. I am
sending along three pages so that your Prudence can see that what I am saying is not a dream or an empty rumour.

I will not condescend to quarrel with such rogues. But if I did not fear
God more than St Francis, I would treat them as they deserve, since they   50
never put an end to it. It lies rather within your sphere of responsibility to
suppress their impudence, not so much for my sake (since you already lend
me considerable support) as for the sake of public tranquillity. For where can
such unrestrained arrogance lead but to rebellion? Therefore I earnestly beseech your reverend Lordship to use the authority of the court to rein in their   55
shamelessness.[7] For if such rogues can do whatever they like there, I do not
see how it would be any advantage for me to live among you. I have in fact
determined to come to see you towards the end of April, if the Lord deigns
to grant me even moderate health. In the meantime I beg you to continue in
your accustomed favour towards me.   60

Given at Freiburg im Breisgau, 1534

2900 / From Christoph Gering   Augsburg, 30 January 1534

This letter was first published as Ep 200 in Förstemann/Günther. The autograph was in the Burscher Collection of the University Library at Leipzig (Ep

* * * * *

5 The reference is to the colloquies *Funus* 'The Funeral' (CWE 40 763–95) and
  Exequiae seraphicae 'The Seraphic Funeral' (CWE 40 996–1032), in the latter of
  which Erasmus lampooned Alberto Pio's burial in the garb of a Franciscan.
6 Ie to be treated as animals rather than men; cf *Adagia* III 1 91.
7 See Ep 2896 n8.

1254 introduction). Christoph Gering (documented 1534–41) was the trusted secretary of Johann (II) Paumgartner (Ep 2882), authorized to sign letters on Paumgartner's behalf. In addition to this letter, he also wrote Epp 2949 and 2989 to Erasmus.

At the command of my master, who is currently absent, I am sending you, Erasmus, singular ornament of our age, gatanaric wine,[1] which he himself arranged to be sent to your Excellency before his departure. I hope that you will find it acceptable. But he himself will soon be writing you more about it. May God long keep you hale and hearty for us.   5

Given at Augsburg, 30 January in the year 1534 after the Virgin birth
The wagoner has been paid down to the last penny.
Your most humble servant, Christoph Gering, secretary of Johann Paumgartner
To the most renowned and excellent gentleman Desiderius Erasmus of   10
Rotterdam, the best and greatest professor of true theology, his most venerable master. At Freiburg im Breisgau

2901 / To Bonifacius Amerbach   [Freiburg], 4 February [1534]

This letter (= AK Ep 1800) was first published in the *Epistolae familiares*. The autograph is in the Öffentliche Bibliothek of the University of Basel (MS AN III 15 87). Allen assigned the year-date on the basis of the reference to 'the position offered,' that is, the job of legal adviser to the city council of Strasbourg, negotiations concerning which continued until January 1535, when Bonifacius rejected the offer; see Ep 2873A n3.

* * * * *

2900
1 The adjective *gatanaricus* does not exist, and Allen offers no explanation. Gerlo, on the other hand, suggests plausibly that the word should be read as *gattanaricus* (as in Allen Ep 2989:4, also from Gering), which would imply that the reference is either to wine from Gattinara, a town in Italy northwest of Novara in Piedmont, or to wine that the imperial chancellor Mercurino di Gattinara may have arranged to be shipped to Augsburg in preparation for his attendance at the imperial diet of 1530. Gattinara died at Innsbruck on his way to the diet, but his wine could very well have arrived safely and then been purchased by local notables like Paumgartner. In a letter of 22 December 1530 to Johann Koler in Augsburg, Erasmus wrote: 'I would be surprised if the princes had left no good wine behind [after the diet]. But I do not want our friend Anton [Fugger] to be too concerned about this.' (Fugger, Paumgartner's brother-in-law, had offered to supply Erasmus with wine from Italy). See Ep 2415:20–2 with n9.

Cordial greetings. The quittance pleases me greatly.[1] I will burn the other one. I would not dissuade that friend of ours from accepting the position he has been offered,[2] as long as the salary is appropriate. For he seems to be too familiar with that most seductive of the Sirens, Apatheia.[3] Therefore it will be expedient for him to be dragged into activities, so that he will shake off that indolence. I keep the matter in my heart and will not set it free.[4]

    Farewell, 4 February

    Yours truly, Erasmus of Rotterdam

    To Doctor Amerbach. At Basel

2902 / From Bonifacius Amerbach

For the reasons given by the AK editor Alfred Hartmann, this letter (= AK Ep 1904) has been redated to c 4 February 1535 and will appear as Ep 2989A in CWE 21.

2903 / To Bonifacius Amerbach

For the reasons given by the AK editor Alfred Hartmann, this letter (= AK Ep 1907) has been redated to 8 February [1535] and will appear as Ep 2992A in CWE 21.

2904 / From Frans van der Dilft   Mechelen, 11 February 1534

This letter was first published by Johannes Fecht in his *Historiae ecclesiasticae se-culi a. n. Ch. XVI. supplementum plurimorum celeberrimorum ex illo aevo theologorum epistolis* ... (Durlach: Martin Müller 1684) page 821. For Dilft, Erasmus' former secretary and courier, who had recently returned to Flanders from a second sojourn in Spain, see Ep 1663 introduction.

* * * * *

2901
1 A receipt for the sixteen hundred florins deposited with Bonifacius; see Ep 2855 introduction.
2 For the sake of confidentiality, Erasmus refers to Bonifacius in the third person.
3 Ie Apathy or Inertia (Greek in the text). There was no classical siren by that name; this one appears to be Erasmus' invention. He was familiar with Bonifacius' tendency to take a long time to make up his mind; cf Ep 2642:19–20.
4 This sentence echoes passages from Propertius, Cicero, and others cited in *Adagia* I iii 13: *In sinu gaudere* 'To rejoice in one's own bosom.'

TO ERASMUS OF ROTTERDAM, FRANS VAN DER DILFT
SENDS GREETINGS

Greetings. When I was returning from Spain,[1] nothing grieved me more, most renowned master, than that I could not travel by way of Germany, since I very much wanted to see you and had decided to do that above all else. But the mar- 5
riage arranged for me by my parents required me to hasten straight to Brabant, where I now have a wife who is temperamentally most compatible with me and who has a dowry that neither inclines me to extravagance nor binds me to unwelcome parsimony. To be sure, she was a widow, but there is no reason for me to regret my status.[2] May the news that is constantly circulating about your 10 arrival does not turn out to be an empty rumour! I would provide you with a most suitable residence, not only because of the splendour of the buildings but also because of the salubrious location; it is no more than a stone's throw from the city walls of Mechelen, on a low hill and protected by its own double moat. I would leave it all to you alone, since I will be moving to Antwerp. 15

As for Spain, I hardly know what to write you. The support for you there is fervent, but without any outward expression of itself.[3] The arch-bishop of Toledo has been promising much, but his generosity is remarkably slow. I would gladly have extracted, before my departure, a promissory note for the sum intended for you,[4] but since my eloquence was not equal to the 20

* * * * *

2904
1 Dilft was still in Spain in May 1533; see Ep 2876:29–30. According to Allen, who cites no source, he was back in the Netherlands by the following July.
2 Allen identifies her as Cornelia, daughter of Fernando Bernuy, a Spanish mer-chant who had settled in Antwerp. But according to CEBR she was Dilft's second wife, whom he married in July 1535, following the death in September 1534 of his first wife, a rich widow whose name is unknown.
3 By this time it was prudent for Spanish Erasmians, who were facing increasing hostility from the Inquisition, to be reticent about declaring their support for Erasmus. Juan de Vergara (see n5 below) had been arrested on 23 June 1533 and, after a trial that dragged on until December 1535, he was compelled to ab-jure a list of heretical opinions on indulgences, the sacraments, and oral prayer. Erasmus appears to have received his first news of Vergara's difficulties from Juan Luis Vives in May 1534; see Ep 2932:30–1.
4 The archbishop was Alonso de Fonseca (Ep 1748). He had provided a generous grant in support of the publication of Erasmus' edition of St Augustine (Ep 2157 introduction). More recently, because Erasmus had written to Vergara, in a let-ter now lost, mourning the death of his patron William Warham, archbishop of Canterbury, Fonseca had decided to grant him a new subsidy. See Bataillon 494, 530–1.

task, Vergara has taken on the burden of sending it.[5] Because he is waiting to receive it, I have kept his letter till now, so as to send it together with the promissory note. In the meantime, however, no one has come along to whom I could safely entrust it.[6] As for me, I have found faithful friends in Spain but they are all smooth talkers. I am most indebted to the kindness   25
of the archbishop, but so far he has kept himself within the bounds of a benevolent attitude. Farewell, most renowned master and consider me always sincerely yours.

In haste, at Mechelen, 11 February 1534

I am sending you a little speech that we delivered at Barcelona.[7] It is   30
not without pleasure that we submit it to your extremely refined judgment, in the great hope that I can easily gain forgiveness for making any mistake because of your affection for me. But in this matter any rashness must be attributed to the emperor, who did not oppose having it printed. Once more, farewell.   35

Most devoted to your Excellency, Frans van der Dilft

2905 / To Juan Ginés de Sepúlveda   Freiburg, 17 February 1534

This letter was first published in the *Sepulvedae epistolae* folio B. It is Erasmus' reply to Ep 2873, in which Sepúlveda had sought to persuade Erasmus of the importance of Vaticanus 1209, the oldest extant Greek manuscript of the New Testament (see n3 of that letter). For the context of the discussion of which this letter is a continuation, see Ep 2873 nn1–2. Sepúlveda's answer is Ep 2938.

ERASMUS OF ROTTERDAM SENDS CORDIAL GREETINGS
TO JUAN GINÉS DE SULPÚLVEDA
Nothing has been delivered to me, most learned Sepúlveda, but the reverend lord Iñigo, cardinal-bishop of Burgos, had indicated in his letter that he would see to it that whatever in Zúñiga's notes seems pertinent would be   5

* * * * *

5 Juan de Vergara (Ep 2879) was Fonseca's secretary. According to Bataillon 530–1, Vergara attempted to secure payment of the subsidy, but Archbishop Fonseca died (5 February 1534) before he could make good on his promise.
6 The letter is lost, and it is not known whether it was ever sent.
7 The reference is to the *Oratio gratulatoria ad Carolum v* that Dilft delivered in the presence of Charles v, thus earning himself the reward of a knighthood. The text was published at Louvain by Servatius Zassenus Diestens in 1533.

copied;[1] and he did that, but the pages did not reach me before Iñigo himself, after he had set out to visit the emperor, discovered them among the papers of Alfonso de Valdés, together with his own letter,[2] and he sent them to me from there, noting that on his deathbed Zúñiga had explicitly instructed him not to publish any of them but to send them to me to use them as I wish. If you did send anything, please know that nothing has reached me.[3] And in fact, it is better for Zúñiga's reputation that they not be published, not because he did not have many good insights but because, on the other hand, many of them are trifling or make false objections, and some present misunderstandings; I will send you a sampling of such places, if you wish, but only with the proviso that the matter is not made public; of quarrels we have more than enough.

You wonder why I translated συστοιχεῖ as *confinis est* 'bordering on.'[4] Jerome uses the same word when he is explaining this passage,[5] and I wonder why he was not at all disturbed by this difficulty; *confinis est* is less definite than *coniunctus est* 'joined to,' the phrase used by the translator. Chrysostom and Theophylact did not hesitate to translate as *vicinus est* 'is near,'[6] and things that are similar to each other are said to be *vicina* 'neighbouring,' but even more often *confinia* 'bordering.' Nevertheless, since I saw that the translators varied in this place, it did not seem right to explain the expression any further in translating it, especially since no opinion completely satisfied me. But I myself wondered why I did not express some doubt in the Annotations. I wonder why you take Thomas to task. For he did not take Sinai to be a mountain neighbouring Jerusalem, but rather thought that it was said to be joined because of the linkage by journeying. For the Law travelled from Sinai to Jerusalem. Concerning the expression συστοιχεῖ, Budé has a good deal to

* * * * *

2905
1 The letter is not extant, but it had to be earlier than Ep 2705. For Zúñiga's notes, see Ep 2873 n1.
2 The notes and the letter were supposed to be sent from the imperial court by the emperor's Latin secretary, Alfonso de Valdés; see Ep 2705:3–5 with n2. From Erasmus' statement here it is to be inferred that Valdés had in fact not sent them before he died (6 October 1532).
3 The copy of Zúñiga's notes sent from Rome by Cardinal Iñigo López de Mendoza had reached Erasmus by mid-May 1533; the copy sent by Sepúlveda from Bologna seems never to have arrived. See Ep 2873 n2.
4 At Gal 4:25; see Ep 2873:34–73.
5 PL 26 417B
6 For Chrysostom see PG 61 662; for Theophylact see PG 124 1005C.

say in his *Commentaries on the Greek Language,* if you care to consult it.[7] But I am grateful for your admonition.[8]

Most of Zúñiga's notes on my *Jerome* arrived late, for the collected epistles had already appeared at Paris.[9] He was an estimable man, learned 35 and careful, and for many years he promoted scholarly studies and occupied himself with his own inquiries. Now it is clear that throughout his whole life he did nothing but that. I have not yet been able to get the apologia that he wrote against Lefèvre d'Etaples.[10]

Concerning what you write about the Greek codex that you came 40 upon in the papal library,[11] which agrees in so many places with the readings of the Vulgate, see to it that you do not waste time on it. For it is an established fact that when the Greeks entered into a treaty with the Roman church, as is testified in the bull that is called 'Golden,' there was among the articles one requiring that the Greek codices, especially those contain- 45 ing the Gospels, be emended so as to agree with the Roman readings;[12] and I came upon similar codices when I first edited the New Testament. Hence you cannot make any judgments based on this codex. Rather, Greek readings should be sought in Greek authors such as Athanasius, Basil, Origen, Chrysostom, Nazianzus, Cyril.   50

* * * * *

7 Allen cites *Commentarii linguae Graecae* (Paris 1532) 531–2, and notes that in his *Lexicon Graeco-Latinum* (no publication data or page number given), Budé translates *confinis est Hierusalem* as 'borders on Jerusalem.'

8 This exchange with Sepúlveda on the meaning of Gal 4:25 appears to have been responsible for the new, nearly page-long annotation on the passage in the 1535 edition of the New Testament; see CWE 41 345.

9 In the first four volumes of the Chevallon edition, published in 1533 with a preface by Erasmus (Ep 2758)

10 The *Annotationes Iacobi Lopidis Stunicae contra Iacobum Fabrum Stapulen* were published in 1519; see Ep 1128 n2.

11 See introduction above.

12 Cf the passage in the *Contra morosos quosdam* (CWE 41 822–3), where Erasmus advances the same claim. Erasmus may have been thinking of the Council of Ferrara-Florence, which met in 1438–9 to bring about a union between the Greek and Roman churches, but no such provision concerning Greek manuscripts is found in the agreement concluded at the session (CWE 41 345 n1486). In his reply to this letter Sepúlveda informed Erasmus of his error (Ep 2938:98–100), and Erasmus in turn accepted the correction while claiming nonetheless to have been told on good authority that changes in the Greek manuscripts had indeed taken place in consequence of the agreement (Allen Ep 2951:52–5), thus undermining their value as support for the Vulgate.

From a letter of the reverend lord Cardinal Iñigo,[13] who wrote that you would accompany him on his return to Spain, I gathered that you were not in Rome. That was the reason I did not write you.

So much in answer to your letter, which the apostolic pronotary Ambrosius von Gumppenberg, an outstanding gentleman, sent to me, to-   55
gether with a letter from him.[14]

Given at Freiburg im Breisgau, 17 February in the year 1534 after the birth of our Lord

2906 / To Johann Koler   Freiburg, 19 February 1534

This letter was first published in the *Vita Erasmi*. The manuscript, in a secretary's hand throughout, is in the Humanistenbriefe collection of the Stadtbibliothek at Zofingen (MS P 14 I 10). For Koler, see Ep 2814.

Cordial greetings. I received two letters from you on the same day and by the same courier; one was written on 10 January and the other on 1 February.[1] I am responding to both of them, both briefly and in the handwriting of some- one else, for gout has so completely taken over my right hand that I cannot hold either paper or pen with that hand. You write that my *Concord* has dis-   5
pleased some Roman cardinals;[2] I am amazed at the maladroit judgments of some people. But it seems they have decided to heal this worldwide pub- lic affliction by harsh measures. I, however, hoped that the matter could be healed by the authority of a council, with fewer disturbances. To that goal my book seemed to be sufficiently relevant. I do not know what Luther wrote   10
against masses, for I hear that his book came out before mine.[3] If he treats the

* * * * *

13 Not extant
14 No letter from Gumppenberg (Ep 2926) from the year 1533 is extant.

2906
1 Neither letter is extant.
2 Ie *De sarcienda ecclesiae concordia* (Ep 2852)
3 Luther's *Von der Winkelmesse und Pfaffenweihe* (*On Private Masses and the Conse- cration of Priests*) appeared in print around the end of October 1533, approxi- mately two months after the publication of *De concordia* (see Ep 2852 introduc- tion); see *Luther's Works* ed Jaroslav Pelikan, Helmut T. Lehmann et al, 55 vols (St Louis / Philadelphia 1955–86) 38 145.

mass with contempt, how could he have found any pretext for that in my book,[4] for it treats no article more carefully or more reverently than the mass?

But these things are bound to happen. I also have no doubt that the *Anticiceronianus* about which you write is full of poison.[5] Zúñiga has died, but it seems he will be succeeded by Sepúlveda, a fosterson of Alberto Pio and a colleague of Zúñiga, the most boastful of the Spaniards; I think you have seen his remarkably foolish and contemptuous book against me.[6] When the Italians are insane, they are brilliantly insane. Agostino Steuco respond- ed to my letter, but he did so furiously and ignorantly.[7] I really thought I was dealing with a philosopher. I know Nausea only from one conversation and some letters.[8] He brought to the court of Ferdinand the news about the Romans being offended by my *Concord*,[9] as I am led to believe by a letter from Johannes Fabri, the bishop of Vienna.[10] But I am surprised by the busi- ness that was assigned to Nausea by the cardinal of Trent,[11] since, as far as I can judge from his books and letters, he is not outstanding for his wisdom. For before he was summoned to the royal court, he asked me in a letter to dedicate some work to the cardinal and to testify in the preface that there is no one to whom a difficult task could more rightly be assigned.[12] He does nonetheless seem to be one of my supporters.

I see that the affairs of princes and kings are festering wounds, if it is true what they say about the slaying of the count of Mirandola in Italy,[13] to-

* * * * *

4 Literally 'any handle'; see *Adagia* I iv 4.
5 Doubtless the never-published book of Georg von Logau (Ep 2568 n4) men- tioned in Allen Ep 2961:158–61 (24 August 1534): '[Logau] has made a thor- oughly insipid attack on my *Ciceronianus*. The book has not yet been published, but for some time it has been passing rapidly from hand to hand in Rome and has now reached the hands of the pope.' On 18 March 1535 Erasmus reported having received a manuscript copy of it from Rome (Allen Ep 3005:20–5).
6 The book was the *Antapologia pro Alberto Pio in Erasmum* by Juan Ginés de Sepúlveda; see Ep 2637 introduction and n1. For Sepúlveda's connection to Diego López Zúñiga, see Ep 2873:3–6.
7 See Ep 2465 introduction.
8 For Fridericus Nausea see Ep 2823 n1. He visited Erasmus at Basel early in 1526 (Ep 1632 introduction). None of his letters to Erasmus are extant.
9 See n2 above.
10 Not extant
11 His appointment as court preacher to King Ferdinand; see Ep 2823 n1.
12 Cf Ep 2847:14–16.
13 Gianfrancesco Pico della Mirandola, who was assassinated in October 1533 by his nephew Galeotto II Pico, count of Concordia; cf Ep 2917 n6.

gether with his children, about the citadel of Milan attacked by the stratagems
of the French,[14] about the Voivode's many violations of the treaty,[15] about the
Turkish fleet badly damaged by mistake by the by the triremes of Venice.[16]   35
Besides what you mention in your letter, a harsh and savage edict has been
issued in Paris against the Lutherans.[17] Some have been thrown into prison,
some have fled out of fear. Some suspect that one of the fugitives was the son
of Cop, who now lives in Basel, though he had once been the rector of the
University of Paris.[18] I do not know whether that is true, but it is certain that   40
he is now in Basel, for he wrote to Baer from there.[19] Béda and his colleagues
have been recalled and he triumphs in earnest.[20] Some months ago there was
a rumour here that at Paris it is forbidden, by the authority both of the

* * * * *

14 Francis I and his agents never tired of asserting the French claim to the duchy
   of Milan. Francis tried, for example, to get the pope to include it in the dowry
   that Catherine de' Medici brought to her marriage with the dauphin (see Ep
   2917 n4). But there is no evidence of an actual attack on Milan at this time or of
   a plan to do so.
15 In June 1533, John Zápolyai, voivode of Transylvania and ally of the sultan, had
   entered into a truce with his rival for control of Hungary, Ferdinand of Austria.
   Peace between the two would not come until 1538.
16 Venice and the Ottomans were not at war at this point. We have no information
   about this incident.
17 This is evidently a reference to the aftermath of the sermon of Nicolas Cop
   (see following note), in which the Parlement arrested a number of people, and
   the king, furious that 'the damned heretical Lutheran sect' was flourishing at
   Paris, ordered the prosecution of heretics and published two recent papal bulls
   against heresy; see Knecht 245.
18 Nicolas Cop (c 1501–40), third son of Erasmus' friend Guillaume Cop (Ep
   124:18n), studied philosophy and medicine at Paris. From 1530 he taught philosophy at the Collège de Sainte-Barbe and on 10 October 1533 was elected
   rector for a term. At a convocation held on 1 November he read an address in
   which he drew heavily on the works of Erasmus and Luther, denounced the
   'sophists' who had turned theology into a hairsplitting science, and praised
   those who had been persecuted for professing the gospel (see Knecht 244–5). In
   the uproar that followed he fled the country and by February 1534 had reached
   Basel, the birthplace of his father. After three years abroad, his whereabouts
   uncertain, Cop, rejecting the example of his brother Michel, who became a pastor at Geneva, returned to Paris, where his brother Jean was a canon and a
   lawyer. In May 1536 he became a medical licentiate and taught medicine at the
   University of Paris until his early death.
19 Ludwig Baer (Ep 2225)
20 For Béda's exile from Paris see Ep 2841 n5.

theologians and the Parlement, to sell certain of my works.[21] But this seems to me unlikely, and none of my friends have written to me about any such thing. 45

The reign of the Franciscans flourishes under this emperor.[22] As for what will happen to me, let the Lord see to it; nothing concerns me now but to present a clear conscience to Christ, since I am soon to depart from this world. At Bonn there is a certain Franciscan by the name of Nikolaus Herborn,[23] whose jurisdiction is very wide, since he is the cisalpine commis- 50 sary. At Antwerp he published a book of Lenten sermons as if they had been delivered to the people at Cologne, though he is writing in Latin and there is nothing in them for the people; in fact they are so full of absurdities that the people would not put up with someone blathering such nonsense. In that book there is not a speck of intelligence or eloquence, no learning at all, and 55 not even a trace of a devout outlook. He seems to have heaped up this stuff only to have a pretext for pouring out his venom under the name of religion. From the printer's workshop they sent me three pages, as a sample and a taste of this magnificent work.[24] On one of them, apart from other insults, he writes this: 'Luther drew to himself a large part of the church; Zwingli 60 and Oecolampadius drew some; Erasmus drew away the most.' He adds that it would have been better if that man had never been born. On another page he calls Luther, Zwingli, and Oecolampadius the soldiers of Pilate who crucified Christ, numbering me among them and adding that I wrote in the same spirit and with the same purpose as they did, the only difference be- 65 ing that I joke and they are serious. He adds a saying drawn from the choice witticisms of the monks: that I laid the eggs, Luther and the others hatched the chicks.[25] I have no doubt that the whole work is strewn with such pretty little flowers.

My more sincere friends write that there is nothing that such people can- 70 not achieve at the court of the emperor. Mary is nothing other than a daughter of our land.[26] Montigny, who has a great deal of power, is completely

* * * * *

21 This may possibly be a reference to the undocumented incident reported in Ep 2868:13–31.
22 Cf Ep 2896:19–21.
23 Actually Nikolaus Ferber of Herborn, Franciscan of Cologne ('Bonn' is probably Erasmus' slip for Cologne), for whom see Ep 2896 n8
24 For the summary that follows, cf Ep 2899:10–42.
25 See Ep 1528:15–16, which is the earliest known record of the famous saying that Erasmus laid the egg that Luther hatched. Erasmus attributed it to the Franciscans of Cologne.
26 Mary of Hungary, regent of the Netherlands. Cf Allen Ep 2961:46–7: 'Queen Mary is more the child of our native land than its mistress.'

devoted to the Franciscans.[27] The cardinal of Liège is a doubtful friend, and a
bitter enemy if he is offended.[28] The archbishop of Palermo is a smooth talker,
but nothing more.[29] Even if tumults erupt in Germany, I am sitting pretty here,   75
between the anvil and the hammer.[30] But I am not much concerned about
myself, for I will soon be sailing into port. If you can stay there comfortably,
even after a change of religion,[31] I would not advise you to go elsewhere.

I am very sorry about Fugger; he did himself more harm than fortune
or his enemies did.[32] In these stormy times he should have taken heart, hop-   80
ing for better days. Indeed I would gladly encourage him, but because I do
not know the details of the disease, it would be dangerous to do so; like an
unskilled surgeon I might make the wound worse by an inept attempt to cure
it. You ask me to write back to you by this courier, but the one who delivered
the two letters let it be known that he had received them not at Augsburg   85
but somewhere else not far from here – in this very town, I imagine. There is
no news at all from England, nor even from Brabant, except a rumour that is
too true, that the cathedral there has almost entirely burned down.[33] If I hear
any news from the next fair, I will let you know.[34] I only wish I could give
you more cheerful news about my health: I suffer all the time from attacks of   90
gout in the feet, gout in the hands, gout all over, seeking out all my joints, and
going from one to another as soon as it has caused enough torment in one of
them. The unbearable pain lasts about four days. Then, when it has swollen
up, there is some relief, but it acts like a general who has seized many cita-
dels: leaving a guard behind, it occupies another bodily member and rages   95
there all over again, and then, at the slightest prompting, it either retreats or
it grows worse.[35] It does not suffer the slightest touch, so that you would say

* * * * *

27 Antoine de Lalaing, count of Hoogstraten, lord of Montigny, member of the
    council of state and head of finances (Ep 1038 n7), less influential under Queen
    Mary than he had been under Queen Margaret, but still an important figure
28 Erasmus' always stormy friendship with Erard de la Marck, cardinal of Liège,
    had come to its definitive end in 1531; see Ep 2590 n6.
29 Jean (II) de Carondelet (Ep 2899 introduction). On him as a 'smooth talker,' cf
    Ep 2785:59–60.
30 Literally 'between the shrine and the stone' (Adagia I i 15; cf Adagia I i 16)
31 For Augsburg's slow but seemingly relentless progress towards the adoption
    of the Reformation, see Ep 2814 n8.
32 See Epp 2818:39–44, 2845:38–46.
33 See Ep 2876 n2.
34 Ie from the spring book fair at Frankfurt
35 See Ep 2818 n1.

that it is like Anagyrus, which Greek proverbs forbid one to move.[36] But I am
afraid that this poor old body, shaken and tormented so often, will not bear
up very long. My servant Quirinus, about whom you inquire, lives here. He   100
is a student of Zasius and elegantly dressed thanks to British money. He has
his fellow whisperers. Some other time, when I have leisure to do it, I will tell
you more about him, some of which will make you laugh.[37] So much for your
first letter, written on 1 February.

I come to the other letter, written earlier but delivered on the same   105
day. In the letter to Paumgartner I make no mention of the letter in which I
make known his praises;[38] I send only the book *On Preparing for Death*. For I
think it more courteous for him to learn about my praises of him from you
rather than from me. But since you say you are languishing in the desire
for that book, I have immediately sent my servantboy so that you will not   110
die of your desire.[39] I am only afraid that you will find it to be coals rather
than a treasure.[40] I know that Paumgartner is always most generous. But you
should make sure that he does not consign to this boy anything but a letter
or something similar, in case he should want to increase his travel allowance
by a penny or two. For he has not been with me very long – and is not likely   115
to stay with me very long. If the bishop is at Augsburg, see to it that he gets
what I am sending by this courier; if he has departed for Dillingen, tell my
boy to go there on his way back; if the bishop is going from castle to castle,
take everything from my boy and see to it that it is delivered to the bishop
at the earliest opportunity.[41] Likewise, if Paumgartner himself has gone far   120
away, it is not necessary that my boy should follow him, but the items should
be delivered to him by his servant, Christoph Gering.[42]

* * * * *

36 There was a town in Attica called Anagyrus, which may have given its name
   to a shrub that was 'efficacious as medicine' but that emitted a strong and disagreeable odour, 'especially when rubbed with the hand.' See *Adagia* I i 65:
   Anagyrim commoves 'You are moving Anagyrus.'
37 Quirinus Hagius; see Ep 2896 n11.
38 For the letter to Paumgartner (not extant) see Ep 2882 n1. The letter singing
   Paumgartner's praises is Ep 2879, which had embarrassed Koler; see the introduction to that letter.
39 The servant-boy has not been identified.
40 *Adagia* I ix 30
41 Christoph von Stadion, bishop of Augsburg, owned a castle at Dillingen (on the
   Danube, northwest of Augsburg) and often resided there.
42 For Christoph Gering see Ep 2900 introduction.

Many say that this affliction is not gout but a disease in its own right, called *Souch* in the vernacular.[43] They say that many here suffer from it. I am sorry that you and I have so many afflictions in common. Certainly it is true   125
that not the least part of a person's happiness consists in having a faithful and suitable servant. It is our fate: the world is full of wicked men who call themselves 'evangelical.' Besides this one I have also taken in two of them as servants but have quickly got rid of them. You will see to it that the little book is not printed there,[44] so that Froben does not suffer any losses. I hope that   130
this boy will bring back good news about your health. Give my greetings to our friends, if there are still any living there. If my right hand recovers I will write you at greater length. Farewell.

Given at Freiburg im Breisgau, 19 February in the year 1534 after the birth of Christ   135

Yours, Erasmus of Rotterdam, in his own voice but in the handwriting of another

To the most distinguished gentleman Master Johann Koler, provost of Chur. At Augsburg

2907 / From Bonifacius Amerbach

For the reasons given by the AK editor Alfred Hartmann, this letter (= AK Ep 1909) has been redated to [c 8 February 1535] and will appear as Ep 2995A in CWE 21.

2908 / To Bonifacius Amerbach

For the reasons given by the AK editor Alfred Hartmann, this letter (= AK Ep 1916) has been redated to 21 February [1535] and will appear as Ep 2997A in CWE 21.

* * * * *

43 In Ep 2916:8 the same word is spelled *Such*. In Ep 2918:41 one finds the related word *gesucht*. In sixteenth-century German *sucht* normally meant simply 'illness' and required a prefix to make it specific, eg *wassersucht* (dropsy). *Gesüchte*, on the other hand, though it could also have the same generic meaning as *sucht*, was far more commonly used for diseases of the joints or extremities that had Latin names like *podagra* (foot-gout) and *chiragra* (hand-gout). See *Deutsches Wörterbuch* ed Jacob and Wilhelm Grimm et al, 16 vols in 32 (Leipzig 1854–1960) 5 4287–8 under 'gesüchte.'
44 In Allen Ep 2961:13–14 Erasmus reports that *De praeparatione ad mortem* had been published in several places, including Paris.

2909 / From Nicolaus Olahus   Brussels, 23 February 1534

This letter was first published in Ipolyi page 459. The manuscript is page 557 of the Olahus codex in the Hungarian National Archives at Budapest (Ep 2339 introduction).

NICOLAUS OLAHUS TO ERASMUS OF ROTTERDAM

If all is well with you and you are in good health, I rejoice from the bottom of my heart. I am greatly surprised that I have not received any letter from you for quite some time now.[1] I beg you, my dear Erasmus, to let me know about your condition and your safety. Please know that I am your friend, now and   5 in the future, for as long as I live, one whom you have recognized, I think, as genuine. I wish you all joy and happiness, as much as I wish them for myself.

Farewell, from Brussels, 23 February 1534

2910 / From Bernardus Gravius   Cologne, 1 March 1534

This letter was first published as Ep 113 in Enthoven. The autograph is in the Rehdiger Collection of the University Library at Wrocław (MS Rehd 254 27). For Bernardus Gravius, and for the background to the present letter, see Ep 2893 introduction.

Cordial greetings. Why should I here hesitate, my most learned Master Erasmus, to call you the loftiest founder of Roman eloquence, since not only I but all of us who run in the stadium of the Muses give you thanks for extending and opening up for us the great flower gardens surrounding the *pomerium* of the Latin language?[1] It would be the greatest incivility indeed   5 for us not to confess freely that you have watered the meadows from your most salutary springs, and that we have been led by your guidance, assisted by your encouragement, and finally embellished by your reputation. If

* * * * *

2909
1 Cf Ep 2915:3–7.

2910
1 Gravius uses the word *pomerium*, which refers to the area within the sacred boundary of the city of Rome, the only area where the auguries could be taken. It did not coincide with the actual walls of the city or the area of habitation, and was technically closed to habitation or farming. The word seems out of place here, and one wonders, with Gerlo, if Gravius perhaps meant to say *pomarius* (orchard).

St Jerome boasted that he had found Donatus to be a useful teacher,[2] if St Paul
thought he was worthy of praise because he had been instructed at the feet of 10
Gamaliel,[3] why should I not boast that I had the benefit of that great teacher
Erasmus? After the likes of Cicero and Quintilian, no one in this theatre of
mortals has equalled, much less surpassed him in divine and human learning and in wonderful eloquence. And so, my most distinguished teacher,
since through your efforts and learning I have come this far in the stadium 15
of the Muses, it would be most kind of you to provide the culmination of
my studies. That will happen if you will persuade my father (as I earnestly
begged you to do in my last letter)[4] to send me to that noblest emporium (as
it is called) at Louvain. That is what I most ardently desire to do, and I long
for you to advise me about the right studies, especially those right for me. 20
In this matter I implore you with all my strength to remember your protégé
Bernard. You will get the news from my father. Take in good part, O my patron, this monstrous pile of words.

In haste, from my father's house, 1 March 1534

Your most humble protégé, Bernard 25

To the most excellent gentleman Master Erasmus of Rotterdam, my
incomparable patron

2911 / To Jan (ii) Łaski   Freiburg, 5 March 1534

This letter, Erasmus' reply to Ep 2862, was first published in Wierzbowski I 44.
The manuscript was part of the same ill-fated collection at Warsaw as that of
Ep 1954.

ERASMUS OF ROTTERDAM TO THE REVEREND MASTER PROVOST
OF GNIEZNO
Your letter was very much desired, but it didn't want to come into my hands.[1]
I received the ring that had once been worn by the archbishop.[2] I only wish

* * * * *

2 Aelius Donatus was the most influential grammarian of the fourth century AD.
St Jerome was among his pupils (*Contra Rufinum* 1:16), and his works domi-
nated grammatical instruction in Europe until the twelfth century.
3 Acts 22:3
4 Not in Ep 2893 but in another, now lost

2911
1 Cf lines 21–3 below.
2 Ep 2862 n9

that you had succeeded to the dignified status of your uncle.[3] In that you   5
condemn both honours and wealth,[4] I praise your philosophical attitude, but
as things are in our times, high station is an advantage, so that we are not exposed to the mockery of pigs and dogs. Your virtues deserved, if nothing else,
some magnificent stage, where you could be of benefit to the most people.

I am not changing anything about the library; that matter will be at   10
your discretion.[5] It is not safe to write about the new disturbances, but I have
noted a few things (including also something about my condition) on a sheet
of paper that I have sent to Justus Decius, in case anyone should want to
know.[6] For my ill health forces me to write to few, and to write briefly. I hope
that your affairs and those of your family are faring well, seeing that our   15
friendship persuades me to think that I should consider your fortune to be as
great as mine, if indeed mine exists. I would like to know what your brothers
Hieronim and Stanisław are doing.[7] Farewell, my patron and singular friend.

Freiburg, 5 March in the year of our Lord 1534

Erasmus of Rotterdam, in a handwriting not unknown to you   20

Although your letter, which I had keenly looked for and for a long time,
did not come to hand, it finally turned up while I was looking for something
else. I read it at leisure with no small solace to my mind, so much does it
breathe from beginning to end of your genuine and unfeigned kindness. One
of your bishops wrote to me that he had summoned Melanchthon to Poland,   25
which I found rather surprising.[8] True, Melanchthon writes less violently,
but he doesn't depart by a hair's breadth from the teachings of Luther; he is
(I might almost say) more Lutheran than Luther. I have added this in someone else's handwriting because gout has taken over my right hand.[9]

* * * * *

3 Ep 2862 n3
4 Ep 2862:8–17
5 Ep 2862:32–4
6 Doubtless much the same as the sheet of news sent to Erasmus Schets; see Ep
   2913:40.
7 For Hieronim see Ep 2279 n3. After accompanying his two brothers on a diplomatic mission to the French court in 1524, which included a visit to Erasmus at
   Basel (Ep 1341A:1278–84), Stanisław Łaski entered the service of Francis I as a
   diplomat. Following the peace of Cambrai he left French service and returned
   to Poland, where he became closely associated with his brother Hieronim's efforts on behalf of John Zápolyai in Hungary. After Hieronim's death in 1541,
   Stanisław was active in the diplomatic service of King Sigismund I and his successor Sigismund II Augustus.
8 See Ep 2876 n10.
9 See Ep 2818 n1.

2912 / From Jean (II) de Carondelet   Brussels, 8 March 1534

This letter, Carondelet's reply to Ep 2899, was first published in Ipolyi pages 472–4. The manuscript is page 351 of the Olahus codex in the Hungarian National Archives at Budapest (Ep 2339 introduction).

JEAN, ARCHBISHOP OF PALERMO, CHANCELLOR OF THE EMPEROR
IN BRABANT, TO ERASMUS OF ROTTERDAM, GREETINGS

While we were looking forward to your return, which before the past winter you had promised by letter to her royal Majesty and to us,[1] the reverend Master Nicolaus Olahus, treasurer of Székesfehérvár, secretary and counsel- 5
lor of her Majesty, etc delivered to us your letter sent on 23 January. From it we learned for the first time, and not without mental anguish, that since Christmas you had been afflicted by bad health and that you are afraid that the winter thaw might make your health even worse. About this we are sorry indeed. But we hope that this spring you will be restored to your former 10
good health, so that in accordance both with your promise and with our desire to see you, you will be able to come back here as completely healthy as we hope for you to be.[2]

Next you write that you are more than a little disturbed by a recent edition of comments on the Lenten Gospels by a certain Franciscan, Nikolaus 15
Herborn, the general cisalpine commissary, because he subjects you to insults. And to keep us from thinking that you were writing to us about mere dreams, you sent us pages from that publication.[3] You should know that by a firm edict his imperial Majesty has forbidden all printers in his provinces to publish such things, or anything new written either by monks or anyone 20
else, without having the consent or undergoing the censure of his Majesty

* * * * *

2912
1 The letters are not extant, but see Ep 2820 introduction.
2 As Allen points out, these two sentences were written in the margin of the manuscript, presumably as an intended replacement for two sentences that were underlined in the text: 'I was quite disturbed to hear that you are ill and that your body is weak. We believe that in the springtime your body will return to its former health and that you will arrive at such bodily vigour that, just as you promised us and just as we long for your return, you can come back to us in the perfect health that we wish for you.' Allen included both passages in his text, even though both say much the same thing and the marginal correction reads better. We have left the marginal correction in the text and have relegated the underlined sentences to this note.
3 Ep 2899:10–48

or of those whom he has assigned to that function.[4] And I, as part of my
official duty, have been most energetic in seeing to it that this edict of his
Majesty is observed everywhere. Nevertheless, as usually happens, it is not
possible by edicts, however firm, entirely to prevent some of these writings   25
from being published secretly. But still such things should not disturb you.
For who can be completely immune to the lying accusations of malevolent
detractors? What man, however pious or well deserving of the Christian
commonwealth, is not open to thoughtless and reckless insults? And her
most serene Majesty, to prevent you from being the object of such noxious   30
and injurious attacks by the aforesaid Franciscan, ordered in writing that
the margrave of Antwerp should immediately summon the aforementioned
printer and forbid him in the name of her Majesty from presuming to print
such a book or sell it after it was printed, and that then the margrave should
be sure to inflict rigorous punishment on the man for having violated the   35
imperial edict.[5] And so there is no reason for you to be afraid. But rather, go
ahead with your intention and promise of returning here towards the end of
April or any time when you can do so without injuring your health, and do
not have any doubts about your protection. For just as her royal Majesty and
I have written to you in the past, we will take care of your honour and your   40
person so that, together with us in your native land, with the help of Christ,
you will be able to spend the rest of your life quietly, safely, and comfortably.
May Christ preserve you and bring you back to us very soon.

From Brussels, 8 March 1534

2913 / To Erasmus Schets   Freiburg, 11 March 1534

This letter was first published by Allen. The manuscript, in the hand of Gilbert
Cousin (Ep 2381 n1), is in the British Library (MS Add 38512 folio 86).

* * * * *

4 Beginning in 1522 Charles v issued a series of edicts intended to prevent the
   circulation in the Netherlands of unauthorized books on the subject of religion.
   The most severe of these was an edict of 1529, which Queen Mary reissued on
   assuming the regency in 1531. See James D. Tracy *Holland under Habsburg Rule,
   1506–1566* (University of California Press 1990) 160.
5 The 'margrave of Antwerp' (ie the royal government's representative in that
   city) was Willem van de Werve (d after 1559). A city alderman from 1524, he
   was margrave from 1531 to 1550. The instructions to him mentioned here do
   not appear to have led to effective action against the printer; see Epp 2915:42–8,
   2922:16–17, and cf Ep 2896 n8.

Cordial greetings. Through Master Tielmannus Gravius I have received two
bundles from you.[1] The first had your letter, as well as one from your son,[2]
written at the bidding of his mother, which clearly reveals that he is a bright
young man, naturally suited to liberal studies. Do not think I am flattering
his father's ears; I am speaking frankly. I wrote replies to both letters,[3] and   5
I have no doubt that you received them through the same Tielmannus. The
second bundle had no letter from you; it only had one from Grapheus (not
very long),[4] and two from Portugal, one written by Damião de Gois, the other
by someone else.[5] That bundle did not have any other letters.

It is a good thing that my native land Holland promises me at least two   10
hundred and forty florins; I imagine the rest of it will stick in some people's
fingers.[6] The letter in which you indicate that the treasurer Vincent promises
the two hundred and forty florins and says he will investigate the trickery by
which the sixty were diverted arrived later than it should have.[7] For through
Viglius Zuichemus I have already written to some people about the money   15
that was held back and hived off, which I would not have done if I had received your letter a little earlier.[8] I would have been more grateful for the
honorarium if it had remained intact and had been delivered on time. But
I am no less grateful to the Estates for their generous intentions, however
much their munificence has been held back and diminished by some fam-   20
ished individuals, as courtiers generally are.

I am now sending two gilded books,[9] together with some letters, to
be forwarded to England. But because Luis de Castro has left England,[10] it

* * * * *

2913
1 The first bundle arrived on 22 January; see Ep 2896:1–2. The second bundle,
  delivered sometime before 11 March, included the letter of Cornelius Grapheus
  and the two from Portugal mentioned in lines 6–9 below.
2 Gaspar Schets (Ep 2897 introduction). Neither letter is extant.
3 Epp 2896–7
4 Not extant, alluded to again in Ep 2914:20–1, presumably answered by Ep 2916
5 Neither letter is extant. That from Gois is presumably the one answered by Ep
  2914. The 'someone else,' evidently known to Erasmus, has not been identified.
6 This is a reference to Erasmus' suspicion that Pieter van Montfoort, who delivered the honorarium from the Estates of Holland to him at Freiburg, had kept
  some of the money for himself; see Ep 2819.
7 The letter from Schets is not extant, but cf Ep 2896:1–8.
8 The letters are not extant, but Erasmus refers to them in Ep 2896:3–4 and
  2923:5–7.
9 Ie two ornately decorated presentation copies of De praeparatione ad mortem; cf
  Ep 2924:33–4.
10 Luis de Castro, long Erasmus Schets' agent in London, left England early in 1534.

seems more advisable that you should have everything, all gathered together
in one little packet, handed over to Robert Aldridge,[11] formerly the chaplain 25
of the bishop of Lincoln,[12] now the king's chaplain,[13] for he is the most reliable of all my friends and will take care that all items are delivered to those
for whom they are intended. At any rate, I am eager to know whether anyone
has succeeded to the place held by Luis and who that is.[14]

Since Viglius left us I have not been able to find out anything about him, 30
whether he is alive or dead. He left here in the middle of winter, a very harsh
one at that.[15] I would like you to let me know if anything has happened to
him that I would be sorry to hear. If you get a chance, tell Quirinus Talesius
that the letter which he entrusted to you, together with the linen sent by his
wife, has been delivered to me.[16] I employ someone else's handwriting be- 35
cause my right arm has been so taken over by severely painful gout, or some
ailment very much like it, that I cannot make so much as a stroke with a reed
pen. I am glad that you will soon pay Grapheus the amount I have directed,[17]
though I am surprised that the money has not yet come into your hands.

You will get a summary page of news, both general and personal.[18] Best 40
wishes to your dear wife and sweet children.

Freiburg im Breisgau, 11 March in the year 1534 after the birth of our
Lord

My hand swelled up three days ago. The pain hardly allowed me to write
my signature. 45

Erasmus of Rotterdam

To the honourable gentleman Master Erasmus Schets, businessman at
Antwerp, a special friend. At Antwerp

* * * * *

11 Ep 1656 introduction
12 John Longland
13 Since c 1531
14 Following Castro's departure from England (see n10 above) responsibility for
collecting Erasmus' pensions rested with Castro's partner Alvaro de Astudillo
(first mentioned in the correspondence in Ep 3009, 11 April 1535) and the imperial ambassador Eustache Chapuys (Ep 2798).
15 Viglius Zuichemus visited Erasmus at Freiburg in January, on his way home
to the Netherlands from Basel; see Ep 2878 n2.
16 The letter is not extant. For an earlier gift from Talesius' wife, see Ep 2735:23–4.
17 See Ep 2914:21–3.
18 See Ep 2911:11–14.

2914 / To Damião de Gois   Freiburg, 11 March 1534

This letter, presumably Erasmus' answer to the letter from Gois mentioned in
Ep 2913:8, was first printed by Mgr P.F.X. de Ram in the *Bulletin d l'Academie
Royale des sciences et belles lettres de Bruxelles* IX/2 (1842) 433–5. The manuscript,
in the hand of a secretary but with the final sentence and the signature in
Erasmus' own hand, is in the British Library (MS Add 38512 folio 88).

Cordial greetings. I am glad my letter was delivered to you,[1] my most distinguished friend Damião, and that affairs at court are going as you wish.
Your letter and the one from the person who wrote at your request (and did
so in a most friendly way),[2] I laid aside intending to answer them, but they
never seemed to come to hand. In the meantime gout so took over my right   5
hand that I cannot form so much as a single jot, and your letter was of the
sort that didn't require an immediate answer. So I didn't think I needed to
exert much effort in writing, not knowing for sure whether my letter would
reach you there. The other letter I will answer briefly, as soon as the use of
my right hand is restored to me.   10
    I would very much like to know where our friend Resende is living
and what he is doing.[3] I have hardly ever found anyone more generous
than he, though I never deserved anything from him, nor do I see how I
ever could. I have read the poem in which he describes the celebration in
Brussels of the birth of a baby boy to your king; in it he describes every-   15
thing and puts it before my eyes so that I can see more in the poem than
I could have if I had been present.[4] I have read the letter he wrote from
Regensburg,[5] which I did not answer at the time because he was acting in
a lively play.[6] If I learn where he is and if my right hand comes back, I will
write him a long letter.[7]   20

       * * * * *

2914
1 Ep 2846
2 See Ep 2913 n5.
3 André de Resende (Ep 2500 introduction)
4 Resende's *Genethliacon principis Lusitani* was published at Bologna (G.B. Phaelli)
  in 1533.
5 Not extant
6 Acting in a *fabula motoria*, Erasmus' way of saying that he was constantly on
  the move, his whereabouts uncertain; see Ep 2643 n3.
7 Ep 2500 is the only surviving letter to him.

Grapheus still complains about his ill health, and to console him I ordered that fifty Caroline florins be paid to him from my funds. He is a man who deserves better, both in his fortunes and his health.[8]

Bonifacius Amerbach was with me today, but he was already prepared to set out on his travels.[9] He requested that I send you attentive and friendly greetings in his name. He is sincerely devoted to you. So too is Henricus Glareanus,[10] though I do not know if he will be writing to you, for he is very much taken up with the business of the Muses.

Farewell, Freiburg im Breisgau, 11 March 1534

Concerning the Lapplanders, I was about to do what you wanted, but the printer failed me, and not in that venture only. But I did what I could: I saw to it that your letter to the bishop was translated into German and added to a book translated into German that tells of the obedience displayed by the king of Ethiopia to the pope.[11]

My gout is in remission to the extent that I can sign my name, though with difficulty.

Erasmus of Rotterdam, in my own hand

To the most illustrious Portugese gentleman Master Damião de Gois, treasurer to his most serene Majesty. In the royal palace of Portugal

2915 / From Nicolaus Olahus   Brussels, 12 March 1534

This letter, in which Olahus responds to Epp 2877 and 2898, was first published in Ipolyi pages 475–7. The manuscript is page 358 of the Olahus codex in the Hungarian National Archives at Budapest (Ep 2339 introduction). Erasmus' reply is Ep 2922.

* * * * *

8 For the troubles of the humanist, poet, and former secretary of the town of Antwerp, Cornelius Grapheus, see Ep 1299 n24. For the payment of fifty florins, cf Ep 2913:38–9. The Carolus florin was valued in 1533 at 42d groot Flemish; the gift to Grapheus was therefore equivalent to £8 15s 0d or slightly over a year's wage of an Antwerp master mason/carpenter (CWE 12 650 Table 3, 691 Table 13).
9 By 20 March he was back in Basel; see AK Ep 1806.
10 Ep 440
11 See Ep 2846 n29.

THE RESPONSE TO ERASMUS OF ROTTERDAM FROM NICOLAUS
OLAHUS, SECRETARY TO QUEEN MARY

I recently received two letters, my most learned and dearest friend Erasmus.
The one that was sent earlier[1] was delivered to me later by Viglius Zuichemus;[2]
the other one,[3] which was written later, I received earlier, joined to another   5
letter, through the efforts of Erasmus Schets. In the earlier one you recommend Zuichemus. I am so impressed by his learning, his talent, and his
character, and by your letter and recommendation, that I greatly value his
acquaintance and company. I promised to be generous in helping and supporting him, should he happen to need anything, and I will in fact fulfil this   10
promise to the best of my ability, provided he wishes to make use of my help.

You write that there is a rumour spread among you that the king of
England has taken Queen Catherine back.[4] Would that it were so! But nothing is further from the king's mind. For because of love for his Anne and
his anger at the excommunication by the pope,[5] he has shut up the queen   15
herself in a castle,[6] with a few servants. He is so contemptuous of the pope's
authority that every day various infamous books, insulting and full of the
most grievous slanders, fly over to us from England. In them the English
preach about the humility, chastity, poverty, patience, and other virtues of
Christ, but they place before our eyes the pride, impurity, riches, tyranny,   20
impatience, and other vices of the pope, the vicar of Christ. In addition to
that, they say that the king has in recent days forbidden that prayers for the
pope be included in prayers and supplications for the church, as they used
to be until now; that he has distributed monasteries among his barons, to be
torn down and used however they wish; and finally, that he has decreed that   25
no one should recognize or consider the pope to be anything other than the
bishop of Rome only. They also say that three or four of his nobles, following
his example, have repudiated their legitimate wives and entered into matrimony with other women. If this is true, they seem to have far outdone even

* * * * *

2915
1 Ep 2877
2 See Ep 2913 n15.
3 Ep 2898
4 Ep 2877:19–21
5 At this stage, Henry VIII had only been threatened (July 1533) with excommunication unless he abandoned his marriage to Anne Boleyn and took back
  Catherine of Aragon as his wife. The threat was renewed in 1536, but the bull
  of excommunication was not finally promulgated until December 1538. See
  Scarisbrick 317–18, 334, 361.
6 Kimbolton castle, where Catherine lived until her death in 1536

Martin himself;[7] in the manner of the pagan barbarians, they change their   30
wives whenever their lusts prod them. What is to happen next is not certain.
We cannot hope for anything good from such bad beginnings.

In your second letter you indicate that your health has been bad since
Christmas.[8] This state of your health is distressing to me. I would wish to
take some part of your illness upon myself, if such a transfer were possible,   35
provided I could do some good for you and lessen your pain. But with the
help of an allpowerful and allgood God, and now that winter and the present
month of March are gradually coming to an end, I hope you will send away
all those physical sufferings and tell them to go be hanged.

Concerning that rascal and the book he printed at Antwerp,[9] I took the   40
matter up with the queen, with the archbishop of Palermo (to whom I gave
your letter),[10] and with the duke of Aarschot.[11] I saw to it that the queen
gave orders to the margrave of Antwerp[12] that if this book has already been
printed it should not be sold, and that the bookseller should be punished for
violating the edict of the emperor.[13] The nature of that command you will   45
understand from the letter of the archbishop.[14] And you will know the language of the command given to the margrave from a copy of the letter that
I have sent to you.[15] Therefore, do not be disturbed by either the writings or
the speech of such rascals, rogues, and shameless people. By their croakings
they will harm themselves rather than you, and they stir up the hatred of all   50
good men, not against you but against themselves. And do not think that
there is a safer place than this for you to live or die in. For just as in Germany,
so here too there is no lack of patrons such as those who have written to you
and to whom your excellence is most cherished. The more sensible among
the monks also favour you, as I have certainly found by experience. It is the   55
more ignorant ones, those who have hardly read your writings at all but
have merely heard false reports about them from others and whose virtue
consists only in a display of mere pharisaical superstition, who shout against
you, rage against you with indignant fury. But these people, too, what are

* * * * *

7 Martin Luther, who married an ex-nun, Katharina von Bora, in 1525
8 Ep 2898:4–7
9 See Epp 2898:11–21, 2899:11–48, 2906:49–69.
10 Ie Jean (II) de Carondelet (Ep 2899)
11 Philippe de Croy (Ep 2822 introduction)
12 See Ep 2912 n5.
13 See Ep 2912 n4.
14 Ep 2912
15 Not extant

they doing but talking nonsense? You have such virtue and magnanimity that   60
you may scorn them utterly. For who can protect himself from this stupid and
mindless barking? If the emperor, the queen, and other princes are not free of
detractors, certainly you are much less likely to be so. Whoever, even among
the ancients, if you go back over ancient history, was not subject to the cavils
of rascals and worthless rogues? Therefore, my dear Erasmus, it is pointless   65
to delay your return for this reason. As you had earlier resolved to do, and as
you have promised not only me but also the queen and others of your patrons,
come back, either at the end of April (as you write) or as soon as your health
makes it feasible, lest, if you do otherwise, they accuse you of inconstancy, and
conceive I know not what opinion of me, who out of my love for you have   70
always done, sincerely and honestly, what I was able and what I was obliged
to do in your affairs. About that I prefer that you should learn in due course
from the letters of others or from their speech, rather than from me.

You commend Lieven to me.[16] I avail myself of his assistance, as long
and as often as I need it. I had previously arranged that he should have eight   75
groots per day from the treasury.[17] Now I have once again arranged for him
to instruct the young nobles of the queen's court.[18] For that service he receives the same daily amount. The lord duke of Aarschot bids me give you
his regards. He wishes to oblige you in every way he can.

Farewell. Brussels, 12 March 1534   80

2916 / To Cornelius Grapheus   Freiburg, 13 March 1534

This letter was first published in the *Vita Erasmi*. It presumably answers the one
mentioned in Epp 2913:7 and 2914:21. For Cornelius Grapheus, see Ep 1299 n24.

ERASMUS OF ROTTERDAM TO THE MOST LEARNED GENTLEMAN
CORNELIUS GRAPHEUS AT ANTWERP, CORDIAL GREETINGS
Damião cheers me by telling me that things are going better for you, both in
mind and body, and that your circumstances are more favourable.[1] A new

* * * * *

16 Ep 2860:36–9
17 Assuming a year of 365 days, £12 3s 4d groot Flemish were equivalent to a year
   and a half's wages of an Antwerp master mason/carpenter (CWE 12 650 Table 3,
   691 Table 13).
18 He had the title *maitre d'escole des pages d'honneur*.

2916
1 But cf Ep 2914:21–3.

ailment torments me, footgout, or rather all-overgout.[2] It attacks all joints,   5
moving from one to another so that I can hardly ever catch my breath. They
say that it is not footgout, but a disease in it own right, from which many here
are now suffering. In the vernacular they call it 'Such.'[3] My poor old body,
broken down by so many ailments and such varied torments, will not be able
to hold out for very long.   10

      What I need most of all is a reliable servant from our own country, for
the Germans, like poets, are an irresponsible race.[4] I would prefer someone
older rather than an adolescent. I do not care much about learning, as long
as he knows Latin and can write tolerably well. Then too, he should not
be susceptible to any disease, such as scabies or epilepsy. I cannot put up   15
with someone who is superstitious. I do not put up with anyone committed to a sect. The wages will be as much as you have prescribed, twenty or
twentyfour Caroline florins per year.[5] Whether anything is added to this for
clothing, out of spontaneous generosity, will depend on him. But if human
destiny should catch up with me, I will see to it that he has not misplaced his 20
services. He would journey here at my expense, and if it happens that he is
not satisfied with everything, he will be sent back at my expense.[6] You can
talk the matter over with Schets. It seems that Damião has refused the office
the king offers him and will return to us.[7] I hope that he will be making use

                  * * * * *

2 See Ep 2818 n1. Erasmus puns on *podagra* (gout in the foot) and *panagra* (gout
   everywhere).
3 See Ep 2906 n43.
4 Cf Lucian *Pro imaginibus* 18: 'There is an old saying that both poets and painters
   are irresponsible.'
5 The upper limit of the wage Erasmus offered a prospective servant/secretary
   was equivalent to £4 4s 0d groot Flemish, a little under half the annual wage of
   an Antwerp master mason/carpenter (CWE 12 650 Table 3, 691 Table 13).
6 It was in response to this request that Grapheus recommended Johannes
   Clauthus, who entered Erasmus' service in the spring of 1534 but died at
   Rochester (10 September 1534) on a mission to England to look after the collection of Erasmus' annuity and to gather information on Thomas More and
   John Fisher, both of whom had been arrested. Erasmus, who never heard from
   Clauthus during his mission and never saw him again, reacted to the news of
   his death with anger and a series of entirely unjustified accusations of bad faith,
   incompetence, and malfeasance, much to the embarrassment and distress of
   Grapheus. See Allen Epp 2981:1–15, 2997:5–43, 3053:5–22.
7 This is the first reference in the correspondence to the decision of Erasmus'
   new friend Damião de Gois to abandon royal service in Portugal and pursue
   humanist scholarship; see Ep 2826 introduction.

CORNELIVS GRAPHEVS
ANDOVERPIENSIS

Magna tuum celebrat Corneli Antuerpia nomen,
    Tradit & innumeris quos habet hoſpitibus.
Te ciuem canit illa pium fidumque miniſtrum
    Scribere qui bene ſcis, publica qui gerere.   C 4

Cornelius Grapheus

Portrait from Philip Galle *Virorum doctorum de disciplinis benemerentium*
effigies XLIIII (Antwerp 1572)

of your prudent counsel. As for you, take care of your health. I pray that all   25
goes well for you and for your wife and children.

Given at Freiburg, 13 March in the year 1534 after the Virgin birth

2917 / From Franciscus Ricius   Tübingen, 17 March 1534

This letter was first published as Ep 114 in Enthoven. The autograph is in the
Rehdiger Collection of the University Library at Wrocław (MS Rehd 254 142).

Franciscus Ricius (d 1578) was the younger son of Paulus Ricius (Ep 549:16n),
a Jewish convert and Hebrew scholar whom Erasmus had met at Pavia in 1506
and with whom he maintained friendly relations thereafter. In 1530, in consequence of his service as personal physician to Ferdinand of Austria, Paulus was
ennobled as baron of Sprinzenstein. By 1526, Franciscus had, like his brother
Hieronymus (Ep 2131), followed his father into the service of King Ferdinand,
and in 1532 he was made provost of Trent (indicating that he was in holy orders). In 1536–7 he was Ferdinand's ambassador to Constantinople, and later
was sent twice to Spain for negotiations with the government of Charles v.
Franciscus appears to have retired from the court in 1560, though he subsequently undertook the visitation and reform of several monasteries. He resigned the provostship of Trent in 1575, and died three years later in Mantua,
during a journey to Italy. No other letters from the correspondence between
Franciscus and Erasmus have survived.

Most renowned gentleman, most respected master. Today I received your
letter,[1] which was forwarded from Innsbruck, and I found it truly delightful
because I learned from it that you are in good health. For there was for some
time a persistent rumour that you were afflicted *in extremis*, a rumour that
disturbed me not only for your sake but also for the sake of scholars and the   5
common good, which for so many years now you have embellished with
your extraordinary powers, and which even now, when you have reached
an advanced age, you have not ceased to assist and enlighten. Thus, as long
as you survive, Catholics and scholars can go on using the fruits of your lucubrations, which perhaps might not be the case after your death because of   10
the authority and power of wicked and envious people who are mortified by
the splendour of your reputation. But if you endure the injustice of our times
for just a little while longer and conquer it by your bravery, just as up to now

* * * * *

2917
1 Not extant

you have scorned it by your prudence, I already see in my mind how their
wickedness will be routed with fire and sword and you will triumph in glory.   15

And conquer you will, I hope, if you take good care of your health;
in our times the salvation of many depends on it because of your excellent
advice and teaching, and it must therefore be maintained at all costs. If you
yourself neglect it, you will seem to be neglecting not so much your own welfare as that of the public. Therefore take care of your health. And sometimes   20
set aside your unremitting labours and studies, so as to enjoy occasionally
some suitable and pleasant recreation.

It is more out of loyalty than prudence that I give such advice to you,
and I do so out of love for you and concern for the common good. That
you ask for frequent and long letters from me is a never-ending source of   25
amazement, since there is nothing in them that would not bore, rather than
entertain, a man of your great learning. But I am delighted that you have noticed, recognized, and accepted my special good will and undying reverence
towards you by letting it be known that you find my letters not displeasing.
Therefore, when I have something worth telling you, I will be most careful to   30
comply with your request, but in such a way that I will not too often trouble
such an important and busy gentleman with my trifles.

In my letter[2] I made no mention of Velius because on the day before
I left Innsbruck, after I had said farewell to those at court, I gave that letter
to the courier, who was unexpectedly getting ready to set out on his jour-   35
ney, without Velius knowing about it.[3] The pope has promised the duchy
of Urbino to the son of the French king as a dowry for his niece.[4] Since the
duchy is still held by Duke Francesco Maria,[5] who has been summoned to

* * * * *

2 Not extant; the one answered by Erasmus in the letter mentioned in lines 1–2 above
3 Caspar Ursinus Velius (Epp 1810 n6, 2008), professor of rhetoric at the University
   of Vienna, official historian to King Ferdinand, and (since 1530) tutor to
   Ferdinand's children
4 On 28 October 1533 Catherine de' Medici, niece of Clement VII, was married to
   Henry, duke of Orléans, during the conference at Marseille (October–November
   1533) between the pope and King Francis I. Catherine had a claim to Urbino
   through her father, Lorenzo (II) de' Medici, who had been duke of Urbino in
   1516–19. Francis I himself drafted a secret treaty stipulating, among other things,
   that not merely Urbino but also Milan should be taken from their respective
   rulers and ceded to Henry of Orléans. But there is no indication that this was
   seriously discussed or that the pope was committed to it. See Pastor 10 234–5.
5 Francesco Maria Della Rovere had been duke of Urbino in 1508–16 but lost
   the duchy to Lorenzo (II) de' Medici in 1516 (see preceding note). In 1521 he
   reconquered Urbino and ruled it until his death in 1538, after which the duchy
   remained in his family until 1625.

Philip of Hessen
Portrait by Hans Krell
Wartburg-Stiftung Institution

Rome but has not yet appeared there, we must fear that there will be a new
and horrible war in Italy. Moreover, the most serene emperor is so outraged   40
by the horrible and wicked crime of the count of Concordia (I wrote you
about how he treacherously killed his kinsman and his son and seized the
town and citadel of Mirandola) that he will not allow such a crime to remain
unavenged.[6] And so we must fear that the thief will be led by desperation
to join up with profligate allies;[7] and since he holds a town which is almost   45
unassailable, he will cause us no little trouble.

Our friend Cornelis de Schepper was recently sent by his most serene
Majesty to the emperor of the Turks at Constantinople. I hope that he will
bring back something that will please you and all good men.[8]

Since I think you have been informed by the bishop of Augsburg or   50
by Provost Koler concerning the quarrel between William, duke of Bavaria,
and the landgrave of Hessen about the restoration of of the expelled duke of
Württemberg,[9] and concerning the payment of four thousand florins by the

* * * * *

6 The Pico family ruled two principalities in Italy, the counties of Mirandola and
   Concordia. Years of family strife had left Gianfrancesco Pico (Ep 2088 n28) in
   possession of Mirandola, while his nephew Galeotto II Pico (1508–50) ruled
   Concordia. On 16 October 1533, Galeotto and a band of armed men broke into
   the castle of Mirandola and murdered Gianfrancesco and his son Alberto. The
   emperor pronounced an imperial ban against Galeotto but was not able to
   enforce it.
7 Chief among these was Francis I.
8 Cornelis de Schepper (Ep 1747 n23) undertook two missions to Constantinople,
   in 1533 and 1534, neither of which produced a satisfactory result.
9 This is the first direct reference in the correspondence to Landgrave Philip of
   Hessen's campaign to restore the exiled Duke Ulrich of Württemberg (Epp 1554
   n4, 1603 n7) to his duchy, which was the largest, most populous, most prosperous principality in southwestern Germany. (Erasmus would soon hear more
   about the matter from his correspondent in Augsburg, Johann Koler; see Epp
   2936:75–90, 2937:54–71, Allen Ep 2947:9–37.) In January 1519 Ulrich, already
   guilty of a long list of crimes against subjects and fellow rulers, laid siege to
   the free imperial city of Reutlingen and incorporated it into his territory. The
   Swabian League (Ep 2814 n9) reacted by invading Württemberg, driving Ulrich
   into exile, and then (1520) transferring control of the duchy to Emperor Charles,
   who (1522) incorporated it into the possessions of his brother, Ferdinand of
   Austria. In exile – initially in Switzerland and Alsace and then (from the winter
   of 1526–7) at the court of Landgrave Philip of Hessen – Ulrich matured into a
   responsible adult and became a sincere, theologically articulate supporter of
   the Reformation. Landgrave Philip, always alert to any opportunity to vin-
   dicate the rights of territorial princes (the expulsion of Ulrich and the transfer of Württemberg to Austria had been without basis in law), to weaken the

Ulrich, duke of Württemberg
Unidentified painter
Kunsthistorisches Museum, Vienna

emperor's men to Christopher, the son of the expelled duke, and concerning the treasure restored to him by the inhabitants of Ulm,[10] I will not bother you with any useless report about those matters. 55

In other matters, a month has passed since I came to Stuttgart to see Duke Philip,[11] who left three days after my arrival to go to the court. Since I am required to await his return to this province, I went to Tübingen, a place most pleasant and comfortable because of its location and its temperate climate, 60 and also because of its wealth and the way of life of the people. Moreover, I am not to leave here even when the business with the duke is completed unless I am called back for the third time by the king or by my father.

The courier to whom I committed this letter to you and whom I sent to Freiburg will come back here immediately with the money entrusted to me 65 while I was there. If you want to give him a letter to me, and if you ask him to

* * * * *

over-mighty Hapsburgs, and to advance the cause of the Reformation, was quick to exploit the golden opportunity to do all three that presented itself in the early months of 1534. On 2 February, the Swabian League, now riven by internal divisions between Protestant and Catholic members, dissolved itself. The emperor was away in Spain and not paying attention to Germany. King Ferdinand had his hands full in Hungary and did not have the resources for effective defence of his interests in the southwestern corner of the Empire. Catholic but fervently anti-Hapsburg Bavaria favoured the project, though Duke William wanted his nephew, Ulrich's still-Catholic son and eventual successor, Christopher, to be the one restored. Finally, Catholic but vehemently anti-Hapsburg Francis I of France was willing to advance to Duke Ulrich most of the cost of the required military campaign, which neutralized Bavaria's wish for the restoration of Duke Christopher. On 13 May, Philip's hired troops decisively defeated the forces of the Austrian regent (see n11 below) at Lauffen on the Neckar (just south of Heilbronn), leaving the way clear to the occupation of the duchy. The Peace of Kadan (29 June 1534), by which Ferdinand of Austria agreed to Ulrich's restoration as duke of Württemberg, recognized his right to introduce the Reformation but stipulated that only 'adherents of the Augsburg Confession' (ie Lutherans) were to be permitted, not 'Sacramentarians' (ie Zwinglians). Ulrich, whose adherence to the Reformation had been mediated by both Zwinglians and Lutherans, initially attempted a harmonious mingling of both confessions, but it did not work, and by 1538 Württemberg had become what it would long remain, an unequivocally Lutheran principality, the bulwark of Lutheran orthodoxy in southern Germany.

10 We have no information about either any payment to Christopher by the emperor's men or any restoration of treasure to him by the inhabitants of Ulm.
11 In 1532, King Ferdinand appointed Philip, Count Palatine of Neuburg (1503–48), as his regent in the duchy of Württemberg.

stay until it is convenient for you to write a return letter, he will not go away
until he is dismissed by your Benevolence, to whom I wish many happy and
healthy days.

From Tübingen, 17 March 1534   70
Most devoted to your Benevolence
Franciscus Ricius von Sprinzenstein (I have written my own signature)
To the most renowned gentleman Master Erasmus of Rotterdam, most
honourable master and patron. In Freiburg

2917A / To Bonifacius Amerbach   [Freiburg, spring 1534]

This letter (= AK Ep 1810) was first published in the *Epistolae familares*. The autograph, address sheet missing, is in the Öffentliche Bibliothek of the University
of Basel (MS AN III 15 78). Allen assigned the conjectural date 'Summer 1531'
and published the letter as Ep 2509. Alfred Hartmann, however, has argued
persuasively that the letter was more likely written in the spring of 1534, at
which time Bonifacius, having arrived at a position on the Eucharist essentially identical to the one that Martin Bucer had formulated in his effort to reach
an accord with the Wittenberg theologians (cf Ep 2248 n6), had been offered
the position of legal adviser to the Strasbourg city council and was inform-
ing himself concerning the terms of the appointment. The presence of Nicolas
Cop (line 5 below) at Basel in February and April 1534 is documented in Ep
2906:38–40 and in Herminjard Ep 458.

Greetings. Before I take on the task of writing, I would like to inquire whether the tribune is willing to undertake the case in your behalf and if he is going to remain there any longer;[1] also whether Jakob Sturm is away on some

* * * * *

2917A
1 In Erasmus' correspondence the word *tribunus* 'tribune' is the word for the
   magistrate of a German city elected by the guilds (with patricians excluded
   from eligibility), while *consul* is his word for the magistrate who had to be
   a patrician. In Basel and Freiburg the German equivalents for *tribunus* and
   consul were *Oberzunftmeister* and *Bürgermeister*; see Epp 2158 n9, 2372 n1, 2462
   n2. In Strasbourg the equivalent terms were *Ammeister* and *Stettmeister*, with
   real authority concentrated in the hands of the former. In 1534 the *Ammeister*
   was Martin Herlin, merchant and zealous supporter of the Reformation. See
   Thomas A. Brady Jr *Ruling Class, Regime and Reformation at Strasbourg 1520–
   1555* (Leiden 1978) 164, 317. Though nothing is known of Herlin's role in the
   negotiations with Bonifacius, it would presumably have been an important
   one. It is not clear why Erasmus would wonder if Herlin were going to 'remain
   there any longer.'

embassy.[2] My quittance is based on gold to gold; it will be so much less a
burden for the one who is bringing it here.[3] Send a copy of the letter to Cop,[4]   5
and farewell.

2918 / To Georgius Agricola   Freiburg, [early April] 1534

This letter, evidently a reply to one no longer extant, was first published by
Georg Buchwald in the *Zeitschrift für kirchliche Wissenschaft und kirchliches Leben*
5 (1884) 56, from a copy in the Ratsschulbibliothek Zwickau (MS 36 page 217b).
For Georgius Agricola, since 1531 town physician in Chemnitz, Saxony, see
Ep 1594 n23.

The letter is Erasmus' first reaction to the publication of *Epistolae Nicolai
Amsdorfii et D. Martini Lutheri de Erasmo Roterodamo* (Wittenberg: Lufft 1534).
The work was in print no later than 28 March 1534 (see WA-Br 7 27), and Froben
published Erasmus' reply, *Purgatio adversus epistolam non sobriam Martini Lutheri*
before the end of April. Hence Allen's approximate date for this letter.

Since the publication of *De servo arbitrio* in 1525 Luther had refrained from
public attack on Erasmus. But in private he continued to pay attention to
Erasmus, studying carefully some of his works, particularly the fourth edition
of the New Testament (1527) and other works of biblical scholarship. This confirmed him in his already settled view that Erasmus was a religious sceptic
and a bad influence who needed to be exposed as such and discredited. Early
in 1533 Luther declared to the theology students who boarded in his home,
'I enjoin hatred of Erasmus on all of you ... I have decided to slay him by the
pen' (WA-TR 1 446). The opportunity to do so arrived about a year later in the
context of a dispute between the Wittenberg theologians and Georg Witzel (see
n1 below). Since 1532 Witzel, a one-time Lutheran pastor turned irenic Catholic,
had been defending the Catholic teaching on good works in a heated debate
with the Wittenberg theologian Justus Jonas (see n2 below). Hearing that Luther
intended to intervene in the controversy between Witzel and Jonas, Luther's
friend Nicolaus von Amsdorf (pastor and superintendent at Magdeburg), wrote

* * * * *

2 Jakob Sturm (Ep 2510), aristocrat of Strasbourg, was a leading member of its
  city council who served five terms as *Stettmeister* (see preceding note) and was
  the city's chief diplomat. He would have been influential in the determination
  of the conditions under which Bonifacius Amerbach would be appointed legal
  adviser to the city government.
3 This presumably has something to do with the monies deposited by Erasmus
  with Bonifacius; see Ep 2855.
4 See introduction above.

Martin Luther
Lucas Cranach the Elder
Private collection

him a letter, dated 28 January 1534, arguing that since Witzel stole all his ideas
from Erasmus, Luther should ignore Witzel and take aim at Erasmus instead
(WA-Br 7 16–17). On about 11 March Luther responded with the letter (WA-Br 7
27–40) that, together with Amsdorf's letter, was printed at Wittenberg later that
month. Luther's *Epistola* is, in the words of Allen's introduction to this letter,
'a piece of masterly invective.' It is also the most ferocious attack on Erasmus
ever published. The core of Luther's criticism is that Erasmus never openly and
frankly says what he means, preferring to revel in ambiguity; that he continually disparages the Christian religion, in which he only pretends to believe; that
he harbours a fundamental aversion to all religion; and that he is therefore a
pagan sceptic, the devil in human form (cf ASD IX-1 432).

Erasmus, who since the publication of *Hyperaspistes* 2 in 1527 had abstained
from public criticism of Luther and could not imagine what he had done to deserve such an attack, was taken entirely by surprise and deeply offended. After
some hesitation, expressed in the present letter, he published the *Purgatio*, in
which he responded point for point to Luther's 'manifest lies' and misrepresentations (cf Ep 2933:4–9). Erasmus' friend in Augsburg, Johann Koler, who
was incensed by Luther's *Epistola*, found the *Purgatio* much too mild in tone
(Epp 2936:24–74, 2937:12–35, 104–11). All the same, he arranged for a reprint-
ing of the work in Augsburg and sent two copies to Rome, intending that it
become known to both the pope and the emperor (Allen Ep 2947:56–83). In
addition to Froben's *editio princeps*, several hundred copies of which were
shipped to Brabant (Ep 2933:10–11) there were six reprints of the work in
Erasmus' lifetime, including the one arranged by Koler at Augsburg (see the
list in ASD IX-1 439–40).

Even before he had seen the *Purgatio*, Luther announced to Amsdorf his intention to continue the controversy with Erasmus (WA-Br 7 53:16–18), and many,
including Erasmus himself, expected a renewed attack (Allen Ep 2961:15–19). It
did not come to that, however, doubtless in large measure because Melanchthon,
who had been 'displeased' by Luther's *Epistola* and told him so (CWE 78 407 with
n64; cf WA-Br 7 79:1–8), intervened to prevent it. That at least was what Johann
Koler, who knew of Luther's intentions, hoped would happen (see Allen Ep
2947:79–82).

ERASMUS OF ROTTERDAM TO GEORGIUS AGRICOLA, GREETINGS
I received Luther's absolutely furious *Epistola* a while ago. Is the man not
ashamed to lie so shamelessly? And he promises something even harsher.
What are people thinking when they commit their souls and their fortunes
to man subject to such emotions? And at the same time he does not consid-   5
er how much he harms the very cause that he promotes with such fervour.
Georg Witzel has written to me twice, but without giving the place he was

writing from, and so I have not responded.[1] I knew that he did not think well of Luther; I would have advised him not to give rein to his anger.[2] I suspect Luther was offended by my *Apostles' Creed,*[3] which the new fatherinlaw of the   10 king of England asked me to write.[4] For he boasts openly that England has received the word of God.[5]

I have no desire to contend with Luther.[6] As for me, every day I prepare for my last day – I am an old man terribly afflicted by illness, broken down by labours, overwhelmed by rabid and raging books. I don't see what good   15 it would do to exasperate Luther with books. The rope of contention is being stretched by both sides;[7] the matter can never be settled except by monarchs. Right now the Franciscans are in charge.[8] I have made my support of the church sufficiently clear. Let others do whatever they can; my only concern is to save my poor soul. The only thing in which I take pride is that I have never   20 committed myself to any sect.

* * * * *

2918
1 For Witzel, see Ep 2715 introduction. The only extant letters from him, Epp 2715 and 2786, indicate clearly the place from which they were written. This is presumably a reference to recent letters, now lost.
2 From Ep 2786:63–8 Erasmus would have known of Witzel's controversy with Jonas (cf introduction above).
3 Ie the *Explanatio symboli* (Ep 2772). Luther's *Epistola* in fact contains several paragraphs devoted to the *Explanatio* (referred to as Erasmus' *Catechismus*), which served to illustrate Luther's view that Erasmus provided ambiguous, bewilderingly complicated, doubt-inducing answers to fundamental questions of faith requiring clear, definitive answers. See WA-Br 7 30–1.
4 Correcting Erasmus' slip *gener* 'son-in-law' for *socer* 'father-in-law.' Thomas Boleyn, at whose request Erasmus wrote the *Explanatio symboli* (Ep 2772), was the father of Queen Anne Boleyn.
5 This sentence is a puzzle. First of all, Allen's text makes an unwarranted correction of *iactat* 'he boasts' to *iacta[n]t* 'they boast.' Second, 'he' is ambiguous. Was it Luther or Boleyn who made that open boast? Since it is Luther's suspected annoyance that is being explained, he seems the more likely candidate, but he said no such thing in the *Epistola de Erasmo Roterodamo* and is not known to have done so anywhere else. Nor can we find evidence of any such statement from Boleyn. Finally, regardless of who said it, we can find no plausible explanation of what the boast might mean in this context.
6 Erasmus changed his mind about this very quickly, without ever explaining why he did so, and his reply was in print by the end of the month. For an assessment of his likely motives, and the strategy followed in doing so, see CWE 78 404–7 (James Tracy's introduction to the *Purgatio*).
7 Cf *Adagia* I v 67: *Funem abrumpere nimium tendendo* 'To stretch the rope till it breaks.'
8 Cf Epp 2898:11–21, 2906:46.

If Luther throws my books out of his schools and hands me over to Satan,[9] I don't care one little bit about that. How shamelessly he has raged against the English king,[10] against Duke George,[11] and not just once! Since he has thus far escaped with impunity, it is not surprising that he dares to do whatever he wants with the likes of me. I feel that some people are setting deadly snares for me, especially those who lived for some time in my household and were helped by my letters, money, and recommendations. Recently a servant whom I judged to be most faithful has turned against me; he rages against me as if I had murdered both his parents. It seems that he wormed his way into my household precisely to discover my secrets, and there are those in this town who egg him on.[12]

Last autumn I was called back to Brabant in the name of the emperor and Queen Mary, with someone sent to escort me back there bringing with him two hundred florins, but my health would not allow it. Now I am being summoned once more. But many things prevent it, even though I am unhappy being stuck here.[13] For almost a year now I have been repeatedly tormented by a persistent ailment very similar to gout, though they say it is not gout. It wanders through all my joints, sometimes with excruciating and unbearable pain, but after three days it lets up. In the vernacular they call it *gesucht*.[14] In addition to that there is old age itself, an incurable disease. But we are in the hands of the Lord.

I greatly enjoyed having my memory of Egranus refreshed. I knew him at Louvain, when he was not averse to Luther (for at that time who was there who did not favour him?), but afterwards at Basel he had already become hostile to him.[15] Johannes Cochlaeus sent me Witzel's book.[16] I received the

* * * * *

9 This echoes the penultimate paragraph of Luther's letter; see wA-Br 7 38–9.
10 In reply to Henry viii's *Assertio septem sacramentorum* (Ep 2831 n16) Luther had published vituperative treatises in both German and Latin; see Ep 1308 n3.
11 For the acrimonious controversy between Luther and Duke George of Saxony in the years 1528–30, see Ep 2338:12–43.
12 Quirinus Hagius; see Ep 2896 n11.
13 See Ep 2820 introduction, where the amount carried by the escort (Lieven Algoet) is set at three hundred florins.
14 For Erasmus' ill health at this time, see Ep 2818 n1. For *gesucht*, see Ep 2906 n43.
15 For Johannes Sylvius Egranus, see Ep 1377 introduction. In 1520 he delivered Ep 1127A (from Luther) to Erasmus at Louvain, and in 1523 he paid a visit to Erasmus at Basel (Epp 1376:12, 1383:1).
16 In a letter of 28 March 1534 Witzel says that so far that year he had published seven books; see Georg Witzel *Epistolarum ... libri quatuor* (Leipzig: Nicolaus Wohlrab 1537) e iii verso. Gregor Richter *Die Schriften Georg Witzels bibliographisch*

letter; the bundle will arrive tomorrow.[17] Give my cordial regards to Lucas
Scuppegius and Bartholomäus Bach.[18] See to it that this letter does not go any
further. I wrote it with great difficulty and I have not reread it. If any prod-
uct of your talent comes to maturity, remember Froben; no one prints more   50
grandly.[19] Farewell, most learned gentleman.

Given at Freiburg im Breisgau, 1534

2919 / To Damião de Gois   Freiburg, 11 April 1534

> This letter was first published in the *Epistolae familiares*. For Damião de Gois see
> Ep 2826 introduction.

ERASMUS OF ROTTERDAM TO THE MOST RENOWNED YOUNG
PORTUGUESE GENTLEMAN DAMIÃO DE GOIS, CORDIAL GREETINGS
Your letter, my very dear friend, was given to me at lunch.[1] I wrote back right
after lunch – which I usually don't do – because the courier was in a hurry.[2] I
pray that your leaving behind you such magnificent opportunities will turn   5
out happily and well.[3] I am entirely at your disposal. My health is miserable
and I am forced to put up with it. I will turn over to you a part of my house
that is very fine and secluded, where you can live the life of a hermit. But if

* * * * *

bearbeitet (Fulda 1913; repr Nieuwkoop 1963) lists nine works published in
1534, only two of which were in Latin and in print in time to be received before
the composition of this letter: *Sillabus locorum ex utroque testa. de boni operibus*
(February 1534) and *Oratio in laudem hebraicae linguae* (March 1534). See Richter
13–14, items 9 and 10.
17 The reference is without context.
18 For Scuppegius and Bach, see Ep 2529 n14.
19 At Erasmus' suggestion, Froben had published Agricola's *Bernannus sive de re
metallica* in 1530; see Ep 2274 introduction.

2919
1 Not extant, but clearly written from Basel, where his presence on 10 April is
documented; see AK Epp 1814–15.
2 In line 4 of Ep 2920, also written on 11 April, Erasmus reports to Bonifacius
Amerbach that 'Damião is here.' He must have arrived after the impatient courier departed with this letter.
3 See Ep 2916 n7.

my place does not suit you, the counts of Rennenberg have left vacant a part
of the house where I formerly lived.⁴ You will find Erasmus ready to do   10
everything. About clothes, it does not matter very much whether you get
new ones there or here. I'll tell you the rest face to face. Farewell, my very
good friend. .

Freiburg, 11 April 1534. We will drink from your cup,⁵ which will be
brought out the day after tomorrow.   15

Whenever you get here, you will find the place ready. I do not imagine
you will want to keep horses. We have a fine stable, but it is full. Again and
again be well.

2920 / To Bonifacius Amerbach   [Freiburg], 11 April 1534

This letter (= AK Ep 1816), which answers one no longer extant, was first published in the *Epistolae familiares*. The autograph is in the Öffentliche Bibliothek
of the University of Basel (there is a photograph of it in Major, plate 28).

Greetings. As for my health, may the Lord see to it.¹ Please do not waste
words about the offence.² I would sooner distrust myself than lack confidence in you. Some things I put off until you arrive. The torment is gone; my
stomach is upset. This is nothing new. Damião is here.³ The rest I will tell you
face to face.   5

Farewell. Right after lunch, 11 April 1534
Yours truly, Erasmus
The seal on your letter was a mixture of red and green wax. I would like
to know whether this was your doing.⁴
To the most renowned Master Bonifacius Amerbach. At Basel   10

* * * * *

4 See Ep 2810 n54. On 23 April Erasmus reported to Erasmus Schets that Gois
   was living in his house (Ep 2924:39–40). He remained in Freiburg until August,
   when he left for Italy to continue his studies at Padua.
5 See Ep 2826 n19.

   2920
1 See Ep 2818 n1.
2 The remark is without context.
3 See Ep 2919 n2.
4 Erasmus worried that the letter might have been opened and resealed by an
   unauthorized person.

2921 / From Bernhard von Cles Prague, 21 April 1534

This letter was first published by Allen. For the manuscript, and for Cles as well, see Ep 2821 introduction.

TO ERASMUS OF ROTTERDAM

We are sending you a pamphlet (perhaps you have already seen it) that somehow came into the hands of the reverend lord nuncio apostolic residing with his royal Majesty,[1] not for the reason that we think it will detract from your honour in any way (since the thrusts of a gnat against an elephant are 5 pointless),[2] but rather because it seemed to us intolerable that you should be treated with such shameless impudence.[3]

Another book by Luther, on private masses,[4] has been published, with which his royal Majesty is greatly displeased; but his Majesty has refused to assign the refutation of it to you because you are already worn down by old 10 age. We wanted to let you know this in order to make you aware of the attitude of the aforesaid Majesty towards you. If there is any way we can oblige you, neither our zeal nor our efforts will be found wanting. We wish you a long and healthy life.

At Prague, 20 April 1534 15

2922 / To Nicolaus Olahus Freiburg, 22 April 1534

This letter, Erasmus' reply to Ep 2915, was first published in Ipolyi pages 491–3. The manuscript is page 361 of the Olahus codex in the Hungarian National Archives at Budapest (Ep 2339 introduction). Olahus' reply is Ep 2948.

ERASMUS OF ROTTERDAM TO NICOLAUS OLAHUS,
SECRETARY TO HER MOST SERENE MAJESTY
Concerning what you say about affairs in England,[1] I am quite ready to

* * * * *

2921
1 Pier Paolo Vergerio (Ep 2825)
2 *Adagia* I x 66
3 The pamphlet (*libellus*) is clearly Luther's *Epistola de Erasmo Roterodamo*; see Ep 2918 introduction.
4 The book (Cles calls it a *libellus*) is probably Justus Jonas' translation of *Von der Winkelmesse und Pfaffenweihe* (cf Ep 2906 n3): *De missa privata et unctione sacerdotum libellus* (Wittenberg: Johann Luft 1534).

2922
1 Ep 2915:13–32

believe part but not all. Things would not have come to this tragic pass if the
cardinals appointed by the pope seven years ago had given a clear decision.[2]   5
I would hope that we could get along with the English. On the first of April I
began to feel not exactly well but at least a little less bad and my hopes were
raised. But then, eight days later, an enormous pain struck the left side of my
head and the left part of my neck, together with my shoulder and arm, and it
stays there as if it will never go away. For five months I have not set foot out-   10
side my house.[3] Even on Easter Day I said mass in my bedroom.[4] The violence
of the monks would not deter me from returning[5] if it were not that I would
be afraid of being paralyzed. But if the journey were to take four or five days,
I would even see to it that I would be taken there in a litter.[6] You say, 'They
would accuse you of inconstancy.'[7] Would that I could rightly be so accused.   15

The margrave will not do anything to Hillen; he favours the Franciscans.[8] And the books have already sold out.[9] But in fact that stupid book
will hardly do much damage to my reputation. I am afraid of worse damage from the supporters of the sects, who have persuaded themselves that
Erasmus is keeping them from ruling everywhere with impunity. Luther   20
has published an epistle which is simply insane and which breathes nothing
but a parricidal hatred.[10] With respect to your support for me, my most dear
Olahus, you are telling someone who already knows, and I am not unaware
of how much and in how many ways I have been obliged to you. Would that
I could manifest my gratitude by doing you some outstanding service. I am   25
pleased by what you write about Lieven,[11] but I very much wish that he,

* * * * *

2 In June 1528 Clement VII gave cardinals Thomas Wolsey and Lorenzo Campeggi
   full authority to examine the evidence for and against the marriage of Henry
   and Catherine and to render judgment; see Pastor 10 257. This led to Campeggi's
   journey to England in the summer of 1529 to preside over a legatine court,
   which adjourned without coming to a decision when Pope Clement transferred
   the case back to Rome; see Ep 2215 n17.
3 See Ep 2818 n1.
4 15 April 1534
5 Ie returning to Brabant; cf Ep 2915:48–66.
6 Cf Ep 2924:2–9.
7 Ep 2915:69
8 The Latin is *favet funigeris* 'he favours the rope-wearers,' referring to the Franciscan
   custom of cinching their habits with a knotted rope. For the margrave see
   Ep 2912 n5.
9 Cf Ep 2912:24–6.
10 See Ep 2918 introduction.
11 Ep 2915:74–8

holding out his hands in supplication,[12] would call upon Fortune. He informs me that you are getting ready to return to Hungary, and I pray that such a change may work out most happily for you; although for me it will be just as disadvantageous whether I return or not. Friends dwelling far away are no true friends.[13] I beg you to take the place for me of a letter to the most reverend lord archbishop of Palermo;[14] thank him in my name and, if it seems convenient, show him this letter. For I could hardly write this much because of the severe pain. Believe me, my return does not require any exhortations. I will not miss the opportunity. For her serene Majesty I pray that all may be joyful. Give my cordial greetings to the duke of Aarschot.[15] Give my warmest regards to the Dane.[16] Perhaps he thinks that I am angry because I do not write to him. Illness is the reason, not my feelings.

Farewell. Freiburg, 22 April 1534

READ THIS WHEN YOU ARE ALONE   40
I know what Pieter van Montfoort is hunting for, and I do not begrudge him any success.[17] I am not responsible for anyone's support of him. He is a friend to no one but himself. Certainly he is no friend of mine. He is highly intelligent and quick, but crafty, vain, arrogant, and vile. Be careful about trusting him. He extorts recommendations from everyone. He actively solicited the job of delivering to me the honorary gift that the six Estates of Holland had decided to grant me. They had decided upon three hundred Caroline florins. He brought two hundred, but only with words. Even though I was at that time very ill, he kept after me, to the point of making me weary of life, to write long and lying letters of recommendation to the emperor, to some commander I didn't know, to the treasurer of Holland, and to others. I would rather have paid him a sizable sum of money than to torture my health by such labours. He and his companion took

* * * * *

12 Greek in the text (Xenophon *Memorabilia* 2.6.31)
13 Greek in the text (*Adagia* II iii 86). As Erasmus himself observes in explaining the adage, it is the equivalent of 'the saying now on everyone's lips: Out of sight, out of mind.'
14 Carondelet, who had recently sent Ep 2912
15 Philippe de Croy (Ep 2822 introduction)
16 Jakob Jespersen (Ep 2849)
17 For Pieter van Montfoort, see Ep 2812 introduction.

their meals with me for some days.[18] He never thanked me. Through my
servant Quirinus he did not deign to write a single word.[19] These are things, 55
my friend Olahus, that you needed to know. But keep them to yourself. He
is extremely loquacious, and he can do damage (which is easy enough for
anyone to do). Farewell.

2923 / To Vincent Cornelissen van Mierop — Freiburg, 23 April 1534

> This letter was first published in *Illustrium et clarorum virorum Epistolae selec-
> tiores* ed Daniel Hensius (Leiden 1617) 320. The original letter is in the Mary
> Hyde Eccles autograph collection at the Houghton Library, Harvard University
> (MS Eng 1343 [9]). For Cornelissen see Ep 2819 introduction.

Cordial greetings. Although it is clear that the sum of three hundred florins
was decided upon by the Estates of Holland (which even Master Pieter van
Montfoort himself confesses) and that the letter of the advocate of Holland
had only two hundred, etc, I have no suspicion of wrongdoing by anyone,
but the facts themselves make it clear that there has been some mistake. I 5
wrote back through Doctor Viglius, which I would not have done if I had
received the letter of Schets.[1] For in Easter week I received the letter of that
extraordinary gentleman Joost Sasbout, written on 19 October.[2] Now there is
no problem left except the sixty florins, about which from now on I will make
no trouble for anyone, regardless of whether they were not decided upon or 10
whether they are in good hands. The only thing I will do is to offer to you, to
my friends, and to my country some evidence of my gratitude for this honour so freely bestowed on me.

> Given at Freiburg im Breisgau, 23 April 1534
> Erasmus of Rotterdam, in my own hand 15
> To the most renowned gentleman Master Vincent Cornelissen, trea-
surer, etc

* * * * *

18 For Montfoort's visit to Erasmus, the letters of recommendation, and the misunderstanding regarding the honorarium from the Estates of Holland, see Epp
2818:15–21, 2819:1–19, 2896:1–8, 2913:10–21, and 2923.
19 Quirinus Hagius, who returned from his second journey to England in the
summer of 1533

2923
1 This repeats what Erasmus wrote to Erasmus Schets in Epp 2896:1–8, 2913:10–21.
2 Not extant. For Sasbout, see Ep 2844.

2924 / To [Erasmus Schets]   Freiburg, 23 April 1534

This letter was first published by Allen. The autograph, address sheet missing, is in the British Library (MS Add 38512 folio 90). The contents make clear that Schets is the addressee.

I am greatly troubled by the generosity of your wife, who has given me such a wonderful gift.[1] Would that I could have received it there! I had begun to have better hopes by the first day of April. But this sudden, unending hot spell has afflicted me more grievously than the winter cold, and not me alone but many others as well. Hardly ten days had passed 5 when an atrocious pain seized the left side of my head and neck, and also my shoulder and arm, and it persists there as if it will never go away.[2] If Brabant were not further away than a four-day's journey, I would see to it that I be transported there by litter.[3] I am so weary of this region. There are people there about whom they think I should be careful. But a greater 10 danger hangs over me here. I feel that there is a conspiracy to kill me. Like a trumpeter of war, Luther has sent out a letter more furious than the all the Furies, breathing a more than parricidal hatred, stuffed with slanders and lies.[4] Many hope for war. And meanwhile the emperor is hunting in Spain. Unless he comes back to Germany we are in danger of seeing a calamitous 15 state of things here.[5]

I wrote back to your son;[6] I think the letter was delivered.

You write that a diploma exists.[7] Would that it had been sent to me! The Canterbury pension has been paid up to Michaelmas of last year.[8] I will receive nothing unless I send the document to England. Robert Aldridge prom- 20 ised that he would find someone at the court of the archbishop to take care of

* * * * *

2924
1 See Ep 2896 n9.
2 See Ep 2818 n1.
3 Cf Ep 2922:6–14.
4 See Ep 2918 introduction.
5 Charles V had left Germany for Spain in the autumn of 1532 and would not return to his northern dominions until 1540 (the Netherlands) and 1541 (Germany).
6 Ep 2897
7 The 'English diploma' of Ep 2896:26–7; see nn12–13 in that letter.
8 29 September 1533

this business.[9] If I receive the document that was in the hands of Pieter Gillis,[10] I will see to it that that pension is also confirmed.[11]

I am sending back to you your letter to the counts of Rennenberg because I do not know where they are now. They went away eight days before your letter arrived.[12]

I especially need bed sheets. So I would ask you to buy for me 100 or 115 ells of Holland cloth, substantial and closewoven.[13] The bundle should be sent to Hieronymus Froben, if there is no one to bring it here. I will make a note of what you pay out from the Holland grant.[14] I wonder where the letter of Sasbout is being held up for so long.[15]

I have written to Vincent and Sasbout,[16] trying to calm their suspicions. I would like to know whether you have received the two books on the preparation for death, together with a letter, and have sent them on to England.[17]

To you, my most trustworthy of friends, and all who are dear to you I wish the best of health and good fortune.

Given at Freiburg, 23 April 1534

Your Erasmus of Rotterdam

Damião de Gois, an outstanding young man, is living in my house, but because of my poor health we take our meals separately.[18] For that reason especially I am furious at my illness.

* * * * *

9 See Ep 2913:23–8.
10 Erasmus had written to the late Pieter Gillis' brother, who was a canon and cantor at Antwerp, in the hope of securing the document through him; see Ep 2896 n13.
11 This would be the second of Erasmus' English pensions, the location of which is not known; see Ep 2332 n10.
12 See Ep 2810 n54.
13 'Ell' was a synonym for 'yard.' Linen was generally sold by the ell, woollen cloth by the yard, but there was no substantial difference in the length of the measure. See CWE 12 606 n63.
14 Ie the grant from the Estates of Holland, which had been paid to Schets (Ep 2819:3–10). Erasmus reiterated this order on 11 June 1544, but on 30 July it had still not been delivered; see Allen Epp 2944:8–10, 2955:24.
15 See Ep 2923 n2. The letter mentioned here (not extant) is clearly not the letter mentioned there.
16 The letter to Vincent Cornelissen is Ep 2923; that to Joost Sasbout is not extant.
17 See Ep 2913:22–8.
18 See Ep 2919 nn2, 4.

2925 / To Pietro Bembo Freiburg, 25 April 1534

This letter was first published by Pierre de Nolhac in *Érasme en Italie: Étude sur un épisode de la Renaissance; suivie de douze lettres inédites d'Érasme*, 2nd ed (Paris 1898) 129–31. The autograph is in the Vatican Library (MS Barberini Lat 2158 folio 111). For Bembo see Ep 2106 introduction. His answer to this letter is Ep 2975.

Viglius Zuichemus, a protégé of your Muses, has published at Basel the *Institutes* of Justinian translated into Greek.[1] In his preface he praises you with all stops out, as they say,[2] but he always does that, and quite rightly, dear sir, since you of all people now living are the kindest and most ready to give assistance to everyone. 5

I hear, and I am sorry to hear, that the Asulanus press is languishing.[3] But that of Froben is busier every day with the publication of the best authors, not sparing either labour or expense, doing so indeed with greater glory than profit. They have now undertaken the decades of Livy, uncommonly well corrected from manuscript volumes. The one who did most of the work on it 10 is Beatus Rhenanus, a learned gentleman, diligent and extremely judicious. Next to him in the labour is Henricus Glareanus, who is highly proficient in all subjects, but especially in the knowledge of ancient history. The third is Sigismundus Gelenius, by birth a Bohemian but a fosterchild of Italy in his outstanding learning.[4] 15

They have also heard that there is a manuscript there of the first six books of the third decade, which they have not been able to obtain here. If

* * * * *

2925
1 The work was published by Froben at Basel in 1534; see Ep 2791 n22.
2 Literally 'with all the holes open,' said of flute-players who, when they leave the holes of their instrument open, produce a piercing sound (*Adagia* I v 96)
3 By 1533 control of the Aldine Press at Venice (Erasmus calls it the Asulanus Press) had fallen to Paolo Manuzio (1512–74), third son of the founder Aldo Manuzio (Ep 207) and (through his mother) grandson of Aldo's business partner, father-in-law, and immediate successor, Andrea Torresani of Asola (whence the surname often used for him and his sons, Asulanus). Paolo had not yet succeeded completely in arresting and reversing the decline of the press under the management of Torresani and his son Gianfrancesco. This is why Viglius wanted his book published at Basel rather than Venice. See his letters of 4 November 1532 and 17 January 1533 to Bonifacius Amerbach (AK Epp 1689, 1704).
4 The first Froben Livy was published in March 1531 with a prefatory letter by Erasmus (Ep 2435). The three scholars mentioned were working on a new edition that was published in 1535. For Rhenanus, Glareanus, and Gelenius see Epp 327, 440, 1702 n1.

Pietro Bembo
Lucas Cranach the Younger
Private collection
Image courtesy of P. and D. Colnaghi and Co

they get access to it through your intercession, you will not find them lacking
in gratitude. I hope that, if you possibly can, you will not find it burdensome
to do this, out of your innate kindness and your inclination to promote the best 20
kind of scholarship.[5] Farewell. Here we hear nothing but drums and trumpets.[6]

Freiburg. The feast of St Mark, 1534

Erasmus of Rotterdam, in my own hand

To the most renowned gentleman Master Pietro Bembo, patrician of
Venice. At Padua 25

2926 / From Ambrosius von Gumppenberg [Rome, April 1534]

Written in a secretary's hand and signed by Gumppenberg, this is the concluding portion of a letter, the first part of which is missing. First published as Ep
201 in Förstemann / Günther, the manuscript was in the Burscher Collection of
the University Library at Leipzig (Ep 1254 introduction). For Gumppenberg, influential German prelate at the papal court in Rome, see Ep 2619 introduction.

Moreover, my dearest friend Erasmus, I have need of some impoverished
young man whom I can safely trust to write my confidential documents from
this time on. I will provide him generously with divine endowments or else
priestly benefices (if he should wish to dedicate himself to the service of God
in some other way).[1] And so if you have someone who is skilled in Latin 5
eloquence, who is needy (for the rich ones are too haughty), and who will
submit his hand to the rod (for men of a more advanced age are unwilling to
be reprimanded), please send him to me as soon as you can and I will see to it

* * * * *

5 In his reply (Allen Ep 2975:21–3), Bembo reported that he had 'no manuscripts
  of Livy that would not be less correct than those used by Aldus in his edition, which is in everyone's hands.' He did not mention that he owned a fif-
  teenth-century manuscript of the third decade of Livy in the hand of Poggio
  Bracciolini (MS Vat 3330), perhaps because he thought it too recent to be of any
  value. He does, however, seem to have made inquiries about other manuscripts
  in response to direct requests from the Froben press; see Nolhac *Érasme en Italie*
  (as in introduction above) 130.
6 Ie sounds of war. This is doubtless a reference to the reconquest of Württemberg.
  See Ep 2917 n9.

2926

1 The Latin for 'with divine endowments or priestly benefices' is *dotibus divinis
  aut sacerdotiis*. We have no idea of the precise meaning of 'divine endowments.'
  In Ep 2929:28–9 Gumppenberg states simply 'I will provide him generously
  with benefices.'

that, provided he himself is willing, he gets the benefit of your recommendation, for which he will always be obliged to you.   10

Farewell, and in this matter answer as soon as possible.

The same Ambrosius von Gumppenberg signed this.

2927 / To Bonifacius Amerbach   [Freiburg], 25 April 1534

This letter (= AK Ep 1823) was first published in the *Epistolae familiares*. The autograph is in the Öffentliche Bibliothek of the University of Basel (MS AN III 15
58). Bonifacius' answer is Ep 2930.

Greetings. I am terribly afraid that my candour in advising Sadoleto has alienated him.[1] I beg you to see to it that my letter reaches him.[2] I think Episcopius
is setting out for Lyon,[3] and from there it can be sent on through Gryphius.[4]

Farewell. The rest face to face. On the feast of St Mark 1534

You recognize the hand   5

To the most renowned Master Bonifacius Amerbach. At Basel

2928 / To Bonifacius Amerbach   [Freiburg], 27 April [1534]

This letter (= AK Ep 1824) was first published in the *Epistolae familiares*. The
autograph, addressed by Gilbert Cousin (Ep 2381 n1), is in the Öffentliche
Bibliothek of the University of Basel (MS AN III 15 76). Bonifacius' answer to
both this letter and Ep 2927 is Ep 2930.

I beg you, send this letter to Sadoleto the first chance you get.[1] I am waiting
for you to come – and though that is a pleasing prospect, I still wouldn't want
you to be put to any trouble.[2]

Farewell. 27 April

* * * * *

2927
1 See Epp 2816 n3, 2930:1–22.
2 The letter is not extant.
3 See Ep 2930:2–3.
4 The printer Sebastianus Gryphius, who had reprinted a number of Erasmus'
  works, including editions of the *Adagia* in 1528 and 1529; see Ep 2135 n2.

2928
1 Erasmus apparently did not trust the carrier engaged to deliver Ep 2927, so he
  sent with this message a copy of the letter to Sadoleto that he had enclosed with
  the earlier letter.
2 See Ep 2930:27–8.

You recognize the hand.   5

To the most renowned Master Bonifacius Amerbach, doctor and most celebrated professor of law. At Basel

2929 / From Ambrosius von Gumppenberg   Rome, 29 April 1534

This letter was first published as Ep 202 in Förstemann/Günther. The manuscript, written and addressed by a secretary, was in the Burscher Collection of the University Library at Leipzig (Ep 1254 introduction). The secretary dated the letter 'tertio kalendas Maias' (29 April) but enclosed with it a letter from Sepúlveda that seems likely to have been Ep 2938, dated 23 May 1534 (see n3 below). Allen speculated that the secretary's 'Maias' was likely a blunder for 'Iunias' and that the real date of this letter is therefore 29 May 1534. But he did not find his own argument persuasive enough to cause him to redate and renumber the letter.

Greetings. Reverend Master Erasmus, the latest letter I sent you I entrusted to a Strasbourg letter carrier, who promised that he would travel to Freiburg.[1] I will be pleased if you receive it, together with a letter of the reverend lord Cardinal Cajetanus bound together with mine.[2] Yet I did not want to commit to writing things that the letter carrier will tell you in person; you can have   5 complete confidence in him, etc. For the time being there was nothing else worth writing about except that I sent on to you Master Sepúlveda's letter and response.[3] I beg you grant us a reply as soon as possible.

Moreover, Erasmus, best of friends, I once more advise, exhort, and implore you to turn your attention at last to extinguishing these new sects   10 and perverse teachings. Do not depart or withdraw from the teachings of the church, which have until now been piously observed and received from our fathers. Strive to keep the Catholic church unharmed; through your efforts and counsel protect her and her towers or members against the clandestine plots of those who attack her. You will be doing something you will never   15 need to regret (believe me, I am not speaking lightly). Someday you will confess that the advice I gave you was that of a friend. Therefore, whatever else you publish, see to it that you dedicate it to the supreme pontiff; take care to send me one or two copies to be presented to his Holiness in your

* * * * *

2929
1 Probably Ep 2926
2 The cardinal's letter has not survived.
3 Sepúlveda did not answer Ep 2905 until 23 May (Ep 2938).

name, and if you have no other convenient way to do it, send them through   20
your own letter carrier. Do not worry about paying his wages; someone will
be found to respond to that need. Whatever you do or write, remember to
avoid ambiguity, lest your writings seem to be equivocal. In fact, whatever
you think about something, speak your mind openly and boldly. And I earnestly implore you to take my exhortation in a friendly way.   25

Lastly, I repeat what I recently requested,[4] and I ask you once again to
provide me with some educated young man, someone intelligent who writes
a clear hand. As long as he is willing to submit to discipline, I will provide
him generously with benefices, and I will see to it that the benefit of your recommendation will accrue to him, as you will understand more clearly from   30
the letter of Franciscus Rupilius.[5] And so I will await his arrival, together
with your answer. Farewell, most distinguished gentleman.

From the city of Rome, 29 April in the year 1534 after the birth of Christ

Most obediently yours, Ambrosius von Gumppenberg, apostolic protonotary, signed with his own hand   35

To the most renowned gentleman Master Desiderius Erasmus of
Rotterdam, as to a father most worthy of obedience. At Freiburg im Breisgau

2930 / From Bonifacius Amerbach   [Basel, end of April, 1534]

> This letter (= AK Ep 1826) is Bonifacius' response to Epp 2927–8. The autograph
> rough draft is in the Öffentliche Bibliothek of the University of Basel (MS C VIa
> 73 192 verso).

I received your letter to Sadoleto, but somewhat tardily, for eight days before it was given to me, Episcopius, together with some other merchants,
set out from here to go to Lyon. But I will faithfully see to it that it will be
delivered by the very first messenger to Parmentier,[1] whom I have hitherto
found to be reliable in sending letters there and back. As for your fear that   5
your critical remarks and admonitions have turned Sadoleto's mind against
you, I do not believe there is any reason to fear that, primarily because he is

* * * * *

4 In Ep 2926
5 Not extant

2930
1 Michel Parmentier (c 1481–c 1561), bookseller and publisher at Lyon, whose
   shop was a major centre for the circulation of Basel publications in France, and
   who often acted as intermediary in the correspondence between scholars

a man of such great candour and integrity, and because he sent you his commentaries for you to correct. For what could have been more inconsistent
with what he expected to get than not to listen to the very things for the sake   10
of which he had sent them,[2] which you in fact performed as the duty of a
friend? When a friend asked you for your opinion, what else would you do
except to point out what you think in a friendly way, that is, sincerely and
with no deception? Surely he sent these things so that they could be dealt
with severely and he could hear your judgment of them. It would have been   15
quite inappropriate for you to speak insincerely. In fact, he wrote to me at
that time in these words: 'On your part,' he said, 'if you write to me what
Erasmus thinks, you would be doing me a great favour. To be sure, I am of
such a mind that I would rather be justly reprimanded (if that happens to be
the case) than praised unjustly. For the former will make me more careful,   20
and the latter, more ignorant. There is no need to write which of the two is
more useful.'[3]

So much for Sadoleto. I think the reason he does not write is to be attributed to the paucity (or rather the untrustworthiness) of messengers, who
intercept or neglect letters, rather than to such a fine gentleman as Sadoleto,   25
who is one of your most eager supporters.

Take care of your health, my master, and all the best to you. I think I
will be coming there next week.

2931 / From Bonifacius Amerbach

For the reasons given in Allen XI xxiii (addenda to vol X) and in Alfred Hartmann's
introduction to AK Ep 1855, this letter has been redated to 2 September 1534 and
will appear as Ep 2966A in CWE 21.

2932 / From Juan Luis Vives   Bruges, 10 May 1534

This letter was first published in Vives' *Opera omnia* (Basel: Episcopius 1555) II
976. On Vives see Ep 927 introduction. For the circumstances of this letter, and
for the letter, no longer extant, to which it is the reply, see Ep 2892 n40.

* * * * *

2 The sentence to this point is struck through in the manuscript.
3 This is a direct citation from AK Ep 1770:31–6 (10 August 1533).

VIVES TO ERASMUS

The letter you sent to me on 5 January would have pleased me even more if it had let me know that your health has improved.[1] But that your health should be so badly affected in your time of life could not but be most painful for me to hear. I pray for your return to good health, but if that is not Christ's will, 5 then for the strength of mind and body to make your torment more bearable. Last summer I was seriously and dangerously ill with colic. I have become so accustomed to my gout that familiarity now makes it less grievous. I think that I contracted it from the cold rather than from any other cause. These are the sweet little gifts with which this body of ours rewards us for constantly 10 and anxiously taking care of it.

What forbearance or circumspection could be sufficient if a letter written about someone should be sent to that man himself? That would clearly be, as Cicero says, to take away from life life's mutual participation.[2] But as for me, I do not think that you are flagging in friendship and I do not com- 15 plain about your writing to me rather infrequently. That complaint would rebound on me, since I send you letters just as infrequently. And in many of my letters, both to you and to other friends, I have declared that I do not judge friendships by the rather trivial duty of writing (indeed some write all the more diligently the less they love), especially when there is no business be- 20 tween us that is worth writing about. But my intention was to deter Carvajal from mixing in my name if he should in future publish anything against you, understanding clearly from my letter that doing so would displease me. And I did that to keep anyone from thinking that you and I are not on good terms. That would be quite uncalled for, both because of the close friendship 25 between us, which is sometimes made quite clear in works by each of us, and because of the studies we have in common, so that no one should think we are not fellow hunters in pursuit of wisdom. But potter.[3] We live in difficult times, when we can neither speak nor be silent without danger.

* * * * *

2932
1 The letter is not extant.
2 Cf *De amicitia* 17.61.
3 Greek in the text, an allusion to *Adagia* I ii 25: *Figulus figulo invidet, faber fabro* 'Potter envies potter, smith envies smith,' a proverb traced back to Hesiod *Works and Days* 23–6. The competition between men engaged in the same trade can lead either to quarrelling and conflict or to industry and honourable emulation. Vives places himself and Erasmus in the second category.

In Spain Vergara and his brother Tovar have been arrested,[4] and so have 30
other learned men: in England the bishop of Rochester and the bishop of
London, and Thomas More.[5] I pray that you may have an easy old age.

Bruges, 10 May 1534

2933 / To Erasmus Schets   Freiburg, 11 May 1534

This letter, the answer to one now lost, was first published by Allen. The autograph is in the British Library (MS 38512 folio 92).

Cordial greetings. I have received the letters that your servant sent to me and
to Damião from Cologne. On the same day I received both letters from Paris
on the same subject.[1]

I am sorry that the little books reached you so late.[2] Luther seems to
have gone quite insane. He is not ashamed to spread such manifest lies 5
throughout the world.[3] I never wrote that God had intercourse with the
Virgin.[4] What he says about the passage in Hilary is a stupid slander which

* * * * *

4 For the arrest and trial of Juan de Vergara see Ep 2904 n3. In 1530, three years
   before Vergara's own arrest, his half-brother, Bernardino Tovar (Ep 1814 n14),
   an Erasmian long pursued by the Inquisition, had been accused of heresy and
   imprisoned. No record of his trial survives, but it dragged on until 1541, when,
   like his brother, he was compelled to abjure his views and do penance.
5 In April 1534, both Thomas More and John Fisher, bishop of Rochester, were
   imprisoned in the Tower of London. The report of the imprisonment of John
   Stokesley, bishop of London, was false, but Erasmus passed it on in two letters
   written in August 1534 (Allen Epp 2961:87–90, 2965:24–7).

2933
1 None of the letters mentioned is extant, and we have no clue to the nature of
   'the same subject.' It is, moreover, noteworthy that while Erasmus wrote seven
   letters that we know of to Schets in 1534, no letter from Schets to Erasmus during that year survives.
2 Presumably the presentation copies of *De praeparatione ad mortem* sent with Ep
   2913; see n9 of that letter.
3 The reference is clearly to Luther's *Epistola de Erasmo Roterodamo* (Ep 2918
   introduction).
4 Pierre Cousturier said that he had done so, in the Paraphrase on Luke 1:35
   and elsewhere, and called it blasphemous. Erasmus defended himself in Ep
   1687:104–22. It was on that letter that Luther based his accusation in the *Epistola*;
   see CWE 78 439 n160 (*Purgatio adversus epistolam Lutheri*).

I have refuted more than once.[5] All his accusations are similarly fictitious
and distorted.

I think that my response is already available there.[6] For Froben sent   10
several hundred copies by wagon to Brabant. But in the meantime I have not
received my diploma, which Pieter Gillis stored all too well.[7] Tell Grapheus
to remember what I wrote about the young man.[8] To you and your dear ones
I wish every happiness.

Given at Freiburg im Breisgau, 11 May 1534   15
Erasmus of Rotterdam, in my own handwriting
To the most distinguished gentleman Erasmus Schets, merchant. At
Antwerp

2934 / To Fridericus Nausea   [Freiburg], 15 May 1534

> This letter was first published in the *Epistolae ad Nauseam* page 149. For Nausea,
> see Epp 2823 n1, 2847.

ERASMUS OF ROTTERDAM SENDS CORDIAL GREETINGS TO
THE MOST UPRIGHT GENTLEMAN MASTER FRIDERICUS NAUSEA,
COURT PREACHER TO FERDINAND, THE MOST SERENE KING
OF THE ROMANS, ETC
In the letters of friends these words frequently occur: 'You will learn the rest   5
from Nausea.' But no one testifies that he has had access to you. Indeed you
gave me some hope of meeting you in person, though I have so far not had
the privilege of seeing you or receiving a letter from you.[1] But I am aware,
my friend Nausea, of how many labours keep you from writing, and I take
your failure in good part.   10

* * * * *

5 Ie the charge of denying the Trinity because of his observation that Hilary and
   other ancient Fathers had 'not dared to call the Holy Spirit God'; see CWE 78 435–7.
6 Ie the *Purgatio adversus epistolam Lutheri*
7 The reference is to the 'English diploma' of Ep 2896:26–7; see nn12–13 in that
   letter.
8 The reference appears to be to Erasmus' request to Grapheus in Ep 2916:11–22
   to recommend a young man to become his servant. Allen omitted the sentence
   on the ground that Erasmus had erased it, including it instead in his introduction. We have restored it to the text of the letter.

2934
1 All of Nausea's letters to Erasmus are missing.

This young man has devoted himself earnestly to the study of law, and
has earned the degree known as a licentiate.[2] But soon afterwards he put himself under obligation here, with bonds that I hope are pleasant for him. For he
married a young woman who is both well born and good looking. I will not
add anything more, since I do not know where in the world you are residing.   15
    Farewell, on the day after Ascension in the year 1534

2935 / From Giovanni Danieli   Rome, 16 May 1534

This letter was first published as Ep 203 in Förstemann / Günther. The autograph, which was part of the Burscher Collection of the University Library
at Leipzig (Ep 1254 introduction), was without address and written on little
more than a scrap of paper. It was probably enclosed with the letter of Cardinal
Cajetanus mentioned here in lines 11–12.
    Giovanni Danieli, a member of the household of Cardinal Cajetanus (Ep
2690), is known only from the colophons of some of the cardinal's works. The
colophon of Josse Bade's edition of Cajetanus' commentary on the Gospels
(1532), for example, indicates that the work was revised by Danieli.

Both of your letters,[1] my venerable master, were greatly pleasing both to the
cardinal and to the pope, and both of them are extremely well disposed towards you. Concerning the cardinal, I can testify from what I saw and heard
from him when I was with him and read him both your letter and your book
concerning amiable concord.[2] As for the pope, when I spoke to the cardinal   5
today about the subject matter of the said book, he told me, among other
things, that the pope very carefully read your letter to the cardinal and a copy
of it in German,[3] which pleased him greatly, and that, when he had heard

* * * * *

2 Unidentified; perhaps the 'servant' of Ep 2937:77

2935
1 Not extant
2 *De amabili ecclesiae concordia* was the alternative title for *De sarcienda ecclesiae
  concordia* (Ep 2852); see CWE 65 131.
3 Strictly speaking this should mean that Erasmus had sent his letter to the pope
  in both Latin and German versions, but why would he have done that? It is possible that Danieli intended his words to refer to one of the two German translations of *De concordia* that had so far been published (see Ep 2852 introduction).
  Erasmus may have sent it as evidence of popular interest in the subject of re-
  storing peace and unity to the church.

the testimony of the cardinal about the book, he was most enthusiastic and
remained very favourably disposed towards you. It seemed to me that it was   10
my duty, as a humble servant of your Worship, to add these few words to the
letter of the cardinal,[4] and I would add more except that I am afraid I might
be more troublesome than obliging. With best wishes for the health and
happiness of your Lordship.

    Rome, 16 May 1534   15

    Before I had seen the aforesaid book by you, some people here found
fault with it, saying that Erasmus allowed complete freedom for anyone to
indulge in his own judgment, an objection that afterwards in my presence
the cardinal most thoroughly refuted. Certainly I know that they will now be
more just, etc. If I knew that your Lordship still does not have the *Quolibetica*   20
of the cardinal,[5] I would send it to you.

    Your Worship's humble servant, Giovanni Danieli

2936 / From Johann Koler   [Augsburg], 22 May 1534

This letter was first published as Ep 204 in Förstemann / Günther. The autograph was in the Burscher Collection of the University Library at Leipzig (Ep
1254 introduction). For Koler, see Ep 2814 introduction.

    This letter was supposed to be forwarded to Erasmus via Johann (II)
Paumgartner (see line 108 below), using a messenger scheduled to depart on
22 May (see Ep 2937:2–10). But when Koler had written this letter, letters arrived by courier from Erasmus. Koler appears to have sent Erasmus' messenger
to Paumgartner, assuming that the messenger would carry back to Erasmus
both his own letters (Ep 2936–7) and one from Paumgartner to Erasmus. On
26 May Paumgartner did in fact write to Erasmus a letter (Ep 2939) in which
he stated that because he did not trust the messenger he was not sending the
gift that he had promised. Whether Paumgartner's letter was entrusted for delivery to the untrustworthy messenger is not clear. But it is clear from Allen
Ep 2947:1–7 that Koler's two letters were not forwarded at that point, and one
month later Koler, impatient with Paumgartner's unfulfilled promises to provide a messenger, entrusted all three letters (Epp 2936–7, 2947) to a courier who
had been sent by Erasmus.

* * * * *

4 Not extant; cf Allen Ep 3100:70–2.
5 Presumably the 1531 edition of *Quaestiones et omnia (ut vocantur) quolibetica
  Thomae a Vio* published at Venice (L. de Giunta).

SENT WITH CORDIAL GREETINGS

For a long while I was not able to write anything to you because I was suffering from gout in my feet and hands, and also because in the meantime I did
not find anyone whom I could safely trust to carry it to you, especially because
Paumgartner was absent for quite some time, and I usually entrust to him   5
my letters to you, since he always has quite a few messengers at the ready.

But concerning the last letter you wrote to me on the day before Easter,[1]
you seem to complain because I have not yet given you my opinion about
the letter in which you praise Paumgartner.[2] Actually the only reason is that I
wanted to find out what Paumgartner himself thought about it, to what degree   10
he approves of your effort, and from that give you my judgment. But because
I have not been able to meet the man alone, and also because he is exceptionally cunning and very good at simulating or dissimulating, I have not been
able to get anything definite out of him. But as far as I am concerned, I very
much approve of the contents of that letter, for you did not pass over anything   15
that pertains to his importance or dignity. I am afraid that in another setting
it might get a chilly reception. For what point is there in writing to a Spaniard
an encomium of a German completely unknown to him, since you could have
done that more appropriately for another audience or at least as the subject of
a dedicatory letter addressed to someone else? Although I feel certain you had   20
a reason for what you did (though I have not yet been able to figure out what
it was), I would prefer to learn from you what led you to praise Paumgartner
in a letter to a Spaniard rather than to one of our countrymen.

As for that extraordinary *Epistola* of Luther which you wrote about in
your last letter,[3] I finally got it and read through it. Heavens above! I never   25
in my life saw anything anywhere more bitter or insane. I have no idea what
you will do, but as for me, after long thought and much deliberation, I think
that you should not overlook this extraordinary contempt. It is an important
matter (believe me, Erasmus) and more important than can be imagined. For
it is not enough that you have been most unjustly assailed in the eyes of   30
all men of upright character; this outstanding, one-and-only restorer of the
Christian religion adds and even promises that he will leave behind for the
whole world his own judgment about Erasmus. See what you can expect
from such a man! You are not dealing here with hooded friars; if you were,
perhaps it would be better to ignore them completely. But if you are willing   35

* * * * *

2936
1 Not extant, dated 4 April; Erasmus' last extant letter to Koler is Ep 2906.
2 Ep 2879, addressed to Juan de Vergara
3 The *Epistola de Erasmo Roterodamo* (Ep 2918 introduction)

to ignore this insult, inflicted by such a man, I am afraid something more serious might happen to you and that we would have to hear things said about you that we do not want to hear. I know what high expectations your friends have about you, especially here at Augsburg; they often come to me, asking and pressing me about what I have learned from you and whether   40 you intend to reply to Luther or to swallow such outrageous contempt and be complaisant to such an insulting slanderer.[4]

As for me, my friend Erasmus, because of your remarkable and esteemed prudence in all matters, I know you will not do anything recklessly. But since he threatens to leave behind for the world his judgment about you   45 (and you can easily guess what that would be), unless you defend your honour and reputation and also publish your judgment about Luther (which is only fair), I fear that you will cause a great injury to your reputation and entirely lose your good name. For people will not think that you are moved by reason to say nothing, but that you remain silent out of fear, terrified by   50 your own awareness of guilt, because you do not dare to reply when you are assailed by so many and such enormous insults. But what do you think will be said and done by those who envy you? Those who also slander you by saying you were the precursor of Luther and that you provided him with the content of all his dogmas – what judgment, I beg you, do you imag-   55 ine they will advance about you if you are willing to be silent in the face of such affronts? It is not enough for him to call you a doubletongued charlatan, a satanic trickster, the king of ambiguity, Babel in all its confusion, a pagan, and an Epicurean; he loudly proclaims that you are an Anabaptist, a Sacramentarian, an Arian, a Donatist, a thrice-great heretic, and a clever   60 mocker of Christ, and he brands you with hundreds of other unheard-of crimes! If you tolerate such insults, if you can swallow them in silence, then you are not the man I know you to be. Perhaps there may be no lack of other friends who think otherwise and do not think that a madman should be answered with his own madness, lest you be guilty of the same insolence   65 that we find reprehensible in him. Though that can be true, I nevertheless think that what everyone says and thinks about you should not be ignored. If Luther were someone else, I would do as I have often done: I would advise, according to my former opinion, that you should not respond to the insulter with insults. In this case, however, since his writings circulate freely   70

* * * * *

4 By now Erasmus' *Purgatio adversus epistolam non sobriam Martini Lutheri* had already been published; see Ep 2918 introduction. By 25 May Koler had received his copy and read it; see Ep 2937:12–35.

throughout the whole world and reach remote people, I don't think it advisable that you should pass them over in silence. I think that in your prudence you have already decided what you must do; I wanted to present my opinion and that of your friends here. You will do whatever seems most advisable.

You can easily guess what these tumults in Germany portend. You see 75 what French gold can do.[5] As if from a high lookout, I see that all of Germany will come crashing down in total ruin. I do not see what an impoverished king,[6] deprived of all assistance, can possibly do. Until his brother comes from Spain to help him, he is done for. In the meantime they will carry on their own negotiations with the French. Yesterday the dukes of Bavaria re- 80 ceived from France three hundred thousand gold écus brought here via Switzerland.[7] I cannot guess how they are to pay back the large sum of money they have received. But I am persuaded that unless the emperor soon takes thought for his brother and comes to his assistance with troops and money,[8] next month we will have a different king. They openly boast that 85 the election of the king of Rome was paid for and for that reason cannot be legitimate.[9] I am horrified even to think of the tumults, the spoliation, the devastation there will be in all of Germany! I knew that we Germans were

* * * * *

5 The reference is to the war for the restoration of the Duke Ulrich of Württemberg to his duchy, the decisive battle of which had taken place on 13 May 1534. Francis I of France had provided most of the money for the victorious Protestant army. See Ep 2917 n9, and cf n9 below.
6 Ferdinand of Austria
7 Cf Ep 2937:59–61 with n12.
8 Literally 'the sinews of war,' a reference to the Ciceronian phrase 'endless money, the sinews of war' (*Philippics* 5.5)
9 On 5 January 1531, at Cologne, Ferdinand of Austria had been elected king of the Romans, ie heir apparent to his brother Charles v as well as the latter's viceroy during his long absences from the Empire; see Ep 2384 n7. There had been much opposition to the election on the ground that the emperor had no constitutional right to designate his own successor and thus abridge the right of the electors to a 'free election' following his death. (Such 'free' elections routinely involved the purchase of votes with bribes and favours.) Only one of the seven electoral princes, however, the elector of Saxony, remained adamant in his opposition and withheld his vote. This made him the focus of a league of Protestant and Catholic anti-Hapsburg princes aimed at overturning the election, protecting themselves from Hapsburg aggression, and enlisting the support of France for their cause. The most important of the other members of this group were Landgrave Philip of Hessen and Duke William IV of Bavaria, both of whom (encouraged and abetted by France) were also heavily involved in bringing about the dissolution of the Swabian League in 1533–4 (cf n16 below) and the reconquest of Württemberg in 1534 (cf n5 above).

likely in the end to perish through internal discord and civil strife. I fear that
this is the hour I have always dreaded.   90

Gumppenberg informed me that he had sent you the *Anticiceronianus*
from Rome.[10] I would like to see it, if that is possible. But I would prefer it
to the *Epistola* of Luther, which I think you should by no means tolerate.
Everything might seem to be tolerable; but I do not think you should put up
with being called a heretic.   95

We are still stuck here. The Evangelicals have petitioned that our preachers should do battle with them; they even accept the bishop of Augsburg as the
judge.[11] They are trying to set the number, the day, and the place. I do not know
what will happen, except that I think it inadvisable at this time, in such a state
of total disturbance, to want to have a disputation about the faith. For it can   100
easily be seen, from other disputations that have been held, what good can be
hoped for from it. It would be better at this point to disturb Camarina as little as
possible,[12] since everything is otherwise sufficiently disturbed. But such people
can never be calm; they strive only to stir up and reduce everything to ruins.

Fugger has gone away again, with his whole household.[13] He requested   105
that I send you his good wishes. He intended to write to you if anything
should happen.

Paumgartner, to whom I entrusted this letter to you,[14] came back here a
day ago. He is one of your most enthusiastic supporters. We expect our most
reverend bishop in the coming days,[15] though some do not believe he will   110
come because these military tumults do not permit the making of an alliance
among the Swabians.[16]

* * * * *

10 Doubtless the book by Georg von Logau; see Ep 2906 n5.
11 On the plans for a disputation between the Catholic and Evangelical preachers,
   with the bishop as judge, see Ep 2937:41–53.
12 Ie not stir up unnecessary trouble; see *Adagia* I i 64.
13 Firmly opposed to the progress of the Reformation in Augsburg, and in trouble
   with the authorities for disorderly resistance to it, Anton Fugger had taken up
   residence at one of his private estates; see Epp 2818:29–44, 2845:39–44.
14 See introduction above.
15 Christoph von Stadion, bishop of Augsburg, spent most of his time at his residence in Dillingen, a little over 50 kilometres north and west of Augsburg.
16 The bishop of Augsburg was one of the imperial commissioners who presided at meetings of the Swabian League (cf Ep 2937:99–101). At a meeting in
   Augsburg that ended on 2 February, the league, once a force for peace and
   order in southern Germany (Ep 2269 n2) but now riven by internal conflicts
   between Protestants and Catholics as well as between allies and enemies of the
   Hapsburgs, failed to agree on the extension of the alliance. There were attempts
   to salvage something from the wreckage (see Ep 2937 n13), but they failed.

Nothing remains except to wish you well, and if you should have any news (and you have a great deal from all over the world), I beg you, share it with us. Above all, I wish you would let us know how you think all these   115
disorders will turn out. May Christ keep you for us in perpetuity. Farewell.

Given on 22 May in the year of salvation 1534

Yours whatever happens, Koler

To be sent to the most learned and upright Master Erasmus of Rotterdam, a theologian beyond compare. At Freiburg   120

2937 / From Johann Koler   [Augsburg], 25 May 1534

This letter was first published as Ep 203 in Förstemann/Günther. The autograph was in the Burscher Collection of the University Library at Leipzig (Ep 1254 introduction). The references to Ep 2936 in lines 2, 5, and 13 indicate that this letter is essentially a postscript to that letter. For that reason, the Allen editors placed the two letters together, even though this letter is dated two days after Ep 2938.

SENT WITH CORDIAL GREETINGS

The day before I sent this letter to you, Johann Paumgartner announced to me that he had a courier who would be setting out the next day to travel directly to you and that if I wanted to write to you I could do so. Delighted that I had finally procured a courier going to you, I wrote the enclosed letter   5
to you.[1] But before our courier left here the bearer of the present letters intervened, bringing me a packet of letters from you.[2] There were letters to the most reverend cardinal of Trent,[3] to Paumgartner, and to Georg Hörmann.[4] I immediately arranged to send all of them on, having luckily secured a courier to Trent; likewise I sent Paumgartner his letter, and he will undoubtedly   10
reply to you by the present messenger.[5]

I gladly read your *Purgation* and was delighted with it.[6] Of your own accord you did what in the enclosed letter I urged you at such length to do.[7]

* * * * *

2937
1 Ep 2936
2 None of them extant
3 Bernhard von Cles (Ep 2821)
4 Ep 2716 n46
5 Paumgartner's letter is Ep 2939.
6 *Purgatio adversus epistolam non sobriam Martini Lutheri*, Erasmus' reply to Luther's *Epistola de Erasmo Roterodamo*; see Ep 2918 introduction.
7 Ep 2936

But you have handled the man more gently than the shameless wretch deserved; I wish you had sharpened your quill even more. What I especially   15
dislike in your *Purgation* is that you said you have never ceased to give him
your love.[8] How can it be that you love Luther, who has accused you of so
many atrocious crimes and has attacked you with such extraordinary insults?
Moreover, can you love a man who has been the target of so many censures,
so many thunderbolts from the pope and the emperor, a man given over to   20
the Furies, who never in his whole life wrote anything that was not stuffed
with unbridled and insane insults, with monstrous mendacity and seditious
vociferation? Come now, my dear Erasmus, such a man, such an outandout
plague, you have never stopped loving? You will say that as Christians we
should love those who hate us. In fact I can hardly bring myself to believe   25
that you are required to love someone like Luther. Perhaps it would be right
not to hate him, but Christ does not command you to love him, since his
villainy, his foolhardiness, his tenacious clinging to what is evil does not deserve any love at all, nor is it worthy of anyone's good will. Who would love
this man, who, though you have never wronged him with even the slightest   30
word, cuts you to pieces with insults, maligns you with calumnies, falsely
accuses you of so many crimes? In future there is no need for you to lament
the weakness of your stomach; it is only too strong, your stomach, which is
able so easily to digest such outrageous slanders, so many affronts. I am not
Christian enough for that; you far surpass me with this patience of yours.   35

    Further, concerning what you want to understand about the state of
things here, you should know that it is not so much that we remain here as
that we are stuck here, and it is not clear to me how long we will stay, since
that depends on the choice of utterly rebellious men who are our enemies.
Following this latest sedition things have been a bit quieter, since in the   40
meantime they have been negotiating about the disputation. Actually those
Evangelicals asked that our preachers be silenced, and, if that cannot be
done, they want our preachers at least to be forced to render an account of
their teachings and their faith. Finally, after various disagreements, it came
down to having a disputation, with our bishop as the judge and having both   45
sides present their arguments in his presence. They actually agreed to this,
claiming that they could readily allow our bishop to be the judge, as long as
he did not preside as the diocesan ordinary but only as a good man and a

* * * * *

8 Erasmus does not actually say this in the *Purgatio*. It appears to be Koler's ten-
   dentious reading of one or two passages in which Erasmus expresses preference for defending himself rather than attacking Luther. See CWE 78 405 n53.

Christian prince. The business has still not begun. Our preachers requested
that they be presented with the articles to be disputed, so that they might   50
know the points about which they want to raise doubts or questions. But
there has not yet been any answer. I think all these warlike gestures may
bring forth other plans.[9]

The duke of Württemberg and his friend the landgrave of Hessen will
perhaps cause us to think about other things. Everyone is waiting in sus-   55
pense. No one can even imagine what will finally happen or how these up-
risings will proceed.[10] The landgrave increases his forces day by day and is
said to be making a new recruitment now that he is rich and rolling in French
gold.[11] Finally, the Bavarians are said to be actors in this play; there is a persistent rumour that the French king has recently granted them three hundred   60
thousand ducats.[12] The king is completely deserted and will be hissed from
the stage unless the emperor comes to his aid. An assembly of the Swabians
has now been announced for this very day. But no one has come yet and I

* * * * *

9 The disputation does not appear to have taken place. On 22 July 1534 the city
council took the first decisive step towards the formal establishment of the
Reformation in the city: henceforth only the Evangelical preachers appointed
by the council itself were allowed to preach, and mass was permitted only in
eight churches under the direct control of the bishop.
10 The decisive battle in the reconquest of Württemberg had already taken place
on 13 May; see Ep 2917 n9.
11 By the terms of the treaty of Bar-le-Duc (20 January 1534), Francis I agreed to
pay Philip of Hessen 125,000 écus towards the cost of the campaign to reconquer Württemberg; see Brendle 145, Knecht 232. As might be expected, this was
an astronomical sum: 125,000 écus au soleil were equivalent to £39,583 6s 8d
groot Flemish or the annual wage income of 4,564 Antwerp master masons/
carpenters (CWE 12 650 Table 3, 691 Table 13).
12 The ducat was officially valued in 1534 at 80d groot Flemish and therefore this
sum was equivalent to £100,000 groot Flemish or the annual wage income of
11,530 Antwerp master masons/carpenters (CWE 12 650 Table 3, 691 Table 13).
This appears to be a somewhat garbled account of the renewal in December
1533 of Francis I's long-standing offer to contribute 100,000 écus d'or au soleil
(to be deposited at Munich) to the cost of a war against King Ferdinand. To this
Bavaria added the stipulation that its participation in such a war would neces-
sitate Francis' contribution, in addition to the 100,000 écus already committed,
of one third of the total cost of the war. See Brendle 106, 136, 144. Despite receipt
of the promised 100,000 écus, Bavaria remained neutral in the war to reconquer
Württemberg; see Brendle 161.

don't think anyone will come.[13] This French gold will destroy the Germans. Everything seems to have been devised out of hatred of the emperor and es- 65 pecially of King Ferdinand. The other imperial princes are sitting there with their hands folded; they present themselves as spectators. In the meantime those two are dealing with their own business, or rather, that of the French. Until the emperor brings some remedy to a desperate situation (if indeed he ever does want to do that), we are lost. I see a huge storm taking shape that 70 will devastate and crush Germany.

Paumgartner has been gone for several days. But Fugger, who stayed in Augsburg for many months, now at last, on the day before Ascension,[14] departed from here with his household to his village and castles at Weissen-horn.[15] I think he was mindful of the old trouble and did not want to wait 75 this year for the hanging Christ.[16]

As for your servant,[17] who you think came to us, you should know that no one came, and it is not clear to me which servant you mean. But you should know that none of your servants (after that young man)[18] came here. If anyone should come, I cannot fail to know about him. 80

In your last letter you seemed to lament that you have too freely used up your nutmeg kernels, so that you had to do without them. And so I am sending you several pounds of nutmeg kernels by this same messenger.[19] I got them from Fugger (lest you should think I bought them myself). I would have sent a larger batch, but they did not seem to be quite fresh, and fresher 85 ones were expected any day now from Portugal. When they come, if they are fresh, I will send more, for Fugger has arranged for me to take for your use whatever I want or whatever I know you would enjoy.

* * * * *

13 A meeting of the now-defunct Swabian League (Ep 2936 n16) had in fact been called for 25 May (Klüpfel 354–5), but it did not actually meet until June. On the agenda were the reestablishment of the league and the mediation of a settle-ment of the conflict over Württemberg. The delegates had no success in resur-recting the league, but their efforts at mediation were helpful; see Alfred Kohler *Antihabsburgische Politik in der Epoche Karls v. Die reichsständische Opposition ge-gen die Wahl Ferdinands i. zum Römischen König und gegen die Anerkennung seines Königtums (1524–1534)* (Göttingen 1982) 356–8.
14 14 May 1534
15 About 22 kilometres southeast of Ulm
16 See Ep 2818:29–44.
17 Possibly the young man of Ep 2934:11
18 Unidentified, probably the 'bearer' mentioned in line 6 above
19 A note in the margin of the manuscript specified four pounds.

Notice has come to us here that in Brabant and in Lower Germany a number of virgins of great holiness, strong in the spirit of prophecy, live un- 90 der a vow of chastity but not subject to any religious order; instead they live a most holy life in private dwellings under tutelage of their parents and are famous for their miracles. Things are told about them that are almost beyond belief (though I do not doubt that God has his saints everywhere).[20] I only wanted to inform you about them so that, if you know anything certain 95 about them, you will be willing to tell us about it.

As soon as you get a courier coming to us, please write back so that I may know whether or not the nutmeg kernels were delivered.

Today I sent your *Purgation* to our bishop Christoph. I hoped he would come here to the meeting of the Swabians, over which he usually presides in 100 the name of the emperor. But I do not know if he will come, since he has not yet received any commission.[21] I cannot even imagine how things will turn out, not only here but in all of Germany.

I do not think Luther will be quiet. He will be provoked rather than placated by your response.[22] He will do what he promised: leave to the world 105 his judgment about you. But if he does respond to this *Purgation* of yours, or continues to rage against you with his usual shamelessness, I beg you to sharpen your pen so that he will finally know that you are a man – unless you would rather plead with Melanchthon to keep Luther from plotting against you! For that is what the jealous slanderers here say you have done. 110 You have no idea what these gossips bandy about.

Nothing is left but to say 'farewell' and to ask you to write back as soon as possible, so that I can know how you are and what you are doing. You can promise yourself anything whatever from me. Farewell. May Christ keep you safe and sound. 115

Given 25 May 1534

You recognize the hand of your friend Koler.

* * * * *

20 This sounds like a somewhat embroidered reference to the lay religious communities of women known as Beguines, whose houses were particularly common in the towns of the Netherlands (here referred to as *Germania inferior* / Lower Germany). Although they promised not to marry as long as they lived in the community, Beguines were not nuns, did not take vows, and were free to leave at any time if they wanted to marry. They devoted themselves to pious devotion, manual labour, care of the poor and sick, and other good works.

21 The bishop of Augsburg, who spent most of his time at his residence in Dillingen (Ep 2936 n15), was one of the imperial commissioners who presided at meetings of the Swabian League (Ep 2936 n16). For the intended meeting of the league, see n13 above.

22 Luther did not publish a response to the *Purgatio*.

2938 / From Juan Ginés de Sepúlveda   Rome, 23 May 1534

This letter, Sepúlveda's' reply to Ep 2905, was first published in the *Sepulvedae epistolae* folio B3. The manuscript, in a secretary's hand and signed by Sepúlveda, is in the Rehdiger Collection of the University Library at Wrocław (MS Rehd 254 69). Erasmus' reply is Ep 2951.

Cordial greetings. I am surprised that my letter, together with the annotations of Zúñiga, has not been delivered.[1] You would have perceived that I did not send anything separately but was being strictly careful to see that the pages I received from Cardinal Iñigo at Bologna should be sent to you once again as soon as possible.[2] You write that you had learned from his letter that on his deathbed Zúñiga ordered that none of his notes should be published but should be reserved for you to use for the common good; I was aware of this, as I had testified to you in the *Antapologia*.[3] I would have no difficulty agreeing with you that it would be best for the reputation of Zúñiga that they not be published, since there is much in them that is superficial and wrongly censured. But you know in turn that publication has no less bearing on your reputation, since you grant that he had many good insights. Therefore, although I do not think anyone would incur the blame of publishing anything against the wishes of the dead man, expressed in his dying words, it would nevertheless be in keeping with your kindness to let it be known, when occasion offers, that you have not completely cheated Zúñiga of his praise; thus at the same time you would play the part of an honest man, as you usually do, and also forestall anyone who might seize the opportunity to publish it as a pretext for accusing you of ingratitude. But there is no reason for you to send me (as you promise to do if I wish it) examples of places where Zúñiga has wrongly criticized you. I am far indeed from wishing to defend Zúñiga in every case, especially against you, a powerful adversary whom I have always judged to be the equal of the greatest men, and whom I therefore respect and lovingly cherish. And I have no doubt that in your prudence,

* * * * *

2938
1 See Ep 2905:3–11.
2 Iñigo López de Mendoza had sent to Erasmus from Rome the annotations of Diego López Zúñiga on Erasmus' edition of Jerome and his Annotations on the New Testament; see Ep 2810:87–92. Sepúlveda here wants to make clear that the documents he sent to Erasmus from Bologna were merely another copy of the notes on the New Testament, not an independent version; see Ep 2873:3–6 with n2.
3 *Antapologia pro Alberto Pio*; see Ep 2637 introduction.

apart from all contention, you will frankly accept whichever of the dead 25
man's admonitions you consider to be just.

As for Paul's word συστοιχεῖ,⁴ it should be enough just to have pointed
it out.⁵ But for me, sound reasoning is always more valuable than all the
explicators or translators, none of whom I will approve if they use doubtful
or figurative words to translate what the author expressed in proper and di- 30
rect language. I will not accuse Thomas of linking places very far from each
other (for how could I do that?), separating them by a journey of twenty
days, but rather for pointlessly imagining an unbroken journey of the Jews,
contrary to the mind of Paul, to say nothing of the fact that no journey was
ever less unbroken than that of the Jews, who spent so many years in the 35
deserts of Arabia.⁶

But this passage reminds me to urge you, out of my singular good will
and high regard for you, not to be careless when you have to discuss the
location of cities, but rather should revisit Strabo, Mela, Pliny, and Ptolemy.⁷
For while I spent a few days recently looking through Jerome's letters I came 40
across some of your annotations where I found a more serious lack of preci-
sion. In the letter to Evagrius you write that Rhegium is a town in Greece
and that Constantinople is in Macedonia, when in fact Constantinople,
which was formerly called Byzantium, is undoubtedly located in the part
of Thrace that is directly opposite Macedonia, and Rhegium is in Bruttium, 45
where Italy is separated by a narrow strait from Sicily.⁸ But if you meant
Magna Graecia, an old expression used by Cicero,⁹ you should still have
remembered that when someone says simply 'Greece' he is not referring
to that part of Italy but to Attica and the neighbouring territory. I also remember (but the exact place escapes me) what I read in another one of your 50
notes, that the city Nicopolis (named after the victory of Augustus), is a city
in Thrace, though it is quite clear that it is in Epirus near Actium, where

* * * * *

4 Gal 4:25
5 See Ep 2905:18–27.
6 See Ep 2905:28–33.
7 Strabo (d AD 23), Pomponius Mela (d AD 45), Pliny the Elder (d AD 79), and
  Ptolemy (AD 100–170) were the foremost ancient writers on geography.
8 Bruttium is the ancient name for Calabria, and Rhegium is now called Reggio
  di Calabria.
9 Magna Graecia ('Greater Greece,' but invariably used untranslated in English)
  was the term commonly used by Roman authors to refer to southern Italy.

Anthony was defeated in a naval battle.[10] You were probably misled because there is another city of the same name in Thrace. On Cicero's book *De senectute* I noticed that you identified Capua as a city in Apulia,[11] though it is the chief city of Campania and was once, apart from Rome, the noblest city in Italy. There is a similar carelessness in the *Ciceronianus,* where you number me among the Portuguese,[12] though you knew that I am from Cordoba, as I informed you in the book I mentioned above.[13] Concerning these difficulties, which are both very slight and quite easy for you to avoid when you are not nodding off but which indicate considerable carelessness, I thought I ought to admonish you out of friendship (as I said) and out of duty, being myself admonished by that saying of Paul,[14] which some people do not understand very well, not paying heed to considerations of geography.[15] As for you, you should take everything as well intentioned. And if I understand that you have taken it otherwise, I will not bother you anymore with unwelcome services.

I can give you no information about Zúñiga's apologia against Lefèvre. I don't think he wrote any such thing, since, as far as I know, he had nothing to do with Lefèvre.[16] As far as the book in the papal library is concerned,[17] it is undoubtedly true that the Greek manuscripts of the New Testament were, as you write, corrupted by the malice or the fickleness of some Greeks, because

* * * * *

10 This has to have come up in reference to Titus 3:12, where St Paul mentions his plan to spend the winter at Nicopolis. Since there were in the ancient world quite a few cities by that name (which means 'city of victory' in Greek), biblical exegetes wondered which one was meant. Jerome identified it with the city founded by Emperor Augustus in 29 BC near Actium, where in 31 BC he had won a great victory over Anthony and Cleopatra. But Greek commentators (Chrysostom, Theophylact) identified different places, one in Thrace in northern Greece, one on the Danube in modern Bulgaria; cf Allen Ep 2951:24–8, where Erasmus says that he had mistakenly followed Chrysostom and Theophylact and that the error was corrected in the fifth and final edition of the New Testament Annotations.
11 Sepúlveda is mistaken. In his reply to this letter Erasmus points out that he had never edited or commented on *De senectute*; see Allen Ep 2951:28–9.
12 See CWE 28 596 n761.
13 See n3 above.
14 Ie Gal 4:25; see lines 27–36 above.
15 Allen mistakenly enclosed this final phrase in quotation marks, as though it were 'that saying of Paul.' The words, as should have been clear, are not Paul's but Sepúlveda's.
16 Sepúlveda is mistaken; see Ep 2905 n10.
17 Ie the Codex Vaticanus of the Greek New Testament; see Ep 2905:40–2.

in the treaty entered into with the Roman church by the Greeks when they returned to sound doctrine it was provided that the Greek codices be corrected
to agree with the Roman readings.[18] For how could both sides attest any more   75
clearly that the Roman copies were true and genuine and that the Greek ones
were corrupt? For when you say that the Greek readings should be sought
in Greek writers, this would make some sense if you were asserting that the
meaning of the Greek language is explained more fittingly by Greeks than by
Latins. But as for the archetypal books containing the basis of our religion,   80
which were written in Greek by their authors, why should we not consider
them to be preserved in a holier, weightier, more uncorrupt form in the shelves
and the libraries of the Roman church (which is the head of Christianity and
has always been the norm of Catholic piety) than in Greece, which has often
been disturbed by the deception of heretics and fickle-minded men and by   85
revolutionary movements? Certainly that is what happened to the seventy
decrees of the Council of Nicaea, which were preserved in their true form on
the shelves of the Roman church but in the East were burned by the heretics
in some churches and in others were reduced to a smaller number – that is,
those decrees that seemed to block their plans and their efforts were removed.   90
Athanasius and other bishops at the Council of Alexandria make this complaint in a letter to Pope Mark, from whom they had received a copy of the
decrees that they had requested from him.[19] Moreover, books are usually less
likely to suffer harm or to be corrupted by ignorant people who confuse commentary with text when they are read or understood by fewer people – unless   95
perhaps you are saying that the treaty intended to have Greek words corrected in accordance with the Latin. That is not likely – except in one specific
place – and I am quite sure it was never done. As for the article you cite from
the Golden Bull, I have never been able to find it, even though I read through
the two Golden Bulls in the book containing the councils.[20] And so I beg you   100
to be so good as to write to us indicating which bull you mean and where it
can be obtained.

* * * * *

18 See Ep 2905:42–50 with n12.
19 Pope St Mark, about whom little is known, reigned from 18 January to 7 October
    336. There does not appear to have been a council at Alexandria in that year.
    Athanasius was bishop of Alexandria 328–73 (but with several periods of exile
    under emperors Constantine, Constantius, and Julian). For the undated letter
    referred to here, see PG 28 1445, where it is included with the *dubia* attributed to
    Athanasius. It says that the Arians burned the decrees.
20 See n18 above.

Farewell. At Rome, 23 May in the year 1534 after the birth of Christ
Your completely devoted Juan Ginés Sepúlveda.

To the renowned gentleman Master Desiderius Erasmus of Rotterdam,   105
etc. At Freiburg

2939 / From Johann (II) Paumgartner   Augsburg, 26 May 1534

This letter was first published as Ep 206 in Förstemann / Günther. The original
letter, in a secretary's hand but signed by Paumgartner, was in the Burscher
Collection of the University Library at Leipzig (Ep 1254 introduction).

Greetings from your most obliging servant in all matters. My most outstanding and learned friend Erasmus, I have received the letter you sent me and
I have delivered the other letters to those to whom you wrote them.[1] I know
how much you love and respect me. For that reason I also recognize that I am
indebted to you in many ways. I would have sent you a small gift now, but   5
I did not dare to entrust it to this messenger. If a faithful messenger presents
himself in two or three days I will send by him the small gift I wanted you to
have, or, if I do not find anyone, by a special messenger just for you.

I have no other news to write you except that the duke of Württemberg
is taking possession of his dukedom by force.[2] We must fear that this evil, led   10
on by the French king and the pope,[3] will spread out further. Farewell and
accept my best regards, as you usually do.

From Augsburg, 26 May 1534

Yours as much as his own, Johannes Paumgartner von Paumgarten, etc

To the most outstanding and learned gentleman Master Erasmus of   15
Rotterdam, the best and greatest professor of true theology, his most venerable master

* * * * *

2939
1 Cf Ep 2937:7–11. None of the letters is extant.
2 He had already done so; see Ep 2917 n9.
3 Rumour had it that at his meeting with Francis I in Marseille (Ep 2829 n7)
  Clement VII, annoyed by Charles V's incessant demand that he summon a
  general council, indicated his support for Francis I's alliances with German
  Protestants and the project for the restoration of Duke Ulrich. He had of course
  done no such thing. See Pastor 10 235–6.

THE DONATION TO GOCLENIUS (EP 2863)

On the face of it, Ep 2863 appears to be a deed of gift to Conradus Goclenius, professor of Latin at the Collegium Trilingue in Louvain, conveying to him, in full right, all the monies deposited with him by Erasmus up to the date of the letter (28 August 1533). Erasmus had made such deposits on three occasions. In 1521, when he left Brabant, he deposited 450 gold florins (Ep 2352:41–2; documents A1 and A2 in this appendix; and cf Ep 1437:132–5). In May 1522 he deposited, through Hilarius Bertholf, monies with a total value of 330 Rhenish florins and 12 stuivers (Ep 2352:43–55; A1). At a later, unspecified date he deposited through Quirinus Talesius 909 gold Philippics (Ep 2352:62–70; A2). In 1539 Bonifacius Amerbach reckoned the total value of monies for which he had receipts from Goclenius at about 1,960 gold coins (A13).

When Goclenius died, the deposited monies became the subject of a protracted litigation, the history of which remains in many respects unclear but the end result of which was the determination that the monies transferred to Goclenius were not a bequest to which his heirs had title but rather a trust to which binding conditions had been attached. The relevant surviving documents, here numbered A1–A14, are preserved in the Öffentliche Bibliothek of the University of Basel. One of them, A9, P.S. Allen himself had transcribed in 1924. Transcripts of the rest were supplied to the Allen editors by Alfred Hartmann, the founding editor of the Amerbachkorrespondenz (AK).

The sequence of events was essentially as follows. Goclenius died intestate on 25 January 1539. Pending the arrival of family members who might claim to be his heirs, the University of Louvain took possession of his goods, including the monies that Erasmus had deposited with him. In his last will, made at Basel on 12 February 1536, Erasmus had directed that the monies deposited with Goclenius were to be expended in Brabant in accordance with instructions that he himself had given to Goclenius, namely for pious purposes, including the financial support of poor students at the Collegium Trilingue (A14:4–11). Goclenius and Amerbach exchanged letters on this subject in August and September 1536 (A3, A13, A14). But at the time of Goclenius' death, most of the money entrusted to him by Erasmus had still not been expended. On 7 April 1539 Amerbach, in his capacity as trustee of Erasmus' will, addressed to the University of Louvain a letter (A4) giving them full authority to dispose of Erasmus' money according to the terms of his will. Amerbach's letter was read to the university on 7 June, but because of pending litigation it was not answered until 15 October (A6). The imperial fiscal procurator gave the university permission to sequester Goclenius' property until a suit for the possession of it had been decided by the council of Brabant. There were three claimants: the University of Louvain, Goclenius' family, and the treasury of Brabant. The treasury of Brabant claimed that

Erasmus' will was invalid in Brabant because he had not received a licence to make one from the duke of Brabant, the licence granted him by the emperor being deemed insufficient (A9).[1] This claim was quickly set aside by the council of Brabant. The explanations of the council's decision in the surviving documents (A9–10) are not entirely consistent in their account of the weight assigned to Ep 2863 in them. Be that as it may, the decision terminated the power given to the university to sequester Erasmus' money, and Goclenius' family now deemed themselves entitled to it as his heirs. But the university managed to secure a restraining order, claiming that the donation to Goclenius was 'counterfeit' and that Ep 2863 had from the beginning been understood by both Erasmus and Goclenius to be not a deed of gift but rather a deed creating a trust (A6:16–29). On 15 October the rector, representing the university, wrote to Amerbach a letter asking him to send to Louvain any documentary evidence he might have that the donation of 1533 was 'counterfeit' (A6:30–7). Amerbach replied with a letter (A7), written c 16 November, accompanied by copies of the documents he himself listed in A13. On 2 December he sent a further letter to the university (A8) explaining some of the details in the earlier one.

Before writing that second letter, however, Amerbach had received at the end of November two letters written on behalf of Goclenius' family: one from their legal agent Johannes Altenanus (A9), and one from Konrad Heresbach, counsellor to the duke of Jülich-Cleves (A11). In reply Amerbach furnished Altenanus with copies of the documents already sent to the university, and he included on the list of documents the relevant sentences from Erasmus' will (A14:4–8). In the letter to Altenanus accompanying the documents (A10) and in his reply to Heresbach (A12), Amerbach left Goclenius' brothers in no doubt of his view that they had no claim whatever to the money that Erasmus had deposited with him.

The records of the University of Louvain show that on 23 July 1540 Goclenius' family still maintained their claim and were planning to take it to court. After that, however, the matter disappears from the record,[2] and there is evidence that at some later point two thousand ducats of the

* * * * *

1 The duke and the emperor were the same person; Emperor Charles v was also Duke Charles ii of Brabant.
2 See Henry de Vocht *Literae virorum eruditorum ad Franciscum Craneveldium 1522–1528* (Louvain 1928) 248–9.

monies deposited with Goclenius by Erasmus were distributed to the poor of Brabant.[3] It is thus apparent that Goclenius' family had not been able to sustain their claim at law.

The interpretation of Ep 2863 given by Amerbach and the University of Louvain represents accurately the understanding of the matter by both Goclenius and Erasmus. Goclenius' deed of acknowledgment (A1), written on 17 September 1533, was clearly written immediately on receipt of Ep 2863, dated 28 August 1533. Goclenius' primary aim was to provide for the unlikely event of his dying before Erasmus, in which case all the monies would go back to Erasmus. It seems clear from this that he understood the monies to have been given to him in trust. Erasmus himself stated his intention in clearer language. His memorandum of 8 April 1534 (A2) makes plain that he regarded all the deposits of monies with Goclenius as fiduciary, intended to create a trust, disbursements from which would be made according to his instructions. There would have been no point in writing the memorandum if he thought he had disposed of the monies in question by means of a free and irrevocable gift. Both the memorandum and Erasmus' will (cited by Amerbach in A14) make his intention clear beyond doubt. Goclenius' letter to Amerbach, the penultimate paragraph in particular (A3:48–57), show that, in 1536 at least, he interpreted his office as a trustee even more rigidly than did Amerbach. His failure to execute the trust in the three years before his death is difficult to explain. But one must be sceptical of Altenanus' statement (A9) that he could produce witnesses who would testify that Goclenius had often spoken and sometimes acted as though he recognized no trust and could use Erasmus' money as he pleased. Altenanus was, after all, arguing the case of Goclenius' family, and it is not clear that the testimony of the witnesses would have survived cross-examination.

Ep 2863 and Erasmus' memorandum of monies deposited with Goclenius (A2) are best seen in light of the two memoranda printed in the introduction to Ep 2855. Those memoranda record a deposit of sixteen hundred gold florins by Erasmus with Bonifacius Amerbach. The first of them (drawn up on 13 August 1533) is just over two weeks older than Ep 2863. The second one, composed as an improved version of the first, was executed on the same day (8 April 1534) as memorandum A2 below. Both memoranda for Amerbach make clear that the monies deposited with him had been given to him in trust and were to be disbursed according to Erasmus' intentions and instructions.

* * * * *

3 See Pieter Opmeer *Opus chronographicum orbis vniversi a mundi exordio vsque ad annum MDCXI* (Antwerp: Hieronymus Verdussius 1611) I 476b.

THE SUMS DEPOSITED WITH CONRADUS GOCLENIUS BY ERASMUS
The sums described in the documents appended to Ep 2836 – A1 (Goclenius'
acknowledgement of receipt), A2 (Erasmus' own memorandum on the sums
deposited with Goclenius), and A14 (a memorandum by Amerbach of documents sent to Altenanus regarding the deposit) – do not entirely correspond.
All three documents refer to five sums with a total value of £329 1s 10d groot
Flemish; documents A2 and A14 mention two further sums with a total value
of £98 9s 7.5d groot Flemish that are not included in A1; and, finally, A1 notes
six sums totalling £55 11s 4d groot Flemish that are not listed in A2 and A14
and omits the two sums unique to A2 and A14. As is clear from the table below, the sums unique to A1 do not correspond in value to the sums unique
to A2 and 14.

Amerbach declares in A13 that a total of 1,960 'gold' coins (*aurei*) were
deposited with Goclenius, but a later source suggests that 2,000 ducats were
distributed to the Brabantine poor from the deposit in Erasmus' name after his
death. Amerbach's gold coins were almost certainly Rhenish florins, the most
common gold coin in circulation in the Burgundian-Hapsburg Netherlands.
The sum of 1,960 Rhenish florins (equivalent to £481 16s 8d groot Flemish)
corresponds almost precisely to the total of the sums mentioned in A1, A2,
and A14 – if we count sums common to three or two documents only once –
that is to say, £483 4s 11.5d groot Flemish, an amount equivalent to the annual wages of fifty-six Antwerp master masons/carpenters (CWE 12 650 Table 3,
691 Table 13). The figure of 2,000 ducats was therefore probably an approxi-
mation, since, if we take it literally, the amount said to have been distributed
was significantly greater (£666 13s 4d groot Flemish or seventy-seven years'
wages of an Antwerp master mason/carpenter) than Amerbach's estimate
and the total of the amounts detailed in documents A1, A2, and A14.

For the reader's convenience, all sums are tabulated below.

Document	Coin	Number	Official exchange rate in d groot Flemish	Value in d groot Flemish	Value expressed in money of account (groot Flemish)
A1/A2/A14	Rhenish florin	450	59	26,550	£110 12s 6d
A1/A2/A14	ducat	6	80	480	£2 0s 0d
A1/A2/A14	Philippus florin	130	50	6500	£27 1s 8d
A1/A2/A14	Philippus florin	909	50	45,450	£189 7s 6d
A1/A2/A14	stuiver	1	2	2	£0 0s 2d
Subtotal				78,982	£329 1s 10d
A1	demi-réal	140	60	8400	£35 0s 0d
A1	Philippus florin	53	50	2650	£11 0s 10d
A1	Carolus florin	30	42	1260	£5 5s 0d
A1	angel-noble	5	119	595	£2 9s 7d
A1	Rhenish florin	7	59	413	£1 14s 5d
A1	stuiver	9	2	18	£0 1s 6d
Subtotal				13,336	£55 11s 4d
A2/A14	Rhenish florin	346.5	59	20,443.5	£85 3s 7.5d
A2/A14	écu au soleil	42	76	3192	£13 6s 0d
Subtotal				23,635.5	£98 9s 7.5d
Grand total				115,953.5	£483 4s 11.5d
A13	Rhenish florin	1960	59	115,640	£481 16s 8d
	ducat	2000	80	160,000	£666 13s 4d

A1 / Acknowledgment by Goclenius of monies deposited
with him by Erasmus

Basel MS C VIa 71 110 verso   17 September 1533

The manuscript is a notarized copy. For the sums mentioned in the text see the
introduction.

A copy in the handwriting of Goclenius (as was clear)[4]
May Christ turn this to the good.

Desiderius Erasmus of Rotterdam donated to me all the money that I have
until now held in my possession as deposited by him with me, and I accepted such great munificence all the more willingly because it proceeded   5
from such a great man. But in order that such a great outpouring of money
should be no loss to him if I should die (for while I am alive I consider all I
possess to belong to him), I proclaim, signify, and declare by this receipt in
my own handwriting (which I wish to be equivalent to my last will according to any law, custom, or value whatever) that, if it should happen that I   10
depart this life before the death of Desiderius Erasmus, at that time I either
return or donate to him whatever I have received as a gift from the same. But
to make perfectly clear what I have received from him, I will list the items
here in detail. First: I received from him 450 gold florins; but from those I
paid Jacobus Ceratinus 25 for a Greek dictionary,[5] on behalf of and at the   15
request of Desiderius Erasmus. Accordingly, from that sum my heirs will
pay Desiderius Erasmus 425 gold coins. In addition, I had from him six simple ducats, besides 130 Phillipics. Likewise, out of the money that Hilarius
Bertholf deposited with me on behalf of the same Desiderius Erasmus, I had
this money as coins, which were worth more then than at the present time,   20
but in coins there were, first of all, 140 half-royals of the Emperor Charles
(constituting a simple Caroline and a half), 53 Phillipics, 30 Carolines, 5 angels,
7 gold Rhenish florins of the Electors, 9 simple stufers. Finally, I received from
Quirinus Talesius 909 Phillipics with one stufer. This entire sum of money I
either render to him as a grateful follower or donate to him according to my   25
last will, and not only the sum listed above but also beyond the listed sums

* * * * *

4 '(as was clear)' added by the notary
5 Cf Ep 1437:168–9, perhaps a reference to the new edition of Craston's *Dictionarius*
   Graecus prepared by Ceratinus; see Ep 1460.

I give and bequeath to the same Desiderius Erasmus 20 ducats,[6] testifying in
my own handwriting that this is my last will in so far as concerns the sum
listed above.

I wrote this with my own hand in the year of our Lord 1533, 17 September.   30
Conradus Goclenius

A comparison shows that the copy agrees with the original. This is at-
tested by me, Johann Duykens, notary licensed by the council of Brabant.

A2 / Memorandum by Erasmus of monies deposited with Goclenius

Basel MS Goclenii epistolae (Erasmuslade) folio 34 verso   8 April 1534

The manuscript is a notarized copy.

I, Desiderius Erasmus of Rotterdam, professor of theology, have deposited
with the most excellent gentleman and my truest friend Conradus Goclenius,
professor of Latin in the Busleyden College at Louvain,[7] 450 gold florins
in actual gold, 6 simple ducats, 130 Philippics, and also 346 1/2 florins of
Brabantine money. Four écus à la couronne, which I instructed him to give to   5
Maarten Lips, should be deducted from this sum. Moreover, I deposited with
him 42 écus au soleil, 909 golden Philippics with one stufer, as is testified
by receipts provided by the same Goclenius. Of this sum, if I do not make
a different decision before my last day, I will that he keep 400 for himself,[8]
and that he either hand over the rest to the trustee I have designated and to   10
the executors or distribute it himself for pious purposes.[9] And I will that this
document have no less weight than if it were inserted in my will, and to accomplish this even more fully I have written it with my own hand and have
sealed it with my own Terminus ring. At Freiburg im Breisgau, 8 April in the
year of our Lord 1534   15

* * * * *

6 Twenty ducats were equivalent to £6 13s 4d groot Flemish or seventy-six
  percent of the annual wage of an Antwerp master mason/carpenter (CWE 12
  650 Table 3, 691 Table 13).
7 Ie the Collegium Trilingue
8 Rhenish florins, equivalent to £98 6s 8d groot Flemish or eleven years' wages of
  an Antwerp master mason/carpenter (CWE 12 650 Table 3, 691 Table 13)
9 When speaking of his will, Erasmus distinguishes between the trustee (*haeres
  sive fidei commissarius*) and the executors (*executores*). Bonifacius was the trustee
  of his last will; the executors were the Basel publisher Hieronymus Froben and
  his business partner Nicolaus Episcopius; see Allen XI 364:6–9. The '400' in
  question were presumable the 400 gold florins mentioned in Ep 1437:132–3.

A comparison reveals that the above copy agrees with the original written by Desiderius Erasmus. It is thus. Egidius Martin of the fostering University of Louvain, in his function as a licenced notary

A3 / Letter of Goclenius to Bonifacius Amerbach
Basel MS G2 II 67   Louvain, 19 August 1536

   The manuscript is a notarized copy.

+ Copy
Heading: To the most renowned Doctor Master Bonifacius Amerbach.
At Basel

Contents of the letter:
Cordial greetings. Although the death of our Erasmus caused me more bitter   5
grief than any death except that of my father, reflection has restored me to
reason, and I am beginning to endure it with more understanding. For what
did he have to expect in his lifetime that he did not fully accomplish? He
was always steadfast in refusing honours; he was held in highest favour by
princes of both orders;[10] all scholars, now and in the future, must attribute 10
to him as if to a parent all learning and the pursuit of true piety. He receives
the reward of his diligent application not only now in heaven, but he also
left behind in the world his most honourable reputation and his undying
fame, to which I do not see how anything could have been added by a longer
life. But I have no words to tell you, my dear Amerbach, how much joy was   15
mingled with my tears, how much consolation I found in seeing how calmly
he considered death, how he departed from life like a true Christian, how he
left his goods to be dispensed for pious uses. In order to carry out his will in
that matter, which with me is no less powerful now than when he was alive,
and also to satisfy your wishes and those of his executors, I immediately   20
set out for Antwerp to visit Erasmus Schets, a businessman and – as is not
always the case with people of that sort – a gentleman of the utmost inter-
grity and admirable humanity. Once he had received your letter,[11] he immediately agreed to deliver all the money, but in the currency in which he had
received it, namely that of Brabant. But because I thought that might be in- 25
convenient and troublesome to you, and because I saw that such a sum could
not be transported to Frankfurt without considerable expense and danger, I

       * * * * *

   10 Ie both ecclesiastical and secular princes
   11 Not extant

followed another plan which, it seemed to me, would be a good deal safer and less expensive. For I got Schets to agree to pay to you at Frankfurt the money that he would receive from his debtors at the next Frankfurt fair, cal- 30 culating the value in terms of the Brabant money and paying it in German gold coins or in French écus à la couronne.[12]

Concerning the bequest and the deducted payment to Lambert Coomans, Erasmus Schets or his son Gaspar or certainly his agent will produce a quittance.[13] But one difficulty remains: there is a mistake in each list, 35 both that of the sums deposited with Schets and that of the sums to be paid by him. For among the sums deposited, 81 florins with 15 stufers (as we say here) is erroneously listed twice; and in the sums to be subtracted for linens, 20 florins should have been written instead of 15. Then, too, Schets did not pay Maarten Lips 80 florins but thus far only 40.[14] But if Desiderius Erasmus 40 bestowed 80 on Lips by his promissory note, Lips trusts in your good faith not to diminish the generosity, certified in writing, of Desiderius Erasmus. Schets would not have refused to pay Lips the remaining 40, relying on your instruction, but I wanted to bring the matter to your attention first, since this discrepancy would be immediately resolved by examining the documents 45 written by Erasmus, and you would have done your duty in this matter as in all others.[15]

As for what you go on to say, that you would be pleased if I would be willing to promote your plan with some of the money deposited with me,[16]

* * * * *

12 For the sums that Erasmus had on deposit with Erasmus Schets and their transfer to Bonifacius after Erasmus' death, see AK Ep 2052:10–18 (Schets to Amerbach, 18 August 1536).
13 Lambert Coomans of Turnhout (d 1583) was from August 1535 Erasmus' last famulus. Greatly pleased with his services, which included a good deal of nursing care, Erasmus included a bequest of two hundred gold florins to him in his will. Presumably these were Rhenish florins, equivalent to £49 3s 4d or just over five and a half years' wage income of an Antwerp master mason/carpenter (CWE 12 650 Table 3, 691 Table 13). For the payment to him by Schets, see AK Ep 2052:13–15.
14 In a letter of 8 May 1536 Erasmus instructed Schets to pay Maarten Lips (Ep 2566 introduction) forty gold florins (*quadraginta Caroleos*); see Allen Ep 3119:21–3.
15 Lips himself later testified that 40 florins, not 80, was the amount that Erasmus had actually offered him; see his letter to Bonifacius Amerbach of 5 February 1539 (AK Ep 2303).
16 Amerbach had requested that some portion of the monies deposited with Goclenius be made available for distribution at Basel; see lines 50–7 below, A13:10–14.

I hardly know whether I could do this in good faith, since the testator himself   50
in the language of his will limited his bequests to a specific place, saying that
he wants me to distribute them in Brabant; and several years before he made
his will he also clearly dictated to me, in a directive mentioned in his last
will, what I should confer and on whom.[17] Otherwise I would be happy to
yield this task to those who are more honourable and endowed with greater   55
wisdom. If you think something else is permitted me, I will not dismiss the
authority of a highly respected man.

One thing remains, my dear Amerbach. Since, as you write, we have
been deprived of a friend we had in common, one who loved both of us in
an extraordinary way, let us not struggle against the necessity of fate, but   60
strive with all our care, effort, and thought to be able to follow him eagerly
when Christ calls us. In the meantime, while we have our dwelling place
here, it would be an extraordinary gift if you would count Goclenius – whom
Erasmus himself did not find wanting (to speak of myself rather too grandly)
– among your friends, a friend who will not fail to respond with any kind of   65
service he can provide. Furthermore, it would be not only an initial but a complete token of your good will if you would see to it that all my letters written
to Erasmus are completely destroyed; some malicious people in these regions
might be able to use them to injure me, since I did not permit him to remain
ignorant of anything that concerned him. For what could be more fitting than   70
that Erasmus' trustee should do everything he can to keep me from being in
any danger after his death, since I often took such care to preserve his reputation and safety that there was no danger to which I was not willing to subject myself, and he in turn so loved me that if I suffered some misfortune he
grieved for my affliction as if it were his own. If you consider how much less   75
freedom there is here than there among you, you will not be surprised that
I am concerned about a matter that can injure many people if it is neglected;
and by the same token, you will understand that I will be extremely grateful
to you for the removal of all fear and the preservation of my safety.

Farewell, my most distinguished friend Amerbach, at Louvain,   80
19 August 1536

Yours, however little he may be worth, Conradus Goclenius

The present copy agrees word for word with its original; this I confirm
by my seal, and by my usual and customary name and cognomen, Jodocus
Grimberga, notary licenced by the sacred authorities both apostolic and im-   85
perial, and also by the council of his imperial Majesty in Brabant.

* * * * *

17 For the language of the will see A14:6–8 below.

A4 / Letter of Bonifacius Amerbach to the University of Louvain
Basel MS Erasmuslade C no 13   Basel, 7 April 1539

> The manuscript is a draft written by a secretary and corrected by Amerbach, the
> address and signature autograph.

To the magnificent and most learned rector, and to the doctors and professors of every faculty at the famous University of Louvain, my most honoured masters

Cordial greetings. Magnificent Master Rector, most illustrious doctors of all
faculties, most outstanding gentlemen. Three years ago, shortly before he   5
departed to join the saints in heaven, Erasmus of Rotterdam, singular ornament of our native land and of literary culture, having been provided with
diplomas of the Roman pontiff and of the august emperor,[18] made a will in
which, among other things, he took care that I, who had been named trustee,
should leave with Conradus Goclenius the money deposited with him, as he   10
had received it in trust, with the mandate that it be distributed in Brabant.
      Immediately after the death of Erasmus, I did indeed inform Goclenius
of this wish, being fully persuaded that he would carry out the last will of the
testator as soon as possible. But since it is becoming known here more clearly
every day that Goclenius breathed his last not long ago without having done   15
so and that the treasury is plotting to seize the deposited money, I cannot
refrain from grieving that after his death the mandate of a man so extraordinary for his learning has not yet been satisfactorily carried out.[19]
      And so I think that because of such delay the authority to distribute
the monies there has devolved upon me, I wish to assign this task to you,   20
who are gentlemen of the most upright character, and I beg and beseech
you not to refuse to take upon yourselves the task of distributing the aforesaid money, which I am confident you will do all the more willingly because
you are not unaware that it is for the common good that the last wishes of
testators should be fulfilled, and then, too, because this is a pious legacy   25
that was bequeathed by someone who deserves most highly of you and
of the whole literary community, and finally because it will turn out to be

* * * * *

18 Ie the *diplomata* authorizing Erasmus to make a will: the papal brief of Clement
   VII (Ep 1588) and the letter patent of Charles V (Ep 2318)
19 Thanks to the omission of *post* before *mortem*, and the substitution of *possum*
   for *possim*, the Latin of the part of this sentence following the final 'that' is
   ungrammatical.

advantageous to the university. For I desire nothing other than that the deposited money be applied to the uses prescribed to Goclenius or that, if you
should have no specific stipulation, you should, in your prudence, invest   30
it so as to supply an annual revenue that can foster and support some poor
students at your university.

Thus, if I perceive that you do not refuse to undertake this task, I am prepared, if necessary, to transmit to you transcripts or faithful copies of the will,
and likewise of the papal and imperial diplomas, and, in brief, of everything   35
that you consider pertinent to invalidating and eliminating the intrigues of
the treasury.

I am writing this pressed by the lack of time, since by chance the most
illustrious Master Johann, the bearer of this letter,[20] greeted me yesterday
evening on his return from Italy and is about to set out very early this morn-   40
ing to travel there. And so, with your customary benevolence, take in good
part this my extemporality, and let me know by your own letter carrier what
I ought to hope for from you.

Farewell, illustrious gentlemen, on the day after Easter 1539, at Basel,
in great haste   45
Your most obedient servant, Bonifacius Amerbach, doctor of laws[21]

A5 / Letter of Bonifacius Amerbach to the University of Louvain
Ms Bibliothèque municipale at Nantes[22]   Basel, 2 October 1539

> The letter is in the hand of a secretary, the date and signature in the hand of
> Amerbach. Following the address Amerbach noted: 'Not sent, the messenger
> having changed his mind.'

To the magnificent, most illustrious, and learned rector, and to the doctors
and professors of all the faculties at the famous University of Louvain, my
most honourable masters

Cordial greetings. Magnificent lord rector, most illustrious doctors of all the
faculties, most distinguished gentlemen. Last April I wrote to your Lordships   5
that Desiderius Erasmus of Rotterdam, having made me the trustee of his

* * * * *

20 Unidentified
21 Here, as at the end of A5, Bonifacius signs himself 'VV. pp. paratiss.' as the ab-
    breviation of 'Viris perfectisimis paratissimisque.'
22 The transcript supplied to the Allen editors by Alfred Hartmann was based on
    a photograph of the original in the Basel Erasmus collection at Nantes.

will, instructed me to leave with Conradus Goclenius a certain sum of money deposited with him in Brabant to be distributed according to the instructions he had been given. Since the same Goclenius afterwards expressly acknowledged in a letter of his that he had in his possession what had been deposited with him, accepting the duty to comply with the injunction as soon as possible, I had no doubt that he would immediately fulfil his commission. In the meantime, however, when the rumour arose here that Goclenius had died and had not yet distributed the money, I resolved, according to my duty as trustee to fulfil the sacrosanct will of the testator, to ask you, as men of the most upright character, not to object to accepting the task of distributing the money, which I was confident you would not decline because it is a holy legacy and because I wished that it should be so invested as to yield annual revenue to support students in the trilingual college there (if it was clear that it should not be used for some other purpose prescribed by Desiderius Erasmus), desiring to learn your wishes through your own messenger. But since you have thus far not replied, and since I have procured a messenger who is going in that direction, I beg and beseech you, in the name of Christ and sacred studies (which you undoubtedly wish to provide for), that in your kindness you do not refuse to send me at least some word of what you expect me to do. For if I learn that you are not disposed to undertake this task, I will have to look for another way and proceed according to a different plan to see to it that money ordained for pious uses should not be profaned or granted to the undeserving. Certainly I will do everything I can to satisfy the last will of the testator. Farewell, most illustrious and outstanding gentlemen.

At Basel, 2 October 1539

Your most obedient servant, Bonifacius Amerbach, doctor of laws.[23]

A6 / Letter of the University of Louvain to Bonifacius Amerbach

Basel MS G2 II 67 50   Louvain, 15 October 1539

Allen provides no description of the manuscript. This is the university's response to A4 (see lines 3–7 below).

To the most renowned and learned gentleman Master Bonifacius Amerbach, most expert professor of both laws at Basel, our dear friend

Cordial greetings. We have received your letter, most illustrious sir, sent to us on the day after the past Easter. In that letter you assigned to us the

* * * * *

23 See n21 above.

distribution of the monies that Desiderius Erasmus of Rotterdam, a man of   5
admirable erudition, had deposited with the excellent gentleman Conradus
Goclenius, professor of the Latin language in the Busleyden College,[24] and
had entrusted to him to be expended for pious purposes in Brabant, prescrib-
ing to us that, if we had no other specific purpose to which it ought to be
applied, we should invest it so as to produce annual income that can foster   10
and support poor students in this university. We have accepted this assignment all the more willingly in order that that the task of distribution desired
by such an outstanding gentleman can be carried out with greater trust, diligence, and care, according to his desire and your prescription.

But after a prolonged litigation in the council of Brabant, conducted by   15
our syndic and Johannes Altenanus, procurator of the heirs of Goclenius,[25]
we secured the exclusion of the treasury of the prince by decree of the council. Then lo! a new controversy suddenly arose. The aforesaid Johannes
Altenanus, on behalf of the heirs of Goclenius, under the pretext of a certain donation that he claimed had been made to Goclenius by Erasmus on   20
28 August in the year 1533, according to a document written and sealed by
the same Desiderius Erasmus (a copy of which we are sending to you), tried
to have the money withdrawn from the trust and transferred to Goclenius'
heirs as their own. We intervened to keep him from succeeding in doing this,
and, as much on behalf of this university and the poor as of the trustee and   25
executors of the testamentary assignment made by Desiderius Erasmus, we
managed, through the efforts of that magnificent gentleman, the rector of the
University, to have that money placed under restraint or (as it is commonly
called) sequestration.

But, because there are many indications that the aforesaid donation   30
is counterfeit, especially because of a letter written by Desiderius Erasmus
himself at Freiburg im Breisgau on 8 April in the year 1534,[26] which, though it
is later than the letter giving the alleged donation, nevertheless still mentions
the money that had been previously deposited, we are sending you a copy

* * * * *

24 See n7 above.
25 Altenanus was a native of Altena, to the west of the county of Waldeck in
    Westphalia. Goclenius and his brothers were natives of Mengeringhausen, in
    the neighbourhood of Bad Arolsen in Waldeck. Altenanus worked as a notary
    in Louvain and was a friend of his countryman Goclenius. He also appears
    to have looked after business on behalf of the duke of Jülich-Cleves, and in
    that connection was well acquainted with Konrad Heresbach, whose interven-
    tion with Bonifacius on behalf of Goclenius' heirs he instigated (A9:124–5, and
    A11). See de Vocht CTL III 591 n2.
26 A2

of it, with the request that if there are any other documents there that can be   35
used to show that the said donation is fictitious and counterfeit, you would
be good enough to send them to us.

And because with your outstanding learning you have ascertained that
the commission given to us concerning the distribution of the aforesaid monies according to the intention of Erasmus is not sufficient to support the suit   40
that must be undertaken against the heirs of Goclenius, you will also be able,
in order to remove any opportunity for them to slander us and to prevent
them from evading us, to cede to us the right to distribute the prescribed
monies intended, according to the last will of Erasmus, for the use of poor
students (since we have no other plan for distributing the aforesaid money),   45
so that in a judicial proceeding we can take the part either of the plaintiff or
the defendant, whichever is more convenient.

So that all of this can be carried out more securely, we are sending to
your Excellency the bearer of this letter, who will faithfully report to us whatever is entrusted to him. Farewell, most illustrious sir.   50

From Louvain, 15 October, in the year 1539
The Rector and the entire University of Louvain. A friend

A7 / Letter of Bonifacius Amerbach to the University of Louvain

Basel Erasmuslade c folio 12   [Basel, c 16 November 1539]

The manuscript is an autograph rough draft. The approximate date was assigned on the basis of the location of the manuscript in the archive, ie immediately preceding a letter dated 16 November 1539.

As is clear from the signature (line 17 below), this letter is actually nothing
more than a postscript. In the main letter, now lost, Amerbach will have given
to the University of Louvain the authorization requested of him in document
A6; in document A10:13–25 he informs the legal representative of Goclenius'
heirs that he has done so. Other documents in Amerbach's hand confirm that
the notary of the University of Louvain, Jodocus Grimberga, visited Basel
15–18 November and had been entrusted by Amerbach, acting in his capacity as Erasmus' trustee, with a letter conveying to the University of Louvain
full authority to disburse the monies deposited with Goclenius as prescribed in
Erasmus' will; see AK Ep 2360 introduction.

Most distinguished gentlemen. Because Desiderius Erasmus was in failing
health when he undertook to make his will according to the testamentary
laws of Basel, those laws had to be observed as strictly as possible. Since
those laws agree almost entirely with canon law, which requires that every
word be spoken in the presence of two or three witnesses, and in order that   5

your Highesses may be properly informed against any slanderous sophistry,
I affirm that nothing can be found lacking in the number of witnesses provided when Erasmus made his will. I had also intended to send copies of the
documents in which the Basel magistrates granted to Erasmus the right to
make and revise a will and proclaimed after his death that it had been cor-   10
rectly drawn up, except that they had been issued in our native language,
and Jodocus Grimberga, the notary who was sent here, stating that the controversy is not about the validity of the will but about the alleged donation,
thought that even if the documents were translated into Latin they would be
of no use to your Highnesses. Otherwise I would have been the most willing   15
and obedient servant of your Lordships in this matter as in others.

 The very same Amerbach

A8 / Letter of Bonifacius Amerbach to the University of Louvain
Basel Erasmuslade c no 14   Basel, 2 December 1539

 The manuscript is an autograph rough draft.

To the magnificent and most renowned rector and to the doctors of all the
faculties at the University of Louvain, honourable gentlemen

Cordial greetings. Magnificent lord rector and most renowned gentlemen.
I recently sent to you, via the public notary, Jodocus Grimberga, copies of
whatever documents are in my possession regarding claims to the monies   5
deposited with Goclenius.[27] But since at that time I was overwhelmed with
innumerable occupations and my mind was preoccupied by many thoughts,
I forgot to point out that acknowledgments of the deposited monies written in the hand of Goclenius were also found in the papers of Erasmus. But
because Goclenius did not deny that the sum had been deposited with him   10
and did not refuse to distribute it, I sent the acknowledgments to the same,
as you will understand from the copy I sent of the inventory and of my letter
to him, authorized by the public notary.[28] I wanted to inform you about this
just in case some objection was made to the quittances.

 * * * * *

27 For Jodocus Grimberga see A7 introduction. It is he who notarized the copy of
 A3 sent to Louvain (see A3:83–6).
28 The list of the documents sent, signed by a notary named Saltzmann, is item
 A13.

Similarly, the most illustrious Master Johannes Altenanus sent me his   15
greetings in a letter.[29] And since he sent me copies of everything that seems
to favour his clients, I thought it would be proper for me to respond to his
request by sending in return copies by which his are overthrown and foiled,
so that he would learn that his case is inferior and that there is very little basis
for litigation. Farewell, most renowned gentlemen.   20

At Basel, in haste, 2 December in the year 1539

For an excerpt from the inventory, etc, turn the page.

I sent this by the letter carrier of Altenanus, but secretly, to Schets,
wrapped in another covering, through Froben to Schets at Antwerp.

A9 / Letter of Johannes Altenanus [to Bonifacius Amerbach]
Basel MS C VIa 71 111–12   Louvain, 28 October 1539

> The manuscript is the original letter, autograph throughout, with the address-
> sheet missing. For Altenanus see n25 above. The postscript (lines 131–42 be-
> low), in the hand of Altenanus, is on a loose sheet (Basel MS C VIa 71 117).

Cordial greetings. That I, an obscure man not known to you even by sight,
did not hesitate to interrupt you, a most distinguished man distracted by
arduous labours, with a verbose letter, I hope you will, in your well known
kindness, forgive me, once you know that it was necessary for me to write to
avert any blame.   5

We have learned from letters you have sent here that you are aware
that Master Conradus Goclenius, to the very great loss of the commonwealth
and the grief of scholars, has withdrawn intestate from this most corrupt age,
strangled suddenly by a deadly inflamation of the throat. A noxious absess
had produced severe throbbing in his head for several months, but he him-   10
self, trusting the promises of a certain doctor, thought it would heal. In the
meantime he had called together his heirs, namely his brothers, of whom he
had seven in the county of Waldeck, upright indeed but obscure, poor, and
burdened with numerous children, to be the witnesses of his last will, since
he was not unaware that for a foreigner, not to say a German, to end his days   15
here is difficult, not to say dangerous. But the sudden death of this good man
threw his affairs into the greatest danger.

* * * * *

29 A9. Here and in line 23 below, Amerbach calls Altenanus 'Altinaus.'

For the rector, through the syndic of our university, made an inventory of his goods and took them in hand himself, waiting for the arrival of the heirs. When they arrived, their claim to inherit was denied because Rutgerus 20 Rescius,[30] together with some of his followers, had made his way into the private documents of the dead man, which were preserved in a box in the library at the College of Busleyden, and had brought out from the pile of other letters one by Erasmus, saying that a sum had formerly been placed in the possession of Goclenius, his truest friend;[31] at the same time, suppressing the 25 letter about the donation,[32] he insisted that the money found in Goclenius' chest belonged to Erasmus – and you know that Erasmus' reputation is not favoured by everyone here and that Goclenius is detested for his steadfast loyalty and love for the great man. They castigate the virtuous Erasmus, calling him a greedy man who, while he was alive, did not want the sum to be 30 spent for the poor, and calling Goclenius wicked because he had not conformed to the commission of the testator about distributing the money deposited with him. But you, most illustrious sir, will judge otherwise from the letter about the donation which, after much pleading and putting myself in danger from the treasury, I finally obtained, having been named the procura- 35 tor of the heirs by the order of the count of Waldeck and the lady of Cleves.[33] I am sending you a copy of it, and if you so wish, I will also send what was said by the most illustrious witnesses before whom Master Goclenius exonerated himself right after the death of Desiderius Erasmus, asserting, when you asked him for subsidies for students and young girls drawn from 40 the adjusted revenues of that pious ordinance, that he had no money deposited with him by Master Erasmus, as he would effectively demonstrate by many letters from the donor, which he had displayed, if anyone made trouble for him in this matter, adding that it was at his discretion to distribute that money for pious purposes, and that no testamentary power to dispose 45 of the money remained to Desiderius Erasmus, but that he, Goclenius, had nevertheless distributed a good part of it, so as suitably to fulfil the pious

* * * * *

30 Rescius (cf Ep 2876 n24) was professor of Greek at the Collegium Trilingue (referred to below as the College of Busleyden).
31 A2
32 Ep 2863
33 Until his death on 20 June 1539, the count of Waldeck was Philip III. If, as seems certain, Altenanus was appointed procurator to Goclenius' heirs soon after the latter's death in January 1539, then Philip would be the count in question, and his wife, Anne of Cleves (1495–1567), sister of Duke John III of Cleves, would presumably be the 'lady of Cleves.'

intention of Desiderius Erasmus. And at the same time, in the presence of the
witnesses, he sent three hundred gold florins to his native land[34] in order to
buy an income to support his little nephews in elementary school or, if there   50
be no nephews, to provide dowries for the marriages of his nieces. But our
doctors do not recognize such a distribution because it was done outside of
Brabant, as if it were a crime to promote piety in a foreign province and to
provide help for notable talents in mountainous Westphalia. I have no doubt
that he also described to your Prudence what he intended.   55
    Hence I urgently implore your Kindness to share with us a copy of that
letter, and that you not allow the innocent shades of such illustrious men to be
tormented and the wretched heirs of Goclenius, who have rescued that sum
from the treasury at their own expense, to be so unjustly persecuted. Agitated
by clamours, it would have taken the money away had not Goclenius' heirs   60
defeated it in the council of Brabant, not without great expense and effort,
by means of the letter of donation. The treasury had thundered that the licence to make a will had not been obtained by the illegitimate Erasmus from
the duke of Brabant, since the duke is different from the emperor and is not
bound by an imperial letter.[35] Perhaps the treasury had heard of a genealogy   65
that Master Erasmus, the prince of all learning, had written in his own hand
during his lifetime, which Rescius had also taken away.[36] If you wish, I will
send you a copy of it. Therefore, when the judgment was given, confirming
that the donation had been *inter vivos et ex causa*,[37] the heirs thought that, after
intolerable troubles, the matter had been completely settled, hardly expect-   70
ing that there would be any other harpies, and they sought to possess the
inheritance they were owed (from the possession of which they had been

* * * * *

34 Presumably Rhenish florins, equivalent to £73 15s 0d groot Flemish or eight
   and a half years' wages of an Antwerp master mason/carpenter (CWE 12 650
   Table 3, 691 Table 13)
35 See n1 in the introduction to this appendix.
36 An apparent reference to the *Compendium vitae*, the account of his life that
   Erasmus had written at the request of Conradus Goclenius and included in a
   letter to him of 2 April 1524 (Ep 1437: 233–406 / CWE 4 403–10). One need read
   only the first two paragraphs to reach the conclusion that Erasmus was born
   out of wedlock.
37 Ie it was a contract concluded by the mutual consent of the donor, who had
   divested himself of something in order freely to transfer title of it to the donee,
   who in accepting the thing had acquired legal title to it. It was a *donatio inter
   vivos et ex causa* because the parties to it acted by title (*ex causa*) and the donor
   was not in immediate apprehension of death (otherwise it would have been a
   donatio mortis causa).

excluded by the rector, who held the goods), leaving also behind in the university the annual income from the money that had been found, which was being used to support one or two of Master Goclenius' nephews, so that in 75 this way (provided the university deserved this through its kindness) they might fulfil the wishes of the brother,[38] to which he had often testified while he was alive. But the wretched heirs are making no progress at all: the doctors consider that the money should not be given to Germans; some judge that it should be divided among the faculties of all ranks, others, that it should 80 be converted into revenues to be distributed among doctors presiding over new disputations that they wanted to establish; they say that the heirs, who lacked any favour or friends, in order to facilitate a settlement,[39] should bring a suit if they want to get anything, submitting that the donation made to Goclenius was fictitious, considering the intention of Erasmus. They produce 85 your letter to defend themselves,[40] asking you to offer stronger defences. A letter of Episcopius to a certain Nannius (who, as I hear, was appointed by the theologians to Goclenius' professorship)[41] is also being read, in which it is said that the virtuous Goclenius is castigated, greatly to the displeasure of some of his pupils. I would wish that the man had been advised not to 90 be so ready to believe malicious tale bearers. They have no doubt that he did keep the money. On the other hand, I contend they should demonstrate clearly, with solid arguments, that the donation is fictitious, and even if it is, I contend that the heirs of the intestate person should undertake the task of disposing of it, and that a good part of it has already been distributed, and 95 that the doctors ought not to become involved, in the name of the university, in tasks that do not concern them.

But what I say falls on deaf ears. Hence I beg and beseech you, most illustrious sir, on behalf of that truth which never fails, to lend your patronage to the heirs, in the name of justice and truth, by sending from the possessions 100 of Desiderius Erasmus those documents by which the donation, of which I send you a copy, can be either confirmed or refuted. But if there are no such documents, please deign to write to the university that in all fairness you would not impede such a donation (provided they recognized it as in the

* * * * *

38 Ie Goclenius, brother of their fathers
39 The Latin is obscure; this is a guess.
40 Presumably A5
41 For Episcopius see n9 above. Petrus Nannius (Pieter Nannick, 1496–1557), Goclenius' successor as professor of Latin at the Collegium Trilingue, was appointed by the responsible authorities at the Collegium Trilingue, not by 'the theologians.' See de Vocht CTL III 566.

hand of Erasmus and confirmed by his Terminus seal) and that you do not   105
want there to be any legal dispute that would unjustly burden the poor heirs
of that most distinguished gentleman, Master Goclenius. For this service of
yours Christ will reward you, and the heirs themselves will give you thanks
as long as they live. Someday you will hear in person how shamefully the
affairs of this excellent gentleman have been handled and you will detest   110
the falsehood and wickedness of many people.

You once wrote to Master Goclenius about obtaining from Schets what
Erasmus had deposited with him. We are not unaware of how much that was
and what Goclenius received. Gaspar Schets, the son of Erasmus Schets, owed
a debt to Goclenius.[42] We managed to get our hands on this, not without great   115
difficulty, for the documents confirming the debt had been stolen. Our friend
Karl Harst recently wrote to us from Spain, where he acts as the ambassador
to the emperor from our prince of Cleves,[43] concerning the commentary of
Master Goclenius on Terence, mentioning his compatriot Episcopius.[44] But
all the efforts of this gentleman were to no avail. Nevertheless, I think some   120
things are in safe hands and will at some time or other come to the Frobens.
A while ago I was with Johann von Vlatten,[45] who has just returned from the
electoral princes,[46] and he asked me to greet you for him as your obedient
servant. I will reveal the state of affairs to Konrad Heresbach and I have no
doubt that he will add a letter to you.[47] Remain, O most illustrious ornament   125
of the commonwealth, hale and hearty to the age of Nestor,[48] and write back

* * * * *

42 See A3.
43 The prince was John III, duke of Cleves-Mark-Jülich-Berg. For Karl Harst, see
    Ep 2804 n1.
44 Goclenius is known to have done some work on Donatus' commentaries on
    Terence. Erasmus solicited his help with a projected edition of Terence by
    Froben (Ep 1890:30), but Goclenius thought that the job should go to Johann
    Sichard, who had access to a better manuscript (Ep 1899:28–57). Harst and
    Episcopius (n41 above) were both Alsatians.
45 Ep 2804
46 The electoral princes, or simply the electors, were the seven German princes
    who participated in the election of a new emperor and were a separate college
    in the imperial diet. The reference is unclear, but it could be to some diplomatic
    journey undertaken to the three nearby Rhenish archbishops (Cologne, Mainz,
    Trier) who were electoral princes and were also heavily involved in the politics
    of the region.
47 See A11.
48 Ie to a very great age: see *Adagia* I vi 66.

to us what you think through this messenger, whom I have especially sent
to you.

Louvain, 28 October in the year, etc 1539

Johannes Altenanus, the servant of your most excellent Lordship   130

Certain vile friends of Goclenius would almost have undermined his
status as heir because books of Melanchthon, printed at Wittenberg, which
have been prohibited here by a most severe edict,[49] were discovered in his
library, and they are still a threat if those who list the goods force the heirs to
justify themselves. I rather think that those blinded by hatred would prefer   135
that the treasury take the money away rather than that the heirs should enjoy
it by a just inheritance. Throw this into the fire.

A certain counsellor in Brussels would like to see Erasmus' will, if you
can give him a copy without any difficulty or danger. You will not find him
ungrateful for this service, if he can ever return the favour in some way. For   140
he is a very great admirer of Erasmus.[50] But you, in your prudence, should do
whatever you judge is best. He asked me to let you know.

A10 / Letter of Bonifacius Amerbach to Johannes Altenanus

Basel MS C VIa 71 115 verso   Basel, 2 December 1539

The manuscript is an autograph rough draft. The version of the letter subsequently published by Alfred Hartmann as AK Ep 2365 contains additions and
one correction that were not in the text that he supplied to Allen. We have incorporated those changes into the text below.

To the most illustrious gentleman Master Johannes Altenanus, doctor of both
laws, etc, his most honourable master

Cordial greetings, most illustrious sir. When last April the news circulated
here that Goclenius had left to join those who dwell on high, and that the
treasury was scheming to obtain the goods of Erasmus of Rotterdam that   5
had been deposited with the deceased, I began to feel immense sorrow, not
so much because such a learned man was dead as that the money that had
been deposited with him was not being devoted to its proper uses, considering (as I did) that the dilatoriness of Goclenius should be replaced by my
diligence, and that the duty of a good trustee is to see to it that somehow   10

* * * * *

49 See Ep 2912 n4.
50 The counsellor has not been identified.

or other the solemn intention of Erasmus should be kept unimpaired. Since, however, no other remedy was available to me, located as I am at such a great distance from these places, I addressed the governing authorities of the University of Louvain,[51] doing so specifically to assure that Erasmus' money be applied to the uses Erasmus had prescribed to Goclenius, or if no specific   15
prescription existed, that in their wisdom they should arrange that it be used to provide an annual income that would serve to support poor students. And when they later took it upon themselves to do what I had prescribed, I yield-ed and transferred to them in the prescribed way every right to distribute the money, which, because of Goclenius' delay, had devolved upon me as   20
the designated trustee; and I did so in the presence of a notary and witnesses and with the consent of the executors,[52] adding and stipulating one rule, that the remainder of the bequest be invested so as to provide an annual income assigned to support poor students, intending that special consideration be made for the young people in the trilingual college there.   25

Since the things I have recounted, most illustrious sir, have been car-ried out, you will in your wisdom easily gather the rest. Accordingly, when in a lengthy letter you commend to me the heirs of Goclenius, whose claim you are defending, and when you wish that documents be presented to you by which the donation that those same heirs allege will be proved genuine,[53]   30
I would indeed be most willing to gratify you if I had anything pertaining to your undertaking. But since neither in Erasmus' will nor in the instruc-tions he left me on his deathbed in his own handwriting is there a single word mentioning a donation, and since in fact he entered the whole amount of money in his records as deposited with Goclenius and ordered that the   35
same sum should be distributed in Brabant, it seems to me that the sort of donation of which you sent me a copy (and I say it with all respect to you) smells faintly of forgery. What about the fact that we also found in Erasmus' papers documents written by Goclenius acknowledging the deposit of the same money,[54] which I did not hesitate to send to the same, as you will easily   40
learn for yourself from copies of letters and other documents to be lawfully published by the University of Louvain.[55]

And so, most illustrious sir, since Erasmus wished all his goods, apart from legacies, to be distributed at my discretion for the benefit of the poor,

* * * * *

51 A4
52 See A7. For the executors see n9 above.
53 A9
54 A1
55 For the list of documents sent, see A13.

and since it seems proper that the aim in investing it should primarily be the   45
will of the testator, it is appropriate, I think, that money gained from scholarship should be placed so as to benefit scholars. It seems to me, moreover, that
the trustee should stick religiously to his duty; both divine and human law
exhort me to do this.

Farewell, most illustrious sir. 2 December in the year 1539. At Basel.   50
Lest you should find me lacking in any way, most illustrious sir, I will send
you copies (verified for you by a public notary against the autographs) of
all the documents that refute and disarm the accusations of your clients,[56]
and, if I possessed anything that would be favourable to these same clients,
I would do the same with equal sincerity. Erasmus Schets, a gentleman of   55
complete integrity, has conducted himself in such a way that I have no doubt
he is a man with whom you could play morra in the dark.[57] With respect to
this matter,[58] I pronounce Goclenius, together with his heirs, completely free
to act. Please give my best regards to Master Johann von Vlatten, greatly
distinguished for his ancestry, his learning, his honours – a gentleman of   60
excellent character.[59] Your letter carrier was stuck here for three days because at this time I am overwhelmed with innumerable tasks. But I do not
want my delay to cause you any expense; I have paid out of my own pocket
whatever he spent at the inn.[60] Once more, farewell, and number Amerbach
among your friends.   65

A11 / Letter of Konrad Heresbach to Bonifacius Amerbach

Basel MS C VIa 71 113   [6 November 1539]

> Allen supplies no information about the manuscript (nor does AK, which only
> mentions the letter in the introduction to Ep 2358 without providing the text)
> and does not justify the date, which appears to be based on Altenanus' state-
> ment in A9:124–5, written on 28 October, that Heresbach would write to him

* * * * *

56 See A14.
57 Ie an honest man who would not cheat even if he could get away with it. Morra
   was a game that entailed guessing the number of fingers that one's opponent
   was holding up. An honest man would not cheat even if the cover of dark permitted him to do so. See *Adagia* I viii 23.
58 See A9:112–16.
59 See Ep 1390 introduction.
60 Actually, he paid the letter carrier's expenses out of the income of the bequest
   from Erasmus of which he was the administrator; see AK Ep 2365 n12.

soon on the matter of the donation to Goclenius. For Konrad Heresbach see Ep 1316.

To the most distinguished gentleman Master Bonifacius Amerbach, public professor of law at the University of Basel, once my most affable companion, now my revered and respected friend

Cordial greetings. Although we have not had contact with one another for a long time, so that your memory of me, I imagine, has long since faded into 5 oblivion, nevertheless, relying on our intimacy of old, I have not hesitated to refresh your memory of me and to call upon a friend for the sake of a friend. I have had business dealings with Johannes Altenanus, a man both learned and well thought of in this region. Although you did not know him, he knew that I had formerly associated with you at Basel,[61] and he persistently begged me 10 to recommend him, a stranger, to you. I did so all the more willingly because I was persuaded by the nature of his case and your well-known kindness. Since he was a friend and compatriot of Conradus Goclenius while the latter was alive, he wanted to assist the heirs of Goclenius after he died, simple and needy people, so that they would not be cheated of both their brother and 15 his goods. For first of all, as I hear, the treasury cast longing glances at those goods. And now that the treasury has lost its suit, the sophists at Louvain,[62] harpies even more rapacious than the treasury, are trying to lay their hands on the same goods, basing their claim, as I hear, especially on some kind of authority from you, on the grounds that certain monies were deposited by 20 Erasmus with Goclenius to be distributed for pious purposes, which money the attorney representing the heirs claims he will prove, by means of relevant documents, was legally donated at that time by Erasmus to Goclenius. Now in fact, whether the money was deposited by Erasmus with Goclenius to be distributed for pious purposes or whether it was left to Goclenius him- 25 self as a *donatio inter vivos*,[63] it would certainly be well placed with the heirs, who are poor and are working very hard to provide for numerous offspring,

* * * * *

61 From c December 1520 Heresbach had worked as a corrector at the Froben press in Basel, before being appointed lecturer in Greek at Freiburg in June 1521. Bonifacius refers to Heresbach as 'our Konrad' in a letter of c June 1521; see AK Ep 790:1.
62 Cf the reference in line 32 below to 'those theologians.' The reference appears to be to Rutgerus Rescius and others at the Collegium Trilingue who supported the claim of the University of Louvain to Goclenius' money; see A9:18–27.
63 See n37 above.

although, as I understand it, they will allow themselves to be defrauded of
the money that came from Erasmus as long as this does not become the occasion for excluding them from what was left them by Goclenius, and as   30
long as Erasmus' money is applied to the support of poor students and is not
seized by those theologians.[64] You can well imagine what use the theologians
would make of it, namely theological symposia, no doubt to offer these as an
acceptable sacrifice to the shades of Erasmus and Goclenius.

And so your Benevolence would be acting piously if you if you would   35
assist the pious endeavours of Altenanus to rescue Erasmus' money from
these harpies. If, in this matter, you would deign to write a letter in support
of Altenanus at the University of Louvain, you would be doing a great service to many good men, certain to be repaid some day, if the occasion arises,
with some splendid reward.   40

Farewell, most distinguished sir. If it is not too much trouble, I would
most strongly desire that you offer my most dutiful good wishes to the venerable Froben family. But I would especially like to be remembered to Beatus
Rhenanus.[65] Also please take the trouble to give my best wishes to Episcopius
and Artolf and my other delightful friends of long ago.[66] And if I feel that   45
you are not displeased by my letter, I will write more often. I have learned
that all of Erasmus' writings are to be republished[67] and distributed among
appropriate volumes. I would be glad to learn about it. Once more farewell.
In haste, extemporaneously
        Konrad Heresbach   50

A12 / Letter of Bonifacius Amerbach to Konrad Heresbach

Basel MS C VIa 71 115   Basel, 2 December 1539

The manuscript is an autograph rough draft.

* * * * *

64 It was the entire university, not 'those theologians,' that had laid claim to the
   money deposited with Erasmus.
65 Ep 327
66 For Episcopius see n9 above; for Hieronymus Artolf see Ep 2012.
67 Literally 'put back on the anvil,' ie remade, altered, corrected; see *Adagia* I v 92.
   Erasmus' last will made no provision for the publication of his works. But after
   his death Bonifacius Amerbach and the other executors of his will decided to
   put into effect the plan that Erasmus had outlined in his first will. The result
   was the Basel edition of 1540. See Ep 2754 n8.

To the most distinguished and learned gentleman Master Konrad Heresbach, counsellor of the most illustrious prince of Jülich, honourable gentleman and honourable friend

Cordial greetings. I found your letter, most illustrious Heresbach, quite pleasing and delightful. I learned from it that even though you have been el- 5 evated to a high position, and thus are provided with quite splendid friends, you have not at all forgotten your old ones. Even if I respect this generosity of yours and am most eager to comply with it in every way, nevertheless, in the matter about which you write to me, I am sorry to say that it would in all honesty be impossible for me to satisfy your wishes unless I were fully 10 assured that you are not aiming at anything except what is just.[68] For it is necessary to cooperate with friends, but only so far as the gods allow.[69]

For since it serves the common good, according to the opinion of Paulus, that the last wishes of men must be fulfilled,[70] and that they are especially to be protected by their trustees, I think that I, having been named as the trustee 15 of the incomparable gentleman Erasmus, must remember the duty I have undertaken and not fail to perform it scrupulously, in those matters as well that have devolved upon me through the default of others. For that reason, when I learned that following the death of the most learned gentleman Goclenius, the treasury was scheming to get control of the goods of Erasmus that had not 20 yet been distributed there, no more suitable plan occurred to me in a matter I knew nothing about than that the distribution of such monies be committed with certain stipulations to the governing authorities of the University of Louvain. Since they clearly did not refuse to undertake this task, I yielded to them my full right under the law, so that all the money should be used for the 25 purposes laid down for Goclenius by Erasmus or, if nothing is especially laid down, it should be both applied and invested so as to provide an annual income to serve and foster poor students, paying special attenton to the young men at the trilingual college there. But, as for the donation of some sort alleged by the most illustrious gentleman Johannes Altenanus, the advocate 30 of the heirs of Goclenius, I suspect (and I want it to be said with all respect to you) that it is a forgery. For if the money had already been donated to

* * * * *

68 The language of this last clause, Bonifacius' attempt to express his refusal politely, is an impenetrable series of negatives that cancel one another out. The translation is very free, but it says clearly what Bonifacius said obscurely.
69 Greek in the text.
70 Bonifacius is citing the Roman jurist Julius Paulus (*Digest* 29.3.5): 'Publica expedit suprema hominum judicia exitum habere' (It is advantageous to the public good that the last wishes of men be fulfilled).

Goclenius, in what will of Erasmus could there be any mention of money deposited with Conradus Goclenius and to be distributed in Brabant? Or why
should the same Erasmus, a man of unblemished character, record not long   35
before his death, in his own hand, the same amount of money, entering it in
the account-book of his payments and receipts, and why would he have allowed it to be left unrevised to me as his trustee? I add that Goclenius, when
he was reminded by me about the task of distribution, did not at all deny
that it had been entrusted to him. Since he accepted the duty of distribution,   40
I did not hesitate to return to him all the quittances for the deposited money
that were found here among Erasmus' papers, as is perfectly clear from our
exchange of letters.[71] And how, I ask you, will a donation not sworn to and
beyond the amount set by law be maintained?

Thus, most illustrious sir, just as your letter in support of others has great   45
weight and authority with me, since I am very devoted to you, so too, because
of your uprightness, I am fully persuaded that you desire nothing from me except what would do no injury to the justice that gives to each his own or to preserving my reputation. Farewell, most illustrious sir. All your old friends, just
as you wished them well, return your good wishes reverently and lovingly.   50

Basel, 2 December 1539

A13 / Memorandum of documents sent to the University of Louvain
by Bonifacius Amerbach

Basel MS Erasmuslade C folio 14 verso   [2 December 1539]

The manuscript is in the hand of a secretary, corrected by Amerbach.

To the University of Louvain[72]
From the inventory of the goods of Erasmus written and executed by the
undersigned notary on 20 July 1536:

Likewise, some documents in the handwriting of Goclenius when he was living
at Louvain, containing the sum of approximately 1,960 gold coins committed to   5
the same Master Goclenius for distribution.'[73]

* * * * *

71 See A3 and cf A8:9–14.
72 In Amerbach's hand
73 This is a somewhat abbreviated citation of a passage in the inventory of Erasmus'
    possessions prepared (in German) by the notary Adalberus Saltzmann follow-
    ing Erasmus' death; see Major 54. The text of the inventory published by Major
    is dated 22 (not 20) July 1536.

Excerpt from a letter written in the hand of Doctor Bonifacius Amerbach to Conradus Goclenius that begins 'Your letter brings the good news, etc,' dated at the end of the letter '1 September 1536, at Basel':[74]

As for my having asked you to share with me a portion of the money to be dis-   10
tributed by you for the sake of giving substantial support, please take in good
part this false thought. Having considered the matter more carefully, I think
that in fulfilling final wishes one should not recklessly depart from the written
document, unless some different intention of the testator is apparent. For that
reason, in order that you may act more freely in carrying out your plan as pre-   15
scribed, I am sending via Froben, bound together in a packet, as many of your
quittances or acknowledgments (as they are called) as we have found.[75]

Signed by Saltzmann, as in his protocol.[76]
These were sent.

A14 / Memorandum by Bonifacius Amerbach
of documents sent to Altenanus
Basel MS C VIa 71 folio 116   [2 December 1539][77]

The manuscript is an autograph, roughly written.

Sent to Altenanus

Passages which show that the money of Master Erasmus of Rotterdam found
in the possession of Goclenius was not donated but rather deposited.

From the will of Erasmus of Rotterdam written in his own hand at Basel
on the twelfth day of February in the year of our Lord 1536 and signed and   5
sealed with the Terminus seal of his own ring: 'The trustee, etc. He will leave
with Conradus Goclenius the money deposited with him to be distributed in
Brabant in the manner that I ordered him to follow.'

* * * * *

74 The letter from which the following excerpt was taken is not extant. It was evidently Bonifacius' answer to A3.
75 This is Bonifacius' apology for the request courteously refused by Goclenius in
A3:48–57.
76 In Amerbach's hand. For Saltzmann, see n73 above.
77 Not dated by Allen, but presumably sent with A10

From the account book of Master Erasmus written in his hand and found
among his papers at his death: 10

    Monies in the possession of Goclenius
        More than 450 gold florins
        6 simple ducats
        130 florins of St Philippe
        346 and 1/2 florins of the Rhine [or of the four electors], in the currency of   15
        Brabant
        42 écus au soleil
        909 gold florins of St Philippe, with one stufer

    To be subtracted from the above
        4 écus à la couronne, which he gave to Lips[78]   20
        5 gold florins, which he gave to Lambert[79]

From the inventory of all the goods, written and executed after the death
of Erasmus by the undersigned notary, on 11 July in the year of our Lord
1536, after the death of Erasmus: 'Likewise, some documents in the handwriting of Goclenius when he was living at Louvain, containing the sum of   25
approximately 1,960 gold coins committed to the same Master Goclenius for
distribution.'[80]

From the letter of Conradus Goclenius in his handwriting to Doctor
Bonifacius, written at Louvain on 19 August 1536: 'As for what you go on to
say,' etc.[81]   30

From a letter in the hand of Doctor Bonifacius, 1 September in the year 1536,
written to Conradus Goclenius: 'As for my asking you to share,' etc.[82]

* * * * *

78 See nn14–15 above.
79 See n13 above.
80 The date of the inventory given here (11 July 1536) differs from those in A13 and
    in Major; see n73 above.
81 Here followed lines 48–57 of A3.
82 Here followed lines 10–17 of A13.

ERASMUS' ILLNESSES IN HIS FINAL YEARS
(1533–6)

During the last three years of his life, beginning in February 1533, Erasmus complained regularly of terrible pain in his feet, hands, and indeed his entire body, combined with severe gastro-intestinal discomfort.[1] In conformity with the then prevailing view that illness was caused by external influences that disrupt the balance among the bodily humours, he attributed the pain in his feet, hands, and other joints to unfavourable weather,[2] and almost always referred to them as 'gout.'[3] The stomach discomfort, though not always clearly distinguished from the joint pain, he attributed to bad wine.[4] In some respects, at least, Erasmus' description of his symptoms is sufficiently specific and detailed to permit a reasonably confident diagnosis from the perspective of modern medicine.

It seems clear that Erasmus did indeed suffer from gout, and that he had done so for some time. He gives a classic description of what is known to modern medicine as acute gouty arthritis: 'My left foot [is afflicted] with such sharp and constant pain that I can neither sleep nor eat. I have experienced this ailment once or twice before, but it went away after three days and didn't extend above the foot.'[5] Acute gout occurs when crystals of uric acid precipitate in a joint, most commonly in the big toe. Uric acid crystals can also precipitate in the urinary tract, causing kidney stones, an ailment from which Erasmus had suffered frequently and severely in earlier years.[6]

Some individuals who have suffered episodic attacks of acute gout develop what is known as an asymmetic polyarthritis of chronic gout. This appears to be what Erasmus describes in the following passage: 'I suffer all the time from attacks of gout in the feet, gout in the hands, gout all over, seeking out all my joints, and going from one to another as soon as it has caused

* * * * *

1 Cf Ep 2818 n1.
2 See, for example Epp 2827:5–7, 9–10 with n6, 2858:2–3.
3 For his passing doubts on this subject, see Epp 2906:123–4, 2916:6–8, 2918:37–41.
4 See Ep 2818:1–6 with n2. Erasmus had long insisted that certain light red wines from Burgundy were essential to the well-being of his digestive system and of his urinary tract (Epp 1342:504–41, 2057 n1, 2115, 2241–2, 2329–30, 2348:9–12), and one of his stated reasons for hesitating to return to his native Brabant was the fear that he would not have a reliable supply of such wines (Ep 2689:8–9).
5 See Ep 2770:1–5; cf Ep 2776:62–5.
6 On the history of his affliction with calculus ('the stone') see Epp 1989 n4 (where the reference to Ep 2022:55–6 is out of place), 2263:11–12, 2271:3–4, 2277:12–13, 2278:10–12, 2290:54–5. One of Erasmus' recent references to his gout includes mention of 'a stone [calculus] in my right lower back' (Ep 2782:9–10). On the other hand, in Allen Ep 2965:5 he reports that 'attacks of the stone are rarer and less severe than before.'

enough torment in one of them. The unbearable pain lasts about four days. Then, when it has swollen up there is some relief, but [later it returns and] occupies another bodily member and rages there all over again, and then, at the slightest prompting, it either retreats or it grows worse.'[7] In the last year of his life, the gout in his hands made it increasingly difficult for Erasmus to write, or even to sign, his own letters.[8]

Some of Erasmus' aches and pains, however, are less easily categorized. Shoulder pain, for example,[9] is an unusual manifestation of gout. So his sense of having a diffuse illness that affected 'all the inner parts' of his body,[10] combined with his description of an 'enormous pain' that would not go away on the left side of his head, the left part of his neck, as well as his shoulder and arm,[11] suggests the possibility that a second illness, like polymyalgia rheumatica combined with temporal arteritis, may well have been involved.[12]

As for Erasmus' gastro-intestinal complaints, they need to be treated as something distinct from gout, even though the symptoms frequently occurred simultaneously. If any of his 'excruciating pains' were abdominal rather than articular, one could conclude that Erasmus was suffering from a peptic ulcer. But with respect to his stomach he talks of nausea and vomiting rather than pain.[13] At all events, the combination of gout with gastro-intestinal distress continued into the last months of his life, with the latter becoming worse. In March 1536 he complained that in addition to the usual gout he had been weakened 'for more than twelve days by diarrhea,' his stomach 'rejecting any kind of food.'[14] After his death in July, Bonifacius Amerbach reported that the end had come as the result of having suffered 'twenty days and more from dysentery.'[15] In the sixteenth century infectious diarrheal diseases were common, and the term 'dystentery' appears to have been applied to them all without distinction. It is therefore impossible to say whether or

* * * * *

7 Ep 2906:90–8. Cf Epp 2916:4–6, 2918:37–40. See also Allen Ep 3000:18–21.
8 See Allen Epp 2971:48, 3000:71–2, 3106:15, 3108:14, 3109:12–14, 3125:12, 3126:9, 3130:39.
9 Complained of in Ep 2783:18–19, 22
10 See Ep 2788:3–4.
11 Ep 2922
12 Polymyalgia rheumatica, a syndrome affecting older individuals, is an inflammatory condition that typically causes shoulder and neck pain. It is frequently associated with temporal arteritis, a painful inflammation of the temporal arteries, one on each side of the head.
13 See especially Ep 2818:1–8.
14 See Allen Ep 3106:11–12; cf Allen Ep 3108:3–6.
15 See AK Ep 2059:10 (29 August 1536).

not the dysentery that led to Erasmus' demise was linked to the earlier episodes of gastro-intestinal illness involving nausea and vomiting.

Thanks are due to Michael A. Hutcheon, MD, FRCP(C), professor of medicine at the University of Toronto, for his expert assistance in the preparation of this appendix.

JME

TABLE OF CORRESPONDENTS

WORKS FREQUENTLY CITED

AK   *Die Amerbach Korrespondenz* ed Alfred Hartmann and
B.R. Jenny (Basel 1942–   )

Allen   *Opus epistolarum Des. Erasmi Roterodami* ed P.S. Allen, H.M.
Allen, and H.W. Garrod (Oxford 1906–58) 11 vols and index

Analecta Belgica   C.P. Hoynck van Papendrecht *Analecta Belgica* (The Hague
1743) 3 vols in 6

ASD   *Opera omnia Desiderii Erasmi Roterodami* (Amsterdam 1969–   )

Bataillon   Marcel Bataillon *Erasme et l'Espagne* (Paris 1937)

Bellaria   Ambrosius Pelargus *Bellaria epistolarum Erasmi Rot. et
Ambrosii Pelargi vicissim missarum* (Cologne: H. Fuchs 1539)

Brendle   Franz Brendle *Dynastie, Reich und Reformation: Die württem-
bergischen Herzöge Ulrich und Christoph, die Habsburger und
Frankreich* (Stuttgart 1998)

CEBR   *Contemporaries of Erasmus: A Biographical Register of the
Renaissance and Reformation* ed Peter G. Bietenholz and
Thomas B. Deutscher (Toronto 1985–7) 3 vols

CWC   *The Correspondence of Wolfgang Capito* trans Erika Rummel,
ann Erika Rummel and Milton Kooistra (Toronto 2005–15)

CWE   *Collected Works of Erasmus* (Toronto 1974–   )

Enthoven   *Briefe an Desiderius Erasmus von Rotterdam* ed L.K. Enthoven
(Strasbourg 1906)

Epistolae ad Nauseam   *Epistolae miscellaneae ad Nauseam* (Basel: J. Oporinus 1550)

Epistolae familiares   *Des. Erasmi Roterodami ad Bonif. Amerbachium: cum nonnullis
aliis ad Erasmum spectantibus* (Basel 1779)

Epistolae floridae   *Des. Erasmi Roterodami epistolarum floridarum liber unus
antehac nunquam excusus* (Basel: J. Herwagen, September
1531)

Epistolae palaeonaeoi   *Desiderii Erasmi Roterodami Epistolae palaeonaeoi* (Freiburg:
J. Emmeus, September 1532)

Epistolae universae   *Des. Erasmi Rot. Operum tertius tomus epistolas complectans
universas* (Basel: Froben 1540)

Farge *Biographical Register*   James K. Farge *Biographical Register of Paris Doctors of Theology* (Toronto 1980)

Förstemann/Günther   *Briefe an Desiderius Erasmus von Rotterdam* ed. J. Förstemann and O. Günther, XXVII. Beiheft zum *Zentralblatt für Bibliothekwesen* (Leipzig 1904)

Gerlo   *La correspondance d'Érasme traduite et annotée d'apres l'Opus epistolarum de P.S. Allen, H.M. Allen, et H.W. Garrod* ed and trans Alois Gerlo and Paul Foriers (Brussels 1967–84) 12 vols

Herminjard   Aimé Louis Herminjard *Correspondance des réformateurs dans les pays de langue française: recueillie et publiée avec d'autres lettres relatives à la réforme et des notes historiques et biographiques* (Paris 1817–1900; repr Nieuwkoop 1965) 9 vols

Ipolyi   *Oláh Miklós Levelezése* ed Arnold Ipolyi, Monumenta Hungariae historica: Diplomataria xxv (Budapest 1875)

Klüpfel   *Urkunden zur Geschichte des Schwäbischen Bundes, zweiter Theil 1507–1533* ed Karl Klüpfel (Stuttgart 1853)

Knecht   R.J. Knecht *Francis I* (Cambridge 1982)

LB   *Desiderii Erasmi opera omnia* ed J. Leclerc (Leiden 1703–6; repr 1961–2) 10 vols

Major   Emil Major *Erasmus von Rotterdam* no 1 in the series *Virorum illustrium reliquiae* (Basel 1927)

MBW   *Melanchthons Briefwechsel, kritische und kommentierte Gesamtausgabe* ed Heinz Scheible et al (Stuttgart-Bad Canstatt 1977–   ) 27 vols to date. The edition is published in two series: *Regesten* (vols 1–12 in print); and *Texte* (vols T1–T15 in print). The letter numbers are the same in both series. In both series, the letters have identical sub-sections marked by numbers in brackets.

MSA   *Melanchthons Werke in Auswahl* ed Robert Stupperich et al (Gütersloh 1951–75) 7 vols

OER   *The Oxford Encyclopedia of the Reformation* ed Hans J. Hillerbrand et al (New York / Oxford 1996) 4 vols

Opuscula   *Erasmi opuscula: A Supplement to the Opera Omnia* ed Wallace K. Ferguson (The Hague 1933)

Opus epistolarum   *Opus epistolarum Des. Erasmi Roterodami per autorem diligenter recognitum et adjectis innumeris novis fere ad trientem auctum* (Basel: Froben, Herwagen, and Episcopius 1529)

Pastor   Ludwig von Pastor *The History of the Popes from the Close of the Middle Ages* ed and trans R.F. Kerr et al, 6th ed (London 1938–53) 40 vols

PG   *Patrologiae cursus completus ... series Graeca* ed J.-P. Migne (Paris 1857–66; repr Turnhout) 161 vols. Indexes F. Cavallera (Paris 1912); T. Hopfner (Paris 1928–36) 2 vols

PL   *Patrologiae cursus completus ... series Latina* ed J.-P. Migne, 1st ed (Paris 1844–55, 1862–5; repr Turnhout) 217 vols plus 4 vols indexes

Pollet   Julius Pflug *Correspondance* ed J.V. Pollet (Leiden 1969–82) 5 vols in 6

Redlich   *Jülich-Bergische Kirchenpolitik am Ausgange des Mittelalters und in der Reformationszeit* I. *Urkunden und Akten 1400–1553,* ed Otto R. Redlich (Bonn 1907)

Scarisbrick   J.J. Scarisbrick, *Henry VIII* (Berkeley and Los Angeles 1968)

Sepulvedae epistolae   *Io. Genesii Sepulvedae ... Epistolarum libri septem in quibus cum alia multa quae legantur dignissima traduntur, tum varii loci graviorum doctrinarum eruditissime et elegantissime tractantur* ed Juan J. Valverde Abril (Salamanca: J.M. de Terranova and J. Archario 1557)

Sieber   Ludwig Sieber *Das Mobiliar des Erasmus: Verzeichnis vom 10. April 1534* (Basel 1891)

Van Heussen   *Historia episcopatuum foederati Belgii* ed Hugo Frans van Heussen, vol 2 part 4: *Historia, seu notitia episcopatus leovardiensis* (Leiden: Vermey 1719)

Vita Erasmi   Paul Merula *Vita Desiderii Erasmi ... Additi sunt epistolarum ipsius libri duo ...* (Leiden 1607)

Vita Viglii Zuichemi   *Vita Viglii ab Aytta Zuichemi ab ipso Viglio scripta = Analecta Belgica* I / 1

de Vocht CTL   Henry de Vocht *History of the Foundation and the Rise of the Collegium Trilingue Lovaniense, 1517–1530* (Louvain 1951–5) 4 vols

VZE   *Viglii ab Aytta Zuichemi Epistolae selectae = Analecta Belgica*
                        II/1

WA   *D. Martin Luthers Werke, Kritische Gesamtausgabe* (Weimar
                        1930–80) 60 vols

WA-Br   *D. Martin Luthers Werke: Briefwechsel* (Weimar 1930–78)
                        12 vols

WA-TR   *D. Martin Luthers Werke: Tischreden* (Weimar 1912–21) 6 vols

Wierzbowski   Teodor Wierzbowski *Materyały do dziejów piśmiennictwa
                        polskiego i biografii pisarzów polskich* (Warsaw 1900) 2 vols

Titles following colons are longer versions of the same, or are alternative titles. Items entirely enclosed in square brackets are of doubtful authorship. For abbreviations, see Works Frequently Cited.

Acta: Academiae Lovaniensis contra Lutherum   *Opuscula* / CWE 71
Adagia: Adagiorum chiliades 1508, etc (Adagiorum collectanea for the primitive
   form, when required)   LB II / ASD II-1–9 / CWE 30–6
Admonitio adversus mendacium: Admonitio adversus mendacium et
   obtrectationem   LB X / CWE 78
Annotationes in Novum Testamentum   LB VI / ASD VI-5–10 / CWE 51–60
Antibarbari   LB X / ASD I-1 / CWE 23
Apologia: D. Erasmi Roterodami apologia   LB VI / CWE 41
Apologia ad annotationes Stunicae: Apologia respondens ad ea quae Iacobus Lopis
   Stunica taxaverat in prima duntaxat Novi Testamenti aeditione   LB IX / ASD IX-2
Apologia ad Caranzam: Apologia ad Sanctium Caranzam, or Apologia de tribus
   locis, or Responsio ad annotationem Stunicae … a Sanctio Caranza defensam
   LB IX / ASD IX-8
Apologia ad Fabrum: Apologia ad Iacobum Fabrum Stapulensem   LB IX / ASD IX-3 /
   CWE 83
Apologia ad prodromon Stunicae   LB IX / ASD IX-8
Apologia ad Stunicae conclusiones   LB IX / ASD IX-8
Apologia adversus monachos: Apologia adversus monachos quosdam Hispanos
   (Loca quaedam emendata in second edition, 1529)   LB IX
Apologia adversus Petrum Sutorem: Apologia adversus debacchationes Petri Sutoris
   LB IX
Apologia adversus rhapsodias Alberti Pii: Apologia ad viginti et quattuor libros
   A. Pii   LB IX / ASD IX-6 / CWE 84
Apologia adversus Stunicae Blasphemiae: Apologia adversus libellum Stunicae
   cui titulum fecit Blasphemiae et impietates Erasmi   LB IX / ASD IX-8
Apologia contra Latomi dialogum: Apologia contra Iacobi Latomi dialogum
   de tribus linguis   LB IX / CWE 71
Apologia de 'In principio erat sermo': Apologia palam refellens quorundam
   seditiosos clamores apud populum ac magnates quo in evangelio Ioannis
   verterit 'In principio erat sermo' (1520a); Apologia de 'In principio erat sermo'
   (1520b)   LB IX / CWE 73
Apologia de laude matrimonii: Apologia pro declamatione de laude matrimonii
   LB IX / CWE 71
Apologia de loco 'Omnes quidem': Apologia de loco taxato in publica professione
   per Nicolaum Ecmondanum theologum et Carmelitanum Lovanii 'Omnes
   quidem resurgemus'   LB IX / CWE 73
Apologia qua respondet invectivis Lei: Apologia qua respondet duabus invectivis
   Eduardi Lei   *Opuscula* / ASD IX-4 / CWE 72
Apophthegmata   LB IV / ASD IV-4 / CWE 37–8
Appendix de scriptis Clichtovei   LB IX / CWE 83
Appendix respondens ad Sutorem: Appendix respondens ad quaedam Antapologiae
   Petri Sutoris   LB IX

Argumenta: Argumenta in omnes epistolas apostolicas nova (with Paraphrases)
Axiomata pro causa Lutheri: Axiomata pro causa Martini Lutheri   *Opuscula* /
    CWE 71

Brevissima scholia: In Elenchum Alberti Pii brevissima scholia per eundem
    Erasmum Roterodamum   ASD IX-6 / CWE 84

Carmina   LB I, IV, V, VIII / ASD I-7 / CWE 85–6
Catalogus lucubrationum   LB I / CWE 9 (Ep 1341A)
Christiani hominis institutum, carmen   LB V / ASD I-7 / CWE 85–6
Ciceronianus: Dialogus Ciceronianus   LB I / ASD I-2 / CWE 28
Colloquia   LB I / ASD I-3 / CWE 39–40
Compendium vitae Allen I / CWE 4
Conflictus: Conflictus Thaliae et Barbariei   LB I / ASD I-8
[Consilium: Consilium cuiusdam ex animo cupientis esse consultum]   *Opuscula* /
    CWE 71
Contra morosos: Capita argumentorum contra morosos quosdam ac indoctos   LB VI /
    CWE 41

De bello Turcico: Utilissima consultatio de bello Turcis inferendo, et obiter enarratus
    psalmus 28   LB V / ASD V-3 / CWE 64
De civilitate: De civilitate morum puerilium   LB I / ASD I-8 / CWE 25
Declamatio de morte   LB IV / ASD I-2 / CWE 25
Declamatiuncula   LB IV / ASD IV-7
Declarationes ad censuras Lutetiae vulgatas: Declarationes ad censuras Lutetiae
    vulgatas sub nomine facultatis theologiae Parisiensis   LB IX / ASD IX-7 / CWE 82
De concordia: De sarcienda ecclesiae concordia, or De amabili ecclesiae concordia
    (on Psalm 83)   LB V / ASD V-3 / CWE 65
De conscribendis epistolis   LB I / ASD I-2 / CWE 25
De constructione: De constructione octo partium orationis, or Syntaxis   LB I /
    ASD I-4
De contemptu mundi: Epistola de contemptu mundi   LB V / ASD V-1 / CWE 66
De copia: De duplici copia verborum ac rerum   LB I / ASD I-6 / CWE 24
De delectu ciborum scholia   ASD IX-1 / CWE 73
De esu carnium: Epistola apologetica ad Christophorum episcopum Basiliensem
    de interdicto esu carnium (published with scholia in a 1532 edition but not in
    the 1540 Opera)   LB IX / ASD IX-1 / CWE 73
De immensa Dei misericordia: Concio de immensa Dei misericordia   LB V / ASD V-7 /
    CWE 70
De libero arbitrio: De libero arbitrio diatribe   LB IX / CWE 76
De philosophia evangelica   LB VI / CWE 41
De praeparatione: De praeparatione ad mortem   LB V / ASD V-1 / CWE 70
De pueris instituendis: De pueris statim ac liberaliter instituendis   LB I / ASD I-2 /
    CWE 26
De puero Iesu: Concio de puero Iesu   LB V / ASD V-7 / CWE 29
De puritate tabernaculi: Enarratio psalmi 14 qui est de puritate tabernaculi sive
    ecclesiae christianae   LB V / ASD V-2 / CWE 65
De ratione studii   LB I / ASD I-2 / CWE 24

De recta pronuntiatione: De recta latini graecique sermonis pronuntiatione
LB I / ASD I-4 / CWE 26
De taedio Iesu: Disputatiuncula de taedio, pavore, tristicia Iesu LB V/ ASD V-7 /
CWE 70
Detectio praestigiarum: Detectio praestigiarum cuiusdam libelli Germanice scripti
LB X / ASD IX-1 / CWE 78
De vidua christiana LB V / ASD V-6 / CWE 66
De virtute amplectenda: Oratio de virtute amplectenda LB V / CWE 29
[Dialogus bilinguium ac trilinguium: Chonradi Nastadiensis dialogus bilinguium
ac trilinguium] Opuscula / CWE 7
Dilutio: Dilutio eorum quae Iodocus Clichtoveus scripsit adversus declamationem
suasoriam matrimonii Dilutio eorum quae Iodocus Clichtoveus scripsit ed Émile V.
Telle (Paris 1968) / CWE 83
Divinationes ad notata Bedae: Divinationes ad notata per Bedam de Paraphrasi
Erasmi in Matthaeum, et primo de duabus praemissis epistolis LB IX / ASD IX-5

Ecclesiastes: Ecclesiastes sive de ratione concionandi LB V / ASD V-4–5 / CWE 67–8
Elenchus in censuras Bedae: In N. Bedae censuras erroneas elenchus LB IX / ASD IX-5
Enchiridion: Enchiridion militis christiani LB V / ASD V-8 / CWE 66
Encomium matrimonii (in De conscribendis epistolis)
Encomium medicinae: Declamatio in laudem artis medicae LB I / ASD I-4 / CWE 29
Epistola ad Dorpium LB IX / CWE 3 (Ep 337) / CWE 71
Epistola ad fratres Inferioris Germaniae: Responsio ad fratres Germaniae Inferioris
ad epistolam apologeticam incerto autore proditam LB X / ASD IX-1 / CWE 78
Epistola ad gracculos: Epistola ad quosdam impudentissimos gracculos LB X /
CWE 16 (Ep 2275)
Epistola apologetica adversus Stunicam LB IX / ASD IX-8 / CWE 15 (Ep 2172)
Epistola apologetica de Termino LB X / CWE 14 (Ep 2018)
Epistola consolatoria: Epistola consolatoria virginibus sacris, or Epistola consolatoria
in adversis LB V / ASD IV-7 / CWE 69
Epistola contra pseudevangelicos: Epistola contra quosdam qui se falso iactant
evangelicos LB X / ASD IX-1 / CWE 78
Euripidis Hecuba LB I / ASD I-1
Euripidis Iphigenia in Aulide LB I / ASD I-1
Exomologesis: Exomologesis sive modus confitendi LB V / ASD V-8 / CWE 67
Explanatio symboli: Explanatio symboli apostolorum sive catechismus LB V /
ASD V-1 / CWE 70
Ex Plutarcho versa LB IV / ASD IV-2

Formula: Conficiendarum epistolarum formula (see De conscribendis epistolis)

Hyperaspistes LB X / CWE 76–7

In Nucem Ovidii commentarius LB I / ASD I-1 / CWE 29
In Prudentium: Commentarius in duos hymnos Prudentii LB V / ASD V-7 /
CWE 29
In psalmum 1: Enarratio primi psalmi, 'Beatus vir,' iuxta tropologiam potissimum
LB V / ASD V-2 / CWE 63

In psalmum 2: Commentarius in psalmum 2, 'Quare fremuerunt gentes?'   LB V /
    ASD V-2 / CWE 63
In psalmum 3: Paraphrasis in tertium psalmum, 'Domine quid multiplicate'
    LB V / ASD V-2 / CWE 63
In psalmum 4: In psalmum quartum concio   LB V / ASD V-2 / CWE 63
In psalmum 22: In psalmum 22 enarratio triplex   LB V / ASD V-2 / CWE 64
In psalmum 33: Enarratio psalmi 33   LB V / ASD V-3 / CWE 64
In psalmum 38: Enarratio psalmi 38   LB V / ASD V-3 / CWE 65
In psalmum 85: Concionalis interpretatio, plena pietatis, in psalmum 85   LB V /
    ASD V-3 / CWE 64
Institutio christiani matrimonii   LB V / ASD V-6 / CWE 69
Institutio principis christiani   LB IV/ ASD IV-1 / CWE 27

Julius exclusus: Dialogus Julius exclusus e coelis   *Opuscula* ASD I-8 / CWE 27

Lingua   LB IV / ASD IV-1a / CWE 29
Liturgia Virginis Matris: Virginis Matris apud Lauretum cultae liturgia   LB V /
    ASD V-1 / CWE 69
Loca quaedam emendata: Loca quaedam in aliquot Erasmi lucubrationibus
    per ipsum emendata (see Apologia adversus monachos)
Luciani dialogi   LB I / ASD I-1

Manifesta mendacia   ASD IX-4 / CWE 71
Methodus (see Ratio)
Modus orandi Deum   LB V / ASD V-1 / CWE 70
Moria: Moriae encomium   LB IV / ASD IV-3 / CWE 27

Notatiunculae: Notatiunculae quaedam extemporales ad naenias Bedaicas,
    or Responsio ad notulas Bedaicas   LB IX / ASD IX-5
Novum Testamentum: Novum instrumentum 1516; Novum Testamentum 1519 and
    later (Greek and Latin editions and Latin only editions)   LB VI / ASD VI-2, 3, 4

Obsecratio ad Virginem Mariam: Obsecratio sive oratio ad Virginem Mariam in
    rebus adversis, or Obsecratio ad Virginem Matrem Mariam in rebus adversis
    LB V / CWE 69
Oratio de pace: Oratio de pace et discordia   LB VIII / ASD IV-7
Oratio funebris: Oratio funebris in funere Bertae de Heyen   LB VIII / ASD IV-7 /
    CWE 29

Paean Virgini Matri: Paean Virgini Matri dicendus   LB V / CWE 69
Panegyricus: Panegyricus ad Philippum Austriae ducem   LB IV / ASD IV-1 /
    CWE 27
Parabolae: Parabolae sive similia   LB I / ASD I-5 / CWE 23
Paraclesis LB V, VI / ASD V-7 / CWE 41
Paraphrasis in Elegantias Vallae: Paraphrasis in Elegantias Laurentii Vallae
    LB I / ASD I-4
Paraphrasis in Matthaeum, etc   LB VII / ASD VII-1–6 / CWE 42–50
Peregrinatio apostolorum: Peregrinatio apostolorum Petri et Pauli   LB VI, VII / CWE 41

Precatio ad Virginis filium Iesum   LB V / CWE 69
Precatio dominica   LB V / CWE 69
Precationes: Precationes aliquot novae   LB V / CWE 69
Precatio pro pace ecclesiae: Precatio ad Dominum Iesum pro pace ecclesiae
   LB IV, V / CWE 69
Prologus supputationis: Prologus in supputationem calumniarum Natalis Bedae
   (1526), or Prologus supputationis errorum in censuris Bedae (1527)   LB IX /
   ASD IX-5
Purgatio adversus epistolam Lutheri: Purgatio adversus epistolam non sobriam
   Martini Lutheri   LB X / ASD IX-1 / CWE 78

Querela pacis   LB IV / ASD IV-2 / CWE 27

Ratio: Ratio seu Methodus compendio perveniendi ad veram theologiam (Methodus
   for the shorter version originally published in the Novum instrumentum of 1516)
   LB V, VI / CWE 41
Responsio ad annotationes Lei: Responsio ad annotationes Eduardi Lei   LB IX /
   ASD IX-4 / CWE 72
Responsio ad Collationes: Responsio ad Collationes cuiusdam iuvenis
   gerontodidascali   LB IX / CWE 73
Responsio ad disputationem de divortio: Responsio ad disputationem cuiusdam
   Phimostomi de divortio   LB IX / ASD IX-4 / CWE 83
Responsio ad epistolam Alberti Pii: Responsio ad epistolam paraeneticam Alberti
   Pii, or Responsio ad exhortationem Pii   LB IX / ASD IX-6 / CWE 84
Responsio ad notulas Bedaicas (see Notatiunculae)
Responsio ad Petri Cursii defensionem: Epistola de apologia Cursii   LB X / Ep 3032
Responsio adversus febricitantis cuiusdam libellum   LB X

Spongia: Spongia adversus aspergines Hutteni   LB X / ASD IX-1 / CWE 78
Supputatio: Supputatio errorum in censuris Bedae   LB IX
Supputationes: Supputationes errorum in censuris Natalis Bedae: contains
   Supputatio and reprints of Prologus supputationis; Divinationes ad notata Bedae;
   Elenchus in censuras Bedae; Appendix respondens ad Sutorem; Appendix de
   scriptis Clithovei   LB IX / ASD IX-5

Tyrannicida: Tyrannicida, declamatio Lucianicae respondens   LB I / ASD I-1 /
   CWE 29

Virginis et martyris comparatio   LB V / ASD V-7 / CWE 69
Vita Hieronymi: Vita divi Hieronymi Stridonensis   *Opuscula* / ASD VIII-1/ CWE 61

CORRIGENDA FOR CWE 19

Page 315 (Ep 2791) line 37: delete question mark (?) after 'mutual friendship with you'

Page 364 (Index), after 'Henry VIII' insert: 'Heresbach, Konrad, counsellor to the duke of Jülich-Cleves 192, 192–3n, 207, 233, 259n, 293'

Page 364 (Index), after 'Julianus Antoninus' insert: 'Jülich-Cleves 46n, 103, 189n, 190n, 192n, 292'

Page 366 (Index), after 'Padua' insert: 'Paul, St, apostle 37, 63n, 136, 178, 194, 199–200n, 219n, 306, 326'

Index

The design of
THE COLLECTED WORKS
OF ERASMUS
was created
by
ALLAN FLEMING
1929–1977
for
the University
of Toronto
Press